Praise

AN UNQUENCH

D1254703

Named One of the Best Books of 2011 by *Kirkus Reviews*

"*An Unquenchable Thirst* is a candid, generous, and profound spiritual memoir by a woman who chose a life of service alongside one of the great religious icons of our time. Somehow, in the midst of this humbling, austere life of devotion, Mary Johnson found herself, even as her doubts about her faith grew. Johnson's writing is always gentle yet honest, detailed yet compelling. This is a book that deserves a great deal of thoughtful discussion."

—ANNE RICE

"If I had a personal list of the best books of 2011, *An Unquenchable Thirst* would be on it. [It] has everything a memoir needs: an inside look at a way of life that most of us will never see, a physical and emotional journey, and suspense. . . . *An Unquenchable Thirst* is much more than a single Catholic journey, and it's far from a book only for current or former Catholics. . . . An incredible coming of age story."

—Slate

"Mary Johnson writes with heartbreaking honesty, inviting us to share her innermost hopes, doubts, and longings. She offers us a humanizing and humanistic exploration of how hard it can be to do good in this world, to be true to oneself, and to chart a new path. And she beautifully balances a cultural connection to Catholicism with the need for a far less dogmatic world: a world where she can be free to question, change, love. Her work here and in the future should be considered must-read stuff for anyone who ever looked critically at their own religious tradition and asked 'Why?'"

—GREG M. EPSTEIN,
Humanist Chaplain at Harvard University and author of
Good Without God: What a Billion Nonreligious People Do Believe

"*An Unquenchable Thirst* is an eloquent and moving tale that is an extraordinary testament to the enduring power of love—beyond faith and dogma."

—MIRA BARTÓK, author of
The Memory Palace

"Incredibly, Johnson writes with a deep empathy for the women with whom she shared twenty years, as if by revealing to us their faults and their kindnesses, their failures and their triumphs, we, too, might forgo judgment and accept them as simply human."   —*The Dallas Morning News*

"It is unusual to find the voice of someone as committed to their faith as Mary Johnson. . . . Johnson writes about her fears, doubts and her thirst for God's mercy as Sister Donata. . . . The writing of *An Unquenchable Thirst* is so lovely that it reads like a prayer for reconciliation."
—*Austin American-Statesman*

"After spending more time as a nun than she had spent in the outside world, [Johnson] left to find her own path and her own way of knowing and loving herself and others. . . . The courage it took to walk away from that life as a nun and to embrace a new way of thinking, living, and loving is almost unimaginable, the courage to share her story in this book even more so. Mary Johnson is a brave, good woman, and she has written a fascinating, compelling book which will raise important questions in the mind of any person with interest in spiritual matters."   —*Seattle Post-Intelligencer*

"Johnson's memoir is a page-turner. . . . She is candid about her experiences as both a woman and a Christian. She shares intimate aspects of the female experience and the terrors and joys that come with it. As for her faith journey, there is nothing easy about it. It is just as serious, questioning, doubting and struggling as Thomas Merton's."   —*Concord Monitor*

"Absorbing . . . Much of [Johnson's] personal life is explored, including the dark nights of the soul, as well as the light-bursts of love, written as if her discoveries and revelations connect to readers one at a time."
—New Hampshire *Sentinel*

"An extraordinarily revealing and intimate portrait of [Johnson's] daily struggle to balance the spiritual with the worldly . . . a remarkable, elegant spiritual memoir."   —*Library Journal*

"Readers . . . will find themselves transported into another world by this powerful, revealing memoir. An aspirant to the Missionaries of Charity at age nineteen, the author spent twenty years living a life both extraordinarily simple and heart-wrenchingly complex. Johnson skillfully demonstrates this juxtaposition through her writing—mundane events, such as gathering eggs or learning to play the piano, often have tragic or miraculous implications. . . . Throughout the book, the author describes her interactions with Mother Teresa . . . [who] actually emerges as a fairly normal person rather than a saintly archetype. . . . [Johnson's] memoir is exceptional."

—*Kirkus Reviews* (starred)

"[Johnson] brings readers close to her story, showing her triumphs and temptations, limning characters as compelling as those in any novel. . . . Her mesmerizing account of trying to orbit the sun that was Mother Teresa vividly captures a life in turmoil." —*Booklist* (starred review)

"A luminous, extraordinary account of one woman who devoted her life to Mother Teresa's Missionaries of Charity, saw the organization from the inside out, and decided to walk away after twenty years of service as a faithful and obedient nun . . . as compulsively readable as a good novel . . . an extraordinary story told with skill. And although the painful process of shedding twenty years of indoctrination and becoming an atheist is only mentioned in the last pages of the book, it's described with all the beauty and grace of the sun breaking through storm clouds. . . . One of the best biographies I've read." —Big Think

"A heartfelt, personal story of the gradual awakening of a person who comes to see that preferring the human to the perfect does not alienate her from authentic spirituality but allows her to live more fully."

—KATHLEEN NORRIS, author of
The Cloister Walk

"Opening up the soul's deep core on the page is always an act of bravery. Mary Johnson is bravery writ large. She writes expertly about the myths and misperceptions of women's religious vocations and the sacred validity of human intimacy." —BREENA CLARKE, author of
Stand the Storm

"This is not your grandmother's ex-nun story. Johnson speaks openly and frankly about her experiences as a nun in the order founded by Mother Teresa. While working closely with Mother Teresa, Mary Johnson experienced the holy joy of prayer, and the angst-filled pull of sex. No sugar coating here: Johnson examines the entire experience with staggering honesty."

—BARB JOHNSON, author of
More of This World or Maybe Another

"Mary Johnson writes from a place of deep love—that unquenchable thirst—and when she finally gives voice to it, you want to stand up and cheer."

—LESLEY HAZLETON, author of
Mary: A Flesh-and-Blood Biography of the Virgin Mother

"We see in this story the great thirst, the girl's romantic sense of the world, the attraction of a life with Jesus. We see ecstasy. And we meet such fragile and struggling women and men in the rhythms of a dedicated life over days and seasons and years, and the costs that life exacts. *An Unquenchable Thirst* is an extraordinary gift to readers, a moving, tender, searching, and generous piece of writing. Love saturates this book."

—MEREDITH HALL, author of
Without a Map: A Memoir

An
Unquenchable
Thirst

AN
UNQUENCHABLE
THIRST

ಹಿ

A MEMOIR

ಲ

MARY JOHNSON

To Eugenie,
our stories are our gifts
Keep writing! Mary Johnson
NYC 2013

SPIEGEL & GRAU TRADE PAPERBACKS · 2012

To all my sisters everywhere

2013 Spiegel & Grau Trade Paperback Edition

Copyright © 2011 by Mary Johnson
Reading group guide copyright © 2013 by Random House, Inc.

Published in the United States by Spiegel & Grau, an imprint of The Random
House Publishing Group, a division of Random House, Inc., New York.

SPIEGEL & GRAU and Design is a registered trademark of Random House, Inc.
RANDOM HOUSE READER'S CIRCLE & Design is a registered trademark
of Random House, Inc.

Originally published in hardcover in the United States by Spiegel & Grau,
an imprint of The Random House Publishing Group, a division of
Random House, Inc., in 2011.

LIBRARY OF CONGRESS CATALOGING-IN-PUBLICATION DATA
Johnson, Mary.
An unquenchable thirst : a memoir / Mary Johnson.
p.   cm.
ISBN 978-0-385-52748-4
eISBN 978-1-5883-6986-4
1. Johnson, Mary.   2. Nuns—United States—Biography.   3. Nuns—
Italy—Biography.   4. Missionaries of Charity.   I. Title.
BX4705.J6723A3   2011
271'.97—dc22
[B]   2010038858

Printed in the United States of America

www.randomhousereaderscircle.com

2 4 6 8 9 7 5 3 1

Book design by Liz Cosgrove

AUTHOR'S NOTE

I chose these stories from many. So that the reader may enter more seamlessly into my experience, I've reconstructed conversations; dialogue is not meant as a direct quotation. No one who appears in these pages expected that I would one day recount conversations and events that they assumed would remain private. Out of respect for them, I've sometimes disguised names and identities. Missionaries of Charity who in these pages held elected or appointed office appear under their real names, as do others who played largely public roles.

All people hunger for love,
whether they are Christian or Muslim, Hindu or atheist.

MOTHER TERESA OF CALCUTTA

Everything that is hidden shall be made known.

JESUS OF NAZARETH

INTRODUCTION

SUMMER 2007

I was in New York on my way to meet a literary agent when Mother Teresa's stubborn brown eyes stopped me at a newsstand on West Twenty-third Street. I handed five dollars to the guy in the kiosk. If I'd still believed in signs, this would have been a big one.

Mother stared out from the cover of *Time* magazine with nearly the identical expression her face had borne the last time we'd spoken, a little over ten years earlier. I saw the disappointment in her eyes. Mother would have no more approved of the meeting I was about to have than she would have approved of the cover of that magazine, which promised to reveal her "Secret Life." Mother's secrets weren't the type normally associated with magazine covers—no adulterous affairs, no shady financial profiteering. Mother's were secrets of the soul.

Though Mother Teresa was one of the most admired women in the world, she always kept her inner life close. She discouraged questions about her original inspiration or about her prayer life, usually by simply smiling in response. She instructed us to keep quiet, too, especially about events in the convent. When I was handed two sheets of paper to write my first "home letter" as an aspirant in the Missionaries of Charity, the sister in charge issued detailed instructions: "Write an uplifting letter. Don't tell your family of your difficulties, and never mention what happens in the community. Urge your people to pray the rosary every night." My letters home were so boring I was sometimes ashamed.

The fine print on the cover of *Time* read, "Newly published letters reveal a beloved icon's 50-year crisis of faith." Mother Teresa's spiritual crisis was not news to me. Several years earlier, I'd read a report of the "dark night" Mother had described in letters to her spiritual directors. Some sisters had been shocked to imagine that the sweet certainty we'd heard in Mother's prayers had been the result of stubborn faith, not ecstatic vision. During my days as a sister, nothing had wrapped me more surely in the presence of God than Mother's steady voice intoning, "In the name of the Father and of the Son and of the Holy Spirit" as she traced the cross over her sari.

Yet I hadn't been too surprised to learn that Mother sometimes wondered where God was, even whether God was out there at all. Desolation in prayer was not uncommon, especially when one lived and served among the desperately poor, slept less than five hours a night, as Mother did, and deliberately deprived oneself of human intimacy as we all did, or were supposed to do. Mother's feelings of desolation distressed her all the more because they contrasted so dramatically with the consolation she'd known when she heard Jesus ask her to found a community of sisters to care for the poorest of the poor. Mother eventually came to see the feelings of abandonment as a gift, a way of sharing Jesus' passion. She often referred to herself as "the spouse of Jesus Crucified" and to suffering as "the kiss of Jesus."

On my way to the literary agency that day, I crossed West Twenty-fifth Street and glanced again at the magazine in my hand. As I looked at Mother's frown, I remembered another *Time* cover, some thirty years earlier.

I had first met Mother on the cover of *Time* in 1975, an image that rendered Mother in watercolor under the headline "Living Saints." When I'd spotted the magazine in my southeast Texas high school library, I'd dropped into a chair to read it, skipping French class, drawn by the magnetic call of the nun's soulful eyes. I read of the desperate needs of the poor dying on the streets, of babies abandoned in dustbins. The photo that impressed me most showed a young Indian nun peacefully bent over a man whose legs, nowhere thicker than a baseball bat, were bound in rags. The man's ribs formed prominent ridges on his bare chest, while his eyes, sunk deep in their sockets, were riveted on the face of the nun cutting his nails. I felt as if the world had suddenly opened itself and revealed my place in it. Since my preparation for First Communion, I'd known that loving others was life's most important calling. That conviction had grown through the years as I'd experienced love's power, and the pain of its lack, for myself. There in the library, with a seventeen-year-old's clarity, I knew that I was meant to follow this nun in Calcutta who loved those most in need of it.

That week I wrote my first letter to her, addressing it simply *Mother Teresa, Missionaries of Charity, Calcutta, India*, begging her to take me as one of her own sisters. Eighteen months later, in a convent in the South Bronx, over my parents' objections, Mother pinned a crucifix to my blouse, saying, "Receive the symbol of your Crucified Spouse. Carry His light and His love into the homes of the poor everywhere you go." I did just that for twenty years.

I tucked the latest issue of *Time* under my arm and climbed the agency's front steps. I uttered no prayer. Through years of wrestling with my own dark nights, I'd replaced marriage to God with a different sort of integrity. I reached to ring the bell, ready to tell my secrets to the agent and to anyone else who would listen. I would have told them to Mother if I could. Mother Teresa would have called my secrets blasphemy, but I call them freedom. I even call them love.

An
Unquenchable
Thirst

I

DAY ONE

SUMMER 1977
SOUTH BRONX, NEW YORK CITY

The cardboard box on the rack above my bus seat held what was left of my possessions. In a few hours they would belong to God, and so would I.

I watched the street outside, mesmerized as cars wove through eight lanes of traffic. On a billboard, an electric blonde advertised cigarettes, then suddenly morphed into a giant banana flaunting a reed skirt and long, dark eyelashes.

"You been to the city before?" A man with a black T-shirt waved his hands, brushing my shoulder with his too-broad gesture. He stared, waiting for an answer.

"Yes, I was here in January."

"Really? You look like you never seen a city before. Where're you from?"

I shifted in the seat. Was it supposed to be this personal between passengers on buses in New York?

"Texas."

"Texas?" The man was loud. Other people in the bus turned their heads to look. "What's a kid from Texas doing in New York?"

I wasn't a kid. I was nineteen and I'd just finished a year in the honors program at the University of Texas, with good grades. I didn't see why I should explain to a loud man on a bus that I was in New York because the only thing I'd been thinking of for the past year and a half had been coming to this city to give myself to God. But not answering would have been rude.

"I came to see some sisters."

"Oh, you got relatives here." He seemed satisfied, but his conclusion wasn't accurate.

"Not those kind of sisters. Catholic sisters. Nuns."

"You're coming to New York City to see nuns?"

"To become a nun."

He drew in a whistle as his eyes traveled my body, perhaps looking for some sort of deformity, or maybe, if he was Catholic, a halo. I possessed neither. I didn't expect him to understand. Even my family didn't understand.

The man grew quiet, and I grew less tense. Soon I didn't see the buildings or the billboards anymore. I saw Mom, Dad, my five sisters, and my brother all lined up on the tarmac that morning, waving their eldest off. Four-year-old Heather's hand had never stopped waving—only she seemed to understand the joy of my adventure. Kathy, just thirteen months younger than I, had cried most of the night. She'd said, as she had for weeks, "Mary, you're wasting your life." I'd told her that I'd chosen the best life possible, a life of love, but that morning she'd refused even to look at me. Mom waved but didn't smile. She'd been so insistent that I at least finish college. I'd explained that when God calls, you don't put Him on hold, but she didn't get that, either.

It had been even worse when Dad had taken me to the airport in January for the preliminary week the sisters called "come and see." The plane was delayed, and while we sat waiting, he put his hand on my knee and looked into my eyes, then at my suitcase, the floor, then me again, without saying anything. When tears began to puddle in his eyes, he left without a word or a glance back.

The bus jerked to a halt at Grand Central Terminal. I reached for the rack above, but the man in the black T-shirt saw me and lifted the box before I could. "Best of luck, kid," he said as he placed the box in my hands, then added under his breath, "Pray for me, okay?"

I nodded and smiled, edging my way along the aisle. I told myself to be more careful about judging people in the future. As I stepped off the bus, a wave of heat slapped me—not the familiar heat heavy with refinery fumes and Gulf Coast humidity, but an undulating heat of asphalt, steel, and bodies. I looked for the man in the T-shirt, but he was gone. All I saw were swarms of people—hurrying, determined people who all seemed to know where they were going.

I knew where I was going, too. I'd taken a taxi in January, though the first three cabs to stop had refused to venture into the South Bronx. This time the sisters had sent directions, and I'd memorized them: shuttle bus to Grand Central, the #5 subway, a five-block walk. *God*, I prayed, *lead me through this scurrying city. Lead me to You.*

I walked down steps that smelled of urine. On the platform, I flinched a little as trains rushed past, then marveled at their jackets of neon graffiti. I clutched the strings on my box. I'd heard stories of men with knives on subways, and lately the evening news had dwelt on the "Son of Sam." The serial killer, who police said believed he was possessed by the devil, shot women with long dark hair. My hair was sort of dark but short. According to Walter Cronkite, women in New York had bought out the city's entire stock of blond wigs and were on the verge of panic. *God, take care of me. I'm working for You now.*

When the #5 pulled up, I found a seat and cradled my box. A suitcase would have been easier, but the sisters had said they didn't use them, or purses, either. *I'm going to live free*, I told myself, *like the lilies of the field and the birds of the air.*

The heat and the crowds and the news stories had made my stomach queasy. I checked my pocket for the envelope I'd safety-pinned there—my passport and money were safe. I'd collected the $700 from my summer job as a technical writer, my savings, and money from selling my French touring bike and electric typewriter. The sisters had insisted on money for airfare to return me home if things didn't work out, or to send me to Rome if they did.

My friends had thrown a "penguin party" for me a week earlier, a beach party—"black and white dress required in honor of Mary's new wardrobe." These public school classmates of mine didn't even know my nuns wore white saris trimmed in blue, yet they squatted around the campfire debating the odds of my perseverance. Some claimed the girl who took on the school board in editorials was constitutionally incapable of a vow of obedience, that a star of the debate team, known for humiliating her opponents, wouldn't last ten minutes in a convent. Others countered that I was the kind of person who, once she decides something, will see it through, even if it means taking the layouts of the school newspaper home with her, working on them all night, strapping them to her bicycle the next morning, and delivering them personally to the printer to avoid missing a deadline. They said once I put the habit on, I'd die in it.

I enjoyed confounding their expectations. These were the people who had voted me Most Likely to Succeed. I wondered if they knew how little that title meant to me. That gathering on the beach was only the second party I'd been to since moving from Michigan when I was twelve. My first act at my new junior high had been to speak to a group of kids in a corner of the gym. Seconds later a spitball smacked my head and I heard—as did everyone else—a boy on the bleachers shouting, "Nigger lover." No one, not the five black kids at school nor the seven hundred white kids, accepted any of my approaches for the next three years. When I started earning debate trophies some of my teammates began to tolerate my presence, and Kathy and Kelley and Monica seemed to enjoy working on the newspaper with me, but boys continued to spit on me on the bus, where I was the only rider over sixteen. My classmates all had cars or hitched rides with friends. The penguin party was a nice gesture, probably prompted by their curiosity about my choices, but I doubted these acquaintances understood my outsider's pride in values beyond the mainstream. They didn't know the secret thrill I felt on the streets of Austin when, watching couples walk hand in hand, I savored my relationship with the Creator of the Universe, who shared my every moment, awake or asleep. They didn't know that living the gospel of poverty and love with God constituted real success.

I got off the train at Third Avenue and 149th Street and began the five-block walk from the subway to the sisters' house. Pulsing Spanish lyrics pushed thoughts of home away. A fruit stand hawking mangoes and papayas caught my eye, until I sensed boys in front of an electronics shop eyeing me. I shifted my box nervously from hand to hand. *God, keep me safe*, I prayed.

A train passed overhead. Kids my own age break-danced under the el, their boom box momentarily overpowered by the train. The smell of hot dogs increased my nausea. I stepped around some broken glass and turned onto East 145th Street. My heart beat a little faster when, midway down the block, I spotted a three-story building behind a high brick wall, barbed wire coiled at the top, a small sign to the left of the gate: *Missionaries of Charity*. I opened the gate and stood before the door. I swallowed, and hesitated just a moment.

I juggled the box, smoothed my hair, then rang the bell, my hand trembling. Staring at the door, I saw Heather's last wave, Kathy refusing to look.

Dear God, I prayed, *please send someone to open the door.*

I set the box on the sidewalk—and the door swung open.

A short, dark woman with puffy cheeks, a blue apron over her white sari, smiled at me. "Welcome," she said. The door clicked as she shut it behind me.

Sister Rochelle took my box and nudged me up a short flight of stairs toward the chapel. "Say hello to Jesus," she whispered.

I knelt on the rough carpet. A large wooden crucifix hung behind the altar, with two words pasted on the wall next to Jesus' head. When I read them, I felt as though Jesus spoke those words directly to me: *I thirst.*

I'd barely begun my silent prayer when Sister Rochelle said, "Come now. We'll take your things." She led me upstairs, climbing quickly. I heard chickens clucking. Nuns keeping chickens in the South Bronx—what surer sign of self-sufficiency and disregard of convention could I have asked for?

"This is the refectory for you aspirants," Sister Rochelle said as we entered a room with a long wooden table, benches on either side. "These are your plates." She pointed to a bookcase marked with numbers cut from calendars. Above each number sat a large white enamel bowl with a small plate, an enamel teacup, and a saucer. Everything was simple, clean, orderly. Above the shelf a plaque read, *The Aspirancy Motto: He must increase; I must decrease.*

"There are going to be twelve of you," Sister Rochelle said. "You are number nine." There'd been nine of us at home. Nine was a good number.

Another bookcase stood nearby. "Your Bible goes here. Number nine."

She took me up another flight of stairs. On the landing, we set my box down in front of a large wooden bookcase with a sheet hanging over its shelves. Sister Rochelle pulled back the sheet to reveal clothes folded more neatly than any I'd ever seen, each little pile above its own number.

"Number nine?" I asked, and she nodded.

The next door led to a room with a slanting ceiling, a linoleum floor, and thirteen cots crowded close, with barely room to walk between them. A bare bulb hung from a black wire, and simple muslin curtains covered the lower halves of the room's three small windows.

"This is your bed, number nine." Sister Rochelle smiled again as she patted a thin mattress in the corner. "I hope you brought your sheets," she said, and I nodded. "The dormitory is a sacred place and no talking is allowed, but your mistress will tell you all that."

Sister Rochelle headed for the stairs. Over her shoulder, she said, "Now unpack your things and feel at home." Already halfway down, she added, "The bell will ring soon for adoration."

I sat for a moment on bed number nine, eager to absorb the quiet. The attractions of the convent were pure, minimalist, essential—life without the additives. Everything about the convent seemed to proclaim: Only God matters.

I was stacking my clothes on shelf number nine, as neatly as I could, when I heard footsteps. A tall woman with straight, shoulder-length brown hair and sparkling green eyes rounded the corner.

"Hey, Mary!" she said, stretching out her hand. "Sister Carmeline told us to expect another aspirant today—I'm so glad it's you."

"Louise! Great to see you." Louise had been in charge of the catechism program at St. Rita's Church, just next to the convent, and we'd met in January. She was just a few years older than I—a recent graduate of the University of Virginia—and played the guitar at Mass. Her hand was warm in mine. "What's an aspirant?"

Louise laughed, throwing her arms up in the air. "I'm developing a new vocabulary. We're aspirants because we're aspiring to be sisters, or something like that."

We walked together to the dormitory, and Louise pulled back the blue and white checked bedspread on number nine, revealing a homemade mattress, not more than an inch and a half thick, resting on the cot's iron netting. As we stretched out the bottom sheet, the smell of fabric softener reminded me of home. "You mean you're joining the sisters, too?" I asked Louise. "I thought you'd decided not to."

"Yeah, well, I talked to Sister Andrea about it a lot. It's been great to work in the parish, but I do feel something missing. I want to give God everything, and I guess it's worth a try." Louise pushed the tiny pillow into my way too big pillowcase and fluffed it up as much as she could. "The sisters are excited that we'll be the first group of aspirants in the U.S. Till now they've only had a few American vocations, and they've all gone to London for aspirancy."

Suddenly a short woman stepped up so close that I nearly lost my balance. A finger to her lips, small crucifix pinned to her blouse, she shook her head with its closely cropped black hair and whispered with a light Hispanic accent, "The dormitory is a sacred place. We do not speak in the dormitory."

I froze, but Louise shook her head and laughed lightly. "Sister Elvira," she said, "this is Mary. She's just come, and I think we ought to say hello."

Sister Elvira turned on her heel and walked away.

"Don't mind her. She's on her second round of aspirancy and thinks she knows everything. She's helping us become holy, making sure we keep all the Rules."

As Louise spoke, five bells sounded. I pushed the box with my remaining things under the bed and we made our way downstairs for adoration. Outside the chapel door, an Indian nun stood, arms folded across a generous chest. Her dark eyes looked right through me. Louise pulled my arm and whispered, "The mistress."

"You must be Sister Mary." The nun forced a smile, her arms still folded.

"I'm Mary Johnson. I arrived a little while ago." I extended my hand, but she kept her arms against her chest. I let my hand fall limply.

"Welcome. We are having adoration now. Jesus is waiting." She unfolded her arms, revealing a piece of black lace in her hand. "This is for wearing in the chapel," she said, handing the lace to me as she turned and walked through the chapel door.

Louise pushed me in, guiding with her arm around my waist. The chapel had no pews. Six nuns in saris knelt in three neat rows on the left side of the chapel. Louise steered me to the right, where seven young women in skirts and blouses of various colors knelt on the carpet, heads covered in black lace mantillas. I set the mantilla on my head, where it swiftly slid to one side. "We'll get you a bobby pin later," Louise whispered. I hadn't worn a mantilla since my First Communion. The lace on my head felt strange, like I was an old lady in a movie. I knelt on the carpet.

A tall, elegant sister—the superior, Sister Andrea—approached the front of the chapel and genuflected before the small gold tabernacle. In a series of fluid gestures, she rose, knelt, bowed. She removed a golden canister from the tabernacle, fixed her gaze on it, and carried it to the altar. Again she knelt, bowed, rose. She removed the canister's lid and lifted the Eucharist into the monstrance: the Body of Christ in the form of bread, the center of every Missionary of Charity's life, Jesus Himself. Everyone prostrated and I joined in, head to the ground, arms stretched forward, hands flat to the floor in an expression of complete surrender. The mantilla slid off, and I replaced it as gracefully as I could.

The gentle song of the sisters mingled with the street sounds floating in from the open windows: the Grateful Dead, cars backfiring, jump rope jingles, an ice cream truck. I hoped that on the other side of the windows, they could hear our song: *Jesus, my Lord, my God, my all, how can I love Thee as I ought?*

The sisters pulled out rosaries from their saris, the aspirants taking theirs from their pockets. In that moment I panicked. I should have remembered to bring a rosary, but in my family we didn't pray the rosary—I was more accustomed to the Mass and to quiet prayer with the Bible. Louise noticed my confusion and fetched me a string of blue plastic beads from somewhere in the back of the chapel.

As I looked at the Host and repeated the prayers, my knees grew tired, my nausea increased, and my lower back began to ache. I leaned on my heels, and the mantilla slid off again. As I reached for it, I realized I was the only one in the chapel not kneeling. Directly in front of the altar, Sister Elvira knelt as straight as a steel rod. I wasn't sure I liked her. I wanted to get along, to fit in. I struggled back to my knees and prayed for strength, strength not only for my knees but strength to live this new life well, the life I had yearned for, a life of love.

After the final hymn, I followed the young women to our refectory without a word. They lined up on either side of the table, facing a print of Jesus—the one with His flaming heart in His hand, one of my least favorite images. To the right was a picture of Mother

Teresa, with a little homemade plaque: *I will give Saints to Mother Church.* Some of the women smiled and made space for me in line. I felt part of some solemn ritual on a peaceful planet, where everyone but me knew the script. After grace, they all turned to me, singing and clapping their hands: "We welcome, welcome sister, we welcome, welcome sister. We welcome, welcome sister from our he-a-rt."

I felt my face flush. The sister who had given me the mantilla sat squarely on a stool at the head of the table, her arms crossed over her chest again. Louise nudged me toward her, saying, "Go sit near Sister Carmeline."

The others filed in on either side. One of the women placed a large aluminum dish—almost a handleless bucket—in front of Sister Carmeline.

"How was your journey?" Sister Carmeline asked with a lilting Indian accent as she ladled soup into her enamel bowl. Carrots and potatoes swam in the red broth; bloated tortilla chips and something—it looked like little pieces of scrambled egg—floated on top. Just from looking at it, my nausea doubled.

"Mother says"—Sister Carmeline lifted the ladle—"a good appetite is the sign of a good vocation." She filled my bowl.

"Thank you, but I'm not hungry," I said. "My stomach is upset, from the heat and the ride, you know."

Sister Carmeline scowled.

"You should eat it," the woman on my right whispered, with a heavy accent. "She won't let you up until it's done."

Some hard French bread came next, and I took a piece. The rough, square woman on my right touched my arm and introduced herself as Jeanne Dubois, from Quebec. She spoke of hockey, which engaged another woman two places down. Soon three or four lively conversations increased the noise level considerably.

I was left with the soup, my first test. I took spoon in hand and, according to Jeanne's advice, swallowed the lukewarm concoction quickly, trying not to think about it. When I took the last spoonful,

Jeanne nodded. Louise stretched her hand out and said, "Congratulations."

Sister Carmeline stood, and all conversation stopped immediately. After another prayer, everyone filed out of the room, plates in hand. At the bathroom sink we silently washed our plates with a homemade plastic scrubber and some yellow bar soap, then dried the plates back in the refectory, one woman handing the dish towel to the next. Each woman moved in silence. Each plate had its place. I stacked mine on place number nine. My soup had settled, and seemed as though it would remain. So, I thought, would I.

Aspirancy Timetable, Summer 1977

Monday through Friday

4:40	Rise
5:00	Morning Prayer and Meditation
6:00	Bed Making
6:10	Housework
6:30	Washing
6:50	Mass at St. Pius M, T, W; St. Rita Th, F
7:40	Breakfast
8:00	Apostolate
12:00	Lunch
12:40	Midday Prayer
1:00	Rest
1:30	Tea
1:40	Common Work
2:10	Study
3:15	Instruction
4:15	Spiritual Reading
4:45	Instruction
6:30	Adoration
7:30	Dinner
8:10	After Dinner Prayer
8:30	Recreation
9:00	Night Prayer
9:20	Bathing
10:00	Final "Praised be Jesus Christ"

Sunday

The same as above except:

1:00	Rest
2:00	Tea
2:15	Spiritual Reading
2:45	Hospital Visiting
6:00	Adoration
7:00	Dinner
7:40	After Dinner Prayer
8:00	Recreation
9:00	Night Prayer, etc.

Saturday (Our Day In)

4:40	Rise	2:00	Tea
5:00	Morning Prayer and Meditation	2:20	Recreation
6:00	Personal Hygiene	3:20	Father's Talk
6:15	Common Spiritual Reading	4:00	Adoration and Confession
7:00	Mass, Convent	5:00	Study
7:50	Breakfast	6:00	Common Work
8:15	Housework	7:00	Dinner
9:15	Washing	7:40	After Dinner Prayer
10:15	Bed Making	8:00	Recreation
10:30	Choir Practice	9:00	Night Prayer
11:30	Free	9:20	Bathing
12:00	Lunch	10:00	Final "Praised be Jesus Christ"
12:40	Midday Prayer		
1:00	Rest		

2

BOOT CAMP

As the rhythm of my new life took over, I came to think of aspirancy as Missionary of Charity boot camp: six months of total immersion, sink or swim. The eleven women with whom I ate, slept, worked, and prayed became my new sisters. From me, age nineteen, to the eldest aspirant at thirty-five, we came from every region of the country, as well as Puerto Rico and Canada. Louise, already familiar with the Bronx and the sisters, was our levelheaded leader. She'd majored in English literature, and sometimes I talked about books with her. I was happy with these good-natured women and felt ready to give myself to the poor.

Our aspirant mistress had another agenda. Sister Carmeline was determined to form us in the two true essentials: discipline and humility.

She taught us to jump out of bed at the first stroke of the bell at 4:40 every morning, to kneel on the wooden floor next to our cots, and to recite the day's first prayers loudly and with joy. We threw our sheets over our heads as a modesty tent while we wiggled into skirts and blouses. After brushing our teeth, we hurried ("Waste no time, but never run—you are not wild elephants") to the chapel for an hour of vocal prayer and meditation, then half an hour of housework—squatting awkwardly to swab the floors with an old potato sack and water, a trick I found hard to master—then twenty minutes to scrub our clothes in the same five-gallon plastic buckets we'd used for housework. At 7:00 we had Mass, sometimes in one of the parish churches close by and sometimes in the convent chapel with a visiting priest.

During breakfast, one of us read aloud from Mother Teresa's *Instructions* while the rest of us gnawed on stale bread and Crisco, which I couldn't swallow without a generous sprinkling of salt. We washed it all down with weak coffee, the milk and sugar already added. Though poverty was difficult, I found its simple strength attractive. Sharing the poverty of the poor proclaimed that God and love were what mattered.

Obedience was less alluring. In the summons of the convent's large brass bell we were to hear "the voice of God" and obey without delay. The *Constitutions*, the Rules, and our superiors were also God's voice and governed when we could speak, what we could read, how to sit, walk, or kneel, sometimes even what to think.

By 7:50 we aspirants joined the professed sisters for apostolate, serving the poor and proclaiming the Gospel as Jesus' original apostles had. We were to accept our assignments cheerfully, for they, too, came from God. I was good with kids and longed to work with the children. But while the other eleven aspirants scattered to summer day camp or to our homeless women's shelter, Sister Carmeline assigned me to the convent kitchen. Alone, I concocted soup from rotting vegetables donated by the local supermarket, then sorted food, clothing, and other donations in the go-downs.

A plaque in the basement proclaimed Mother's words: *Do little things with great love.* I understood this to mean that my activity didn't matter as much as my attitude. Still, I wanted to do big things: feed the hungry, comfort the dying, perhaps even bring the Gospel to a Communist country—or at least work with the kids at the day camp.

Every afternoon we aspirants sat around the refectory table, try-ing not to slump, while Sister Carmeline, at the head of the table, instructed us in the ways of the Missionaries of Charity. When we weren't engaged in work that required speech, we observed silence. The quiet seemed to root life deeply in God, and the Grand Silence after Night Prayer at 9:00 until breakfast the next morning brought a small measure of privacy to life in cramped quarters. The simplic-ity of our life mirrored the life of Jesus in the Gospels, and for the most part I liked it. The minor irritations were nothing in light of God's call. God had a plan for me.

One day Sister Carmeline passed out sheets of paper. "I want you to write why you want to be a Missionary of Charity," she said. "Not many sentences, no big words. Our life is simple."

How did one write about electromagnetism? That's what the pull had felt like, ever since that day I'd spotted the nun with watery eyes on the cover of *Time*. I'd read the article over and over, until I had certain sections memorized. After that I read everything I could about Mother Teresa. Though my parents thought I was too young for the convent, as a high school graduation present they gave me a trip to the International Eucharistic Congress in Philadelphia, where Mother Teresa would speak. My mother and I packed our-selves into a friend's station wagon. I urged Mom's friend to drive faster and make fewer stops, but we missed Mother Teresa's first speech. I had to find her. I scanned the crowds for a nun in a white sari. Mother's image hung everywhere—smiling from posters in barbershop windows, swaying on key chains at souvenir stands, hug-ging babies on mugs and plates—but I couldn't find her.

One morning I squeezed myself against the back wall of a packed auditorium where Archbishop Hélder Câmara of Brazil stopped his speech to kiss the hands of a small woman in a sari. Everyone rose, clapping wildly as the tiny nun stood. I could hardly believe it—I was in the same room as Mother Teresa! She stepped behind the podium and disappeared. Someone brought her a box to stand on.

The applause continued. Finally, her strong, deep voice hushed the crowd. "God loved the world so much that he gave His Son, Jesus— the beginning of Christianity, the giving. And Jesus kept on saying, 'Love one another as I have loved you.' Every human being created by the loving hand of God has been created in His image to love and to be loved.

"One of our sisters, she had just joined, and the next morning they had to go to the home for the dying. . . . They went, and after three hours they returned and she came to my room and said, 'Mother, I've been touching the Body of Christ for three hours.' Her face was shining with joy. I said, 'What did you do, Sister?'

" 'Well, just as we arrived they brought a man, covered with maggots. He had been picked up from a drain. And for three hours I was touching the Body of Christ. I knew it was He.' "

As Mother spoke, my desire grew. I wanted to be the sister who tended Jesus' wounds.

"I ask you one thing," Mother continued. "Never be afraid in your giving, and don't give from your abundance. Give until it hurts. It hurt Jesus to love you and me. Never turn your back to the poor, for in turning it to the poor, you are turning it to Jesus Christ."

My throat tightened. Mother Teresa's simple words came straight from her heart, with unwavering conviction. While everyone stood and applauded, I pushed my way to the front, where I told the two men blocking the stage that I had to speak to Mother Teresa. "You and eight thousand other people," one of them said.

Back home, I sent another letter to Calcutta. The day I finally received an envelope with *Missionaries of Charity* in the upper left-hand corner, I slammed the mailbox shut and rushed onto the streets of Austin. I didn't know where I was going and I didn't care. Envelope in hand, I sang as I ran, revising Simon and Garfunkel for the moment, "Jubilation! He loves me again! I fall on my knees and I'm laughing." I ran past a Moonie selling carnations at the corner, past couples holding hands, past the physics building, and around the fountain in Gregg Park. As I crossed the overpass, the wind threw my letter against the overpass' wire mesh. I grabbed it back, folded it tightly, and shoved it in my jeans pocket. The sunset that evening was a particularly vibrant orange and pink and purple—it seemed as though the sky knew my secret—and I stood for a long time on the overpass saying, *Thank you, thank you, thank you.* Finally, behind the biology building, under the streetlight near the goldfish pond, I opened the letter.

That letter had invited me to the South Bronx, where, pen in hand, I sat that June day, nearly a year later, answering Sister Carmeline's question: "Why do you want to be an MC?"

> God is love. I believe that love is the most important thing in the world, without which life has no meaning. I want to love as Jesus loved, to show people who do not know love that someone cares about them. I believe God has called me, and I have given Him my life.

I put down my pen feeling very good about my essay. The good feeling continued even in my sleep throughout the night, to the next morning. I felt better about this tiny paragraph than I had about all the articles and editorials and research papers I'd ever written. This paragraph "in simple words" came straight from my heart.

The next day, our papers in hand, Sister Carmeline announced, "One of you has written beautifully." I prepared to be recognized.

"Jeanne, would you please read your answer?" My jaw dropped. I closed it quickly, but not before the others noticed, I was sure of that. Jeanne stood. Her skirt was too tight.

> I come to serve Jesus and to be taught the ways of love. I am an unworthy sinner, but I trust the mercy of the Sacred Heart of Jesus to make me faithful of this great vocation. I pray that, living a holy life and doing penance, I will expiate my sins and the sins of the whole world. I want to pass my life in prayer

and reparation. I pray to Mary, the Mother of Jesus, to make me meek and humble.

Sister Carmeline nodded. "You are here *to be taught* the ways of love. You don't know how to please God, but if you are simple and humble and try very hard, you can learn. I am so surprised that only Sister Jeanne wrote that she is a sinner. You all need mercy from the Sacred Heart. Remember, without the Immaculate Heart you can do nothing."

I felt humiliated, judged. I knew I was a sinner, even if I hadn't written it down. Though I'd always considered myself a good Catholic—independent study of Vatican II documents when I was sixteen, daily Mass in Austin, always finding ways to serve my neighbor—I knew I was way behind on other things. I'd never even heard of "the Immaculate Heart," the sisters' favorite way of referring to Jesus' Mother. The rosary, the Sacred Heart of Jesus, personal sacrifices (not only during Lent but every day), weekly confession—these essentials of piety had been absent from my life.

Had my life until then really amounted to nothing?

One day, not more than two weeks after I'd left home, Sister Carmeline handed me an envelope, raising her eyebrows. The envelope was addressed to Sister Mary God.

"The postmark is Beaumont, Texas," Sister Carmeline said. "We thought it must be yours."

I opened the envelope and unfolded a sheet of orange construction paper scrawled with purple crayon.

Dear Mom,
    We miss you. Please come home soon. We are all hungry and Daddy cries all the time.
                                                    Love,
                                                    Angela

It was Kathy, trying to give me a laugh. Or hoping someone would intercept the letter and send me home. Sometimes I missed her so much it hurt. She still didn't understand that living for God was the best possible life. I slipped her letter into my Bible, where I looked at it every day.

Sister Carmeline announced that in a few days we would have a visitor—Mother Teresa! I'd barely been in the South Bronx for two weeks and already the woman whose example had brought me here was visiting. We shouted so loudly that we drowned out the boom boxes outside. Sister Carmeline said Mother visited the mission houses whenever she could, to check on the sisters in person. She said we were very privileged because Mother would stay more than a week in New York. The thought of meeting Mother Teresa made the interminable kitchen work seem almost enjoyable.

But as the day wore on, my excitement gave way to unease. What if Mother didn't like me? If she was a living saint, as *Time* magazine hinted, perhaps she would have supernatural knowledge, like Padre Pio, the Italian priest with the stigmata who read people's souls. If Mother knew I used to lie to get myself out of trouble and that I often thought critically of Sister Carmeline, she might send me home.

Even worse than Mother not liking me, suppose I didn't like her. What if she wasn't who everyone said she was?

On the appointed day, Sister Andrea and the other professed sisters went to fetch Mother from the airport. As the time for her arrival drew near, some aspirants went to the chapel, while others lingered in the refectory. I staked out a perch on the staircase above the front door and hoped Mother Teresa would like my cooking.

When the door finally opened, my heart nearly stopped. I watched a short, bent woman press through a crowd of sisters straight to the chapel. "I must say hello to Jesus," she said.

When she stooped to unfasten her sandals, I thought of Moses preparing to walk on holy ground. Mother reached for the holy water and blessed herself. She genuflected with focused determination, bowing deeply, her chin resting on her chest. Though the boom boxes thrummed outside, in the convent the world stood still, as if existing only for this moment of union with God. I felt myself enveloped in the presence of the Holy. I was ready to be a better person than I had ever been before, and all Mother had done was walk through the door.

When Mother finished her prayer, she emerged barefoot from the chapel and placed her wrinkled hand on the head of the closest aspirant. In a deep, throaty voice, she intoned, "God bless you," then she smiled at the rest of us. Rooted to her spot just outside the chapel door, Mother waited for us to squeeze past each other so she could bless us individually.

As I pressed closer, I searched frantically for something to say— *I want to be like you,* or *Teach me to be holy,* or *I just can't believe I'm here.* When my turn came, I looked into Mother's eyes and said, "Welcome, Mother."

"Very good," she replied, placing both her hands on my head. "God bless you." She gently but firmly pushed me to one side so she could bless the sisters behind me.

Sister Carmeline ushered us to the professed sisters' refectory for dinner. It looked remarkably like ours—long tables, benches, open shelves for the plates, pictures of Jesus, Mary, and Mother, without frames, covered in clear plastic—with the table pushed to the wall and old rugs scattered on the floor to make space for us aspirants to sit. Mother bowed her head low and began grace in a firm, commanding voice: "Bless us, O Lord, and these, thy gifts, which of thy bounty we are about to receive, through Jesus Christ, Our Lord. Amen." She traced the sign of the cross deliberately over her forehead, her chest, and her shoulders, more deliberately even than a priest at Mass.

Mother sat at the head of the table, Sister Andrea next to her. I chose a spot on the rug close to Mother, but I couldn't hear them talking over everyone's excited chatter.

"Isn't she just so cute?" an aspirant asked.

"Cute?"

"I mean she's so small, and so old, and she's in charge of everything, and she's not making a big deal of it. She's eating soup just like everybody else, and the way she holds her spoon—it's just so cute."

I could see her point, though I would have described Mother as focused, eager, happy, humble. I was pleased that she ate my soup with what seemed like gusto.

After her last spoonful, Mother rapped the handle of her knife on the table, and immediately everyone was silent.

"I bring you all the love of the sisters in the Mother House." Her voice was enthusiastic, without any trace of tiredness. She gestured widely. "In the Mother House there are over three hundred novices." She raised three fingers. "Three hundred—imagine that. And the sisters feed three thousand people in Calcutta every day." Mother seemed to delight in the numbers.

"Take us to Calcutta, Mother," one of the aspirants begged.

"There's still time for that." Mother gripped both sides of the table. "And Jesus is everywhere, also in New York." Her smile and her eyes sparkled.

"We are visiting many shut-ins, Mother," Sister Andrea said, "and we have many children in the summer camp."

"*Ah cha,*" Mother said, looking down the table, nodding and smiling. I wondered if I would ever make Mother smile like that. The way Mother said *ah cha*—a Bengali expression meaning "well" or "okay"—really was cute.

Over the next few days, Mother took her meals with the professed sisters. Whenever Sister Carmeline took her plate downstairs, we all wished she would take us, too. I stole glimpses of Mother in chapel. At morning Mass, after receiving the Host, Mother bent her chin to her chest, palms together in prayer, gaze fixed on the floor. When she returned to kneel in her spot at the back, she remained very still. I had never seen anyone so deeply immersed in God.

One day Mother went to see Cardinal Cooke, the archbishop of New York. Another day she visited Eileen Egan, who worked for

Catholic Relief Services, which Mother said provided rice and bul-
gur for the poor in Calcutta and in Africa. Every now and then
someone came to speak with Mother in the parlor. I remembered
how people had crowded around her in Philadelphia, and I was surprised that more people didn't come to visit. I supposed they didn't
know she was here. Once Mother visited the summer camp, and she
accompanied one of the professed sisters to visit an old, sick woman
in the projects. She didn't come down to the kitchen, at least not
while I was there.

A few evenings into Mother's visit, a tiny Indian sister with
bright eyes took Mother away. Sister Nirmala had co-founded the
contemplative branch of the Missionaries of Charity with Mother
just the previous year. The house on Union Avenue, two rosaries
north of us (we measured distances by the number of rosaries we
said while we walked), was the first MC contemplative convent.
The MC contemplatives dressed the same as the MC active sisters
and followed the same basic way of life but devoted more time to
prayer.

Mother's absence filled our house. I missed the sense of wonder
and stability that had pervaded the convent as long as she had been
around. When Sister Nirmala finally brought Mother back at the
beginning of morning Mass, they both knelt quietly in the back of
the chapel, and everything seemed right again.

A week after Mother had first arrived, I was in the hallway when I
saw her climbing the stairs. Mother was coming to us! I nearly
tripped over myself to make way. Mother sat down on Sister Carmeline's stool, at the head of our table, and we aspirants jockeyed for
the best seats. Closing her eyes, Mother began, "Hail Mary, full of
grace, the Lord is with you." The words had power and sweetness,
as if she were speaking to someone she saw.

As we answered with the Holy Mary, Mother kept her eyes
closed and folded her hands until her knuckles turned white. "Sisters," she began, "Jesus has chosen you to belong to Him. Imagine

that. Out of all the people in the world, Almighty God has chosen you.

"God did not call your sister," Mother said. "He did not call your neighbor. God called you." Each word penetrated my soul. I was afraid to breathe, afraid some inadvertent movement might disturb the joy and conviction I felt growing within me. "You must give Jesus your whole heart and soul, your body, everything." Mother looked intently at each of us as she touched the crucifix at her shoulder, caressing Jesus' body.

"You have a choice: Stay and be faithful for life, or pack up and go home right now." Her voice was firm, her tone serious. Her words scared me a little, but mostly they excited me.

Mother held up a small book covered with brown paper and shook it at us. "This book is God's will for you. Put the *Constitutions* into practice and you will become holy, guaranteed. Certain passages you must learn by heart. Soon we will go to the chapel and Mother will give you the cross." Mother's references to herself in the third person, as *Mother* instead of *I*, emphasized mission over individuality. She was living the motto of the aspirancy: *He must increase; I must decrease.*

"When you put on the cross each morning, you must always remember: You are the spouse of Jesus Crucified. Nothing and nobody will separate you from the love of Christ. Holiness is not a luxury for the few but a simple duty for you and me. Mother has promised to give Saints to Mother Church, and Mother cannot fulfill that promise without you."

We moved to the chapel in silence. No one had ever expected so much of me. With each step, my heart sang, *Thank you, God, for choosing me, for loving me.*

We all knelt across the front of the chapel and were handed slips of paper. Sister Carmeline held a plate with a dozen three-inch crucifixes, each bound by wire to a large safety pin, just like the ones the sisters pinned to their saris.

We sang,

I have decided to follow Jesus.
No turning back, no turning back.

The noise of neighborhood girls playing jump rope on the street drifted in,

"Cinderella dressed in yella,
Went downstairs to kiss a fella."

We sang all the louder:

The cross before me, the world behind me.
"Made a mistake and kissed a snake . . ."
No turning back, no turning back.
"How many doctors did it take?"
Though none go with me, still I will follow.
"One, two, three, four . . ."
No turning back, no turning back.

Mother stood at the front and asked, "My dearest sisters, what do you desire?"

We read from the papers in our hands: "To follow Jesus in humility and simplicity and to serve the poor with wholehearted love."

Moving to the first aspirant, Mother took a crucifix from the tray and kissed it, then pressed the crucifix to the aspirant's lips for her to kiss. Mother pinned the crucifix to the aspirant's blouse, and said, "Receive the symbol of your Crucified Spouse. Carry His light and His love into the homes of the poor everywhere you go, and so satiate His thirst for souls."

Mother went on to the next aspirant, and the next, to the women who were becoming my sisters, my friends. From the window, we heard, "Give me my money, motherfucker," and the sound of a brawl. I tried to concentrate on Mother's words: "Your Crucified Spouse . . . His light and His love . . . the homes of the poor." As

Mother made her way down the line of kneeling women, the outside noises died down, and those last words—"the homes of the poor"— drew me in. I imagined myself picking up the dying from the streets of Calcutta or the Congo. I imagined myself becoming a woman who was valued for the love she shared.

As my turn approached, my forehead and palms began to perspire. Suddenly Mother was in front of me, pressing the cross so strongly to my mouth that my lips weren't free to respond with a kiss. Almost before I knew it, Mother pinned the symbol of my Crucified Spouse to my blouse.

Mother left New York shortly after the ceremony of reception. I missed her strong, steady voice in the back of the chapel, her hands on my head in blessing. The crucifix she'd given me bobbed against my chest each time I moved. I was a Missionary of Charity. I belonged.

3

THE RULES

SUMMER TO FALL 1977
SOUTH BRONX, NEW YORK CITY

The day after our official reception as aspirants, Sister Carmeline stood at the head of the refectory table, peered over her spectacles, and told us that certain things had changed. She passed out rubber bands and told us to pull our hair back, like decent girls. We would now address each other as *Sister* Louise, *Sister* Jeanne. We must avoid "worldly conversation," which included talking about our pre-convent lives and books other than assigned spiritual reading. Louise looked at me, a grimace on her face.

Sister Carmeline went on: We were to rise whenever our mistress or superior entered the room, and we were never to pronounce the name of anyone in authority. Mother Teresa was always simply "Mother." When addressing Sister Carmeline or Sister Andrea, we were to say no more than "Sister." We were now members of the family.

From that day forward, for use during daily Rule Class, Sister Carmeline passed out one copy of the official *Constitutions of the Missionaries of Charity* for every two aspirants. Though she told us this small book was meant to guide our every act, we weren't yet permitted personal copies. She told us exactly which pages to open and supervised the reading of one Rule at a time; I wondered what she didn't want us to see. Occasionally she assigned us specific passages from *Mother's Instructions*, transcriptions of talks Mother had given the sisters over the years.

I was sometimes confused by the myriad references to the Rule, the rule, the Rules, or the rules—singular or plural, capitalized or not, without any apparent change in meaning. Though Sister Carmeline referred to both the *Constitutions* and a seemingly endless number of unwritten customs and traditions as Rules, only the *Constitutions* carried what she called "the Church's stamp of approval"; the Vatican's Congregation for Religious had authorized the *Constitutions* as an infallible path to holiness. Failure to observe the *Constitutions* could be sinful, especially in matters connected with the vows. All religious (it felt strange to think of that word not as an adjective but as a noun referring to vowed sisters and brothers and some priests) took vows of poverty, chastity, and obedience. Missionaries of Charity were privileged to take an additional vow of wholehearted and free service to the poorest of the poor. We aspirants wouldn't make these vows until we had completed three years of training, but we were to practice them already.

Some Rules formed the foundations of MC life, such as the one that stated, "Our particular mission is to labour at the salvation and sanctification of the poor not only in the slums but all over the world wherever they may be." I sometimes resented the implications of other Rules: "Our correspondence will be marked with uprightness, clarity, and strength of character. Letters sent by or addressed to the Sisters must be handed over to the Superior that they may be seen by her." Ungrammatical Rules, of which there were more than a handful, bothered me in an official document like the *Constitutions:* "We shall walk whenever opportunity offers to take the cheapest means of transport available to the poor as far as possible."

One day when pontificating about the Rules' importance, Sister

Carmeline replaced her usual drone with a far more tender tone. Sister Carmeline looked almost dreamy as she told us, "When Mother started the Society, she wrote the Rule little by little, at night, after working all day in the slums." Sister paused, then said with even greater reverence, "Mother wrote the Rule on her knees."

The pontifical drone reappeared the day Sister Carmeline read from the *Constitutions* about "particular friendship." She explained that in religious life every sister belonged to every other. Though we might like certain sisters better than others, never, under any circumstance, could we become emotionally attached to any sister. The Rules—Sister Carmeline shook the *Constitutions* book in our faces—forbade sisters touching each other, even in jest. We were not to shake hands, nor so much as tap an arm or touch a shoulder, and certainly never to embrace.

The Rules against touch seemed overblown but didn't annoy me the way the prohibition against friendship did. As my hopes for a friend among the sisters were dashed, I also realized that banning the joy of friendship meant freedom from the pain of exclusion as well. We would all belong to one another. Any subtext buried in the Rules on particular friendship escaped my 1970s southeast Texas sensibility.

I avoided dwelling on the annoying Rules and focused instead on those that fascinated and inspired: "Silence gives us a new outlook on life. In it we are filled with the energy of God Himself that makes us do all things with joy."

Sister often repeated, "Keep the Rule, and the Rule will keep you."

Breaking the Rules was considered a betrayal of the community and its ways. Though some Rules seemed minor, the Rules fit together like a house of cards. If you removed the wrong one, the whole house might come tumbling down.

One sticky July night after Mother left, I peeled off my blouse and skirt for a shower. A candle threw flickering shadows on the bathroom walls. Candlelight in the bathroom seemed romantic, even if the candle was a two-inch stub left over from the altar and the candlestick was the lid of an old pickle jar turned upside down to catch the drippings. MCs didn't use electricity after Night Prayer.

The icy water from the showerhead stung my skin. My muscles seized. Even after nearly a month of "sharing the poverty of the poor," the cold water still surprised me. I soaped and rinsed as quickly as I could, dried myself, slipped on my white nightdress, and tossed my dirty clothes into my bucket. On my way out, the bathroom door hit something. Glaring, Sister Carmeline blocked the threshold.

"Sister Mary, what have you been doing?" Her words during Grand Silence alarmed me—only an emergency merited speaking after Night Prayer.

"Taking a shower," I said.

"You are not ashamed to say it?" Sister Carmeline's eyes narrowed.

Was I supposed to feel shame for taking a cold shower after hours of boiling vegetables into soup, after sweating through the afternoon sitting upright on backless benches while Sister Carmeline lectured us on the spiritual life?

"I'm sorry, Sister," I said. "Did I take too long?"

She hissed, "You did not use the bucket."

I looked down at my bucket—dirty clothes and towel stuffed inside, as they were every other night. "Excuse me?"

The candle cast weird shadows across her face as Sister Carmeline said, "I heard the water falling from the shower, and you did it last night, too."

"Yes, Sister. I've taken a shower every night since I arrived."

"We use the bucket." Sister Carmeline shoved her bucket at my belly. "Selfish, disobedient, and immodest."

Mystified, I searched for an explanation. Perhaps Sister Carmeline had issued a crucial instruction on showers before I'd arrived. I opened my mouth to protest my innocence, but then remembered her instruction that afternoon. When a sister is corrected, Sister Carmeline had explained, even if the accusation is unjust, she is to remain silent, like Jesus before Pilate. I knew that wasn't quite right—Jesus had been silent before Herod, not Pilate. I'd raised my hand to mention this discrepancy, then lowered it. As she'd suggested, dying to self and to pride was more important than getting the facts right. I would remain silent, as required, like Jesus before Pilate.

If Sister Carmeline was testing me, I didn't want to fail. I breathed deeply and limited myself to the five words she had approved as answer to a reprimand: "Thank you, Sister. Sorry, Sister."

"Vain." Sister Carmeline pushed past me into the bathroom, shaking her head and mumbling. "Lazy. Lazy and vain." She slammed the door behind her.

Angry and baffled, I climbed the stairs to the dormitory. *Disobedient and selfish, lazy and vain*—those were fighting words. I sidled between the beds to my cot in the corner. Some aspirants were in bed; others knelt silently to pray the Paters. I knelt, too, bare knees on the bare floor, and stretched my arms in the form of the cross, as we had been taught. I silently prayed the prescribed Act of Contrition, five Our Fathers, five Hail Marys, and one Glory Be. I was then supposed to unpin the crucifix from my blouse and kiss Jesus' wounds while reciting a prayer for perseverance, but instead I shoved the crucifix under my pillow.

In bed, I wondered if Jesus had felt this angry when He'd been accused of blasphemy for calling Himself God's Son—which had only been the truth. Truth was important. Jesus called Himself "the Way, the Truth, and the Life," and told His apostles, "You will know the truth and the truth will set you free."

I took the crucifix from under my pillow and ran my fingers up and down Jesus' bruised body, my thoughts restless. In the morning I would ask Sister Elvira, who prided herself on knowing all the Rules, how taking a shower could be a mortal offense. I raised the crucifix to my lips, kissed Jesus' five wounds, and asked for the grace of perseverance. When I finally fell asleep, I dreamed of buckets and candles, shadows and pointing fingers.

The next morning, after I dried my breakfast plate, I elbowed Sister Elvira and whispered, "What am I supposed to do with the bucket at night?"

Sister Elvira looked to see if anyone was close enough to hear her whispering outside the approved times. "Why, you take the bath," she said. "Did no one tell you?"

"Sister Carmeline mentioned something last night, but, I mean, how do you do it?"

Sister Elvira led me to the plate shelf. She grabbed a plate and a dish towel and began rubbing the plate, though it was already dry. She whispered, "You fill the bucket with water and pour the water over you with the tin can, the one sitting on the side of the tub. It conserves the water. You know, the Indian way."

She steered me into the hall, looked to see that no one was there, then continued, "Don't stand in the bucket. Put the bucket in the tub, stand in the tub, then pour." As we descended the stairs, Sister Elvira continued, "Sister Lilly, she stood *in* the bucket on the floor the first night. She made a terrible mess."

I squeezed Sister Elvira's hand in silent gratitude. She pulled back. "Don't touch," she said.

One afternoon not long after the bucket bath episode, Sister Carmeline stood at the head of the refectory table before instruction. For several long seconds all she did was look at the refectory floor. Finally she looked up and said, "Sister Carol and Sister Lilly have gone home today."

Gone home? They'd been at table with us for lunch and for tea.

"You must pray for them," Sister Carmeline continued, "and you must beg God for the grace of perseverance for yourself. Don't pass judgment on them, and"—she raised her voice for emphasis—"don't talk about it."

Sister Carmeline looked each of us in the eyes. She seemed unbearably sad, defeated. "The devil will try to tempt you. You must be strong." After a long pause, she said, "Do not give sorrow to the Sacred Heart of Jesus." She turned and left the refectory.

We sat in silence, stunned. Sister Carol and Sister Lilly had seemed happy.

From the top of the table, someone murmured, "We didn't even get to say good-bye."

Then, from the other end, "Did anyone know they were going?"

"I knew Sister Carol was thinking about it," someone replied. "She had such a hard time with the food."

The murmurs rose louder, but through it all I sat silent. *Why did I never contemplate that one of our group might leave? Where, exactly, did Sister Carol and Sister Lilly go?*

"That Crisco in the morning nearly makes me vomit."

"We're not supposed to talk about it," Sister Elvira hissed.

If God has called us here, can we leave? Should we leave?

"Does Sister Carmeline think we're babies, telling us not to talk about it?"

"Sister Lilly was so compassionate with the children," Sister Louise said.

"If I get one more rotten apple, I'm leaving, too."

How do we know if God has called us? What am I doing in this strange place?

The bell rang for adoration, and we filed out of the room. I moved to the chapel as though in a dream. From my place in the last row, the carpet seemed to melt away. I didn't know if I was rooted or floating or both. Together, we prostrated. Together, we rose. As the beads slipped through my fingers, my mouth moved in time with everyone else's, but I spoke and listened within. *God*, I said, *Sister Carol and Sister Lilly—they're gone.*

Don't worry. There are many ways. I'd heard this soundless voice before. I did not pause to question its reality.

If there are many ways, God, should I be here? Is this really what You want?

I want you to be happy.

Well, I'm mostly happy—I like the sisters and I like the challenge and this is supposed to be a great vocation—but sometimes things seem really weird. And I'm only working in the kitchen. I don't get it.

Something within me wanted God to say, "It's all a big mistake. You don't belong here. I'll take you where your gifts will be appreciated, back to your friends and family, to your freedom."

But God didn't say that. Instead, He wrapped me in His love, washed me in peace, and stilled my questions—at least for the moment.

Sister Carmeline chose the books for our daily half hour of spiritual reading. I'd grumbled my way though her first two choices, a dusty life of St. Luigi Gonzaga and a book of Marian piety. While her third choice was sometimes dry, it was also thought-provoking: *The Catholic Catechism*, edited by Father John A. Hardon, S.J.

We'd heard Father Hardon speak a few times at the contemplatives' on Union Avenue. He hobbled to the front of the chapel, feeble and white-headed, wearing the traditional black Jesuit soutane, cinched with a long sash. He sat at a table and spoke in a radio announcer's voice about prayer and the Blessed Virgin, saying things like, "My dear sisters, never forget that the Church is our Mother." His explanations were clear and logical. In his catechism, I one day read:

Catholic Moralists have always given due attention to sexual experiences outside of marriage that are called "unnatural," notably masturbation and homosexuality.... The Church has consistently proscribed homosexuality and masturbation as objectively contrary to the will of God.

Objectively contrary to the will of God? That would make masturbation a mortal sin! My college biology text had said masturbation was normal—"as natural an act among primates as is the

removal of insects from the body." The book had described masturbation briefly, and I'd tried it, without much effect. Now it appeared
I'd committed a mortal sin by accident.

Of course, I knew—and had read in Father Hardon's book—that
it was impossible to commit a mortal sin by accident. For a sin to be
mortal, three conditions must be met: grave matter, full knowledge,
and deliberate consent. Father Hardon made it clear that masturbation constituted grave matter, and since no one had forced me and
my faculties hadn't been impaired, my consent was deliberate. My
sinfulness hung on the question of whether I had *known* masturbation was seriously wrong.

No. I hadn't known masturbation was seriously wrong until I'd
read so just moments earlier. But if I had been willfully ignorant, my
lack of knowledge was culpable. If I'd had even the slightest doubt
that masturbation was sinful, I should have taken the trouble to find
out. I tried to remember. I had once run across a reference to masturbation in Ann Landers' column in the newspaper, and she'd mentioned that some religions objected. I had never taken the trouble to
find out if my religion objected or not. But I hadn't really known
what masturbation was when I read the column. I only knew it was
something sexual, and since I was too ugly to ever have a boyfriend,
I had figured it wouldn't apply to me anyway.

But I knew I shouldn't make excuses for my ignorance. My ignorance was culpable. I had offended God.

Our regular confessor came once a week, and venial sins could
wait until then, but I needed to get rid of this mortal sin immediately. Father Hardon had explained that receiving any sacrament
(except the sacrament of penance) when one was in the state of mortal sin was to add another mortal sin, the sin of sacrilege. I'd have to
confess before Mass the next morning—which presented another
problem. Only a thin curtain separated the sacristy from the chapel.
Sisters passed that curtain to enter the chapel. I didn't want them to
hear me say *masturbation*.

That evening I carefully tore a piece of paper from my notebook,
wrote a note confessing my sin, folded the paper several times, and

put it in my Bible. Before morning Mass, I stepped into the sacristy and asked the priest to hear my confession. I followed him to his side of the screen, handed him my folded note, then went to kneel on my side.

I heard him unfold the paper.

Sotto voce, he whispered, "Yes, Sister, it's a mortal sin. Don't do it again, and don't worry. For your penance offer a rosary for the holy souls in purgatory." He gave me absolution. As I got up, he reached around the confessional and put the note in my hand. "Flush it down the toilet," he said.

Two more aspirants left. My sadness at their departures soon gave way to selfish joy—Sister Carmeline needed someone to take their places at summer camp. I didn't know if I'd passed her nearly two-month test of my obedience and humility on KP duty or just lucked out, but I couldn't have been happier. Each morning, after throwing together a quick lunch for the sisters, I joined the throng of children and sisters in the basement of St. Rita's Church.

I'd glimpsed the children's lives briefly during my "come and see" week in January. Packed into tiny apartments in the projects, the kids were as likely to live with a grandmother or aunt as with their mothers. Few had contact with their fathers. Families squeezed by on food stamps supplemented by canned goods from the sisters. We supplied camp kids with breakfast and lunch—a big draw. When we played kickball or jump rope in the park I often spotted men dealing drugs under the sole shade tree—something I'd seen before only on television. I never witnessed a gunfight in the South Bronx, but three or four times a week, while we knelt for evening adoration or tossed in the heat on our cots, I heard shots. Sirens were omnipresent: ambulances racing to Lincoln Hospital, fire trucks rushing to yet another blazing tenement, police cars every now and then. That summer, the Son of Sam still ran free. The South Bronx in 1977 was a scary place for a girl from Texas, but exciting, too.

The kids and sisters loved my camp songs—I knew dozens, com-

plete with gestures and sound effects. My popularity at camp
brought a new and unexpected danger. Sister Carmeline had warned
that pride was a major enemy of the spiritual life. The joy of making
these kids happy could lead me to think more of myself and less of
God. So while I sang at the front of the room or turned the jump
rope or taught the kids to braid lanyards, I silently repeated the
prayer Sister Carmeline had taught us: *Jesus, meek and humble of
heart, make my heart like Yours.*

The heat at camp and in the convent grew unbearable. Sweat saturated my clothes and sometimes dropped from my forehead onto
the pages of my prayer book. Like the poor, we had no fans or air-
conditioning. I was annoyed with the extra decade of the rosary after
Night Prayer on July 13—MCs chanted extra prayers on the thir-
teenth of every month in honor of Our Lady of Fatima. I wanted my
bucket bath and my cot. When I finally hoisted the bucket to pour the
last remaining trickle, I heard shouts from outside, as if the neighborhood had erupted. I squatted to look through the sliver of open
window—and couldn't see anything. No streetlights, no lights in the
projects, though boom boxes continued, a testament to battery power.

I was used to power outages. When tropical storms and hurri-
canes knocked the lights out back home, people lit candles and
Coleman lanterns, watched the rain and the wind, and prayed water
wouldn't fill their living rooms. Here people shouted.

The clamor from the streets grew angry. The candle stub still
flickered above the bathroom sink even though everything outside
went dark. I said a silent prayer for people stuck in elevators or subway trains.

In the dormitory I pulled back the curtain just enough to peek outside. Some headlights shone, and someone had started a small fire.
People were streaming out the project doors and onto the street.

I heard the crack of broken glass, more shouts, and laughter,
then sirens. Sisters tossed restlessly on their mattresses, keeping silence as the Rule required, until Sister Louise elbowed in next to me
at the window. "They've gone crazy," she whispered.

"They're emptying the grocery store," Sister Elvira said. "Look." A little girl carried fistfuls of bread, a teenager lugged six-packs, and a kid pushed an overflowing shopping cart through the street. People shouted, dogs yelped. At the edge of the crowd, people ran, letting out angry howls.

Sister Carmeline peered over our shoulders, and we made way for her at the window. "My God," she said loudly. Soon all the aspirants were up, bumping into each other in the dark, craning for views from the dormitory's three small windows.

An aspirant at a far window announced, "Don't worry. The police are here." I could see lights flashing from a single parked squad car.

"Go back to bed," Sister Carmeline said. "And pray. That's all you can do. Pray."

No one moved. Even Sister Carmeline lingered at the window.

"Are you sure you locked the doors?" Sister Carmeline asked Sister Jeanne, who had this week's lock and key duty.

"Of course," Sister Jeanne said.

Sister Carmeline snorted. "We're going to check. The rest of you, back to bed." Sister Carmeline lit a candle. In the other hand she clutched a rosary.

From my cot I heard sirens, more yelling, more breaking glass. I smelled smoke. One of my fellow aspirants whimpered. A few remained near the window until Sister Carmeline's returning candle flickered in the hall.

"All locked," Sister Carmeline announced.

"I told her so," Sister Jeanne muttered near my bed.

House locked or not, I was scared. Those fires were big and the mob wild. I didn't want to go up in smoke from a bed on the third floor. If I'd been home, I would have checked the radio for reassurance that the lights would soon return, that the authorities were getting things under control. In the convent all we could do was pray and wait.

I must have fallen asleep eventually, because when the bell rang at 4:40 I didn't want to open my eyes. The smell of smoke lingered in the air as we dressed in the dark. Only an occasional passing car or a few words from the street broke the silence. In the bathroom I peeked through the window. A few people lingered on the streets, but the mob had disappeared.

In the chapel we said Morning Prayers in the dark, from memory, and waited to pray the Divine Office until the sun rose. After breakfast sisters packed candles for families and old folks in the projects. To walk the half block to summer camp, we picked our way through an obstacle course. Trash blocked the gutter, so the water that always flowed from the open fire hydrants backed up, creating a huge puddle of wet cardboard boxes, beer bottles, soda cans, and God knew what else.

One of our boys leaned against the church door. His left cheek sported a large bruise. "Hector," Sister Katey asked, "what happened?"

"Bricks," Hector said.

The kid next to him said, "Lots of bricks last night, Sis. They were trying to brick the cops."

Inside, the kids were even more antsy than usual. It took half an hour to get them to settle onto mats in the semidarkness, lit only by slivers of light shining into the basement through small windows at ground level.

At breakfast, one of the girls asked, "What does God have to do with the lights going out?"

"What do you mean?"

"On the radio they said God put the lights out," she said, wrinkling her forehead.

"Some power lines in Westchester County got struck by lightning," a volunteer answered. "They're calling it an act of God."

One of the other girls cut in, "God wanted us to have lots of new things, so He put out the lights. My uncle brought my mama a big necklace and a color TV."

Sister Katey shook her head. "Losing the lights is a test. God wants to see if we'll be good and help whoever needs help or if we'll

be selfish and take things that don't belong to us. It's always wrong
to steal."

I didn't say anything, but I wondered what I would do if the only
way I had to get a TV was to take one when opportunity offered.

We were in bed that night when the lights finally came on. A
cheer resounded through the neighborhood, with loud whoops and
shouting. From our cots in the dormitory, we all broke the Rule to
shout and sigh, too.

Late in July I was assigned chicken duty. On my first day at the task,
which intimidated me more than I wanted to admit, I looked out the
window to the coop (a few wooden crates the sisters had nailed together) as it perched on the flat asphalt roof. I tucked the corners of
my apron into the waistband of my skirt, making a kind of pocket.
Then I filled the pocket with chicken feed, said a prayer, and
stepped out the window. I lifted my skirt higher than modesty permitted, but no one was looking—no one but twenty pecking chickens, who immediately surrounded me. I threw handfuls of feed into
a corner and the chickens scurried after it.

When I tried to lift my feet, my flip-flops stuck on the roof—the
sun had softened the tar. Walking required pulling up hard on my
flip-flops and moving quickly. I entered the henhouse. Remembering Sister Rochelle's instructions, I looked for eggs both on and
under the straw and found three. I placed the eggs, warm and brown
and beautiful, into my makeshift pocket.

The chickens returned, pecking at my ankles. I ran stickily across
the asphalt, holding the eggs in the apron close. As I lifted one foot
through the window, a hen flew in beside me. I pulled in my other
leg, leaving a flip-flop lodged in the tar. As I reached to close the
window to keep the other chickens out, I lost hold of the apron. The
eggs splattered in a gooey mess all over the floor—and I raced after
the renegade chicken.

Rounding a corner, I nearly crashed into Sister Carmeline, the
hen dangling upside down from her fist. She was not smiling.

Sister Carmeline marched past me. I ran behind her, hoping at least to open the window for her, but the look in her eyes forbade me. She threw the hen out and shut the window.

Then she saw the broken eggs.

"Sister Mary," she said, still not a trace of a smile on her face, "you have destroyed community property. You must make reparation."

I stood there, egg goo on my legs, trying not to giggle.

"You must do penance," she repeated.

"Excuse me, Sister?"

"You have destroyed the property of the community. You must do penance."

Penance? For an accident? "Yes, Sister."

"Say, 'Please, may I have a penance for breaking the eggs?' "

I hated this schoolgirl repetition, but one look at her face made me swallow my protests. I repeated, "Please, may I have a penance for breaking the eggs?"

"Yes," Sister Carmeline said, crossing her arms over her chest. "You will pray three rosaries, and you will offer them for your sisters, for perseverance in their holy vocations, and that you might learn humility."

This was absurd—one rosary per egg broken, more than an hour of extra prayer! If I hadn't been so afraid of getting assigned another six months of aspirancy, I would have laughed. Instead I took a deep breath and issued the standard reply: "Thank you, Sister. Sorry, Sister."

I filled a bucket with water, fuming. Hadn't I already humbled myself, leaving academic accolades and a promising future to join these sisters? Hadn't I— I froze, my hand still on the spigot.

Wait, Mary. Listen to yourself. You don't need to learn humility because you've done something so great as to condescend to join a group of women somehow beneath you?

No, that's not what I meant. I tossed the rag in the bucket and headed back to the room. *It's not that I'm better than them, it's just that, well, I know more about some things.*

I squatted among the broken eggs, reproving myself: *Why am I still struggling with such pride? These sisters are the experts, and I'm here to learn the ways of love from them. Why can't I get that through my head?* As I reached for the bucket once more, I thought of Jesus taking the water bowl and towels to wash the apostles' feet, determined to give them an example of humble love.

I finished cleaning the floor and headed to the chapel to begin my penance. My anger still smoldered, but I could see the battle lines more clearly now. I had two enemies: Sister Carmeline's unreasonableness and, more insidious, my pride.

A few days later, I was first in line to wash my lunch plate at the bathroom sink. I was rubbing the scrubber across my plate when I heard Sister Carmeline's voice over my shoulder. "Sister Mary," she said, "you behave like a rich girl. MCs wash with cold water, like the poor."

This insult was too much. All the aspirants used hot water on their plates. If she thought cold water could dissolve the chicken fat that ringed our soup plates, she had a screw loose. Did she want us to get food poisoning? And what did she know about rich and poor? My dad had a decent job, but with seven kids the checking account always reached zero before the month was over. Besides, the poor in the South Bronx had hot water. I tried to calm down enough to spit out the expected apology, but I couldn't. Enraged, I turned on my heel and climbed the stairs to the dormitory for afternoon rest.

While the others dozed, I stared at the ceiling and took deep breaths. When I'd calmed down, I asked myself, *Where is Sister Carmeline coming from?* Literally, from Calcutta. I supposed that in Calcutta the poor used cold water to wash their plates, if they had plates or access to cold water. Germs weren't an issue, because there were so many bigger issues. I was in the convent not just to serve the poor but to live like them.

I'd read that Mother had originally planned for the sisters to live on rice, salt, and water, like the destitute. The Medical Mission Sisters in Darjeeling had helped Mother understand that if we lived like the destitute, we wouldn't have the strength to serve them.

A distinction began to form in my mind. All the destitute were poor, but not all the poor were destitute. A family in the South Bronx who depended on food stamps but had a color TV and hot water was poor in New York but would be considered middle-class in Calcutta.

Unlike poverty, destitution was an absolute: lack of the basic necessities of life. The destitute in the Bronx slept in alleys or under overpasses, eating whatever they begged or found in dumpsters. Destitution in India couldn't have been much different, except that Indians had to deal with tropical diseases instead of frostbite.

As the daily Good Humor jingle floated up through the dormitory window, I realized that I was being asked to live not like the poor in New York but like the poor in Calcutta—which meant I would have to trust the sisters, because I'd never been to Calcutta. I had built a reputation for myself as a person who made insightful intellectual distinctions, but now I was being asked to leave the judgment making to others.

God was asking me to believe the improbable and surrender the valuable. He had done that before, when he'd asked Abraham to believe that sterile Sarah would bear a son, and then demanded Abraham kill that same son. God's angel stayed Abraham's hand at the last moment, but the point was that Abraham believed even when it didn't make sense. Abraham offered God not a trifling sacrifice but what he valued most.

After the evening meal I took my soup plate to the sink. I washed it with cold water.

The day Sister Elvira didn't show up for dinner, we were told she had been sent home. Sent home—that was new. We never got an explanation, but I hoped it meant that scrupulosity wasn't really approved behavior.

Seven aspirants had returned home; five of us remained. A few of the sisters had managed furtive good-byes, pulling us aside one by one in the corridor or washing place. I missed each one.

Not long after, Sister Carmeline announced that she had been appointed superior of a new MC community in Port au Prince, Haiti. She and several other sisters would leave within the week. "I'll be working with the truly poor," she said, smiling broadly.

The day we packed her box into the van and said good-bye, Sister Carmeline told us, "Show your new mistress you know how to do as you are told. Make me proud." I was surprised to find myself choking up a little. At the same time, I was excited to imagine a new mistress who might be less intent on teaching me humility.

On her way back from leaving Sister Carmeline at the airport, Sister Andrea fetched our new mistress from the contemplatives on Union Avenue. A quiet sister with a heart-shaped face, Sister Doris didn't give us many instructions; instead, she assigned us readings and essays while she prayed in the chapel. She never raised her voice, never scolded us in public, rarely talked about "MC ways." As the days passed, I found myself missing Sister Carmeline. Sister Doris was pleasant, but Sister Carmeline had challenged us to grow.

A few weeks after she arrived, Sister Doris announced, "Today I have a gift for you." With a big smile, Sister Doris said, "Sacrifice beads."

She handed each of us a small string of ten blue plastic beads. An aluminum medal of Mary hung from one end, and a small safety pin was attached at the other. Sister Doris told us to pin the beads, in our skirt pockets or under our waistbands, so they'd be accessible without drawing attention to themselves. Whenever we made a sacrifice, we were to slide one bead down the string. Then twice a day, at noon and before retiring at night, we should count the number of sacrifices we'd made and record the number in a small notebook. At the end of each month, we were to show Sister Doris the notebook.

"How big does a sacrifice have to be before it counts?" one of the aspirants asked.

"Size doesn't matter," Sister Doris replied. "As Mother says, 'Do little things with great love.' Help a sister carry a bucket of water or keep silent when you want to speak. Put extra salt on your food, or don't add salt when you want to. Serve yourself an extra spoonful of something you don't like. When it is really cold, cover with one blanket instead of two." Sister Doris' eyes sparkled. She seemed to enjoy this list. "Choose the worst place in the chapel—the place where there is no breeze, or where the carpet is rough, the place near the front if you prefer the back, or near the back if you prefer the front."

I was pretty dazed by this point, but Sister Doris continued. "Did you all see Mother's feet when she was here?" I nodded. Mother's feet angled in a weird manner, the first two toes on each foot curled up over the others. I'd never seen feet like that before.

"When Mother was in Loreto," Sister Doris explained, referring to the convent in which Mother had served before beginning the Missionaries of Charity, "she was given a pair of shoes that were too small. No one even knew they didn't fit."

I couldn't imagine it. Mother must have worn those shoes for years in order to have permanently disfigured her feet. There was no way I would have worn shoes like that, even for a day or two. But Mother had a motive.

The theology of sacrifice as popularized in the early twentieth century owed a lot to the three child visionaries at Fatima. Mary had appeared to Lucia, Francisco, and Jacinta in Portugal, during the First World War, asking them to pray the rosary and offer sacrifices. Mary said their sacrifices would convert sinners, save souls from hell, make reparation for sin, and speed world peace. So the children ate pinecones and bitter acorns, stung themselves with nettles, and wore ropes that made them bleed. As the nuns who taught me in grades one through three (after which my parents could no longer afford Catholic school) explained it, sacrifice was necessary because people offended God by giving free rein to their pleasures. We could make up for their pleasure seeking by choosing what was unpleasant. Even as a second grader, I hadn't bought into this theology: Let those who'd eaten too much ice cream earn their own extra-credit points.

But now the same sort of theology was being spouted by Sister

Doris, and seemed woven into the culture of the new family I'd joined. Even Mother Teresa, a woman nominated for the Nobel Peace Prize, believed that by wearing shoes several sizes too small for her, she pleased God and saved souls.

"Should we really count?" an aspirant asked, wrinkling her nose. "I thought Jesus said when we do good we shouldn't let our left hand know what our right hand is doing."

"You count so that you'll do better every day," Sister Doris said. "No matter how many sacrifices you make, you'll never love Jesus as He deserves. We must take up our cross."

Jesus had said, "Take up your cross and follow me," but it seemed ludicrous to equate consuming extra salt with dying on the cross. The cross wasn't a series of inconveniences. The cross was an instrument of torture used by an imperial enemy against native insurgents—a means of capital punishment, like the electric chair, but public, and the pain was far more prolonged. I couldn't think of any time Jesus deliberately tried to make life harder for the sake of making it harder. If being faithful to the truth meant that He upset people so much that they eventually decided to kill Him, He would accept that—but nowhere do the Gospels record that Jesus ate pinecones or deliberately chose sandals too small for His feet.

While I couldn't make logical sense of the whole notion, there was also something strangely alluring about pleasing God and serving my neighbor by offering up inconveniences I couldn't avoid anyway. If I could turn kneeling into something that would save someone from hell, well, why not? I decided to give it a try.

As the days passed, I found that I could transform almost anything into an opportunity to love. I didn't have to get annoyed by an ill-timed bell, or by a sister who inadvertently splashed water on me while washing clothes. I could offer God my attempts at forbearance as acts of love. I would never practice sacrifice the way some sisters did, deliberately looking for the worst. I adjusted the concept to fit my own understanding, a trick I would apply frequently to practices whose professed rationale I found illogical. When I moved one of my sacrifice beads down the string, I didn't say, "For the poor souls in purgatory" or "In reparation for sins against chastity committed in the world today." Instead, I said, "I love you."

The day the eighth aspirant left, we remaining four pushed one of the refectory tables against the wall. Even so, the benches seemed full of empty places. Doubt gnawed at my resolve. Since I'd first read about Mother, entering the Missionaries of Charity was the only thing I'd wanted to do. But was an attraction that bordered on obsession the same thing as a call from God?

One afternoon I approached Sister Doris in her little office and asked, "Sister, how does a person know if she's doing the will of God?"

Sister Doris smiled. She had a wonderful smile—the sort of smile Mother might have called "the sunshine of God's love."

"Oh, that's the greatness of religious life," she said. "You never need to worry about the will of God. Just follow the timetable, keep the Rules, and do what your superior tells you."

"But, Sister, I don't mean just the day-to-day things. How do I know that God has called me, that He wants me to be an MC?"

"It's the same thing," Sister Doris replied, again with that smile that made everything look easy. "You felt that God called you here, so you came. As long as your superiors don't tell you to leave, you can be sure God wants you here. Leaving because it's hard or because you don't like something is doing your own will. Remaining faithful until the day you die, that is doing God's will."

I bowed my head and accepted her blessing but didn't understand how staying as long as no one told you to leave could be a sign of God's call, especially when superiors didn't send many away. I knew that the opportunity to escape both a painful social life and the financial burden of my schooling had made a religious vocation more attractive. How could I be sure I hadn't invented God's call? Absent objective criteria, believing what I felt when I prayed would have to suffice.

By October, only three of us remained: Sister Louise, Sister Jeanne, and me. Recreations were no longer the loud, boisterous occasions they'd been when I'd first arrived. I lived on hopes that we'd all be sent to Rome, where, if we received approval, we would join six Europeans who were completing their aspirancy in London.

Then one Sunday on the way to the projects to pick up the kids for Mass, Sister Louise halted the rosary and said, "I just want you to know. I can't bear all the Rules anymore. I need my freedom," she said.

I begged her to reconsider. The kids in the parish and the people in the projects loved her. Wasn't the choice to belong to God just a very particular exercise of our freedom? If we were going to become holy, didn't we have to sacrifice something, and why not something valuable?

But Sister Louise would not be swayed. "I love the sisters," she said, "and all the people. But I need my own life. I'm going tomorrow."

In the damp basement kitchen the evening Sister Louise left, after dinner with just Sister Doris, Sister Jeanne, and me, my tears fell on the pots I was supposed to be drying.

Why were they all going? What were they doing now? Even more mysterious, why was I still here? Through my tears, in the kitchen, I tried to hum the hymn from the day Mother had received us all. *Though none go with me, still I will follow, no turning back, no turning back.*

I feared I wouldn't last much longer. It wasn't that I wanted to go—at least, not most of the time—but I was so lonely, and the work was so hard, and I missed using my mind. A friend and a calculus book would have helped a lot. But at nineteen I didn't want a life like the one my friends back home had, an ordinary life with its predictability and compromises; I wanted a life with purpose, a radical life that didn't settle for the easy way. I wanted to make the world a better place. I wanted to stay. And I believed God wanted me to stay, too.

As I ran the dishcloth over the pots and pans, I prayed. *God, I'm scared. This is my life we're talking about. To tell the truth, I'm not liking it much right now. I know You move in mysterious ways, but is this really what You want? Speak to me.* Then I added words I hadn't used since I'd been a little kid. I told God, *Give me a sign.*

Other sisters entered the kitchen. I didn't look at them, but dried my eyes with a corner of the dish towel.

When I reached to put a pot back on a low shelf, Sister Rochelle squatted next to me and whispered in my ear, "Don't be sad, Mary. Many are called, few are chosen." She stood up and went away, but her words echoed in my ears: *Many are called, few are chosen.* Was this the sign I'd asked for? Had God called twelve of us, then decided to choose only two? That didn't seem right—if God had called us all, certainly He wanted to keep us all, didn't He?

That evening I searched my Bible for those words in context—a parable in Matthew's Gospel. A king sent servants to invite people to his son's wedding, but many refused his invitation. Some of them even killed the servants. In return, the king ordered his army to slaughter these people. Then the king sent other servants to call people off the street into the wedding. But when the people came, the king found one without a wedding garment, and had him thrust out into the darkness, with weeping and gnashing of teeth, "for many are called, but few are chosen."

The longer I looked at this parable, the more it disturbed me.

Why would anyone kill a person who delivered a wedding invitation? The people who did that must have been really angry at whoever sent the invitation—and understandably so, since the king didn't seem a nice fellow at all, inviting people in off the street and then throwing one out because he didn't have the right clothes. The king didn't offer to help him find better clothes, or ask him politely to leave. He had him thrown out to a place so dark, so scary, and somehow so evil that he would weep and gnash his teeth—for an offense that didn't even look deliberate.

Under this scenario, it seemed that being chosen just meant surviving somehow through the chaos, being the one left standing when the final bell rang.

As Thanksgiving approached, Sister Jeanne and I carried canned goods and frozen turkeys to hundreds of families, and prepared and delivered scores of meals to shut-ins. Our backs ached and our feet developed blisters. God had seemed so close before, but now even prayer became dry and unsatisfying. I couldn't understand what I'd done to drive God away. True, I hadn't mastered generosity or silence or swabbing the floor, but God must have known I was trying my best.

I decided to tell Sister Doris everything. Maybe this distance I felt was the sign I'd asked for, the sign that I didn't have a vocation. If Sister Doris told me to leave, I could go back to my family and my studies with a clean heart.

I entered her office and told her how difficult prayer had become, how lonely I felt, how I missed thinking and books, how I wondered where God was—and if He had called me.

Sister Doris smiled. That caught me off guard, but not as much as what she said: "So soon. That's a good sign."

"Excuse me, Sister?"

"Sister Mary," she replied, "this is a trial. God sends trials to test the faith of all generous souls. He has given you this dark night as a reward for your generosity. You must be faithful and persevere, that's all. Continue to behave as you did when you felt close to God, and your faith will grow. In the beginning, God gives feelings of consolation to help souls along, like giving sweets to a child. But when God sees you are strong enough, He removes the consolations so that your faith can grow. In the spiritual life, feelings are not important. Faith is everything."

"Dark night" sounded a bit melodramatic, but I liked hearing that I was making progress. So I tried to feel happy about feeling empty, and often reminded myself of all the things I was still doing wrong so that I wouldn't get proud. I decided to believe that God knew what He was doing. I'd come to give God everything, and now it looked like He was taking me at my word.

One evening in mid-December, Sister Doris took us downstairs for dinner with Sister Andrea and the other professed sisters, an event until then restricted to a big feast day or Mother's arrival. On the way, I spotted Sister Nirmala with another, taller sister. The taller sister stood very straight, shoulders back, head erect. She craned her neck, as if inspecting each corner, and tapped her forefingers together at waist level in what looked like disapproval.

At dinner, Sister Nirmala introduced the imposing sister as Sister Priscilla. They had trained together, like Sister Jeanne and me, but decades earlier in Calcutta. They were both daughters of military officers, and Sister Nirmala told how her Hindu father had arrived at Mother House in Calcutta with a contingent of soldiers to take his daughter away, but Sister Priscilla had stuffed her in a closet.

Through all the stories, Sister Priscilla remained remarkably quiet, adding only an occasional correction of detail. Every now and then she looked down the table, pausing on each sister's face as though examining us. Sister Nirmala explained that Sister Priscilla had most recently been regional superior in Bangladesh, where she had overseen all six MC houses there. Now, Sister Nirmala announced, she had come to take Sister Andrea's place as superior in the Bronx.

The sisters let their jaws drop, then forced smiles onto their faces. I knew the sisters loved Sister Andrea, and I could see that it would be hard to warm to Sister Priscilla.

Sister Andrea explained that Mother was transferring her to Manila, where she would be superior of the new novitiate—superior of the house in which young novices would spend two years of intense preparation before first vows.

Sister Priscilla looked at the dismayed faces around the table. "Well," she announced with a sigh, "I wish I were going to Manila instead of coming here, but we must do what God wants."

Sister Andrea then called Sister Jeanne and me into the little office off the refectory. She thanked us for being brave and for working hard, for persevering while others had left. Then she told us the words we'd longed for: "I'm sending you both to Rome, for postulancy."

We'd passed! This was the clear sign that God had called me, that He wanted me, that He chose me. If I'd had a cap, I would have thrown it in the air.

4

STRETCH

I smelled the laundry before I saw it—a potent blend of urine, sweat, feces, dirt, and bleach. Dirty sheets were piled chest high in one corner. Three large vats—one for washing and two for rinsing—stood against a cement wall, and the first vat was already full. I pulled on an apron, applied yellow bar soap to the sheet on top, and began rubbing. I beat the sheet against the stone scrubbing surface built into the vat, wrung it out, and tossed it into the rinse water. I spent four hours that morning washing, rinsing, and wringing sheets, then hauling them to the roof to hang in a fierce wind that often carried the pillowcases away as I tried to clip them to the line. Four hours that morning and two hours that evening.

Laundry wasn't what I'd imagined when Sister Jeanne and I had arrived in Rome a week earlier. I still hoped for a closer look at those exciting places we'd driven past—Nero's Palace, the Circus Maximus, the Roman Forum in the distance. We'd pulled off the Aventine Way onto a steep, tree-lined driveway, then emerged onto a pretty square. From the square rose an expanse of marble steps at least fifty feet wide and several stories tall. Atop the steps sat a huge building of white marble. One of the professed sisters who'd come to fetch us announced, "Your new home—the Basilica of San Gregorio al Celio." This church looked like an ancient mansion, massive, with eagles above three impressive archways, a balcony running around the second story, and a pitched roof. I was impressed.

The sisters helped us lug our boxes up the stairs. At a landing two-thirds of the way up, one of them said, "Turn around." Not half a mile away, the Colosseum stood tall and majestic. It took my breath away. God had brought me to this city packed with architectural and artistic masterpieces, where the Pope lived and history stood on every corner—Capitoline Hill, the Sistine Chapel, St. Peter's Basilica, the catacombs, the river Tiber, masterpieces of Michelangelo and Bernini and Raphael.

Sister Jeanne and I followed the sisters across a small gravel yard. I spotted a hand-painted sign, *Missionarie della Carità*, next to a massive wooden gate. The woman who opened the gate for us was young and quite pretty—though I wasn't supposed to notice that. A cross hung from a safety pin on her sweater, just like the crosses Sister Jeanne and I wore.

"Welcome," she said, extending her hand. "I'm Sister Alberta, a postulant from Milan."

We stepped through the gate and into a cement corridor, stunning for the soulful silence that seemed to fill it, and for the clear blue sky above—so unlike the gray pallor we'd occasionally glimpsed above the South Bronx projects. Squat cement buildings crouched on either side of the corridor; those remodeled chicken houses were our new convent.

We followed Sister Alberta into the room that served as a chapel, a little larger than our chapel in the South Bronx, and much colder. I shivered as I said a quick prayer. Sister Alberta then led us back to the corridor while she went "to call Sister." A numbing wind turned our cheeks red as we waited.

A few minutes passed before we saw, down at the far end, a door open. A thin, pale sister with a gray sweater stepped out and marched down the corridor. As she passed the chapel, she genu-flected so quickly that her sari barely brushed the pavement. She began her "God bless you" while she was still several yards away from us, then skimmed her hands over our heads. Inspecting us through tortoiseshell glasses perched on a prominent nose, she raised her arms in the air, shook her head at us, and asked, "Only two?" Her voice was high-pitched, with a tremor and an almost British accent.

The nun, whose age I placed at a vigorous sixty, turned to Sister Alberta and said, "We were expecting twelve. They distinctly told us twelve postulants from America. Now only two."

"Yes, but we are the best two," Sister Jeanne answered, smiling. "You will not be disappointed."

"The best, are you?" The sister's white eyebrows rose, as did her voice. "We shall see." She told Sister Alberta to take us to the refec-tory and give us some tea, then turned on her heel and marched away. We had just met Sister Frederick, originally of Malta, daugh-ter of a British military officer, superior of San Gregorio, and re-gional superior for all the MC houses in Europe.

Things went downhill from there. The other six postulants had already bonded, and Sister Jeanne and I felt out of place. I'd never acquired a Texas accent (my family had moved from Michigan when I was twelve and I'd resisted the drawl), but the postulants couldn't understand my American English. I cut my vocabulary by about 80 percent and tried for pure vowel sounds and crisp consonants, but again and again my fellow postulants begged me to repeat myself.

Our postulant mistress was a tiny nun whose large, sorrowful eyes seemed to have inspired her name: Sister Dolorosa. Sister Dolorosa had never left India before arriving in the San Gregorio chill to take charge of her first group of postulants. Though we didn't mean to intimidate, Sister Dolorosa seemed to cower before the eight of us relatively tall, often loud white women, half of us older than she. To make matters worse, Sister Frederick's nervous nature kept everyone on edge.

Each morning and evening, two or three postulants accompanied professed sisters to visit the poor in their homes or in hospitals. Another postulant went to the soup kitchen, one stayed in the convent to cook for the sisters, and the rest of us went to the shelter for previously homeless men and women. The shelter, which the sisters always referred to as the "Home," was located in a wing of the San Gregorio monastery. The Camaldolese monks occupied most of the monastery, and had loaned us space to shelter about sixty men and thirty women.

I was excited when Sister Dolorosa assigned me to the Men's Home, but the sister in charge directed me to the laundry. The laundry room was lonely. The skin on my knuckles cracked and my back ached. While I scrubbed and rinsed and hung, I tried meditating on Jesus' life. When he'd been my age, Jesus had passed his days wielding a hammer and saw. I did laundry.

Each evening when the last vat drained and I swept out the corner where the sheets had been piled, a sense of satisfaction filled me. Each morning, with a new pile of sheets high in the corner, I felt a sense of dread.

About ten days into laundry duty, Sister Alberta came to help me scrub. This tall Italian postulant who had opened the gate for us when we arrived plopped a soapy sheet into the rinse water and smiled. Though we weren't supposed to talk, I was pleased when she turned to me and asked, "Sister Mary, what do you think of the discipline?"

I rubbed my sheet with the bar soap. "Well, discipline's important," I said. "But sometimes keeping up with the timetable is really hard."

"Not the timetable, silly. I mean the discipline. You know, for your sins."

I didn't know what she was talking about. I rubbed my sheet harder.

She continued, "In London we had a ceremony in the chapel, with hymns and readings. Then we knelt in front of the altar and the superior gave us each the discipline."

"Did she?"

Sister Alberta pulled on my sleeve and looked into my eyes. "Haven't you ever heard the slapping noise the professed sisters make when they go to the bathroom after dinner?"

"I guess they're washing their underwear." I pounded my sheet against the scrub board.

"No, silly, they're taking the discipline." Sister Alberta's voice was soft but authoritative, and I turned to look at her. "To make up for their sins and the sins of the whole world." She had an earnest look on her face. "They beat themselves. With rope. All of us postulants from London have a discipline, too, but we don't take as many strokes as the professed sisters." She shook her curls from side to side. "Did they really not tell you anything in New York?"

My stomach contracted. I stopped scrubbing.

"What's wrong?" Sister Alberta asked. "Did I shock you?"

I couldn't reply. Kneeling on the chapel carpet till my knees ached was bad enough. But beating myself with rope? Every day? In the bathroom?

Sister Alberta laughed. Then she put her hand on my shoulder, which we both knew was a violation of the rule of touch, but I didn't shrug her off.

"I'm sorry," she said. "I really thought you knew."

"I can't believe people still do things like that."

"People still sin, don't they?"

My sense of sin had been growing steadily during the past eight months. I had never realized there were so many ways to offend God.

Sister Ivana stomped in with an armload of dirty sheets. Her big blue glasses slid down her nose. Sister Alberta looked at me and winked knowingly, nodding in Sister Ivana's direction. "She's not easily convinced," Sister Alberta said.

"No, I'm not so easy convinced of anything," Sister Ivana replied. "What you talking about now?"

"The discipline."

"Ridiculous. This is from dark age. What kind of God they think of, anyway?" Sister Ivana's voice was crusty, made even brusquer by her Croatian-flavored English.

"That's why she's always in trouble with our mistresses, wherever we go," Sister Alberta said as Sister Ivana rolled up her sleeves.

"They say I think too much," Sister Ivana said, hands on her hips. "But why God give us brain if don't want use it?" She picked up some of the sheets she'd dropped and moved toward the vat. "Anyway, this beating self is ridiculous. God doesn't need my bruise."

"Did God need Jesus to die on the cross?" Sister Alberta pulled her hands out of the soapy water and placed them on her hips, imitating Sister Ivana.

"I am Ivana, not Jesus, and God do not need me beating self." Sister Ivana pushed herself into Sister Alberta's place in front of the dirty sheets, just to my right. Sister Alberta moved behind us and down to the rinsing tub on my left. I was about to be sandwiched in an aggressive discussion on a topic that was already making my mouth dry.

Sister Ivana, elbow deep in soapy water, turned to me. "So what you think, Mary?"

I grabbed another sheet and tried to concentrate on soaping it up.

"Give her time," Sister Alberta said. "They never told her anything in New York. I've only told her just now."

"Mary"—Sister Ivana stopped scrubbing to look at me—"all I say is, don't let them to take brain away. Very dangerous."

I'd heard the scoldings Sister Ivana received regularly from our postulant mistress. Sister Dolorosa said Sister Ivana questioned too much, that obedience should be blind. I wanted to agree with Sister Ivana, but weren't we supposed to look at everything with eyes of faith? So much of the catechism didn't make sense—the Trinity, the

Eucharist. You just had to believe it. The sisters were supposed to be
the experts on pleasing God.

I wrung out a soapy sheet and tossed it to Sister Alberta. "Anything that can help me make up for my sins has to be something
good," I said.

Both Sister Alberta and Sister Ivana eyed me, as if to calculate
what sins I could have committed to need that much expiating.

After two weeks of sheet scrubbing, Sister Dolorosa assigned me to
the kitchen in the Home. My new assignment had many advantages:
the gas stove warmed the kitchen, the smells were incomparably
better, and I wasn't alone. The short, plump Indian sister in charge
grinned a lot, like a Smurf. Sister Sajani had a nervous laugh, buck-
teeth, and on her forehead a green cross tattoo about the size of a
nickel, a mark that distinguished Christian girls from Hindu ones in
her Indian state of Ranchi.

Sister Sajani was so short that she had to stand on a step stool to
ladle *caffelatte* from a pot on the stove into large aluminum teapots.
To drain the huge pasta pot, we each grabbed a handle and shuffled
down the corridor to the bathroom, where we drained it in the bath-
tub.

After breakfast, the men of the Home helped cut the day's vegetables. (Most of the women suffered from mental illness and
couldn't be trusted with knives.) The men took great pride in their
chopped potatoes and carrots, their sliced fennel and eggplant—
cases and cases of them—but they refused to touch onions or garlic.
Sometimes I, too, longed for the pleasure of drawing a line: "This I
will not do." Instead, called to obedience, each day I took a knife to
the mounds of onion and garlic the men had spurned.

Back in the convent, onions and garlic were reserved for feast
days. Vegetables for the sisters were usually overcooked by one of
the postulants in the convent kitchen. I resigned myself to rarely enjoying convent food, though the olive oil that replaced the Bronx
breakfast Crisco was a welcome improvement. We sisters ate a lot of

beans, and sometimes eggs, but in the Home Sister Sajani and I prepared chicken for our people once or twice a week.

The birds arrived fresh and whole—head, feathers, feet, and all. Decapitating them was hard for me, and burning the feathers and gutting the birds made my stomach turn, so on chicken days Sister Sajani enlisted the help of Sonia from the Ladies' Home. Sonia was a lovely, enormous woman of the street, of very sound mind and extremely efficient with a cleaver. She taught me all the Italian names for the various chicken parts and often made me laugh.

Sister Sajani only let me near the stove to clean it. She was a decent cook, but boiled pasta until it was limp, and added saffron and curry to her vegetables. Spaghetti sauce had been one of my specialties at home, and after a couple of weeks I suggested she might want to add some basil. Sister Sajani regarded my suggestion as insolent.

Somehow, the more efficient I became, the more Sister Sajani scolded me. I wasn't fast enough, I missed that spot in the corner, the dish towels hung here and not there. I began looking for ways to get away. When Sister Sajani sent me to the monks' kitchen with a hunk of mortadella to slice on their machine, I loitered before the paintings in the corridors, reveling in the stillness of the ancient stone walls. The monastery breathed a quiet passion for God.

On the one bathroom break per morning that Sister Sajani permitted, I would wander to the end of the corridor and look out the window onto the Colosseum. I watched cars and motorbikes skirt the Circus Maximus. The tall pines and the wide, blue sky would beckon, then I'd go back to the pots and pans.

That my world had become so small scared me. That my world had become so small in Rome infuriated me. I was beginning to understand that fairness had nothing to do with convent life. Living in the convent meant accepting whatever came your way as though it came from the hand of God. When Sister Frederick told us to pray for Aldo Moro, a leader of Italy's Christian Democrat party whom the Brigate Rosse had kidnapped in Rome, I began offering my captivity in the kitchen for his release and mine.

I knew also that my desire for more interesting work proved that pride was still my biggest problem. Like Sister Carmeline, Sister Dolorosa recommended repeating this simple prayer: *Jesus, meek and humble of heart, make my heart like Yours.* When I mentioned that Jesus had commanded us not to hide our lights under bushel baskets, she said, "Yes, use your gifts, but only in obedience, in the tasks assigned to you. God loves obedience above all other virtues."

On Sundays I led the singing for the Mass in the Home. I loved the Italian hymns, and singing got me out of the kitchen for an hour. Heading up the monastery stairs after Mass one March Sunday, I heard a loud crash and a chilling scream. I ran to the kitchen, but it was empty. I ran to the bathroom—and found Sister Sajani lying in a puddle of macaroni and boiling water.

I steadied my plastic flip-flops so they wouldn't slip on the starchy water and told Sister Sajani to hold my hands. She whimpered as I dragged her out, habit and sari steaming. She stood still, face blank, in shock, as I pulled at her clothes.

"Sister's going to be so upset," she said.

As I unwound her sari, the professed sister in charge of the Ladies' Home appeared and sent me to the kitchen. As I put more water on the stove, I couldn't get the memory of that scream, those steaming clothes, that look on Sister Sajani's face out of my mind.

That afternoon, I saw Sister Dolorosa trying to swallow her tears as she left the dormitory where one of the professed sisters was bandaging Sister Sajani. I asked how Sister Sajani was; she just shook her head in reply. I knew better than to ask if I could enter the professed sisters' dormitory to see her.

The next morning at Mass, Sister Sajani shuffled into chapel with bandages on her hands and sat on a chair at the back. I asked to leave early for the Home, knowing I'd be working in the kitchen by myself. "Of course," Sister Dolorosa said. The men and Sonia were all eager to help, and though we were a little late with lunch, we managed everything just fine.

The next morning, with breakfast bread already in the baskets and jam on the table, I was ladling *caffèlatte* into teapots when Sister Sajani hobbled in.

"Sister, what are you doing here?" I said, laying the ladle down. "You should be resting."

"A missionary does not rest," Sister Sajani replied, voice flat.

"Sister, you can't work. If you stand near the stove or get your hands wet, you'll never heal."

Sister Sajani turned her back to me and reached for her apron.

"Sister," I pleaded, "please go home. I'll manage here. We'll be fine."

"A missionary does not rest," Sister Sajani repeated, her apron hanging from her neck.

"Sister, this is silly." I put the teapot down. "I'm going back to the convent to tell Sister that you are here."

As I pulled my apron off, I heard a small voice: "Sister is the one who told me to come."

I turned to look at Sister Sajani and saw tears in her eyes.

"A missionary does not rest," Sister Sajani repeated softly, wiping a tear with her apron. "Sister says that when Mother had fever, she just kept working. We are not here to pamper ourselves."

"Pamper? Sister, you're burned from head to toe."

Sister Sajani grabbed my arm with her bandaged hand. She pleaded, "Don't tell Sister anything. I am a missionary. I will offer it to Jesus, okay?"

I would not ask for a new assignment. Sister Sajani needed me now. I marveled at her strength and her restraint. She never complained, and she never mentioned Sister Frederick again. I never again suggested she rest in the convent, though I couldn't help criticizing Sister Frederick in my mind. Maybe she was trying to make Sister Sajani strong—which she might consider love—but it didn't seem like love to me.

After dinner each night, I heard the *slap slap slap* from the bathroom stalls. I would cringe, then feel my pulse race with something verging on excitement.

A voice inside insisted that I tell Sister Dolorosa that I didn't
have a discipline yet, that no one had mentioned this in New York.
But that wasn't really my responsibility, was it? The oversight might
have been God saying to me, *I don't want you to suffer.* Or maybe it
was a divine test to see if I'd be faithful to the interior voice that insisted on duty. Maybe the discipline was what I needed to beat my
heart into generosity and submission.

One evening I found Sister Dolorosa and asked to see her. We
went into the dormitory.

"Sister, I just wanted to tell you that I've heard that as postulants
we're supposed to use the discipline, but nobody ever gave me one."

Her mouth opened slightly. "I see," she finally said. "I'll take care
of it."

The days grew longer and warmer. Flocks of swallows flew over the
monastery, and I could hear their chatter from the kitchen. The
April sky at the end of the corridor was a bright cloudless blue. Sister Sajani no longer winced when stirring soup. She'd begun lifting
pots and putting her hands in the dishwater.

I hadn't yet said a word to Sister Dolorosa about my time in the
kitchen, but I had spring fever so badly that if it had been measured
in degrees, I would have pushed the mercury right out of the ther-
mometer.

Sitting opposite Sister on a bed in the dormitory, I said, "I'm
only nineteen. I'm not used to being inside all the time. I'd like the
chance to learn some of the other apostolic work, too."

"I'll think about it," Sister Dolorosa promised. I left the dormitory imagining the sun on my face again, the wind in my hair.

After a few days, Sister Dolorosa smoothed the bedcover nervously when she called me for another chat. "I'm sorry," she said.
"I'd like to change your assignment, but Sister Sajani won't accept
any other postulant—she wants only you."

"But, Sister," I said, "anyone can do the work in the kitchen—it's
just cleaning and odd jobs. Shouldn't the others have their chance?"

She hadn't looked up yet. "Sister, I can't take it anymore," I said. "I need another assignment."

After a pause, Sister Dolorosa raised her head, narrowed her deep brown eyes, and looked straight at me. "Mother always says, 'Love, to be real, has to hurt.' "

Her words hit me like a slap.

Love has to hurt. Well, love didn't seem to be hurting my sisters who came back from apostolate every day with stories of cleaning the home of an old man who cried in gratitude, stories of praying with the dying in the hospital, of convincing a Gypsy family to send their children to Mass on Sundays.

I tried to calm down. Before I'd joined, God and I had worked as a team. When I was in fifth grade, deciding to take up the flute or the cello, I'd asked God's advice and I'd heard God say in my heart, *I like them both. You choose.* Now no one ever asked what I thought, much less what I wanted.

I stood up and walked away from Sister Dolorosa, without bowing for the customary blessing.

Each day I waited, wanting this to be the day Sister Dolorosa would give me the discipline, and also hoping she would forget. I didn't know if I wanted love to hurt that much, but I wanted to give it a try.

One evening, as we were walking to the refectory, someone whispered my name. I turned in the dark corridor. Sister Dolorosa stuffed something scratchy into my hand and closed my fingers around it. I heard her whisper for Sister Jeanne.

In the refectory, I looked down and saw knotted cords of rough rope dangling from my fist. Trembling, I shoved the wad into my skirt pocket. This wasn't how I'd thought it would be—the London postulants had had a ceremony in the chapel. I saw Sister Jeanne go into the bathroom. I entered the stall next to hers and shut the door. My knees shook. I took the bunch of knotted cords into my hands. From Sister Jeanne's stall, I heard the beating sounds, one, two, three.

I took a whack at my back. That gave a muffled sound, not at all like the sounds coming from Sister Jeanne's stall or the sounds I'd heard behind other closed bathroom doors, either. The sounds I'd heard were of something striking skin, not clothes. But the sisters probably didn't get undressed—they came out too quickly for that.

I lifted my skirt and swung at my legs, just above my knees. It stung, and the sound seemed right, though softer than Sister Jeanne's. I swung harder. The skin of my lower thighs turned red. Then red with white streaks as I hit harder.

I'm doing it right, I thought.

I'm doing penance.

Like all the great Saints.

In the afternoons I escaped the kitchen for a few minutes to prepare for adoration in the Home, where a lanky, slightly awkward Dutch priest often officiated. I set out the vestments for Father Henri Nouwen, and sometimes we exchanged a few words in the sacristy.

Father Nouwen had also written several books. He gave a copy of *Creative Ministry* to Sister Dolorosa, who assigned it to me. I'd never told anyone how claustrophobically lonely I felt in the kitchen, but Father Nouwen spoke to me from the pages of his book, sharing his own struggles and fears, and I began to feel I'd found a friend. I jumped a little from my seat when I read:

> There seems to be a profound resistance to change. . . . In many ways we are resistant to the call of him who says that when you are young you can put on your own belt and walk where you like, but when you grow old you will stretch out your hands and somebody else will put a belt around you and take you where you would rather not go (John 21:18). In complete contrast to our idea that adulthood means the ability to take care of oneself, Jesus describes it as a growing willingness to stretch out one's hands and be guided by others.

My assignment to the kitchen was a call to Christian maturity. The Romans had bound Peter's hands and led him to Vatican Hill, where they crucified him upside down. God was asking me to allow myself to be led to the kitchen every morning, to empty myself for him.

I thought of Mother's words I'd seen printed on a little sign in the hallway: *The less we think of ourselves, the more God thinks of us.* My heart beat quickly. I kept my head down so as not to attract the attention of the other sisters at the table, and I even turned a few pages, but I didn't read any more that day. I was going to be a mature Christian. I was going to stretch out my hands and my soul. I was going to forget myself.

5

EYES OF FAITH

SPRING 1978
SAN GREGORIO, ROME

S ister Frederick stood tall and straight at the head of the table. She had come to the postulants' refectory to make an announcement, and we were nervous. Encounters with the elderly superior of San Gregorio were not typically pleasant.

At Our Lady's statue every night, Sister Frederick stood boldly erect, eyes stern. She would join her palms and hold them close to her face, index fingers pressed against her chin, middle fingers grazing her lower lip. Her quick, British-inflected Hail Marys shrilled like the noise chalk sometimes makes on a chalkboard, and rose in both pitch and volume at the end. "HailMaryfull of grace theLord iswith Theeeeeeee. BlessedartThou amongwomen andblessed isthe fruitofthyWOMB, *Jeeeeeeeeeesus.*" If she hadn't scared me so much, I might have laughed every evening.

That particular April afternoon at the head of our refectory table, after a Hail Mary—complete with her unique *Jeeeeeeeeeesus*—Sister Frederick sat down, folded her hands on the table, and leaned forward, so her face was just in front of the sisters at the top of the table. Her eyes were still hard as marble, but something was different. Her lips turned up a little at the corners.

"Sisters, I've come to tell you something very, very important," she said, pausing to look at each one of us. "It will be exciting news for you, but I've come here not because it is exciting, but because it is very important that you look at what I am about to tell you with eyes of faith.

"Faith, dear sisters—" She raised her chin as if looking down from a place of superior knowledge. "Faith allows us to discern divine reality. Within a few days, our dearest Mother will arrive—"

"*Grazie, Gesú, grazie!*" The shout came from Sister Giosi, a particularly exuberant postulant.

Sister Frederick aimed a frozen stare at Sister Giosi.

"Sorry, Sister. Very sorry." Sister Giosi's head bent until it nearly touched the table. I tried to swallow the smile that rose to my lips, and most of the others around the table did the same.

"I have come to ensure that Mother's visit is something you will anticipate not with your emotions but with the eyes of faith. Mother is the superior general of our Society, and as such she represents divine authority. We owe her deep respect, not emotional gawking. Do you understand?"

"Yes, Sister." We responded in chorus, like schoolchildren.

"But," Sister Frederick continued, bending forward, "I have something far more important to tell you. While Mother is here, we will all be received into the presence"—here she paused, building to a climax—"of the Vicar of Christ."

"*Il Papa Paolo Sesto,*" Sister Giosi whispered.

"Yes," Sister Frederick said, permitting herself a little smile. "Pope Paul the Sixth, visible head of the Body of Christ, is granting us a private audience. We will be received into the presence of he who transmits the Holy Faith that comes from the apostles." I'd never heard anyone speak of "the Holy Faith" the way Sister Frederick did—I could hear the capital letters in her voice, see them in the way her eyebrows rose.

"You must prepare to receive a personal message from Our Lord Himself. We will offer many prayers and sacrifices," Sister Frederick continued. "Our Holy Father has suffered so much from unfaithful priests." Sister Frederick sighed.

I wasn't sure what she meant about the Pope's suffering, but I imagined Sister Frederick was horrified by the sit-ins some American priests had staged to protest *Humanae Vitae*, Pope Paul VI's 1968 encyclical condemning artificial contraception. She probably disapproved of priests who burned draft cards, questioned the virgin birth, or invited the faithful to join hands during the Lord's Prayer at Mass.

Sister continued, "Mother has requested that our people from the Home attend the audience as well, and you will help the professed sisters make them presentable. They must be clean not only of body but also of soul. We must all prepare with prayer and a good confession. Understood?"

"Yes, Sister," we replied.

"Very well, then." She pushed up from the table, said a Glory Be, and disappeared with steps that sounded far too heavy for a person so thin.

Sister Frederick's phrase "eyes of faith" kept coming back to me. Looking at the Pope with eyes of faith, we were supposed to see not just a man but the Vicar of Christ. When we looked at Mother with eyes of faith, we were supposed to see the transmitter of God's will. The Eucharist was not bread but the Body of Christ. The poor were Jesus in His distressing disguise.

Every evening at adoration, we sang, *Senses cannot grasp this marvel; faith must serve to compensate.* God's authority gave faith a logic all its own. This had first become clear to me years earlier, after an impassioned high school discussion of James Joyce's *Portrait of the Artist as a Young Man.* Several of my classmates—including those I respected most—sided with Stephen Dedalus: God didn't exist, and the Church was only out to exploit people. Others said, "Of course

God exists. Creation needs a Creator. Don't you feel Him in your soul?"

I'd been unusually silent. I knew people sometimes misused God, but that didn't prove His nonexistence. I'd often shied away from what I considered my parents' overly emotional religion. They belonged to the Catholic charismatic movement, speaking in tongues and praying for healing. At our home, we prayed together every morning and said grace before every meal. On Sundays we sat together in one of the front pews at Mass, and every Monday we attended prayer meetings. My father studied the Bible the way I studied my schoolbooks, with notebooks and references and various translations at hand. He believed God was with us always. Dad embarrassed me more than once when, chatting with an acquaintance in the grocery store, he laid hands on the person's shoulder and prayed for his or her troubles between the carrots and tomatoes.

Despite my discomfort, part of me understood Dad's easy relationship with God. God had kept me company on my walk to school when I was little, and I'd always talked over important decisions with God, whose answers I heard in my heart. Watching a sunset or the Gulf waters off the Texas coast, God's love had sometimes seemed very close. But these feelings weren't proof of God's existence—they could just mean that looking at nature and imagining God made me feel good.

The evening after that high school debate, I pondered the existence of God. As I dried dinner dishes, I considered Jesus' miracles, especially His resurrection. Jesus said He rose and healed through the power of God, His Father. Good men don't lie and Jesus was a good man.

At that moment in my parents' house, while stacking plates in the kitchen cupboard, I stood before a divided path, though it felt more like a cliff. Kids at school thought God was a bunch of hooey. Still, I couldn't deny logic, nor how my heart felt in what I perceived to be God's presence. Setting myself apart from my classmates to stand on the side that included my parents felt weird, as though my independent teenage self had taken a step backward, but it seemed the only honest choice. Dish towel in hand, without a single spoken word, I turned my life over to God.

A few months after that I'd seen Mother on the cover of *Time* and found my place in the world. Just two years later, I was about to rub shoulders with Pope Paul VI and Mother Teresa, two people widely recognized for being as close to God as a person could get on earth.

We welcomed Mother with songs and garlands. Several postulants shouted; Sister Frederick glared. On the appointed day, we climbed with our squeaky-clean poor into a special bus headed for St. Peter's. It was the first time I'd been out of the San Gregorio complex since arriving in Rome four months earlier. The city looked bright and wondrous, the sky wide enough to hold me. I didn't understand Sister Frederick's admonition against emotion. If she'd been talking about rage or envy or pride, I would have understood, but feeling this gloriously excited might have been a taste of heaven.

We got out near St. Peter's Square. Fabio, an elderly man from the Home, stepped out of the bus behind me. I took his arm, and Sister Giosi clasped the other arm. We rounded a corner, and I nearly stopped breathing when we passed through a massive circle of marble columns and emerged into the square. There I was— gazing upon the vast marble basilica at the heart of the Church. Fabio struggled to put one foot in front of the other. He mumbled something about the church being too far away. We took baby steps across the cobblestones, which suited me just fine. The obelisk at the center of the square, the brilliant dome, the colossal statues of Peter and Paul, the clocks with their mammoth bells—even the pigeons seemed sublime. I could have stood all day in the midst of that massive beauty and symmetry. The columns surrounded us, so broad that it would have taken four or five of us to stretch our arms around any one of them, but I didn't feel dwarfed—I felt enlarged by their splendor. Sister Giosi, a native of Rome, pointed to the window where the Pope blessed pilgrims during the Sunday Angelus, then to the balcony where new Popes appeared for the first time. I marveled at the fact that this girl from Texas was there at all.

When we eventually walked through the massive doors, my eyes took a moment to adjust to the relative darkness. The church was so large that I couldn't see all the way to the end, where we were to have Mass before meeting the Pope. Inside the basilica, I suddenly felt very small. We passed Michelangelo's *Pietà*, and I felt the tenderness and the sorrow of Jesus' Mother as I never had before. Sister Giosi pointed to the statues in alcoves near the top of the walls. "They are the founders of religious orders," Sister Giosi whispered. "One day our Mother will be there."

We approached the main altar, surrounded by oil lamps that marked the tomb of St. Peter, who was buried in the crypt directly below. Only the Pope said Mass at this immense altar with its magnificent canopy. We were headed beyond, to the church's second most important altar, located beneath the chair of St. Peter and the stained-glass window of the Holy Spirit, represented as a dove, golden light spilling through the glass onto the pews where we settled with our poor.

A bishop and over thirty priests concelebrated Mass. The MC novices, all dressed in white and already in place when we arrived, led the singing. I had never heard MCs sing so beautifully, in three-part harmony. It seemed as though the beauty and splendor and history I'd craved were all being packed into this hour in St. Peter's, and I reveled in it. At Communion time, I thanked Jesus for bringing me here, and asked Him to prepare my heart for His message through the Pope.

After Mass Sister Giosi and I helped Fabio out of the church. The novices, unencumbered by the need to guide and assist, wandered freely throughout the basilica, gazing at the mosaics and praying at the tombs. Wrapped in long white habits and saris, rosaries dangling through their fingers, the novices looked—I couldn't avoid the comparison—like angels.

We walked out into the sun again and guided Fabio through the colonnade. We approached another enormous door, flanked by Swiss Guards—silent men with huge axes, bright costumes, plumed hats, and tall boots. The Guards pointed us up three flights of wide marble steps. Colored light from stained-glass saints and angels dappled awestruck faces. For Fabio and many of the older men and women, the climb required several long breaks. I wondered if these steps, probably accustomed to clerics in cassocks and dignitaries in fine suits, had ever seen a crew as motley as ours. Fabio grew short of breath, and Sister Giosi and I hoisted him up the last few steps.

At the top, men in black ushered us past more Swiss Guards into a huge room unlike any I'd ever imagined. Geometric mosaics adorned the marble floor. Gilded garlands framed the ceiling. Several chubby, naked angels flew high in each tall corner, sporting golden fig leaves between their plump legs. On one wall a voluptuous Judith, eyes blazing, ran from a tent, grasping the long hair of Holofernes' bodiless head. On another wall, a muscular Neptune, white beard held aloft by the wind, glared over an angry sea, a huge three-pronged fork in his hand. Several naked women, half wrapped in their own flowing hair, called, beckoned, tempted. A mother nursed her child. I went into overload. This opulent collision of the sacred, the profane, and the mythological was too much to take in. I wondered how the itinerant preacher from Nazareth would have felt.

Ushers guided us to carved oak chairs with pink velvet seats, and Sister Giosi and I sat on either side of Fabio. At the front of the room a large, golden throne with an indigo satin seat stood empty on a raised dais. "It's like a dream," Sister Giosi whispered.

Sister Ivana, trying to separate two of the more unstable women who were prone to fights, whispered back, "It's not a dream. See, Sergio wet the pants already." Sister Ivana and another postulant took the man with the wet pants in search of the men's room.

Before long Mother entered, Sister Frederick by her side, two ushers leading them to seats directly in front of the throne. Novices filed into the section opposite Mother, a solid block of sixty sisters in white. Dozens of Co-Workers, all dressed as though for a wedding, took seats behind Mother. During this audience, the Pope would grant official approval of the Co-Workers' *Constitutions*. The Co-Workers here were spiritual descendants of the Americans in Minnesota who had read about Mother in the 1960s, decided to infuse Mother's spirituality into service to their families and communities, and called themselves the Co-Workers of Mother Teresa. Within a decade this movement of laypeople had spread over the globe. Most of the volunteers who helped us in Rome were more interested in serving dinner to the men than in sitting down to meetings, but some were fervent members of the Co-Workers movement, praying together and discussing how to serve better. Barely a week before our audience, I'd been washing pots when I'd overheard Sister Frederick complain that some Co-Workers had infuriated Mother by raising funds to pay for "newsletters and travel and other such nonsense." I wondered if official Vatican recognition of the Co-Workers' *Constitutions* was an attempt to control the organization.

After nearly three hundred of us were seated, a priest in a black cassock approached a microphone on the floor to the left of the throne. *"In piedi, per il Suo Santitá, il Papa Paolo Sesto."* We all stood, except those like Fabio whose legs refused to move after the climb up the stairs, those whose minds were absent, and Sergio—who had returned drier, but not fully so, and who surely was leaving a wet spot on the velvet.

The Guards clicked their heels and flung their axes upright. Several clerics in cassocks of various shades of red entered, their hands folded, looking neither to the right nor to the left. Behind them walked a diminutive man in white robe and skullcap—Pope Paul VI. We applauded vigorously, and our people shouted, *"Viva il Papa."*

The Pope smiled as he walked. When the procession of clerics neared the throne, the Pope broke ranks to approach Mother, his hands outstretched. Mother bowed and kissed the Pope's ring, and the Pope grasped her hands. I felt very proud.

"Isn't it so incredible?" Sister Giosi covered her cheeks with her hands as she bounced up and down in place. "They are both so small, but so great in the universe."

Mother looked down as the Pope lifted his cassock to mount the steps of the dais. A powerful aura of nobility radiated from him. When the Pope sat, we continued to applaud. As the Pope turned toward us, I could see that his skin looked transparent. He seemed tired and fragile. Nonetheless, he continued to smile, and he waved at us. He was, in fact, the only man near the dais who smiled, and his smile struck me as one of the most genuine I had ever seen.

When we finally stopped clapping and everyone sat down, the Pope spoke into a microphone, "My dearest Mother Teresa and all the beloved Missionaries of Charity." Though his voice was frail, he spoke with obvious conviction and warmth. He greeted the Co-Workers and the poor in Italian. I managed to catch a few phrases: *beati i poveri*, "Blessed are the poor"; *rendiamo grazie a Dio*, "Let us give thanks to God." I wished Sister Alberta had given us more than the two hours of Italian class that Sister Dolorosa had considered sufficient. By listening attentively at Mass and through my attempts at communication with Sonia and the men in the Home, I'd picked up a little Italian, but not much. After the Pope's brief speech, one of the ushers escorted Mother to the throne, where she knelt. The Pope handed her an official document—the *Constitutions of the Co-Workers of Mother Teresa of Calcutta*—and we all rose, clapping even more vigorously than before.

Then the Pope turned to the block of novices, all in white. He glanced at a paper held by a middle-aged priest in a black cassock. Now he was going to give a message from Jesus. I took a deep breath. Sister Giosi leaned forward in her chair.

"Remember always, beloved daughters in Christ"—as he read, his voice quavered—"the value of your religious consecration. Through your consecration to the Lord Jesus, you respond to His love and discover the needs of His brothers and sisters throughout the world." *Yes, that is what I want to do: to serve Christ's poor throughout the world.* Sister Giosi sighed and beat her chest as at the *mea culpa*.

"This consecration, expressed through your vows, is the source of your joy and fulfillment. It is the secret of your supernatural contribution to the Kingdom of God. It is the measure of the effectiveness of your service to the poor, the guarantee that it will last." *A guarantee—how wonderful. I'll still be smiling in God's service when I'm as old as the Pope.*

The cassocked man pulled back the paper, and the Holy Father looked directly at Mother, then at the novices. I supposed he didn't realize that those of us with crosses pinned to our blouses, seated with the poor, were on our way to becoming sisters, too. Still, I knew he spoke to us when he said, "Yes, to belong to Christ Jesus is a great gift of God's Love. And may the world always see this love in your smile."

We all clapped, then knelt for the papal blessing, Sister Giosi holding her rosary high so that it could be properly blessed as well: *"In nomine Patri et Filii et Spiritui Sancti."*

"Amen."

The audience had been shorter than I'd expected, but it had been long enough to understand that the Pope loved the Missionaries of Charity. He had been simple and direct, with a message much like Mother's. Jesus says: "Let me love you. Belong to me forever, and I will make you happy."

A few days later, Sister Dolorosa beamed when she announced that Mother had agreed to meet each of us individually. We were going to be novices, she said. In two weeks we would enter the most important stage of our religious formation, and Mother could help us prepare.

I shuffled nervously in line outside the door of the tiny sacristy that doubled as our parlor. At first I'd been excited. I'd longed for the opportunity to speak to Mother nearly from the moment I'd first read about her. But as I stood in line I scrabbled for something to say. I realized I'd started to feel uneasy in New York, when Mother had insisted that we become Saints, when she'd told us to stay and be faithful for life or to pack up and go home immediately.

The door opened and Sister Giosi came out, hands over her face. She strode straight to the chapel without even a glance to the rest of us in line. I left my place for a better view into the chapel. Sister Giosi knelt in front of the crucifix, head in her hands, crying. She'd been with Mother nearly half an hour. Sister Giosi raised her head, and I saw a half smile through the tears. She rocked from side to side, saying, *"Dio mio, Dio mio, ti ringrazio."* Sister Giosi was thanking God. Sister Giosi tended to be emotional, but seeing her convinced me even more that my meeting with Mother was going to be momentous.

I told myself not to worry. Mother proclaimed love. She would take the lead. I would experience what the British journalist Malcolm Muggeridge had when he wrote that Mother shone with "all the beauty and joy in the universe."

The door opened again, a full fifteen minutes after it had closed. Sister Ivana went in.

"Mother was so beautiful," the postulant who had emerged whispered, tearing up and putting her hand on my shoulder. "I feel she is my own mother. I can tell her anything."

"I don't know what to say," I whispered back, biting my lip.

"Tell her your problems. She is your mother."

I didn't think Mother wanted to hear about my problems. She was important, busy, and tired. I was just a selfish girl, struggling to get all the Rules straight.

Finally Sister Ivana came out. She volunteered loudly, for those of us still in line, "She is *wonderful*. A real mother."

Perhaps the whole "mother" concept was what gave me trouble. My own mother was a wonderful person, and she always did the best she could, but I was born just ten months after the wedding. By the time I was twelve, there were seven of us. When I'd asked why I couldn't go out to play with the others, Mom had told me, "God made you the eldest. That means He wants you to stay and help your mother." In an ideal world a mother consoled, advised, protected, and nurtured, and perhaps I'd once thought Mother Teresa would be like that—but now I knew she expected better of me. Telling this living Saint that I didn't like being assigned to the kitchen was ludicrous.

I was next, and more nervous with each passing minute. I leaned to Sister Jeanne, in line behind me. "I don't know what to say."

"Tell her you want to be a good Missionary of Charity. Ask for her help."

True, I wanted to be a real MC more than ever. Mother's vision of God's love and her determination to love others made me believe a better world was possible. When that door opened, I wanted Mother to say she was happy I wanted to be a Missionary of Charity. I wanted her to look into my eyes and tell me God loved me.

The door swung open, and Sister Jeanne pushed me. "Go on, now."

I closed the door after me. "*Ah cha,*" Mother said, leaning into her hands, palms flat on her knees, as she nodded toward a stool. I waited for her to say something, but she waited for me. She looked tired.

"Mother, I want to thank you for accepting me in the Society."

"Very good," she said, smiling. "You are here to become a Saint. You will enter the novitiate soon, and you must use this time to be very faithful in everything. Faithfulness in little things is a great thing."

Mother has said all this before. "Mother, I was hoping you could tell me something to help me. I really want to live this life well."

"Sister," Mother said, looking for the first time into my eyes, "stay always close to the Immaculate Heart of Mary, and you will never need to worry about anything. Perseverance in your vocation is guaranteed if you stay close to Our Lady."

"But, Mother, how do I do that?" Outside the door, the Angelus bell began to ring. "I've always found it hard to pray to Mary. It never seems like—"

"Sister, they are ringing the Angelus." Mother stood. "The Angel of the Lord declared unto Mary."

"And she conceived by the power of the Holy Spirit."

"Hail Mary, full of grace . . ." Here I was, alone with Mother, praying the Angelus. I was suddenly seized by an insane fear that I would forget some of the words.

"Holy Mary, Mother of God . . ." We finished the Angelus, without any mistakes, and I sat down to continue our conversation. Mother, however, remained standing.

"Sister, the bell has rung."

"Yes, Mother, but—" I rose quickly, realizing that I should not sit while Mother stood. "I had something more I wanted to ask."

Mother looked over my shoulder toward the door. "Sister, the bell has rung."

"I just wanted to know how to stay close to Mary, Mother. She seems so far away."

"Sister, the bell is the voice of God." Mother opened the door.

"May I come back later, Mother?"

"I think you have had enough. There are still others."

"Yes, Mother," I said, swallowing hard. "Thank you." I bowed and her hands rested for a moment on my head, then she left for the chapel. I still hoped, one day, for a message just for me.

The next day, Sister Frederick told us that Aldo Moro, for whose release from the Brigate Rosse I had offered my difficulties in the kitchen, had been found shot dead, abandoned in a car a little more than a mile from our convent.

6

SCISSORS

As my fellow postulants and I knelt before the simple wooden altar, a May breeze swept through the open windows of the novitiate chapel and ruffled our mantillas for the last time. After today we would fuss no more with skirts and blouses that had grown tight from too much bread and pasta. More than anything else, I wanted to belong to God completely. In a few minutes I would be closer to that goal. I wouldn't just be holding a habit and sari in my outstretched arms; I would be wearing them, though without the blue border that marked a professed sister's consecration. I wasn't yet sure if I would miss the feel of the wind on my legs, the sun on my arms, being called Mary.

Mother's words in the refectory moments before had been both firm and consoling. "Sisters, imagine—imagine God so busy with you, so occupied with each one that He gave you a personal call. He said, 'I have loved you with an everlasting love.' " She had nodded sternly and shaken a no-nonsense forefinger in our direction. Mother was forever emphasizing God's call, the one definitive fact

before which all my doubts about worthiness and suitability revealed themselves as mere egotistical preoccupation. God had called
me. He knew what He was doing.

According to Mother's *Explanation of the Original Constitutions*,
the two novitiate years were the most important of our religious life,
a "school of perfection" in which we would "learn to pray continually." The pressure was on, and I felt ready, even eager.

From the corner of my eye, I saw Mother enter the chapel
through a side door. The sisters began a familiar hymn: *I have decided
to follow Jesus, no turning back, no turning back.*

Mother advanced down the line of eight young women yearning
to becoming her spiritual daughters. Sister Alberta knelt first in line,
and Mother locked eyes with her. Our new novice mistress bent to
Mother's ear, and Mother repeated the name Sister Fatima had
whispered: "Sister Maria Lina." Sister Alberta was no more.

As Mother drew closer, my heart pounded. I wanted this. I was
ready. I vowed to make Mother proud one day. Standing just in
front of me, Mother looked into my eyes. Voice firm, she announced the name I had chosen just days before: "Sister Donata."
The new name felt like a wave cresting over me, carrying away that
postulant called Mary who found it so difficult to bend to others. In
her place stood Donata, "the freely given one."

With both hands, Mother lifted the bundle of clothes from my
arms: "Receive this holy habit." She pressed the habit to my face,
and I kissed it. "May this holy habit remind you of your separation
from the world and its vanities. Let the world be nothing to you and
you nothing to the world. Let it remind you of your baptismal robe
and help you to keep your heart pure from sin."

Mother did not wait for my "Amen" before returning the bundle
to my hands. Sister Fatima handed Mother a pair of scissors, and I
held my breath. Mother's fingers closed upon a stray lock of hair.
The blades of the scissors snapped crisply above my ear, startling me
with their finality. Mother laid the single curl on the tray Sister
Fatima held, a token of all the curls about to be shorn. Mother gave
my shoulder a firm shove—time to change into my new clothes.

Once out the chapel door, I ran to the refectory, singing to the sky, "Jubilation! I fall on my knees and I'm laughing."

At the refectory door, a thin Indian novice waited, smiling. She led me to the long refectory table, covered with brown paper. A professed sister, scissors in hand, grasped the ponytail that grazed my back. With a few quick snips, she severed my curls. A novice wrapped my ponytail in brown paper while another tied a headpiece over my head like a kerchief. They led me into the dormitory, where I unbuttoned my blouse and unzipped my skirt.

The novices pulled the habit over my head and I shimmied out of blouse and skirt, letting them fall to the floor. One novice snapped the front placket of my crisp white habit while the other tied a rope cincture around my waist. Then they began the intricate sari dance: tuck, drape, pull, fold, over, under, higher, lower, wrap, adjust, fasten with a pin.

"Turn around." They pulled a little here, tucked a little there. The final verdict: "It's too long, but we haven't time to fix it now."

I walked toward the chapel, stepping on the bottom edge of the sari as I went. "Pull it up and hold it when you walk," one said. The other laid the ponytail package in my hands. I looked at the hair—flimsy, slight, so recently attached—and I flinched, nearly dropping it.

"You are a bride," the novice whispered.

"Those are your flowers," the other said, nodding toward the ponytail.

I hurried to the chapel.

"Hail Mary, full of grace . . ." Mother's firm alto led the rosary. Someone whispered that I should put my hair in the basket in front of the altar. The last of the new novices followed behind me. After she laid her hair in the basket, someone intoned, "Immaculate Cause of our Joy," and we filed out of the chapel singing, *For God and duty we will die, rejoicing all the while.* As our group emerged into the compound, the other novices surrounded us with laughter, clapping, and Jubilate Deo, sung in an enveloping round beneath a budding grapevine.

After more singing, Sister Fatima told us to go behind the parlor to the *asilo*, a large spare room once used as a nursery school for children of working mothers from the neighborhood. As we filed past, I spotted a small mirror in the parlor, a shiny square no larger than a sheet of notebook paper. I grabbed the sari of the novice nearest me and pulled her inside.

"Sister Ivana," I whispered, then corrected myself, "I mean, Sister Jelka—"

"Look at us!" she said, immediately spotting the mirror. "We look like eggs."

A stranger's face grinned back at me. I hadn't seen a mirror since I'd left home.

One of the senior novices pulled us outside. "You're not supposed to be in the parlor, much less looking in the mirror."

"But we look like bald eggs," Sister Jelka giggled.

"You look like angels," the novice answered, shutting the parlor door behind us.

Dinner was noisy, the soup salty, the bread stale, but everyone was very happy. Sister Marcel, formerly Sister Jeanne, looked particularly radiant. After the celebratory chocolate, Sister Fatima clanked a spoon against a water glass, signaling an immediate hush.

Mother sat up a little and smiled. "Today has been a beautiful day, a very important day." As she spoke, the hush in the room deepened. "The cutting of the hair," Mother said, her voice surging with conviction, "is another sign of separation from the world, that we are consecrated. People in the world do not cut their hair. The longer it is, the more shining is their beauty. It's a creation of God for a woman." It took me a moment to realize that when Mother said, "People in the world do not cut their hair," she meant, "Women in India do not cut their hair."

"Some sisters"—she took a deep breath—"grow long hair with the idea of taking back what has been given to God. We cannot do this." Mother emphasized each word, leaning so far forward I feared she might lose her balance. "Always cut your hair, every month. Let it be a renewal of this day for you, an offering." Abruptly Mother concluded with grace after meals and the sign of the cross.

Sister Frederick whisked Mother back to San Gregorio, and the rest of us went to the chapel for Night Prayer, after which one of the older novices silently led us to a dormitory, where she had us remove our saris. Then she ushered us, in our long white habits and covered heads, to a back room. Newspapers layered the floor and a single bare bulb burned from a wire in the ceiling. Four stools sat in the middle of the room. A fire beneath a corner chimney heated large, soot-blackened metal drums full of water for bathing, which made the room very hot.

Other novices tied aprons around our necks, one in the front and one in the back. When the novices left, four professed sisters entered, each with scissors in hand. They tapped the shoulders of four of our group, and led them to the stools. The rest of us watched from a corner.

Sister Fatima began the rosary. The professed sisters unknotted the novices' headpieces, revealing their shorn hair. Each professed sister took a pair of scissors. Sounds of snipping punctuated the prayers, and hair drifted to the ground.

Slowly I realized they were going to cut—everything. They were cutting so close to the scalp that only tiny bristles remained, standing at attention. Tears coursed down the former Sister Giosi's face as her dark curls punctuated the headlines on the paper-lined floor. The words of the rosary circled the room, but I couldn't concentrate. My sisters looked like pictures I'd seen of women in concentration camps.

Head nearly shaved, Sister Maria Lina stood up, untied the aprons from around her neck, and shook them out. A sister with scissors motioned me to the stool.

As I sat, I closed my eyes. I'd never given my hair much attention, but I knew that when I got up from that stool, I was going to be uglier than I had ever been before. I prayed silently, *Jesus, I want to belong to You—body, mind, and soul. Make me Yours.*

I heard the scissors snap, right above my ear. I wanted to open my eyes but didn't dare. I told myself it didn't matter, nothing mattered, no one would see the little bristles under my headpiece anyway. I was now Sister Donata, freely given, a complete donation.

I kept my eyes shut tight. The fire in the corner crackled. I prayed again: *Lord, I give You everything. Make me Yours.* My head began to rest more easily, more lightly on my neck. I opened one eye. The sister with the scissors had moved in front of me. As she cut, she smiled. I tried to smile back.

At the door, I saw Sister Maria Lina and Sister Marcel with their buckets, watching. Our eyes met and they grinned. Sister Marcel mouthed, "Nice style." I tried to tell myself, *It's going to be all right. We're all in this together.*

The sister cutting my hair ran her palm over my stubble. Satisfied, she gave my shoulder a little shove.

In the bathing room, I ran my hands over my head, soaped up my washcloth, and rubbed. My scalp actually felt good—crisp, clean. Two tins of water, instead of the customary five or six, were enough to rinse the soap from what remained of my hair. A few firm swipes of the towel wiped it dry.

As I tossed my nightdress over my shorn head, an acrid stench penetrated the bathing room. From the openings above and beneath the door, thick smoke crept in. I pushed the door and followed the smoke to the room where our hair had been cut and found Sister Fatima pitching a dark ponytail into the fireplace, a stack of ponytails beside her on the floor. I backed out, silent, pulling the door behind me.

The image of Sister Fatima consigning to flame what had so recently been mine haunted me as I tossed on the bed. When I finally slept, a single refrain echoed through my dreams: *No turning back, no turning back.*

7

LIES AND A MIRACLE

SPRING 1978 TO SPRING 1979
TOR FISCALE, ROME

S ister Fatima told us we were to spend the first year of our novitiate falling in love with Jesus. Our novice mistress' dark eyes
were kind and intelligent, and her wry smile seemed to hide secrets
about God and being a good sister. Nothing, she said, could be
more important than to become what Mother (and St. Ignatius before her) called "a contemplative in the heart of the world." To facilitate our transformation into "souls of prayer," first-year novices
were sent for apostolic work only twice a week. In the second year,
the ratio of prayer to apostolate would be reversed. The two years
prepared us for the day we would publicly vow chastity, poverty,
obedience, and wholehearted and free service to the poorest of the
poor. Now we were engaged; then we would become spouses of
Jesus Crucified.

Our Tor Fiscale novitiate, nearly an hour from San Gregorio by
tram and on foot, was nestled in a field of shacks off the Via Appia
Nuova, so poor and so simple that thoughts of God came naturally. Neighbors had helped the sisters construct our convent—

distinguishable from their own *baraccas* of cement and tin only by the fact that sixty of us crowded the enclosed compound. The brick and stone Tax Tower from which the district took its name rose behind the kitchen, and the ancient aqueduct cast a shadow over the first-years' dormitories. I liked everything about Tor Fiscale except the gravel path around the chapel, which cut the bottoms of my bare feet, since poverty forbade using sandals within the convent walls.

Each morning four of us novices pushed wheelbarrows down the dirt road on wood duty. Sometimes Sister Jelka and I were so happy that we skipped like schoolgirls through the wild roses and oleander. Beyond the potato fields, at artisanal furniture shops we filled the wheelbarrows with sawdust and lumber scraps for cooking and winter heating. For Sunday recreation Sister Fatima sometimes let us first-years loose in the field behind the aqueduct—twenty women in white running, jumping, singing, chasing each other through the field. We plucked wildflowers and waved oleander branches in the air when we processed back to the convent, where we laid the flowers at the feet of Our Lady's statue.

Each day, Sister Fatima read to us from *The Way of the Pilgrim*, a nineteenth-century anonymous Russian classic about a man who packed some dried bread in a knapsack and a Bible in his pocket and set off in search of unceasing prayer. Eventually he happened upon a monk who instructed him to repeat at every moment, silently or aloud, these words: "Lord Jesus Christ, have mercy on me." The man did so and found great peace.

Sister Fatima suggested we imitate the pilgrim and—even better—expand the prayer. Sister Fatima suggested, "Lord Jesus Christ, Son of the Living God and Savior, have mercy on me, a sinner."

These words, known as the Jesus Prayer, held little appeal for me. I'd grown accustomed to wordless prayer and enjoyed it. But if those words could initiate me into the transformation Sister Fatima seemed to experience, it was worth a try. When I woke, as I dressed, as I walked to chapel, I repeated, "Lord Jesus Christ, Son of the Living God and Savior, have mercy on me, a sinner." The more I repeated it, the more annoyed I became. Though I could never admit this to any Missionary of Charity, praying to Jesus was hard for me.

When left to my own devices, I directed my prayer to God, without feeling a need for greater specificity. I sometimes experienced something that felt like being in God's womb, but that didn't lead me to picture God as Mother. It was just my way of identifying that feeling of oneness, of protection, of a warm, secure love. The one image that consistently helped me enter God's presence was one I'd never heard any MC mention: God as water. Jesus had called Himself "Living Water," and I especially liked the image of the River of Life flowing through the city of God, with trees on either side for the healing of the nations, as pictured in the Bible's last book, Revelation. I could close my eyes and float on the River of God's Love almost at will.

Praying to Jesus was like praying to someone who wasn't there—I couldn't feel Him the way I often felt God. Mother was *always* praying to Jesus, talking about Jesus, directing her gaze to Jesus. My earlier attempts at repeating "Jesus, meek and humble of heart, make my heart like Yours" had made Jesus seem more distant than ever. The Gospel stories of Jesus' love for the poor moved and inspired me. I was particularly grateful that Jesus had died for me. But if I tried to picture Jesus when I prayed, I came up with a blank, both visually and emotionally. Filling my mind with words calling on Jesus' mercy robbed me of my quiet, leaving my soul thirsty all the time.

Early on in Sister Fatima's instructions, she gave us an unusual assignment, something that brought some solace as I struggled with the Jesus Prayer. "I want each of you to choose a virtue," she announced, her eyes sparkling. "You must think and pray hard about it, because this will be a choice for your whole life, your own special virtue."

A choice! This was one of the first options we'd been offered among the standard-issue prayers, postures, and penances of a Missionary of Charity.

"You could choose the virtue your patron saint was known for," Sister Fatima continued, "or the virtue you see yourself failing in most often, or one you feel particularly drawn to. You'll think of your virtue every day and try to live it perfectly. During your examination of conscience at noon and at night, you'll keep track of your progress so that your failures in this virtue can be special subjects for your confessions. Your practice of this virtue will be your lifelong gift to Jesus."

That afternoon I found a piece of boxboard and some scraps of paper. I folded and stitched them into a little book, about five inches by three. On the first page, I wrote: *"Love one another as I have loved you."* —*Jesus*

Soon the front pages of my little lovebook, as I called it, were filled with quotations. From St. John: "God is love, and he who abides in love abides in God, and God in him." From Mother: "God has made us to love and to be loved." I reserved the back pages for my examination of conscience, using cryptic references: *helped carry; impatient with Sr T; washed J's clothes; late again; kept quiet when corr; pls, God, teach me love.*

Though I enjoyed my fellow novices, I missed my family. Each month I wrote my home letter eagerly, but on Wednesdays and Sundays, when Sister Fatima read out the names on the envelopes, other sisters claimed their letters and I was usually left disappointed. I understood that my family was busy and not used to writing letters. They might have called, had it been allowed. When a letter finally arrived for me, sometimes after two or three or four months of waiting, I tore the envelope open and read it over and over again.

Fairly early in my first year, on a Sunday afternoon devoted to home letters, I wrote:

I don't know whether I should ask this or not, but I'm going to anyway. Would you come see me? I know I'm asking an awful lot, but maybe one or more of you could come—maybe for my profession. It would make me so happy.

Each month I continued to invite them to Rome, always hedging my requests with apologies and caveats. In my letters I complained about their silence, then felt guilty for complaining. Sister Maria Lina and Sister Marcel told me they were praying that I might receive a letter.

Finally, one Wednesday Sister Fatima read my name off a bulky manila envelope. I tore the envelope open and pulled out—a cassette tape. When I approached Sister Fatima, she immediately asked, "What's the matter? Bad news?"

"I don't know if it's bad or not," I said, holding up the cassette.

"Oh," she said. "We don't use tape players."

"Yes, I know—but my parents didn't know. I'll tell them in the next letter. In the meantime," I asked, "I was wondering if I could listen to this at Stefano and Maria's house." Stefano and Maria were our nearest neighbors, and were always blasting Italian pop from a tape player.

"Sister Donata, tape players are against our vow of poverty." Sister Fatima looked stern.

"But it's not our player," I said. "I would just listen."

"Do you remember what the Holy Father said?"

The words of Paul VI served as epigraph to the section on poverty in the *Constitutions*. " 'Let us not look for substitutes which restore to us the wealth we have renounced,' " I quoted.

"Yes," Sister Fatima said, then paused. "But Mother is coming soon. I'll ask her if we can make an exception just this once."

Sister Fatima took the tape from my hand. I never saw it again.

The next month I thanked my family for the tape and apologized for not having listened to it. They wrote back quickly. Mom had taken a job at the hospital. Mom, Dad, and Kathy would come for my profession the next year.

"To practice perfect poverty," Sister Fatima insisted during Rule Class one day, "also means that we own nothing. Like the early Christians, we hold all things in common."

Then she got specific. The two sets of clothes we'd stitched for ourselves, the plate, the bowl, the cup, the tin box with needle and thread, the Bible we'd brought from home, the Divine Office book, the notebook, the prayer book, the sheets, the mattress, the pillow—we used these things, but we did not own them.

Other congregations of sisters approached this situation linguistically, never saying *mine* but always *ours*, even for things given for individual use—*our habit, our pencil.* Sister Fatima summed up the MC way of signifying common ownership in two words: *ask permission.*

Until now, asking permission had been reserved for particular, one-time needs. As aspirants we'd written our requests in a small book: *Please may I have a tube of toothpaste?* Once a week, the mistress reviewed our requests, granted those she thought appropriate, and assigned one of the sisters to distribute the pencils, the socks, the thread. If we were ill, we asked permission for medicine or rest. Asking permission covered occasional requests, but we couldn't go around asking *Please may I* each time we put on our habits or used our plates or our prayer books. To cover these items, we were to request "general permission," a monthly ritual that would mark our lives from that moment forward.

The precise ritual of asking general permission included a request to request permission, then a private meeting with the superior or mistress in which the sister requesting permission knelt, kissed the floor, accused herself of any external fault committed the previous month, and spoke this formula: "I beg a renewal of my general permission and to be admonished for all my faults." The superior then granted the permission, assigned a penance (usually a few Hail Marys), and proceeded to admonish—sometimes an exhortation to do better, sometimes a painful discussion of particular failings, sometimes a simple chat about how things were going.

Technically, if we hadn't renewed our permission by Night Prayer on the seventh of the month (or hadn't requested to renew our permission—sometimes the mistress couldn't manage to see everyone in seven days), then we no longer had permission to use anything. That didn't mean a sister couldn't dress herself or use her fork—it meant something worse. Whenever a sister whose general permission had expired wrapped herself in her sari or sat on a bench or used a bucket, she violated her vow.

One day Sister Fatima called out softly as I returned my plate to its shelf after lunch, "Sister Donata, take this to the kitchen." My novice mistress put a book of matches in my palm, then turned away. As she did so, the bell rang—five strokes for Midday Prayer.

I hated this sort of quandary. The voice of God—represented by both my superior and the bell—had told me to go in opposite directions at the same time. If I went to the kitchen, I would surely be late for Midday Prayer, distracting everyone as I tried to squeeze myself in. If I went to the chapel, I would be delaying obedience to my novice mistress, but no one would need matches in the kitchen until common work in the evening. I stuffed the matches on the shelf between my Bible and my office book, taking my small prayer book with me to the chapel. After Midday Prayer, I followed everyone to rest, without a thought for the matches. After rest, we had tea.

After tea, while we were on our way to wash the cups, Sister Fatima called out loudly, "You didn't put the matches in the kitchen, did you, Sister Donata?"

"Of course I did," I replied automatically.

"I asked you if you put the matches in the kitchen," she repeated, speaking more loudly and looking me in the eye.

"Yes, Sister, I put the matches in the kitchen," I repeated.

"I don't believe you," she said coolly, calmly, laying her teacup on the table.

"It doesn't matter if you believe me or not," I said.

I tried telling myself I hadn't really just lied to my novice mistress, the woman who represented God in my life.

The bell rang for spiritual reading. I grabbed the matches and sprinted to the kitchen. I set the matches on the shelf above the stove and raced back to the refectory. As I entered the refectory, Sister Jelka slid down the bench to make space for me.

Shame made reading impossible. If I had admitted my negligence, Sister Fatima would have scolded me in front of everyone, and I would have had to stand silent, "like Jesus before Pilate." My lie was proof that the good opinion of others was more important to me than a clean conscience before God.

When the bell announced personal prayer, I wanted time with the Lord, but I was too ashamed to go to chapel. I knew I'd just made myself unworthy of my sisters' company. So I went to the little garden behind the chapel and sat on a bench near the tabernacle wall, my head in my hands.

A blatant lie, three times in a row. At least St. Peter had had a good excuse for denying the Lord three times. I was too dependent on others' opinions. Perhaps that was the lesson of Jesus' silence: His dignity was completely independent of what others thought. Why should I have cared if I was scolded? Wasn't I bigger than that?

No, I wasn't bigger than that, at least not yet. Though I'd been trying for nearly two years to stop caring what others thought, indifference remained out of reach. The one thing I could be was honest, even about my failings. Wordlessly, my head against the chapel wall, I promised never to lie again.

I had to apologize. It was early in the month and I hadn't yet renewed my general permission—the perfect forum for apologizing with minimal fuss. After dinner, I followed Sister Fatima into the dormitory. I crossed myself and kissed the floor, then—on my knees, not knowing if I would have the courage to say it—I spoke in a near whisper. I began as usual: "I speak my fault for not having been generous enough to help the sisters and for having been careless with silence, for not always answering the bell promptly, and for not finishing to wash my clothes in time." I paused, took a deep breath, and continued: "I am particularly sorry for not having taken the matches to the kitchen and for having lied when you asked me about it."

Sister Fatima placed her hands on my head, blessed me, and told me, "Rise."

I never knew whether Sister Fatima heard that phrase about the matches, but having said it left me feeling free.

I avoided further lies, but found myself biting my tongue not to make excuses. I still longed to be noticed, appreciated, approved. Despite my obvious pride, when I repeated, "Lord Jesus Christ, Son of the Living God and Savior, have mercy on me, a sinner," I experienced something akin to an allergic reaction, my soul breaking out in spiritual hives. When I did something wrong, I asked God's forgiveness and tried to make it up to whomever I had hurt. Dwelling further on my sins seemed egotistical. More important, begging God for mercy all day seemed insulting to God. God didn't need to be convinced to be merciful—mercy was in His nature. He had sent Jesus to die for me long before I'd had the chance to offend Him. I wanted to dwell on God's love, not my sins.

I became convinced that my annoyance with the Jesus Prayer revealed a serious flaw in me beyond my problems with Jesus. The pilgrim in Sister Fatima's book called himself a sinner constantly. St. Francis called himself a sinner. Sister Carmeline had praised Sister Jeanne's essay because she had acknowledged her sinfulness and her need of mercy. I was so sinful that I didn't even know how sinful I was. I begged God to break through my pride, to show me just how much I needed his mercy.

The discipline began to hold a new attraction for me. As novices, we were allowed additional strokes. Penance became a plea to God to let me know just how bad I was.

When Sister Fatima presented all of us first-year novices with chains one morning, I was ready. The spiked wire armband became the first thing I put on in the morning, and—like all my sisters—I let it gouge my left biceps through Morning Prayer and meditation, housework and Mass. When I took the chain off before breakfast, I did so reluctantly, not yet having been granted the felt knowledge of my sinfulness.

Every night after Night Prayer, we left the chapel for a few final Hail Marys and a hymn before Our Lady's statue in the compound.

One night after the hymn, as I stood in silence, head bowed in the dark, something shifted inside—as though a heavy curtain had been pulled back and I could see what had been hidden. In a single moment, without any reasoning, all of a piece, I knew myself capable, beyond the shadow of any doubt, of all the worst sins ever committed. Murder, deception, promiscuity, larceny—I was capable of all these. That I'd been spared committing the worst of them was a sign not of my virtue but of God's grace, which had prevented me from acting on my potential. Without God, I could have been Hitler or Idi Amin.

God had finally answered my prayer.

On a cold March day, with less than three months left for our first year, Sister Fatima told me, "Sister Julia wants to see you." Ominous words. The last time I'd been called in to see the superior of the novitiate, the elderly sister in charge of both novices and novice mistresses, Sister Julia had accused me, in my performance as Motel the tailor during a novitiate production of *Fiddler on the Roof*, of appearing far too realistically in love with the novice playing Tzeitel. I couldn't imagine what my new fault might be.

"Come in," Sister Julia said, motioning me to a stool in the cramped room with little light. Before I had a chance to fold my hands on my lap, this tiny sister said, "Don Gerardo won't be able to play the organ for first profession, so I want you to play."

I nearly burst out laughing. Only Sister Julia's earnest expression prevented my outburst. "Sister, I've never played the organ before. I don't know anything about it. I've never even played piano."

"But you know how to read music," she said, staring at me through Coke-bottle glasses that made her eyes look huge.

"Yes, Sister, but—"

"Then you will learn to play the organ, too." Sister Julia crossed her arms against her chest. "I will tell Sister Jacqueline Claire to show you how it works, and then you must practice. Professions are at the end of May." Sister Jacqueline Claire had begun piano lessons at the age of six and played the organ beautifully, but she would take vows in May and couldn't play for her own profession.

"Sister, I really can't do this." I'd always liked music but the only Bs and Cs I ever got in high school had been in band. Profession was a big thing, the wedding day for a whole group of sisters, the most anticipated moment of life for many of them. Hundreds of people attended profession. Mother would be there. "I'm sorry, Sister," I said. "Please find someone else."

"I am telling you to do this. God blesses obedience." She was in *I am the voice of God* mode.

"Yes, Sister," I said, bowing for her blessing. Was I really saying yes to something whose only possible outcome was disaster?

I went straight to the chapel. *God*, I prayed, *help me understand what's going on here.* This may have been a great scheme to break my pride, but surely spoiling profession for everyone wasn't worth whatever could be gained by publicly humbling me.

God, I prayed again, *what do You want me to do?*

When I asked Him for explanations, God usually responded. If I was quiet enough, deeply centered within, and not worried about too many things, I usually heard a quiet, wordless answer, often accompanied by courage and trust. Not this time.

The Angelus bell rang, as it did three times a day. *The angel of the Lord declared unto Mary . . .* The story seemed strangely appropriate. Gabriel told Mary that God wanted her to bear His Son. Mary objected, *I know not man.* The angel replied, *Never mind. God doesn't do things the human way.* God made the impossible possible. Was Sister Julia asking me to believe in miraculous music?

Okay, I said.

That afternoon, I met Sister Jacqueline Claire in the chapel for my first, and only, keyboard lesson. She pulled out a stool and I sat in front of a plastic three-octave electric organ with spindly legs and tiny keys, the kind of toy a musically inclined eight-year-old might find under the Christmas tree.

Since I couldn't read bass clef, Sister Jacqueline Claire decided to use guitar music instead. She showed me the guitar chords printed above the melody line of "Morning Is Broken." I was to finger the guitar chords with my left hand and play the melody with my right. She showed me middle C, then told me to play.

"Okay," I said, "but which fingers do I use?"

She gave me an *Ah, you poor, stupid little thing* look. "Use whichever ones you please," she said. "It really doesn't matter. It will be beautiful." Sister Jacqueline Claire patted my shoulder, genuflected, and left the chapel.

I raised my right hand to the keyboard and tried the melody line. Morning really did sound broken. I needed a miracle to fix it.

Mother sometimes told a story about St. Ignatius. One day Ignatius gave a novice a dead stick, telling him to plant the stick and water it and to bring him the flower. The novice thought Ignatius crazy, but he obediently watered the stick for weeks. Eventually the novice plucked a flower off the dead stick and brought it to Ignatius.

I practiced every spare moment I could find, getting permission to forgo my thirty-minute afternoon siesta, bathing and washing clothes as little as possible. Gradually I learned to pick out the melody on the keyboard. I adopted another saying of St. Ignatius: "Pray as though everything depends on God, and work as though everything depends on you."

I had, as early as age six or seven, ceased picturing God as Divine Request Granter. I believed God supplied inner strength and comfort, that He loved me and communicated with me, but I didn't see God as someone who violated the laws of nature for anyone's personal benefit. Now during those weeks before profession my prayers grew desperate. I refused to take no for an answer.

Practice, pray. Practice, pray.

"God sees all your efforts," my novice mistress said. "Trust Him."

With profession only two weeks away, I told God, *I've practiced as hard as I could and I've begged for the prayers of the sisters, but I still make mistakes in every phrase. You can't let this be a disaster. It's not in Your best interests. If Your new brides are unhappy with the wedding, it won't make for a pleasant honeymoon. And if the congregation is so distracted by the ineptitude of the music that they cannot pray, what good does that do You? Think about it, Lord. Don't let us down.*

When the day of profession arrived, the church was crowded—standing room only—and very hot. People had traveled great distances to see daughters, sisters, and friends give themselves to God. I had yet to play a single hymn without several mistakes. Mother and the sisters were lining up outside the church, preparing to walk down the aisle. There was nothing more to do. I turned everything over to God and relaxed. As I did, I felt the presence of God envelop me, a focused peace that seemed to wrap itself first around me, then the sisters in the choir, Mother, the sisters preparing to profess their vows, the priests. God's presence enfolded the bishop, the people in the pews, the altar, the flowers, the incense in the air. We were all one in the momentous act of witnessing twelve women about to give their lives to God.

The cross bearer at the back nodded and raised his right hand. I put my fingers on the little keyboard and began to play. I focused on the melody, without considering the details. We finished the entrance hymn without a major disaster. The Gloria sounded okay. The responsorial psalm sounded really good. I could hardly believe it. I played without a mistake.

The entire profession was beautiful. It was a miracle.

8

DISGUISES

When we became second-years, Sister Sylvia, who had been second-year novice mistress for many years, was appointed superior of a new foundation in Zagreb. Zagreb was as close as the MCs had yet come to Mother's birthplace in Skopje, which made this latest foundation more exciting than usual. Mother returned from Zagreb nearly glowing. She told us the people of Zagreb had been overjoyed, and that by the second day her rusty Croatian had returned.

Mother decided that the Tor Fiscale tertians would be sent to Calcutta that year, freeing Sister Julia to be our second-year mistress. Our hearts sank at the news: we'd been looking forward to the warm, vivacious Sister Sylvia. Though we'd lived in the same compound with Sister Julia for over a year, this tiny, solemn sister remained an enigma behind her Coke-bottle glasses. It wasn't that she was mean; we just had a sense that life with her could get complicated. I hadn't yet decided whether the assignment to play the organ had been a sign of Sister Julia's strong faith or evidence of a deranged mind.

The day Sister Julia gave us our second-year apostolic assignments, she spoke from the head of the table in slow, measured tones. "Sisters," she said, "you have spent an entire year in prayer and contemplation. You have learned to see Jesus in the Eucharist, hidden in the form of bread. During your second year, you must pray to see Jesus in the poor you serve. Only if you see Jesus in the poor can you love Him as He deserves."

Sister Julia's words were very similar to words I'd heard from Mother, but while Mother's passionate, heartfelt intensity made me want to go out and do something for the world, Sister Julia seemed to pull her words from some deep interior well of knowledge. She made me want to discover the secrets of the universe.

I was overjoyed when Sister Julia appointed me Sister Sandra's partner. Sister Sandra was six months senior to me, originally from Venice, kind and practical—and she was assigned to our own Tor Fiscale parish. With her, I felt confident I could learn to see Jesus in His distressing disguise. I strapped on my sandals, stuffed my bag with plastic rosaries and miraculous medals, and followed Sister Sandra out the gate.

We headed that bright spring morning to Adele. I'd often seen Adele, who had lost her eyesight to diabetes, clutching her way from pew to pew in church. When we entered Adele's apartment, she called out, *"Suore, suore,"* but her voice held no joy, her face no smile. She said she needed . . . something I couldn't understand.

I mopped the floor while Sister Sandra talked with Adele in Italian. Adele's tone spoke volumes—now whining, now cajoling, now sharp and critical. Sister Sandra gave Adele an injection in her well-padded rump. I didn't like needles and found it odd that so many Italian drugs were prescribed in injectable form. Even watching made me a little woozy. Before we left, we prayed a decade of the rosary and Adele told Sister Sandra to come back soon. I didn't sense Jesus here, just a lonely, disappointed old lady.

Next, Salvatore stood at the stove of his run-down *baracca*, the starchy aroma of beans filling his little shack. He sat on the bed, and we pulled up two rickety kitchen chairs. The shack didn't hold much else. There were no windows, no electricity, no plumbing. It took a while to adjust to the darkness. Salvatore chuckled a lot and his eyes sparkled, though his knuckles were red and swollen. As Sister Sandra and I hauled buckets to the *fontana*, she told me that Salvatore had once held a good job, but he'd lost his pension and his home. Lately, arthritis made getting around difficult.

When we returned with water, Salvatore thanked us with another toothless smile. After an Ave Maria, Salvatore accompanied us to the door and clipped two roses from the bush in front of his house. *"Per la Madonna,"* he said.

Our encounter with Salvatore had been pleasant, but not mystical.

We headed for the aqueduct, transformed by squatters into an apartment complex, the thick arches boarded up with old billboards advertising Ferraris and Colgate. At the last of the arches, Sister Sandra called out, *"Alvaro, Alvaro. Siamo le suore."*

An old man moaned from inside. *"Non oggi, suore."* Not today.

"Alvaro drinks," Sister Sandra told me. "Sometimes he comes out to speak to us, but he won't let us in. I hope one day he'll let us clean up, so I pass by often." Nodding toward the field on the other side of the aqueduct where nine or ten Gypsy families with small campers had settled that spring, she said, "We don't visit the Gypsies. They have plenty to eat—they beg and they steal."

"We could talk to them about God," I said.

"They're Orthodox," Sister Sandra replied. "They won't go to a Catholic Church and they usually baptize their children, so we don't need to worry about that. If we start going to the Gypsies, they'll be at the convent all the time."

More than a few times I'd opened the convent gate to several barefoot Gypsy children who would stand there asking, "Something to eat, something to wear. Some shoes. Some socks. Lookie, lookie—he has no socks." One day six-year-old Kemo had entered the back door, whisked away a big box full of toys, then turned around to say good-bye and escape untouched—all under the noses of three sisters.

"Maybe if we go to them," I said, "they'll stop coming to us."

Sister Sandra just shook her head.

Back in the convent, I tucked Salvatore's roses into the vase at Our Lady's feet, saying a prayer for the people we'd met that day, and one for the Gypsies. I couldn't say I'd seen Jesus.

We returned often to Salvatore and Adele. We visited many other people, too—poor families, lonely old folks. We called to Alvaro each time we passed his arch, and he continued to refuse to let us in. I bugged Sister Sandra about the Gypsies, but she shook her head and made excuses. I began to think she might be afraid of them. I regretted my poor Italian and ignorance of Roman social services. Certainly some of these people were entitled to government assistance, but we didn't know how to find them.

I continued to wait for my mystical encounter with Jesus.

The October day Sister Sandra and the other second-year seniors began their two months of intensive preparation before vows, Sister Neepa became my partner, which meant I was in charge. Our first stop: the Gypsies.

I walked under the aqueduct and into the field, grass growing high on either side of the path. From the top of the hill, we could see the campers arranged in a loose ring, several campfires sending smoke into the air, mounds of rubbish. I'd wanted to enter that field for months, but walking the path with an Indian sister who knew less Italian than I did, I was scared. Maybe Sister Sandra had been right—the Gypsies only wanted to take advantage of us; they didn't really need our help; they only wanted things. Maybe they were dangerous.

The camp seemed deserted that morning, though it was just past eight. We heard music from one of the campers and knocked on the door. An elderly woman with a single visible tooth pushed the door open.

"*Buon giorno, signora,*" I said. "We are the sisters."

"*Sì, entrate.*"

We stepped up into the camper, which was indeed full of things—piles of clothes, dishes, candles, a kerosene heater, several radios, a framed photo of Mussolini, several clocks all set for different times. Another old woman sat on a mattress in the corner. Both wore voluminous skirts and bright kerchiefs tied around their heads.

"Buon giorno," the other woman said, her breath so foul I nearly flinched.

Now for the hard part—my miserable Italian. I could understand almost nothing of what this old woman in the camper said. It took me a moment to realize she wasn't speaking Italian at all, but Romani, the Gypsy language.

"Parlate Italiano?" I asked.

They both shook their heads. One of them reached for the rosary dangling from my hands. *"Bello,"* she said, "beautiful."

Our rosaries were made of seeds and were nothing special, but she continued to finger mine, repeating, *"Bello, bello."*

Sister Neepa reached inside her bag and pulled out two plastic rosaries—one bright green, another yellow. The women stretched their hands and took the rosaries with obvious delight.

"Preghiamo?" I asked. "Shall we pray?"

The women looked ahead blankly. I made the sign of the cross and folded my hands. The women did the same. I said an Ave Maria, and the women and Sister Neepa repeated the phrases slowly after me. We said several Hail Marys this way, and the women looked quite pleased with themselves. I left the camp feeling pleased with myself, too.

We visited again one chilly October morning. Several younger women were cooking stew in a big pot on the fire and a dozen barefoot children played tag in the field. They all smelled ripe. Even the boys had long hair. Eventually I learned that Gypsy boys frequently disguised themselves as girls, because girls took in more begging money.

The women around the fire had all seen the rosaries we'd left with the older women, and everyone wanted one. I didn't want them thinking the rosaries were jewelry, and promised rosaries on condition that they learn the Hail Mary to pray on the beads. Around the campfire, they all repeated the prayer until they could recite at least the first half by themselves. Sister Neepa passed out the rosaries, which everyone hung solemnly around their necks. I repeated that these weren't necklaces, but one mother kissed the crucifix and patted it against her chest, and soon the others were doing the same. I felt sure Jesus and Mary were pleased.

We returned often to the camp, and the Gypsies started coming—as Sister Sandra had predicted—more frequently to the convent. I made a deal with them: I would bring pasta and clothes for the kids every week if they stopped coming to the convent. The kids didn't stop coming completely, but they came less often.

We offered to clean the kids up, but the mothers said no—clean children didn't make good beggars. None of the Gypsies in this camp knew how to read or write, so I started teaching the kids the alphabet, but when I came for the second class the mothers wanted to take the kids for their usual begging. The next day I approached the Gypsy king, a man in his late forties as far as I could tell, tall and broad-shouldered. "I will be proud to have my children intelligent, my children reading," he said. "Yes, thank you. A thousand thank-yous." He made a fist and struck his chest. "I will guarantee they come."

We began reading classes in one of the caravans every morning. The kids were eager to learn, but the camp was full of distractions. I asked Sister Julia if I could ask the parish priest for an empty room. Soon we had a room, books, pens, crayons. Among ourselves, we sisters started calling the project TFU: Tor Fiscale University.

As the kids progressed, I kept a step ahead of them, learning a few new Italian words a day, repeating them to myself at odd moments, happy to replace the Jesus Prayer with Italian vocabulary. The kids responded with enthusiasm, and the adults were so proud when the children wrote and read simple sentences. I still hadn't seen Jesus in the poor, but it didn't matter so much once I'd seen Kemo write his name in bright red crayon.

I asked Sister Julia if Sister Maria Lina could teach me how to give injections so that I could give Adele her medication. Sister Maria Lina started me practicing on oranges, and she came with me the first time I tried on Adele. I felt like I was making a difference in Tor Fiscale, and Tor Fiscale was making a difference in me. It was exciting.

In mid-October, we received news that Sister Julia had been elected to attend the General Chapter in Calcutta, a meeting held every six years to elect the superior general and her councilors, and to discuss important issues in the Society. After five months, I'd come to appreciate Sister Julia, and she'd given me a free hand in Tor Fiscale. I didn't like to think of almost a month without her around.

One day Sister Julia announced that Mother had been awarded the Nobel Peace Prize. It was a great honor, she said, for which we must thank God. Then she gave an instruction on poverty as though nothing extraordinary had happened.

I couldn't concentrate. Dag Hammarskjöld, Henry Kissinger, and Martin Luther King, Jr., had won the Nobel Peace Prize—and now Mother! I'd always believed my vocation addressed the heart of what this world needed most. Spending so much time washing sheets and cooking had sometimes made me doubt my choice, but my experiences with the Gypsies and now Mother's Nobel Prize were signs I hadn't made a mistake.

Sister Julia returned from the General Chapter a few weeks later. As expected, the delegates had reelected Mother as superior general. Sister Frederick had been elected first councilor, second in charge after Mother, which meant she would move to Calcutta.

Mother arrived in Rome with Sister Agnes and Sister Gertrude, who had been the first two to join Mother. After professions, Mother and her two companions would go to Oslo. All Mother would say about the prize was that she'd accepted it in the name of the poor, and that it meant that works of love were works of peace.

On the day of professions, our little parish church overflowed. People who hadn't managed to squeeze inside stood in the com-

pound and on the street. When Mother walked down the aisle, people reached from the pews to touch her. Sister Gertrude tried to
send the crowds away after profession, but Mother insisted on giving each person a Miraculous Medal and on speaking with those
who wanted to talk with her—which took so long that Mother told
us to start dinner without her. When she finally came in, Mother
was wiping her face with the backs of her hands. I heard her mumbling in disgust, "Kisses, kisses, kisses." She washed, gave the newly
professed their assignments, then swallowed dinner quickly while
the rest of us cleaned up. In six months my family would come and
my group would take vows—I hoped things would settle down by
then. I wanted to spend time with them in peace, without an unruly
crowd spoiling everything.

When Mother returned from Oslo, she wouldn't talk about the
prize unless someone asked her, and then she always repeated the
same three stories. She had passed out the Prayer of St. Francis—
the one that begins *Make me a channel of Thy peace*—and had made
everyone in the auditorium pray together. She had told them that
the greatest destroyer of peace is abortion, because if a mother can
kill her own child, there is nothing to keep us from killing each
other. Finally, she had cancelled the award banquet and asked for
the money so that she could feed the poor instead.

We were all very curious to see the prize. Mother said, "It's not
important, Sisters." Later, Sister Gertrude told us that whenever
Mother received a prize, she never looked at it again. She always left
it in the convent where she happened to be, then later the sisters
quietly brought the award to Mother House and locked it in a cupboard near Mother's room. Mother sometimes asked what was in
the cupboard. The sisters would say, "Nothing important, Mother,"
because that's what Mother always said about awards.

When Mother left Rome she took Sister Julia and Sister Frederick
to Calcutta and assigned Sister Dolorosa, our former postulant mistress, as our new novice mistress.

One of the first things Sister Dolorosa did was to assign two of the novices who spoke Italian to take over Tor Fiscale University. I'd been expecting that. My Italian left a lot to be desired, but the real problem might have been that I'd made my pleasure in this work obvious, with a story at nearly every lunch.

I continued to visit Tor Fiscale, including the Gypsy camp. The parents were warming to the idea of sending the children to regular schools, and told me several times they were disappointed I wasn't teaching the children anymore.

After a few days, the novices who had been assigned to TFU started complaining. They called the kids "wild animals" and said it was impossible to teach them anything. They asked me what I'd been thinking when I'd imagined these children could learn. I replied that the kids had actually learned quite a bit, and that they responded best when learning was more a game than a chore.

A few days later, the parish priest told Sister Dolorosa that if the sisters couldn't keep the children under control, they couldn't use the rooms at the parish any longer. Sister Dolorosa gave the sisters a week to establish discipline, and I prayed that things would improve. Before the week was over, Sister Dolorosa decided to close TFU. I thought of asking her to give the kids another chance with me, but I knew such a request would earn me a reprimand and nothing for the kids. I supposed this was one last trial before my first profession, to deepen and test my obedience. My mistresses had all stressed that any service we might give outside obedience would lack God's blessing and do more harm than good. I wanted to do real good for the Gypsies and begged God to do for them what I couldn't. I avoided visiting the Gypsy camp in the early mornings, so I didn't have to see the kids being sent off to beg.

Alvaro still hadn't let us into his aqueduct apartment, but he had started showing up at the convent at odd hours, asking for me. The first time he'd come, Sister Dolorosa had let me go to the gate, but he'd gotten effusive—he'd been drinking—and he'd kissed my hand. Another sister had seen it, and I was never sent to the gate again, though Alvaro continued to ask for me several times a week. When he asked for me, the portress would say no, then he'd ask for *fazzoletti*—handkerchiefs—and he wouldn't leave without at least one. The sisters began keeping a supply of handkerchiefs in the parlor. When I asked him what he wanted with so many *fazzoletti*, Alvaro smiled and said, "My mamma always told me, 'A true gentleman always has a handkerchief.' "

A week before Christmas, Alvaro finally said we could clean his arch. That evening I stuffed a wheelbarrow with supplies—buckets, brooms, rags, disinfectant, bleach, trash bags, some clean sheets and towels. I added some chipped plates and faded Christmas decorations to the pile. The next morning Sister Neepa and I tied on our aprons and pushed our wheelbarrow toward the aqueduct.

Alvaro was waiting for us outside the arch. "Are you sure you want to go in?" he asked.

"*Sicurissima*," I said, and he pulled the door open. The stench nearly knocked me back. I asked if we could take everything out to air, and he said okay. Sister Neepa and I tied handkerchiefs over our noses and mouths and pulled out everything. We stuffed most of what we found into the trash bags. We removed many, many bottles.

Alvaro stayed close, pacing and mumbling.

"Don't worry," Sister Neepa said. "We make your house beautiful."

The mattress smelled of urine, and we burned it in the field. After scrubbing the walls, ceiling, and floor with water from the *fontana*, we returned to the convent for more trash bags, more rags, a new mattress, a pillow, some candles, and some canned food. I looked for a cot or a bed but didn't find one, so we packed several cinder blocks and strapped a door to the top of the pile. I put a bar of chocolate in my apron pocket.

Back at Alvaro's arch, we started rebuilding his room. The cinder blocks and door became a bed. We put clean sheets on the clean mattress. When Alvaro saw the pillow, he started crying. "A pillow," he said, "a feather pillow."

I hung the plastic holly and set the Nativity scene, the chocolate, and a candle on his little table. Alvaro came in, looked around, and shook his head. He sat on the bed. He lay on the bed. He got up and took our hands in his. We all sat on the bed, and I lit the candle near the crèche. Together, we sang "Tu Scendi dalle Stelle," the Italian Christmas hymn to the Baby Jesus, born amid the cold, with nothing but a cave in which to take shelter.

Singing there, in that archway, I finally saw Jesus in the smelly, bearded alcoholic with a gentlemanly desire for handkerchiefs. My heart filled with that same peace and love I sometimes felt kneeling before the Eucharist or gazing upon a Christmas crib. God made man: Jesus in disguise among us.

9

BRIDE

WINTER TO SPRING 1980
TOR FISCALE, ROME

One February night about eleven, Sister Jelka was snoring in the bed next to mine. The chill permeated every corner of our drafty Roman dormitory. I couldn't sleep. Truth be told, I'd begun to worry about profession again. In a few weeks it would be time to write Mother, asking permission for first vows, scheduled for June. It would soon be too late for second thoughts.

The more I tossed in that cold, dark bed, the more I tried to convince myself, as my novice mistress and my confessor had often reminded me, that my worries were just temptations. The devil was trying to lure me from my vocation. God wanted me to be a Missionary of Charity, and if God wanted it, nothing could be better. He would give me the grace. *All things are possible with God. All things are possible with God. All things—*

"I need a man," someone shouted.

As I realized who it was—Sister Dolorosa, our novice mistress—she repeated the cry several times more. "I need a man! I need a man!" I heard someone get up in the darkness. I lay stunned in bed. Our novice mistress needed *what*?

The words reverberated in my brain, my gut, my bones. Eventually I rolled out of bed and felt my way through rows of beds in the dark. I cracked the shutters open. Moonlight fell on Sister Dolorosa's bed and on her pale face. She sat, headpiece askew, body shaking, her legs under the blankets. Sister Maria Lina sat with her arms wrapped around Sister Dolorosa's shoulders, whispering, "It's all right, Sister. It's all right. You were just having a bad dream." Sister Dolorosa sat silent, tears rolling down her cheeks.

By this time several other sisters were up, too, standing at a distance.

"Go back to sleep, everyone," Sister Maria Lina said. "Sister was just having a bad dream."

"Are you all right, Sister?" Sister Jelka asked. Sister Dolorosa nodded, sobbing silently.

"See, she's fine," Sister Maria Lina said. "Go back to bed."

"Yes, Sisters," Sister Dolorosa quavered. "I'm fine. Go back to bed."

A few of the sisters headed back to bed, and a few of us hung around a little longer.

"Did I say something?" Sister Dolorosa asked Sister Maria Lina.

"No, Sister, you didn't say anything," Sister Maria Lina said. "You just shouted and we woke up. It was a bad dream."

"Go back to sleep, everyone," Sister Dolorosa said.

"Sister needs *camomilla*," Sister Annarita insisted, heading toward the kitchen. Those of us who were still up followed her out, while Sister Maria Lina remained on Sister Dolorosa's bed.

"Did you hear her?" Sister Annarita whispered as she searched for a saucepan.

"Of course. We all heard her," Sister Jelka said, lighting the fire.

"It's only normal," Sister Marcel said. "We are all human."

"But she's our mistress." Sister Annarita shook her head as she filled the saucepan. "We're supposed to learn from her."

"Yes," Sister Jelka said. "Learn from her that humanity does not leave when you make vows. She was just dreaming."

"About men," Sister Annarita said, raising her eyebrows. This was my first discussion about men since entering the convent, except for the Rules about never being alone with a man, not looking at a sick man while you bathe him, and things like that.

"Do you dream only about sheep?" Sister Marcel asked.

"I think Sister is lonely," I said.

"Lonely?" Sister Jelka turned up her nose. "She has Maria Lina by her side all the time. Did you see the way she held her in bed?"

"What would you do if someone was having a nightmare?" I asked. "Throw cold water on her?"

"I agree for tonight it is all right. No problem." Then Sister Jelka shook her head. "But ever since postulancy Maria Lina is Sister's favorite."

"Do you want to be her favorite?" Sister Marcel asked. "Everybody needs companionship."

"Sister Fatima didn't have favorites," Sister Jelka insisted. "Rules are Rules. If the mistress breaks the Rules, what about the rest of us?"

"But what has Sister done that is so wrong?" I asked. "You just said that it was all right. Aren't there exceptions for every Rule, and aren't you usually the first to say not all Rules are useful anyway?"

"You all make big things out of nothing," Sister Marcel said, turning toward the door. "I'm going to bed."

"Sister Maria Lina told Sister that she didn't say anything." Sister Jelka wagged her finger. "That's a lie."

"Sister didn't know what she was saying," I said. "I suppose Sister Maria Lina didn't want her to be embarrassed in front of everyone."

"But we all know anyway," Sister Jelka said. "Everyone heard it. I think she should know, too."

"Why don't you tell her?"

Sister Jelka hesitated. Finally she said, "Mistresses don't like to be told things."

"I'm not going to tell her," Sister Annarita said.

"I'll tell her," I said. "It's not right that we know and she doesn't."

"Tell us what she says, okay?" Sister Annarita smiled.

"If she wants to say something to everyone, I'm sure she will. Or if you want to know, you can ask her yourself."

"Oh, no." Sister Annarita shook her head vigorously. "I'm not getting in the middle of this. Better we forget it."

" 'I need a man, I need a man.' Who can forget that?" Sister Jelka said. "I will think of it every time I see her."

"That's why she needs to know," I said, and Sister Jelka nodded. Sister Annarita carried the saucepan and we followed her into the refectory, where Sister Jelka took Sister's cup and saucer from the shelf.

The next day, Sister got up late for Morning Prayer, appearing in chapel only for Mass. At breakfast she looked tired, and when we came home from apostolate, she didn't come for lunch but stayed in the office, "sleeping," Sister Maria Lina told us, "on Mother's bed." Seriously ill sisters were often sent to sleep on Mother's bed in hopes of curing their illnesses. We didn't see Sister Dolorosa again until after recreation, just before Night Prayer, when she came to bless us. She wore her nightdress. Dark circles framed her eyes, and she did not speak.

I lingered in the refectory as everyone went to chapel. When Sister Maria Lina headed to the office, I pulled her aside. "What's wrong with Sister? Why doesn't she stay with us?"

"She's feeling weak, can hardly sit up."

"But she's not sick?"

"Ashamed."

"Does she know what she said?"

"Yes, she knows—she heard herself saying it as she was waking up."

"Then why did she ask you if she'd said anything?"

"I gave her a way out."

"A way out?"

"She can't accept that she shouted such a thing," Sister Maria Lina said, her voice pleading. "She's the mistress, you know."

"She's human, she was asleep. People say all kinds of things in their sleep. Wouldn't it be easier if she just said something to us, or we said something to her, so that we could get back to normal? She can't stay in bed forever."

"She's not ready."

"Maybe I could talk to her."

"She told me to make sure no one comes in."

"Why don't you just go to Night Prayer and I can sneak in? That way she can't blame you."

"It wouldn't be right."

"She's my mistress, too. I have as much right—"

"It's okay." Sister Dolorosa emerged from the office and placed one hand on Sister Maria Lina's back, the other on mine.

"Sister? We all hope you're not sick."

"I heard your conversation. I've been standing here a while." She said this very matter-of-factly, with a little smile.

"Sister, we need you with us," I said.

"Some of the sisters must have been shocked," she said.

"Well, some were surprised, but we won't get over that as long as you hide."

As I said this, her big brown eyes looked as though I'd bruised them. Then she looked at the floor.

"It's not easy being mistress," I said. "You must get lonely sometimes—no real community of professed sisters close by and all."

"What will everyone think when I say 'Jesus is enough for us' now? No one will believe me."

"But you haven't gone chasing men, have you?"

"Sister Donata!" Sister Maria Lina looked at me with exasperation.

"No, I'm not chasing men," Sister said. "Except those dreams . . ."

"If you come back to us, we will believe more than ever that Jesus is enough for you, because you're not giving in to temptation."

"But Jesus *isn't* enough for me."

She sounded serious. "Sister, maybe you need to talk to somebody," I said.

"Who?"

"Father Charles?" I suggested our confessor.

"He's so old-fashioned, and if I told Sister Stella, she would just kill me, and if I talk to Sister Maria Lina, the group is jealous. I feel like I'm losing my mind."

This was way out of my league, and I knew it. Sister Maria Lina had moved behind Sister so that Sister couldn't see her, and she mouthed to me, *Stop. Stop.*

"Sister, I will pray for you," I said, "but for the sake of the group, please just come back. You could tell us you had a bad dream and things will slowly come back to normal—if not for you, at least for us."

That night I lay awake in bed for quite some time. What did it feel like to need a man so much that you shouted in your sleep? Why wasn't Jesus enough? I hadn't given too much thought to chastity till then. At twenty-one years old, I'd never had a boyfriend, had never been out on a date or to a school dance. Though I'd excelled at schoolwork and in extracurricular activities, I was overweight, had freckles, and wore thick glasses and orthodontic braces. Boys called me "fatso" and spit on me as I made my way to the back of the bus. It hurt, but I tried not to think about it too much.

When I saw couples holding each other and kissing, as they seemed to do on every Roman street corner, it made me kind of excited, sometimes nervous, and sometimes lonely. And sometimes I managed to remember that God loved me even more than those two people loved each other.

Sometimes becoming the bride of Christ seemed like entering a harem. He had many brides, but only one was the chief wife—the superior was the real partner who controlled everything. I didn't want to get all dolled up in a sari edged with blue so that Jesus could show me off as one of His many brides, use me for His pleasure, and submit me to the whims of the chief wife. I wanted to be a partner. I wanted to count for something.

But such ambition was pride. I had to remind myself to look at reality: *Sister Donata, you are nothing, you have always been nothing, and you will always be nothing. Your desire to be someone special is just pride. Everything you have, including your existence itself, is a gift. You breathe only at the pleasure of the Lord. You are privileged to be invited to intimacy with the Maker of the Universe. You will belong to God, and Jesus will be your husband.*

There is no higher honor.

Unlike the boys in school who only liked certain kinds of girls, God had loved me as I was. But as I prepared to become his bride, it became evident that "as I was" was insufficient. Jesus wasn't interested in makeup and long legs—he demanded a complete makeover from the inside out.

As the days drew near for us to write letters asking Mother permission for vows, I began to have my own nightly visitations. It started with a dream of all the boys I'd ever had crushes on— Robert, Lendol, Pat, Steve—but now these boys wanted me. They talked to me and invited me out. Another night I boarded a corporate jet to China to make a business deal. I wore heels, a suit, lipstick. On the flight I donned a lab coat to discover a cure for cancer, and I took off the coat when the media announced that I'd won the contested U.S. Senate seat for Texas.

On one level the dreams were silly. No boy would ever be interested in me, and I'd never had anything vaguely resembling a career. But I liked the way sitting in that corporate jet had felt. I liked the way Robert looked at me, even if it had been a dream. Why was I about to pledge myself to the poorest religious congregation in the Church? Did I really want to follow another's orders for the rest of my life, vow away intimacy with another person forever?

These were the questions I asked at every adoration, at meditation, while I was sorting wood and chopping vegetables. At times I even hoped the sisters would send me away—that would be a clear sign that God had other plans for me. But as my confessor and my novice mistress kept reminding me, my questions and doubts, and even my dreams, were the devil's work.

We wrote our letters to Mother. I asked permission to take vows and told Mother that I wanted nothing more than to be a true MC. We added extra prayer time and doubled the strokes of the discipline and the hours we wore the chains. Each day we awaited Mother's answer.

Meanwhile, my family wrote and told me how excited they were about seeing me in Rome and coming for my profession. I wanted to see them again, too. I missed everyone, especially Kathy, with whom I used to talk over everything.

While we waited for Mother's replies, we washed the saris we'd wear on our wedding day. The white sari of a professed sister had a blue border, called a par. Hand-woven by lepers who lived with our sisters in India, the saris always arrived stiff, with the yellow hue of unbleached cotton. We boiled the saris in laundry soda, scrubbed them, rinsed them in water tinted with blue, and hung them in the sun half a dozen times. If only bleaching away doubt were as easy.

While dusting the library shelves, I ran across a slim book whose title intrigued me: *The Cloud of Unknowing*. Though I wasn't supposed to read without permission, I flipped through a couple of pages and realized that the anonymous English author of the fourteenth-century *Cloud* was talking about my kind of prayer— prayer without images, prayer with very few, if any, words. Whenever I got a chance, I snuck a look at a page or two of *The Cloud*. The author argued convincingly that any image humans could concoct of God would, of necessity, be more unlike God than like God. *The Cloud* recommended a prayer of "simple steadfast attention reaching out towards God . . . with humble love."

After finding *The Cloud*, I gave myself permission to abandon the Jesus Prayer and its irritations. Silently repeating a single word in my mind and heart—God . . . God . . . God or Love . . . love . . . love—often brought great sweetness, and so centered me in peace and courage that worry faded for a while. This permission to once

again open myself with wordless love to the imageless center of reality felt like an engagement gift from God.

When I finally held Mother's answer in my hands, it said yes! A sign
from God. I could take my vows and put my doubts aside forever.

I was so excited that I didn't notice Sister Neepa and Sister Marcel crying in separate corners of the chapel. Their papers read, *Jesus
gives you the gift of six more months in the novitiate.*

This was just plain strange. The rest of our group, even the oft-
scolded Sister Jelka, had been given permission, yet these two sisters
had been postponed. It wouldn't feel right taking vows without Sister
Marcel in line. The previous year, one of our seniors had been postponed. We all knew she lied frequently, but Sister Marcel didn't lie,
wasn't vengeful, never shirked work. Since my first dinner in the
Bronx, when she'd introduced herself as Jeanne Dubois from Quebec,
Sister Marcel had always looked so strong, worked so hard. When
Sister Carmeline had judged her essay the best, I'd been envious.

By afternoon, Sister Neepa wasn't crying anymore. I found her
in the refectory. "It's God's will," she said. "I will have more time to
prepare."

But Sister Marcel was still crying the next day, in the same corner of the chapel. "It's easy for them to say it's God's will. I don't
know where God is in all this. I wanted to take my vows as much as
any of the rest of you, maybe more." Sister Marcel wiped her eyes,
then waved the soggy handkerchief in my face. "Can you get me another handkerchief?"

"Sure," I said, putting my hand on her knee before heading to
the refectory. As I opened the door to the clothes cupboard and
squatted to look for Sister Marcel's shelf, Sister Maria Lina came in
from another door.

"What are you doing?" she asked. "That's not your shelf."

"Sister Marcel asked for a handkerchief. She's crying so much,
ever since yesterday." I located her pile of clothes and searched for
the handkerchief. "I just don't understand."

"What don't you understand?" Sister Maria Lina asked, with a trace of laughter in her voice.

"I can't understand why I'm allowed to take vows and Sister Marcel isn't. I'm not any better than she is. Sister Marcel works very hard and gets more done than all the rest of us put together, because she's so strong."

"There, you're beginning to get it."

"She can't take vows because she works hard?" I found the handkerchief and stood up.

"She's so strong. Strong like what?" Sister Maria Lina stood firm, with a know-it-all look on her face.

"What do you mean? Strong like a horse or an ox, I guess. She can lift anything."

"Strong like a man, silly."

"Huh?"

"Move a bit, won't you?" she asked. "I need to get my sewing box." Reaching for her shelf near the top, Sister Maria Lina looked down at me and smiled. "You're so silly when you say you're no different from Sister Marcel. I mean, just looking at her, you can see she's different."

"What do you mean?"

"Come on! You're curvy—you look like a woman." Sister Maria Lina took her sewing box and closed the cupboard door. "Sister Marcel, she's very straight."

"So what?"

"And her voice is very deep."

"And she works like a man. So what?"

"You don't understand?" Sister Maria Lina leaned over and whispered, "She's inclined to particular friendships."

"How can you say that? She doesn't separate herself at meals and recreations and talk to only one sister—she talks to us all."

"She likes girls." Sister Maria Lina looked at me and shook her head. "They think Sister Marcel is a lesbian."

"Oh." I'd heard this term in high school, whispered about a girl who always dressed in jeans and black T-shirts and never wore makeup, but I didn't know exactly what it meant.

"Finally you see," Sister Maria Lina said, shaking her head. I didn't correct her.

"Somebody found her once," she continued, "with Sister Prapti in a bathing room. They were—" She took a quick look around, and whispered so low that I could barely hear her. "They were kissing."

I raised my eyebrows. That *was* strange. "Mother and the council are actually being very good," Sister Maria Lina explained. "They could have sent her home right then—it's such a sin against chastity—but they're giving her another chance to see if she continues behaving like that or not." Her voice sounded more and more condescending. She enjoyed giving me this information, to which her special relationship with Sister Dolorosa had made her privy.

"You see," she continued, "they can't send anyone home for *being* a lesbian. That's not sinful in itself. But to *act* like a lesbian is always mortally sinful." She shook her head. "It would be impossible to live in community with someone who was continually falling in love with the sisters, wanting to touch them and all. A lesbian would have so many more temptations than the rest of us. I don't know how she would be able to live her vows."

All at once, the pieces fell into place. *Particular friendship* didn't just mean that you wanted to speak to one particular sister to the exclusion of the others. Someone who had particular friends was a woman attracted to other women the way men were attracted to women—a female homosexual, a lesbian.

"I guess we'll just have to pray for her," I said.

"She needs more than prayers," Sister Maria Lina said as she headed out the door in front of me. "Sister Marcel needs a miracle."

Sister Marcel hadn't seemed different from other sisters. If she felt attracted to girls, what was the big deal? The night of Sister Dolorosa's shout, Sister Marcel had been more matter-of-fact than the rest of us. Did she feel a need for women the way Sister Dolorosa dreamed of a need for men? Was that why she'd kissed Sister Prapti?

Yet Sister Prapti hadn't been postponed—she'd taken her vows a year earlier.

When I returned to the chapel, Sister Marcel grabbed the handkerchief from my hand. "What took so long? I needed this."

"I'm sorry. I got interrupted." I bowed my head, not knowing what else to say. "I'm praying for you. It must be really hard."

"You have no idea," Sister Marcel said. I knelt in the chapel, wondering what else I didn't know.

Mother's answer had eased my doubts about God's call but not my concerns about living it. From my blunders with obedience to my inability to make my ration of laundry soap last all week, my practice of the vows was still on shaky ground. Would I wake up one night in the future shouting for a man, or freedom, or respect, or comfort?

At each and every adoration, I prayed, *Lord God, I don't know what I'm doing, but I trust You. Do with me what You will.* As He'd done when He had assigned me to play the organ, God would have to supply what I lacked.

My confessor had warned that the devil might ramp up his efforts, so I wasn't too surprised when during the eight-day silent retreat before our profession, doubt and fear often assailed me. I just pulled out Mother's note giving me permission and reminded myself that God had called me. He would lead and protect me.

The silence of retreat was sacrosanct, especially the retreat before profession. We passed our time praying and listening to the retreat preacher's sermons several times a day. The silence was meant to turn our minds to God—but it also gave me extra time to worry about my vows, to wonder if my family had arrived, to obsess about where I might be sent on my first mission.

Midway through the week Sister Dolorosa surprised us all by announcing that we should put on our sandals and get ready to leave for the Corpus Christi Procession with the Pope. Usually the Holy Father processed with the Blessed Sacrament nearly a mile, from

the Basilica of Maria Maggiore down the Via Merulana to San Giovanni, but this year the city government claimed that the dearth of
interested citizens didn't justify the expense of security and the has-
sle of shutting down one of Rome's central streets for several hours
on a Thursday. So Pope John Paul II called on every Christian in
Rome to show up for a truncated procession in St. Peter's Square to
prove Romans still cared. In silence we walked to the tram stop.

St. Peter's Square was sunny, the atmosphere festive. It was hard to
keep quiet, and almost impossible to keep the custody of the eyes that
Sister Dolorosa insisted was necessary to maintain the spirit of the retreat. I tried hard not to scan the gathering crowds, not to look too
long at the flowers strewn on the steps near the altar, not to eavesdrop
on the conversations of American tourists. I fingered my rosary, trying to refocus on my Fiancé and His Mother. The rosary caught on
my sari, producing yet another hole in the ever-thinner cloth.

I heard some commotion among novices seated a few rows back.
"Sister Donata is over there," they said. I turned and saw Mom and
Dad and Kathy smiling and waving at me. I could hardly believe it.
It was great to see them, but what could I do? I was supposed to keep
silence. I turned around, looking for Sister Dolorosa. She nodded at
me and tilted her chin toward the aisle. I got up and hugged my parents. I hadn't hugged anyone in three years and the hug felt strange,
my body wooden. I knew I wasn't supposed to be doing this—or was
it allowed with family? I couldn't remember—no one had said.

"Mary," Kathy said, "you look strange."

"I'm surprised to see you."

"Not happy?"

"Sure I'm happy." A few novices rearranged themselves and
made space for my family. Mom told me about their flight and their
rooms in the monastery at San Gregorio. Dad looked thinner than I
remembered him.

"Your clothes are weird," Kathy said. "And torn."

"I'll get a new sari in a few days," I said. "My profession clothes
will be beautiful."

"A wedding dress?"

"Sort of."

I felt shy and confused. I hadn't wanted my first meeting with my family in three years to go like this. At the same time, it was wonderful to see them. I asked Kathy about the rest of the family and our friends from high school.

"You have lots of questions," she said.

"I'm actually not supposed to be talking at all," I said. "I'm on retreat."

Finally the great bells of St. Peter's tolled, the organ strains filled the square. While I answered the Italian prayers, Kathy sat silently beside me, my sister but somehow distant, foreign. I longed for the easy closeness we used to have in the days of jeans and T-shirts, before Rules. When God invited me into a new family I hadn't realized how firmly He would require I relinquish my first family. While they were here maybe we could be family again—even with limited visiting, even if we couldn't eat together, even if my letters for three years had all been rather superficial and theirs had been few. Even as I hoped, I knew that to be a good Missionary of Charity I had to let go of the Johnsons.

When Mass and the procession were over, I hugged them and followed my new sisters quickly to the bus. Throughout the rest of the retreat, Kathy's face kept reappearing, and Dad's smile, and Mom's hug, no matter how hard I tried to concentrate on God.

June 10, the day set for our profession, was particularly warm and muggy. We were nervous and anxious to have everything over. Just before lunch, the bell rang frantically, peal after peal, announcing Mother's arrival. We rushed to the compound. Mother smiled as she blessed us, then she disappeared into the house with Sister Dolorosa.

The sisters had spread rugs in the shade, and the eight of us to be professed stood there, waiting for Mother to reappear. Soon we were trying to stifle nervous giggles, with varying degrees of success. Finally Mother walked vigorously across the compound and began grace.

The pasta and vegetable curry were tastier than usual, but none of us had much appetite. I kept stealing glances at Mother. She seemed so happy, so free.

"Today," Mother said, looking at each of us at the end of the meal, "you will become the spouse of Jesus Crucified. On your papers it will say 'for one year,' but each one of us knows in our hearts that it is not for one year; it is for life.

"Jesus has espoused Himself to us in tenderness and love, and we must be faithful. You will profess your vows publicly, before the whole Church. Difficulties and trials will come, but do not be afraid. Never allow anyone or anything to separate you from the love of Christ. You are called to be holy sisters." Mother was so sure, so strong.

While I changed into my best habit, I prayed, *God, I am Yours. I give You everything.* The two professed sisters who helped with my sari didn't understand that my height and width mandated stinginess with the tucks. After the third try, the last layer of the sari still came up short, clinging to my armpit instead of hanging at my elbow. They pinned it there anyway.

We walked the dirt road to the church, and people from Tor Fiscale greeted us as we passed. Many of them recognized me and called out my name, and I felt proud and shy at the same time. At the church, as we stood in the sun waiting for the archbishop to arrive, I admired how beautiful my sisters looked in their wedding saris. All of a sudden, I felt someone tugging at my elbow. Mother wrinkled her forehead and said, "Two years of wearing a sari and you still don't know how to dress?" I wanted to sink into the floor. I searched for a corner where I could readjust, but people were everywhere, and it was nearly time to begin. I just had to accept that my sari and I were both imperfect—God had called me anyway.

When I heard the first strains of the opening hymn, I recalled how, a year earlier, the presence of God had enveloped the church when I played the organ. I tried to quiet my nerves, in search of that same peace and confidence. I kept repeating, *I trust You, Lord, I trust*

You. Hands folded, eyes cast down, we processed through the back door. The novices sang, "*Vieni, vieni, popolo mio. Vieni con me, là nel deserto. Cuore al cuore d'amore, ti parlerò.* Come, come, my people. Come with me into the desert, where I will speak to your heart of love."

Walking down the aisle next to Sister Jelka, I tried to spot Mom, Dad, and Kathy in the crowd, but with my eyes properly lowered I couldn't locate them. Dad was supposed to read one of my favorite passages from St. Paul. I hoped the sisters had found him and that they'd marked the right spot in the Lectionary.

When we reached the steps of the altar, those of us to be professed formed a semicircle, Mother and Sister Dolorosa standing just behind us, dozens of priests and the archbishop filling the sanctuary.

As Dad neared the ambo for his reading, I felt proud. He read solemnly: "Whatever gain I had, I counted as loss for the sake of Christ. Indeed I count everything as loss because of the surpassing worth of knowing Christ Jesus my Lord. For His sake I have suffered the loss of all things"—here Dad looked down at me, and we made eye contact for the first time; I hoped those weren't tears I saw in his shining eyes—"and count them as refuse in order that I may gain Christ and be found in Him." As Dad continued, his voice choked a little, and I felt once again that my decision to join the sisters hadn't been easy for him, or for any of my family. I determined to be worthy of the sacrifice my vocation caused them.

After the readings and the homily, Sister Dolorosa walked to the front and called each of our names. When she called, "Sister Donata," I answered, "Lord, You have called me."

The paper in my hand shook as I read,

I, Sister Mary Donata Johnson, vow for one year chastity, poverty, obedience, and wholehearted and free service to the poorest of the poor according to the *Constitutions of the Missionaries of Charity*. . . . I give myself with my whole heart to this religious family so that, by the grace of the Holy Spirit and with the help of the Immaculate Heart of Mary, Cause of Our Joy and Queen of the World, I may be led to the perfect love of God and neighbor and make the Church fully present in the world of today.

I knelt before the archbishop and kissed the wooden crucifix he gave me—the symbol of my Crucified Spouse. I cradled the palm-size crucifix in my hands and crossed the sanctuary to Mother. She took the crucifix and raised it firmly to my lips, and I kissed it again. Mother lifted the edge of my sari and wedged the crucifix at my left side, between habit and cincture. I knew that I would carry it there every day until the day I died.

Back at the convent the sisters garlanded us with roses gathered from the lanes of Tor Fiscale. I was eager to introduce Kathy and my parents to Mother. When Mother told my parents, as she told the parents of all the sisters, "Thank you for giving your daughter to God," Mom and Dad just smiled. Behind the smiles, I could hear them thinking, *We didn't really have much choice.*

Then Mother turned to Kathy. "And when are you going to give your life to God?"

"I'm engaged," Kathy said, which was the first I'd heard of it.

"Oh, well," Mother said. "Be a good mother, then."

I took my parents and sister to a corner of the garden, where I scolded Kathy. "You didn't even tell me you had a boyfriend."

"You didn't ask," she said. Shyly, she told me about her fiancé, and that they would be married next year, after she had her chemical engineering degree. She said Carroll was wonderful, that he sometimes reminded her of Dad.

I told her, "He may be wonderful, but I've got the perfect husband." She graciously let the comment go unchallenged.

The morning after profession, immediately after Mass and breakfast, our group took the tram to San Gregorio, where Mother would give us our assignments. After we finished the rosary, we

chattered among ourselves. "Where do you think you will go?"
"How long will your parents stay?" "I couldn't believe the archbishop's homily—it was so long and the church was so hot. What
could he have been thinking?" "I hope I don't go to Africa. I really
don't want to go to Africa." I thought Africa would be exciting. The
one thing I didn't want was to be sent back to the States; being an
MC in familiar surroundings would be more difficult.

Sister Jelka entered Mother's office first, and after a few minutes
came out with a smile on her face and a slip of paper with her name,
a quotation from Mother, and in Mother's round script, *Zagreb*. Sister Maria Lina was next, and came out with tears in her eyes: San
Gregorio. "I had hoped for something outside Italy at least," she
said. Sister Annarita emerged with both tears and a smile over her
destination, Palermo. Another sister waved her paper triumphantly
in the air, whispering "Haiti, Haiti, Haiti!"

When I entered, I kissed the floor and spoke my fault, then
Mother told me to rise and take a seat opposite her. She looked me
in the eyes, and seemed to be holding back a smile. "Sister, Mother
is sending you to Skopje. It's a new house. You'll have to work very
hard."

She put the paper in my hand, and I said, "Thank you, Mother,
thank you so much."

Mother smiled some more, and told me what I already knew,
what made this assignment so special. "I'm really happy you're
going there, because Skopje is where I was born. The Communists
have been—"

"Mother," Sister Frederick interrupted, and beckoned Mother to
the back of the office. I heard them whispering and in my excitement could make out only a few phrases:

"Sister Priscilla . . . asked specifically . . ."

"But who . . . why should . . ."

". . . very . . . called twice . . . her there . . ."

"*Ah cha* . . . then we . . ."

Mother came back to the stool I was sitting on and said, "Sister,

Mother is sending you to St. Louis. I'm sure you will do a lot of good there. Could I have your paper back?"

My heart sank. I'd heard the sisters in St. Louis had very little work. Sister Frederick took my slip from Mother and applied a heavy coat of Liquid Paper. The sisters had gone to St. Louis basically because Cardinal Cadbury had asked for them. He was the one Mother always talked about when she told the story, "A big American cardinal asked me one day to write something for him, and I forgot that I was writing for a cardinal and I wrote, 'Let Jesus use you without consulting you,' and he wrote back that he reads what I've written every day." When this cardinal had asked for the sisters, Mother couldn't refuse. Mother took my paper back and began to write, but her pen stuck in the thick coat of correction fluid. Mother picked the paper up and blew on it. I'd passed through St. Louis once on a family vacation—I remembered a bridge and a typical midwestern city. St. Louis seemed the least exciting place I could imagine. Mother handed me the paper, now marked *St. Louis*, and I bent my head for a blessing.

When I left the room, Sister Maria Lina asked to see my paper, and noticed the Liquid Paper immediately. "Hey, Sister Donata, did you see—your paper used—"

"It used to say Skopje," I said, avoiding her eyes.

10

LUCKY

Toting our boxes, nearly twenty of us crowded into the Bronx refectory, the same room in which I'd sat near Mother for the first time. "Wait for Sister," the sister who had met us at JFK whispered. In other MC houses, someone would at least have said, *Welcome, Sisters*, but the three sisters at the table never even looked up from their work. It required a lot of self-restraint to ignore that many sisters at once.

Jet-lagged from the seven-hour flight from Rome, I shifted from one foot to the other, pondering this convent's cold silence. In Sister Dolorosa's last instructions, she'd told us to expect life in the missions to be different from the novitiate, but I hadn't anticipated so much change in the two and a half years I'd been away. Finally the door to the office opened, revealing Sister Priscilla, tall and straight, hands clasped at her chest, chin parallel to the ground. She opened her hands briefly to announce, "Welcome, Sisters," then closed them again. Her lips turned up slightly at the corners, but I couldn't call it a smile.

"Thank you, Sister," we replied. She stood in the office doorway and we approached for her blessing. When I stood before her, Sister Priscilla said, "Ah, Donata, you've come back, have you?"

"Yes, Sister."

"We're very happy to have you." Her face bore the same reluctant half smile.

"Thank you, Sister," I said. "I'm happy to be here, too, if only for a short time."

"For a short time?" Sister Priscilla raised her eyebrows.

"I'm supposed to go to St. Louis," I said.

"Oh, no. I'm keeping you here." With that, the smile spread across her face, showed her teeth.

"But Mother told me to go to St. Louis."

"You're staying here," she said, shaking her head. "Mother gave me permission to keep all the sisters who come to the States in the Bronx for a while."

"Yes, Sister." I had understood that she'd asked for me because she needed an American sister in St. Louis, but I wasn't going to complain. Staying in the South Bronx wasn't as good as Skopje, but it seemed a lot more exciting than Missouri.

At summer camp and during night duty at the shelter, I was in my element. Back in the convent, an unspoken tension hung in the air. The sisters didn't laugh much, and conversation seemed forced. I'd never seen a community more deferential toward their superior.

Sister Priscilla often spoke of the necessity of knowing the mind of the superior, which meant doing everything as the superior would want it done, even if the superior hadn't expressed any particular preference. She spoke frequently with Mother on the phone and claimed to "know Mother's mind." Had Sister really grown so close to Mother that she knew how Mother would respond in every situation? If so, I wanted to learn, too.

Sister Priscilla had accomplished a lot in the two and a half years she'd been in the Bronx. She had opened new houses in Detroit and

St. Louis, and had scheduled a September opening for Miami. In the Bronx, Sister had overseen the expansion of the soup kitchen and night shelter, where I worked sometimes. Unlike Sister Andrea, who had left the convent nearly every day to visit the poor, Sister Priscilla didn't visit the projects or the hospitals. She never showed up at summer camp, just around the corner from the convent. Instead we often saw her at her office window, phone to ear, looking out at the garden—which had been an abandoned lot with a burned-out building when I'd been an aspirant. Sister had leased the lot from the city, then found a contractor with a bulldozer and truck-loads of topsoil; one of the postulants spent every morning water-ing, weeding, and pruning. I'd heard Mother say that sisters shouldn't spend time gardening when they could serve the poor, but Sister Priscilla said the poor people were happy to look out their windows and see the flowers.

In the Bronx I soon found myself violating Rules I'd never heard of. Superiors usually blessed the sisters at the end of evening recre-ation. If a superior wasn't available then, she blessed the sisters after Night Prayer. The first night that Sister was available neither after recreation nor after Night Prayer, I went to bed. The next day, Sis-ter Betsey found me. "What happened to you last night?" she asked. "Sister was looking for you. You must never go to bed without Sis-ter's blessing." Many were the nights this meant waiting an hour, sometimes more. Sometimes I fell asleep on the refectory bench waiting. Sister also insisted that she personally see all donations of food before they were put away. When canned goods blocked the entry and frozen food started puddling the refectory floor, I wrote a list. Sister insisted I had violated my vow of poverty by disposing of things independently when all I'd done was put them someplace cool and out of the way until she could be informed.

The food donations incident had been my first experience as the featured offender in Sister Priscilla's "Some Men Are Lucky" rou-tine. I'd seen it before, when other sisters arrived late for recreation, broke a glass, or forgot to turn out the lights. As prelude, Sister

Priscilla looked long and hard at the offending sister, then at each sister present. Then she slapped the table, establishing the beat. When the atmosphere grew sufficiently thick, she sang: *Some men are lucky*. She expected us to join her on the second and the third lines, slapping the table with her as we repeated: *Some men are lucky*. As she sang, Sister Priscilla narrowed her eyes, while the offending sister's role required her to remain silent and look abject. The next line was a Sister Priscilla solo: *Some men are lucky. Why? Because some women* (slap) *became* (slap) *nuns!*

I'd cringed at the demeaning routine, but when others had joined in, so did I. I preferred this form of correction to the barrage of adjectives other superiors sometimes unleashed.

Several times I saw Sister Priscilla turn a cold shoulder to a sister, refusing to answer the sister's questions, refusing even to acknowledge her presence for days and even weeks at a time. Sister Priscilla also chose to correct through notes. One morning, sleepy and not yet accustomed to my profession crucifix, I'd forgotten to tuck it under my cincture while dressing. When I returned to make my bed, I found a note in Sister Priscilla's neat script: *Only an unfaithful spouse leaves her wedding ring behind*. After breakfast, when I apologized, she said, "I can't believe you would do such a thing." When I told her I wouldn't do it again, she said, "We shall see."

Instead of concentrating on my work, I found myself worrying whether I was violating an unknown Rule. When I went to pray, Sister Priscilla occupied so much psychic space that I labored to empty myself enough to hear God. I had expected life after vows to be filled with hard work and laughter, not preoccupation with my superior. I didn't know if I would ever learn how to navigate this strange new community.

Mother was scheduled to arrive in mid-July. Days before her arrival, Sister Priscilla announced, "I'm transferring Sister Imma to St. Louis." Prone to absentmindedness, Sister Imma had been one of Sister Priscilla's frequent targets. Tension made Sister Imma even more forgetful, leading to an almost daily performance of "Some Men Are Lucky."

Sister continued her announcement: "I can keep only the best sisters in the Bronx."

I felt an immediate impulse to slap her. I'd never heard anyone compare sisters like that, and this final insult seemed willfully cruel.

Sister Imma's assignment to my original post—and her disappearance just days before Mother arrived—confirmed my theory. If Sister Priscilla had told Mother she wanted me in New York, Mother wouldn't have agreed. Three of the seven sisters in the Bronx professed community were Americans, and Mother always avoided concentrations of sisters of the same nationality (or from the same Indian state). Mother would have found it more difficult to refuse a request for an American in St. Louis, which didn't have an American in the community, and still wouldn't. What I couldn't figure out was why Sister Priscilla wanted *me* in the Bronx.

One afternoon before Mother arrived, after we'd dismissed the kids at camp and were cleaning up, I found a tall volunteer sweeping the big room that headquartered the boys. Stan was my age and had just graduated from Notre Dame. He was from Wisconsin, gentle, with deep brown eyes, and the kids loved him. Usually the leaders of the other two boys' groups would have helped Stan clean, but they hadn't yet returned from a field trip to the arboretum, so I fetched a bucket and mop, and started stacking chairs.

"Say, Sister," Stan said, leaning on his broom, "you mind if I ask a few questions?"

Sister Priscilla had given us strict instructions not to "get involved" with the volunteers. If a volunteer had something to say, we were to direct the volunteer to her. I didn't know what sort of punishment talking to Stan might warrant, but I'd been starved for real conversation.

"Sure, Stan," I said. "Ask away, but move that broom while you talk."

"Did you go to parties when you were in school?" Stan spoke loudly.

I stacked the last chair, grabbed another broom from the corner, and left the door half shut after I'd swept behind it. "Not too many parties," I said. "I studied a lot, and I wasn't really a party person, but sure, I went sometimes."

"And did you like it, going to parties?" He swept more slowly.

I picked up the sweeping pace. "It was okay, but like I said, I didn't go all that much. I like being around people, though."

"And what made you decide to be a sister? I mean, it's not something everybody does."

I stopped to lean on my broom. "Becoming a Missionary of Charity was like a fire burning in my heart. Nothing else seemed to have any value when I could help people in need." As I swept again, I added, "To me, life is about love. I want to help people know that they're loved, that they belong, that God is with them."

Stan swept silently for a moment, gathering the last bits into a pile, then asked, "How do you keep on going?" Stan grabbed a dustpan and I swept our pile of dust into it. "You're here with these rowdy kids all the time, in this heat, and you've got so much pressure on you, but you're never nervous, and you always have a good word for everyone."

"Well, I get angry sometimes, and there are moments I can't stand all the noise, but I guess prayer keeps me going. With God I can do anything He asks."

"How do you know what God is asking?" Stan stood still, bucket in hand.

I looked at him for a moment, then said, "You'll know it in your heart, and it will make you happy."

I reached for the mop, and Sister Katey—who'd driven the van to the arboretum—stuck her head inside the door. "Are you two still here? The other sisters and volunteers have left already." She looked at me, and I shrugged. "There was an accident on the bridge," she said. "Traffic was terrible."

As the three of us mopped in silence, I realized that I'd enjoyed my conversation with Stan more than I'd enjoyed anything in recent weeks. For a few moments I'd felt like a person who counted for something—not only because Stan respected me and wanted to hear what I had to say, but also because I had, for a moment, escaped the reach of Sister Priscilla. If Stan wanted to talk again, I would refer him to Sister—speaking again to someone I liked so much could be dangerous—but I was happy for those few moments.

The sisters were all excited when Mother arrived. Sister Priscilla told Sister Katey to bring the summer camp volunteers to the convent so Mother could meet them. When Sister Katey told the volunteers at camp, they were so excited they clapped their hands. One of the Jesuit novices let out a whoop.

I wanted to be there when the volunteers met Mother—but I was a junior sister, and my presence wouldn't have been appropriate. I recalled an altar cloth that needed ironing in the sacristy, just off the hallway where Mother would meet them. I felt slightly guilty about my eavesdropping plan, but excitement trumped my scruples.

After tea, I raced ahead to plant myself in the sacristy before Mother and Sister Katey could see me. As I plugged in the iron, I heard footsteps in the corridor, then the voices of the volunteers: "So nice to meet you, Mother Teresa." "Welcome to New York." "Thank you for seeing us, Mother."

"*Ah cha.*" Mother sounded happy. "So, the sisters tell me you help with the children."

"Yes, it's a big job."

"You are serving Jesus in His distressing disguise. Do you know that?" I could picture Mother wagging her finger at them.

"Yes, Mother. The sisters are patient," one of the girls said. "They show us how to be like Jesus for the kids."

"Sister Katey works really hard," one of the Jesuit novices said. I wondered if Sister Katey was blushing or turning away.

"And Sister Donata has a great personality." That was Stan's voice. *A great personality*. I doubted that made Mother happy—after all, the whole point of the religious life was to decrease so that Jesus could increase in us—but it made me tingle all over.

"Yeah, she's really terrific," the other Jesuit added.

"*Ah cha,*" Mother said. "And which of you will give your lives to God? You?" I heard giggles.

"You?" Everyone laughed. I wondered whom she'd pointed to.

"And what about you?"

"I don't know, Mother." This was Stan's voice again. "I'm thinking about it."

"Thank you, Mother." Sister Katey was calling the meeting to an end.

"God bless you all," Mother said loudly.

I heard footsteps, and Stan's voice again. "Mother Teresa, could I ask you something?"

"*Ah cha.*" They spoke in muted tones and I didn't hear any more—which was right, after all. About ten minutes passed, then I heard the front door open and close, then Mother's heavy footsteps in the corridor. Ten minutes was more than I'd ever spent with Mother.

At dinner that evening, Sister Katey announced, "Mother met the volunteers today."

"Yes," Mother said. "Very nice, all of them." Then she looked up from her soup and asked, "What's the name of that very tall one?"

"With brown hair, Mother?" Sister Katey asked.

"Yes, and so tall."

"That's Stan, Mother."

"He has a vocation," Mother said. "He should be a priest."

I wondered if Mother had told Stan he had a vocation. No one had ever told me, *You have a vocation*. I heard it for myself, deep inside. Knowing that a holy person thinks you have a vocation could create a terrible burden—you might feel obliged against your own judgment. I wouldn't tell Stan what Mother had said. If Stan was going to be a priest, it should be because he believed God called him, not because someone else—no matter how holy—thought he should.

"Oh, Sister," Sister Katey reported one Sunday at lunch, "Father Stanley made the young people act out the parable of the talents instead of reading the Gospel. He had them up near the altar."

"I hope you told him what you thought of it," Sister Priscilla said, licking the remains of chicken curry from her fingers.

Though the food was better on Sundays, I hated Sunday lunches in the Bronx. I'd always enjoyed collecting kids for Mass, but I'd even begun to hate Sunday mornings: I spent all Mass praying that Father Stanley wouldn't get creative, and dreading lunch.

"Yes, Sister, I told Father Stanley that he was being disrespectful," Sister Katey said, "but he didn't seem to listen. Before when I told him things, he paid attention and tried to explain himself. But ever since I told him what you said about the necessity of obedience in the public prayer of the Church, he listens less and less."

"He is a stubborn man," Sister Priscilla said, nibbling her chapatti.

I wanted to say something, but I knew better than to contradict Sister Priscilla. I thought I understood Father Stanley. Father Stanley was more concerned with celebrating Mass in ways that would engage the young people than with ceremonial norms. But Sister Priscilla believed that nothing done outside established Church rules could ever bear spiritual fruit.

When Sister Trudy arrived in the South Bronx after December professions in Rome, she took to Sunday reporting the way a racehorse takes to the track. One of the first aspirants under Sister Priscilla in New York, Sister Trudy was a New Jersey girl with perfect eyebrows—her mother had been an electrologist. Sister Priscilla assigned Sister Trudy to Sunday Mass at Rikers Island's juvenile detention unit. Sister Trudy was practically gleaming the Sunday she reported, "Father made up his own Eucharistic prayer. He said the proper words of consecration, but everything else was about reconciliation and Jesus freeing the prisoners. It was disgusting. And he told everyone to stand, even during consecration."

Sister Priscilla raised her eyebrows, but before she could say anything, Sister Trudy added, "But we knelt, even if nobody else did. He told us to stand three times, but we just folded our hands and stayed where we were. After Mass, I told him it was wrong to change the words like that."

I was boiling inside, but Sister Priscilla nodded in approval. "You see how important it is for us to go to these places, Sisters. The Church in America has strayed so far from the teachings of the Holy Father. We must defend the Church and never be afraid to proclaim the truth."

I found it hard to believe that Sister didn't know special Eucharistic prayers for reconciliation had been approved by the Church and would be appropriate in a prison. I wanted to tell Sister Priscilla that in Roman parishes, even in St. Peter's, everybody stood during consecration. Most of all, I wanted to tell her that it was important we went to Sunday Masses so we could pray with ordinary people and help make the celebration beautiful, not so we could play policewomen.

Sister Priscilla expected me to be a defender of Holy Truth, but I'd begun to doubt my ability to recognize truth. I knew that all the while I accused Sister Priscilla of judging others, I was judging her. Jesus had said, "Don't judge." I was more guilty than she, because judging a superior was especially heinous, but I couldn't help myself. I didn't know how much longer I could manage to keep quiet.

One Sunday Sister Rochelle announced, "Father Harold at St. Pius mentioned evolution in his homily." She wrinkled her forehead and continued, "He started with the Gospel of the mustard seed growing into the greatest of all trees, and then he said that we were all called to continually grow and change. Then he told this story about life coming from the sea."

"And what did you tell him?" Sister Priscilla asked from the head of the table, water glass in hand.

"I didn't know what to tell him. It sounded strange to me." Sister Rochelle's voice was slower, quieter.

"But it's obvious. It's so insulting, this talk about life from water, man from monkeys. I did not come from a monkey." She took a long drink of water, then added, "A priest should be ashamed. It's heretical."

This unfounded accusation of heresy was too much. "Sister," I said, putting my fork down, "the Documents of the Second Vatican Council don't pronounce on evolution. The only thing we are obliged to believe as Catholics is that all human beings are descended from one original couple."

"What in heaven's name are they teaching in the novitiate these days?" Sister Priscilla lifted her palms and her eyebrows toward heaven, then looked down the table. "I don't know what I will hear next."

The other sisters were quiet. Some looked at Sister Priscilla and shook their heads in time with hers. Others stared resolutely at their beans. I didn't want a fight, but maligning the novitiate wasn't fair. We'd studied the Documents of Vatican II, and I knew she was wrong.

"Excuse me, Sister," I said, "but it's in *Gaudium et Spes*. Why, even Genesis doesn't agree about whether man and woman were created on the same day from the word of God alone, or on different days, God fashioning Eve from Adam's side. Genesis wasn't meant as a biology book. The Church leaves science free to investigate such things." I felt a firm, swift kick to my right shin. One of the senior sisters in the community glared at me.

"That novitiate in Rome has misrepresented many aspects of the Church's teaching," Sister Priscilla said, narrowing her eyes at me. "Mother will have to see about placing sisters there who will be more faithful."

I wanted to reply, but Sister Betsey kicked me again. The

Church's refusal to take a stand on evolution was printed in black on white—I thought I even knew on which page. She had no right to slur the novitiate. I hoped Sister Priscilla would look up the Church's real teaching before she talked to Mother.

About a week later, Sister sent Sister Trudy and me to JFK to pick up Sister Felisa, who had been postponed in the novitiate for telling lies. At the airport, Sister Trudy and I scanned the gate, watching scores of weary travelers trudge toward baggage claim. Finally the flight attendants and pilots emerged. I asked if a sister dressed like us was still on the plane, but they said there hadn't been any nuns on the flight, and that the plane was empty. Neither of us knew Sister Felisa's last name, but as far as the representative at the British Airways desk could tell, Sister Felisa hadn't been on the flight.

Back in the convent, I told Sister Priscilla what had happened.

"You bald-faced liar," Sister Priscilla said.

"Excuse me, Sister?" I tried to remain calm.

"Just after you left," Sister said, "I received a call from London. There was a strike and the flight was cancelled. Sister Felisa took a taxi back to the convent."

"Sister," I said, "we saw people get off that flight at the airport. We saw the list of passengers. The flight arrived, but Sister Felisa wasn't on it."

"How can you stand there and lie with such a straight face? I know what you two were doing. I gave you a chance to be together and you've been driving all around the city chatting, having a grand time. Now you have to make up a story about why it took you so long to get back."

Actually, we hadn't chatted at all. We'd said the rosary and we'd kept silent. "I'm sorry, Sister, but that flight arrived," I said. "I'm sure of it. The number matched the one you gave us. It arrived a little late, but it was definitely the British Airways flight from London."

"Are you really so stupid? Can't you see I know what has happened? What are you trying to hide?"

I thought I knew what had happened. Sister Felisa didn't want to come to the Bronx, and I didn't blame her. She'd gone to the airport, chickened out, and made up a story about a strike. But maybe we had made a mistake. Maybe we had the wrong flight number. Maybe there'd been some grand confusion.

"Sister," I said, "I'm not trying to hide anything. We went to the airport, the flight arrived, and Sister Felisa wasn't on it."

"Liar," Sister said.

"If you say so," I said.

Three days later Sister Priscilla sent another sister to the airport with Sister Trudy to pick up Sister Felisa. Before they left, Sister told me, "There was no strike the other day. I called the airport in London and they confirmed it." I said nothing, then she added, "Strange."

A few weeks later, Sister Priscilla sent for me. *God help me*, I prayed. I knocked on Sister's open door.

She sat at a small desk, neither writing nor reading, just staring blankly ahead. After more than a minute she looked up and said, "Come in."

I entered and she indicated a stool. I sat down.

Sister fixed her eyes on me and said, "I suppose you know why I've called you here."

"No, Sister," I said. "I don't."

"Come now, Donata," she said. "How long did you think you could carry on before we found out?"

"Excuse me?" I ran quickly through possible faults I may have committed. None of them merited being referred to as "carrying on."

"Don't play stupid," she said. "It doesn't become you."

I thought for a few moments. One conversation with Stan nine months earlier didn't seem to qualify as "carrying on."

Sister leaned forward with an all-knowing look in her eye and pronounced, "Sister Becky"—the name of one of the aspirants.

"Sister Becky is my night duty partner sometimes," I said.

"And you've been carrying on with her," Sister Priscilla stated firmly.

"I don't have the faintest idea what you mean, Sister," I said.

"You don't? Not the faintest?" she said, drawing out "faintest" in a way that was clearly meant to mock me.

I tried to state the facts as clearly as I could remember them. "Sister Becky comes with me for night duty every other week or so," I said. "Sister Jenny comes the other weeks. I know Sister Becky's sister—Sister Kristina was six months senior to me in the novitiate, and we talked about her one evening during dinner. Sister Becky teaches a First Communion class at St. Rita's, and I've talked with her about her class. I've asked her a few questions about the organ pedals." I racked my brain for anything else I might have said to Sister Becky, anything I might have done.

"You've been carrying on." Sister leaned forward on her chair as she said this.

"What do you mean?"

"Don't make me say it. You know what I mean."

"Sister, if I've done something that I'm not aware of or can't remember, please tell me so that I can avoid it in the future."

"You know what you've done," Sister Priscilla said. "If it's not obvious to you, you don't deserve to wear this habit."

Sister was implying a violation of the vows. Mother always said silence was the best stance before an accuser, so I remained silent.

After a few moments, Sister Priscilla said, "Sister Becky's mistress tells me that Sister Becky is always saying 'Sister Donata this' and 'Sister Donata that.' She says that you asked her to copy some music for you."

I didn't remember asking Sister Becky to copy any music, but it was in the realm of possibility. "Perhaps I did, Sister. I don't remember," I said. "If I did, I apologize. I shouldn't ask an aspirant for anything not directly related to work."

"You must not get involved with the aspirants and postulants. Speak to their mistress if necessary, but never to one of them."

"Sorry, Sister." I waited, assuming there was more to this accusation.

Sister said nothing, waiting for me. The whole time she never took her eyes from me. I marveled at the calm I felt.

"Go and pray for the grace to make amends," Sister said. "If you can't admit to me what you've done, you must at least admit it before God."

I bowed for her blessing. Instead of saying *God bless you*, she said, "I thought you were better than this, Donata."

I knelt in a corner of the empty chapel. Panic quickly toppled the calm that had kept me focused in Sister's office. *God, what is this about? Have I done something to offend You?* I heard no reply. I searched my conscience for something I might have said or done. Sister seemed to imply particular friendship. I didn't even like Sister Becky. If she spoke of me more than she should, was that my fault?

God, take care of me, I prayed. *Give me Your wisdom and strength. Show me Your truth, and show Sister, too, okay?*

In June, Sister Priscilla called me into the office again. "Sister Donata," she said, a weird gleam in her eye, "I'm sending you to Washington for the new foundation. You will be a faithful sister, and you will make both Jesus and me proud, won't you?"

I hadn't imagined I'd be sent to Washington. My head spun. Of course, I didn't have any choice—if Sister sent me to Washington, I'd go to Washington. But if I'd had a choice, I still would have said yes. Never mind that my family was coming to New York to see me and I would be gone. Never mind that the camp I'd prepared would be run by someone else. Never mind that the superior appointed for Washington didn't look quite up to the task. Never mind any of it— Sister Priscilla would not be there!

"I'm appointing you assistant superior," Sister Priscilla said.

"Excuse me, Sister?" Assistant superiors were always finally professed sisters. I'd never heard of a junior sister appointed assistant. I was just one year professed—it would be five years before I would qualify for that position.

"I don't have enough senior sisters, and I've trained you," she said. "It will be your responsibility to make sure that all the Rules are kept in Washington, just as they are here in New York. You must make sure that the sisters are faithful MCs, and that you are a voice of truth in the parish. I'm counting on you," she said.

Sister Priscilla talked as though she trusted me. It felt good to be trusted, but I didn't want to be the voice of her truth. I wanted to be free to voice the truth as I saw it. Still, the appointment as assistant in the nation's capital was flattering.

In contrast to what she'd told Sister Imma, Sister told me, "I have to send my best sisters to the new foundations." Her tactics annoyed me, but none of it mattered. My first year as a professed sister had been far more confusing than my novice mistress had implied it might be. I hoped for a fresh start, a reprieve, fewer complications.

11

PARADISE

When I lugged my wet clothes to the line hung between two apple trees in our new backyard, the grass tickled my bare feet. During our welcome Mass the previous night, Mother had thanked the people of Washington for inviting us. She encouraged them to pray with their families and to help us serve the poor. A gospel choir had rocked the church, delighting me. The ribs and mashed potatoes they offered us afterward had been the best food I'd had in the four years since I'd joined. Mother had seemed to enjoy the ribs and black-eyed peas, but she kept her head down through the music. At dinner Sister Priscilla had disapproved of both gospel music and soul food. Never mind: I already loved this place.

Mother seemed pleased with the two houses perched atop a hill—the smaller for our new community of four sisters and the larger one next door for our work. Sandy McMurtrie had bought and furnished the houses for us. During the ride from New York in the huge Winnebago Sandy had rented, Mother and Sandy and Sister Priscilla chatted around the kitchen table like old friends, though Sandy had met Mother only briefly in Calcutta a few months earlier. In her forties, Sandy dressed simply, smiled easily, and was obviously captivated by Mother. Sister Priscilla told us that Sandy's father, Dwayne Andreas, was rich, the CEO of a grain company called Archer Daniels Midland. Sandy had furnished our convent, and she had gotten nearly everything right: a plain refectory table, two benches, sturdy cots, a rug on the chapel floor. Mother had told our superior, Sister Leonard, to give the refrigerator to a needy family, and the lace curtains were fancier than we were used to, but everything else looked very MC.

After a day with us, Mother went to the contemplatives' new house on V Street while Sister Priscilla remained to supervise Sister Leonard's settling of the convent and to send Sister Reginald and me off to meet people at the local public housing project, Valley Green. The parish priest had said D.C.'s violent crime statistics rivaled New York's, but as we walked past neatly trimmed lawns, southeast Washington felt peaceful and gracious.

At the bottom of the hill, the mood changed. Across the street, a few men leaned against dilapidated buildings, watching with feigned disinterest. On our side, about twenty women sat on benches or stood in small groups, chatting loudly around a prefabricated building labeled *Social Services, District of Columbia.* They all looked rather young, none over thirty-five. Many carried infants. The closer we got, the quieter the women became. A few gathered toddlers to themselves. A knot in my stomach tightened. This wasn't like the Bronx, where everyone knew us. Sister Reginald elbowed me and whispered, "Say something."

"Good morning," I called out.

One of the women replied, "Morning." She balanced a toddler on one knee. Her left cheek was swollen and bruised. The other women continued to stare silently.

"We're sisters from Assumption Church," I said.

"Y'all Muslim?" a woman leaning against the building asked. She

was dressed in black shorts and a black shirt and wore a heavy gold
necklace.

"Ain't you got no eyes?" The bruised woman jogged the toddler
from her right knee to her left. "They got crosses on their shoulders."

"In my church," the other woman answered, shaking her head,
"we're all sisters, but ain't nobody dress like that."

"Your church?" snickered a woman in cutoffs so short the pockets hung through. "You been to church as often as I been to the
White House."

I just stood there, amazed at the way they spoke to each other,
enjoying each word.

"I ain't been in attendance lately," the woman said, "but Mamma
took us all when we was young." She narrowed her eyes and tightened her lips, shaking her shoulders so her necklace caught the
light.

"They're nuns," a lean woman squatting under the building's
eaves said. She dangled a cigarette between long fingers, and a scar
crossed her left cheek. "I been to Catholic school in Northeast. Sister Mary Elizabeth." She took a puff on her cigarette. "And I seen
these on TV. They're nuns. Aren't you?"

"Yes, we're nuns," I said, a slight quaver in my voice. "We just
moved in up the hill, across from the school." They looked at me
blankly. I continued in a voice I hoped was stronger, "We're starting
a summer program for kids tomorrow morning at eight-thirty.
We'll finish about eleven-thirty. If any of you have school-age kids,
we'd be glad to have them."

"How much you charge?" the squatting woman asked.

"Nothing," I said. The discussion continued. Yes, we'd serve
breakfast and lunch. The camp was for kids six to twelve years old.

At a certain point the woman in cutoffs nodded toward Sister
Reginald and asked, "Don't she talk?"

"Hello," Sister Reginald said, taking a step backward.

"Sister Reginald's from India," I volunteered. "She's still getting
used to things."

"India?" The woman in cutoffs laughed. "Valley Green's just another India."

"But we ain't got snakes," another woman said.

"Not the ground-crawling ones, anyway," the woman with the scar said, and everyone laughed.

We headed behind the social services building toward the housing project, stepping over broken glass and discarded syringes. I'd been more nervous with the women than I'd expected to be, but I thought it wasn't bad for a first encounter. I liked these people.

"Do you think they'll come?" Sister Reginald asked.

"We'll see," I said. I slowed my pace and tried to make my voice gentle. Sister Reginald was the most junior sister in the community, professed just a month earlier in Calcutta. "You know, Sister," I said, "I understand you may feel a little strange here, but it would be good for you to invite them, too. It shouldn't look too much like the white sister's in charge. They're used to white people being in charge."

"But you *are* in charge," she said, clutching her rosary more tightly, "and if they're used to it, what's the problem?"

"There's a lot of tension between black people and white people all over America," I said. "The blacks were brought here by the whites as slaves, and the whites didn't treat them well."

"We had the British," Sister Reginald said.

"I just think it's important for them to see us working together on this."

Sister Reginald silently fingered her rosary as we rounded the corner.

"I saw you," a child's voice shouted from three stories above. "On TV. You's with that Mother Teresa lady."

"That's right," I said, nudging Sister Reginald with my elbow.

"Yes," she mumbled.

"We're having summer camp at our house tomorrow," I called out. "Would you like to come?"

"Summer camp?" he asked, leaning out the window so far that I was afraid he might fall.

"Games and singing. You'll get breakfast and lunch."

"Where do you live?"

"Up the street. The big house opposite the school." He nodded, rocking himself back and forth, using his hands on the window ledge as a fulcrum.

I said, "Bring your friends, too. Anyone between six and twelve. Be there at eight-thirty."

A voice behind us stated flatly, "You sure do dress funny." A girl with bright orange shorts and stocky legs, hands on ample hips, arms bulging from a lime green tank top, chewed meditatively and shook her head at us. She looked about ten years old. "Halloween's not till October."

"What's Halloween?" Sister Reginald asked me.

The girl's bubble popped. "You don't know what Halloween is?" She cocked her head to the left on her solid neck. "You from Mars?"

"I'm from India," Sister Reginald replied, "and we're from the Church and you should speak to us with respect."

"I will speak how—"

"What's your name?" I interrupted.

"My name is Shakeesha Wednesday Lewis the Great." She rolled her head. "What's that to you?"

"Well, Shakeesha," I said, liking this feisty girl more and more, "we're starting a summer program for kids at our house tomorrow, and we'd like you to come."

Shakeesha paused for a moment and pulled her tank top down over her shorts a bit more. "You want me to come to your house?"

"Yes. On top of the hill, across from the school." She remained silent, as did Sister Reginald. "We're starting with breakfast at eight-thirty."

"I'll think about it," Shakeesha said, snapping her bubble gum.

"You can bring your friends, too."

"We'll see," she said.

"Okay," I said, turning toward a group of kids near another building who'd been watching us. "That one will come for sure," I told Sister Reginald.

"I hope not," she answered.

Back home, before she left with Mother, Sister Priscilla pulled me aside. "Keep me informed," she whispered. "I'm counting on you." I knew Sister Priscilla was nervous about Sister Leonard, who had never been superior before. Originally from a village in north India, Sister Leonard had worked for ten years in a Venezuelan mission before arriving in New York less than a week earlier. She was bound to feel a little lost. Still, I didn't anticipate any problems. Mostly I was just happy to see Sister Priscilla go.

About fifteen children showed up the first day of summer camp, including Derrick Porter, the boy who had talked to us from his perch on the window, and his two brothers Eric and Jerome. Shakeesha Wednesday Lewis the Great arrived in an orange tank top and turquoise shorts, actually a bit shy in the beginning, nibbling on her Cheerios and looking around the yard. The kids were energetic and fairly well behaved. They liked sitting at the picnic tables under the apple tree and playing on the grass.

After breakfast, Sister Reginald retreated to the kitchen and watched through the window. I'd handed her four boxes of macaroni and cheese and asked her if she knew what to do with them. "Pasta?" she'd said. "Like rice, no?"

I'd told her yes, kind of like rice, and that the instructions were printed on the box.

I played the guitar and taught the kids a few songs. We played kickball and drew pictures. At lunchtime Sister Reginald brought out a pot of what looked like yellow glue. She started scooping it onto paper plates in front of the kids.

"Gross," Derrick Porter said.

"Really gross," the other kids repeated.

She'd thrown the macaroni in cold water and boiled it together with the cheese powder for some forty minutes. I found some peanut butter and we quickly made sandwiches.

After lunch, the kids went home and Sister Reginald and I cleaned up. I told her not to worry about the macaroni, that the kids had been happy with the peanut butter, and that I'd show her how to prepare the macaroni next time.

Each day a few more children came to camp, and after the first two weeks, we divided them into two groups of fifteen each and capped enrollment. Each morning after an all-camp sing-along, I led the boys and Sister Reginald led the girls.

We taught them the Lord's Prayer, which most of them already knew. They wanted to add *For thine is the kingdom, the power, and the glory*, as Protestant churches did. I didn't see the harm in it, since we also added those words at Mass, after an interlude by the priest, but it upset Sister Reginald, and I knew Sister Priscilla wouldn't like it, so I just told the kids that in our house we stop after *deliver us from evil*, and if they wanted to continue, they could do so silently.

No one knew the Hail Mary. I was a bit concerned parents might object, but they knew we were Catholic when they let their kids come, so I went ahead. *Fruit of thy womb* required a brief explanation of anatomy and metaphor. At *Mother of God*, Derrick's hand shot up.

"How can God have a mother?"

It was A.D. 325 and the Council of Nicea all over again. "Was Jesus God?" I asked.

"Yeah," he said. "God and man, too."

"Well, if Mary is the Mother of Jesus and Jesus is God, can't she be called Mother of God?"

"Aw, Sis," Derrick said, turning his head mockingly, "don't you think that's pushing it?" I couldn't tell anyone, but the Porter brothers were among my favorites.

Everyone seemed to have a great time at camp, and Sister Reginald tried really hard. She even made Shakeesha the Great her helper in the kitchen, and once she got the hang of it, the kids liked her macaroni and cheese.

With just four of us in the new community, we had lots of work, not just summer camp but visiting the projects, hospitals, and jails. One afternoon early on when I was preparing to go out, Sister Leonard told me to put my bag away. "I want you to stay home and make curtains for the refectory," my thin superior said. "We need privacy. Make sure the curtains cover almost all the window."

But MC curtains never covered more than half the window.

"Sister, do we really need long curtains in the refectory?" I asked in the most nonthreatening voice I could muster. "No one is ever close enough to the house at mealtimes to see us."

"You think you know everything, just out of the novitiate," Sister said, fire in her eyes. "We don't only eat here. We'll have confession here, too, since we don't have a proper sacristy."

"But no one can hear us," I said, though maybe I should have kept my mouth shut. "What does it matter if they see us?"

"Just make the curtains. And when you finish with the refectory curtains, make some for the dormitories and for the basement."

"The basement?" The basement windows were at ground level, less than a foot tall, and made of frosted glass.

"Yes, no one should be allowed to see that we have things in the basement. We don't want to lead the people into temptation."

As I measured the windows and cut the cloth, I could hear Sister Priscilla's voice: *This is against poverty. MCs don't need curtains in the refectory. You're here to make sure the Rules are kept.* I tried to block out the voice. I had vowed obedience—but to whom?

Weekly confession could be challenging. Not every week was truly notable for its sins, and I was getting along fairly well with the sisters and the people. But weekly confession was the Rule, undoubtedly good for my soul.

One week early on, I confessed lack of generosity, distracting myself with thoughts about camp during prayer times, and having judged my sisters in my thoughts. When I finished, Father Reid on the other side of the screen said one word: "Sister." He waited, then repeated, "Sister." What did he want? "Sister, look here," he said.

I'd always looked down during confession, humble and contrite, but if he insisted . . .

"Yes, Sister, that's right," he said. He smiled, and the overhead light made his white hair look silver. "Don't be so hard on yourself. You're working very hard, and Father Kelley tells me that all the people here are impressed with your enthusiasm." He nodded at me and smiled again. "It's only natural that you think about camp when you go to pray, because you've put your whole heart into it. So talk about the camp with Jesus, and then it will be a prayer, not a distraction, okay?" Again he smiled at me through the screen.

"Okay, Father."

"The more you come to know the sisters, the easier it will be for you to appreciate them. You are all different, and people here need to see your unity. It will happen if you give yourself time. So," he said, drawing up straighter in his chair, "say three Hail Marys for all your sins, and I absolve you in the name of the Father and of the Son, and of the Holy Spirit."

"Amen," I said, feeling more pleased with myself than I could remember having felt after confession. Father Reid was treating me as an individual with real struggles, and he gave good advice. I felt sure he would help me become holy. Mother and Sister Priscilla would be pleased.

Once a week, Sister Leonard scheduled me to cut the grass and Sister Reginald to work in the garden. I loved the smell of freshly cut grass. The roar of the motor and the solitary job gave me some breathing room, time when I didn't need to think about anything. The steep lawn ended at a fence near the street, and to turn the lawn mower on the slope I had to brace myself and pull the mower up hard. I was a little frightened for my feet. We hadn't brought any closed shoes from the Bronx, and we didn't have time to go through the bags of clothing donations in the basement, so I cut the grass in my sandals.

Washington grew hotter and hotter. One day after mowing the lawn in the heat, pushing and pulling the lawn mower up and down the steep grade, I began to bleed heavily, though it wasn't time for

my period. The loss of blood and the heat made me dizzy, and I had
to sit during most of adoration that evening. I often found myself
bleeding again when we worked together to clear the back lot, dense
with brush and vines. I felt myself growing weaker, but I didn't want
to complain—everyone was working hard.

As Mother had requested the day of our opening, when we'd finished the food stocked in the refrigerator by the local Co-Workers,
we gave the fridge to a family in the projects. We used powdered
milk in our coffee and kept fresh produce in the coolest corner of
the basement. If someone donated fresh meat or fish, we cooked it
immediately.

As the weeks passed, people dropped by with cash donations and
occasional gifts of bread and other groceries. We used their money
to buy supplies for the kids at camp, but we had not spent a penny
on the sisters, and we were proud of it. God had supplied all our
needs. However, as we hit the two-month mark, provisions were
running low.

Staples had slowly vanished: flour, powdered milk, sugar, oil,
peanut butter, rice, tea. Sister Reginald, in charge of the kitchen that
month, scribbled out a shopping list. Sister Leonard looked at the
list, and asked, "Chicken, onions, potatoes, bananas, chocolate?" It
was clear that she hadn't expected to see such luxury items on Sister
Reginald's shopping list.

Sister Reginald said, "Society Feast, Sister." The twenty-second
of August was just a few days away, the Feast of the Immaculate
Heart of Mary, patroness of the Society of the Missionaries of Charity. Sisters always looked forward to eating something special on
Society Feast. Sister Leonard nodded, went to the chapel, lifted the
statue of Mary, and left the list under her feet.

We all prayed and went about our business. No one went shopping. The next morning we wet cornflakes with coffee for breakfast
and had crackers with jelly for lunch. We ate apples from our tree,
cutting out the worms.

When we were in the chapel finishing Midday Prayer, the door-bell rang. I opened to a white woman in her seventies, a pillbox hat perched on her head, gloved hands wrapped around a large card-board box. I took the box from her, and she smiled. Poking out from the top of the box were sugar, tea, and bananas. My mouth began to water, and my heart began to sing. God was looking out for us, and we'd have bananas on the twenty-second! As I thanked her, the woman pointed a gloved finger toward the street and said with a lovely southern drawl, "There's more in the car."

Sister Reginald ran to retrieve the other box. The woman with the gloves and pillbox hat introduced herself as Odette Thompson. She and I watched as Sister Reginald emptied the contents of both boxes on the parlor table. Meanwhile, Sister Leonard lifted Our Lady and brought the list in. Every item on the list was accounted for on the table, even chicken and chocolate, plus a few extras, in-cluding a cake, perfect for the feast. Surely this was no coincidence.

Eventually, as the months passed, we did spend money on things for the sisters, and sometimes we even asked Odette Thompson to drive us to the grocery store, but we never forgot that God had sent Odette to us, and that He always looked out for our needs.

Every now and then, Archbishop James Hickey dropped in. He would tell the priest who was scheduled for Mass to take the morn-ing off, and in the scheduled priest's stead, the archbishop surprised us at the door with a big smile, sometimes with a basket of fruit. After Mass, he always wanted to know how we were settling in and how the work was going.

The work was going well, and growing. In the mornings while Sister Reginald and I ran summer camp, Sister Leonard and Sister Fran visited the projects. In the afternoon, we took turns visiting D.C. Village Nursing Home and St. Elizabeth's Hospital for the mentally ill. Once a week Sandy drove us to Virginia, where we taught literacy at Lorton Penitentiary. On Sundays, we taught cate-chism and provided music for the children's Mass in the parish.

Sister Priscilla phoned one fall day and told Sister Leonard to open a soup kitchen in the house we had used for summer camp. A soup kitchen wasn't a bad idea—there were plenty of hungry people in the neighborhood, and D.C.'s soup kitchens were nearly all across the river—but I found it odd that Sister hadn't asked us what we thought people needed before starting another big project. Sister also told us to equip the basement for a clothes distribution center. Father Reid found a contractor willing to donate labor and material, but he wouldn't be free for months.

In the meantime, we readied the soup kitchen—with a lot of help. Eunice Kennedy Shriver sent people to help fix the driveway and paint. Senator Mark Hatfield donated a freezer. General John Pesch of the Air Force brought some of his buddies and installed shelves in the convent basement to store canned goods. Sandy's father sent cases and cases of soy products from Archer Daniels Midland.

Lots of people volunteered at the soup kitchen once we opened. One Saturday I washed dishes with a new volunteer. Henry said, "I've been wanting to come for a long time, ever since I read in the *Post* how Mother Teresa brought you sisters here." He slung the wet dish towel over the handle on the oven door. "I wish I could be here every day, but I'm too busy." He looked out the window and onto the street. "My work—it takes too much of my time. I'm out of town a lot." Turning to me, he spoke with frustration. "What I do is so unimportant compared to what you do here. You sisters do the work of Jesus and Mary. You help a lot of people. I envy you."

"What do you do, Henry?" I asked.

"I'm an advisor to the Senate Committee on Foreign Affairs."

I was floored. This man with what anyone would call an important job recognized what I also knew—serving the poor, face-to-face, was the best job in the whole world.

Summer camp morphed into an after-school program. We helped the kids with their homework, played games with them, and always

ended the day with prayer and singing in the little chapel upstairs. I
played the guitar and Sister Reginald led the prayers.

Sandy helped us arrange an October trip for our kids to a farm in
Virginia. The kids had been excited for weeks, but when the big day
arrived, these forty kids from Valley Green looked at the bus driver
with his blond hair and ruddy cheeks, and I couldn't get a single one
on the bus. Archie Moore mumbled, "They's gonna be white people
there."

For some reason, they hadn't realized until then that this trip
would take them into white folks' territory. All at once, they decided
they weren't taking any chances.

After a lot of convincing, including promises of pony rides and
chocolate, the kids boarded the bus. In town and on the Beltway, I
tried to interest them in songs, but the kids weren't having it. Instead, they yelled at each other, beat the seats, and engaged in ear-
splitting whistling duels from the back to the front of the bus.

When we took Route 610 west, the traffic thinned and the hills
grew woody. The changing leaves glowed orange and red in the
sunlight. Geese flew overhead. The kids looked out the windows
and grew quiet. The only noises came from those on the aisle seats,
who complained that those near the windows blocked their view.

At a certain point, despite my reminder that walking in the bus
wasn't allowed, Shakeesha Lewis' little sister walked down the aisle.
When she reached my seat, this tiny girl with red-ribboned pigtails
whispered in my ear: "Sister, I'm scared. It's too pretty." I got up and
squeezed Shalitha between Sister Fran and me. Too pretty was a
problem I didn't want to solve. I put my cardigan around Shalitha's
shoulders. She closed her eyes and put her head on my chest.

No one spoke. I could hear the bus wheels roll on pavement. I
could hear the kids breathe. I'd never heard that before.

The bus turned down a long winding driveway and pulled up in
front of a large white house. The bus driver honked, and two dozen
white kids appeared—teenagers with scrubbed faces, blue jeans and
T-shirts, football jackets, big smiles. They reminded me of myself a
few years earlier.

I got down and told the kids to follow. No one moved. I urged. I cajoled. I renewed promises of pony rides and chocolate. Even mention of ice cream didn't move them. Finally Joey announced he had to pee. The others hassled him as he left, and watched a white boy lead Joey into the house. When Joey returned, he had a hot dog in his hand and a Redskins cap on his head. Derrick announced, "I'm getting me a hot dog," and the others followed him down.

The kids enjoyed the hot dogs, the pony rides, the ice cream, patting the pigs and goats, fingering the white kids' hair.

On the bus ride home, I sat behind Archie and Derrick. At a certain point Archie turned to Derrick and said, "You know, them peoples ain't white. Them's Sister Donata's color."

Derrick nodded.

We were nearly home, in more ways than one. I was never happier to be a Missionary of Charity than I was those first few months in Washington.

12

SLIPPERS, CURTAINS,
AND A PENCIL

SUMMER 1982
WASHINGTON, D.C.

"Such a big place you have," Mother said, turning in a circle in the yard, hands open wide, eyes sparkling. Apart from the wrinkles, she did not resemble any seventy-year-old woman I knew.

Sister Leonard, who as superior should have responded to Mother, just looked nervously at the grass.

"That house is for our people," I said, wondering how much Mother remembered from the harried days of the official opening the previous year. I pointed: "We live over there."

"*Ah cha*," Mother said, nodding. "In the smaller house. Very good."

Weeks earlier, Sister Priscilla had called to remind us that Mother would be alert to deviation from MC practices. If I were a better assistant superior, I would have known how to convince Sister Leonard to lead prayers more slowly, to conclude recreations at the proper time, to limit her frequent phone calls to Father Reid—phone calls I knew about because after a year of trying she still wasn't able to dial the numbers by herself; I wondered if she was dyslexic. Still, I was proud of our work with the kids and the soup kitchen, and hoped Mother would be pleased.

Mother arrived on a Saturday. She would receive honorary degrees at Georgetown and at Niagara University on Sunday, and speak to four different groups downtown on Monday, then to six thousand people in Arlington on Tuesday. It was futile to hope for a quiet visit like those of the pre-Nobel days. Wednesday morning we were scheduled to have Mother to ourselves for an hour before she left. Perhaps during this visit there would be a moment when Mother would say something special just for me. As the only Westerner in the community, I often felt lonely, and the hormones the doctor had given me for dysfunctional uterine bleeding had darkened my moods even further. I was supposed to ease the sisters' cultural integration, but they took offense when I explained American jokes or holidays or traffic regulations. I hoped Mother's visit would bring renewal and inspiration.

We were all crossing the lawn to the convent when Mother looked down at our feet and shook her head. "Sisters, you mustn't come out of the house barefoot anymore," she said. "There is a new disease. No one knows what causes the disease or how you catch it, but everyone who gets it dies. You must wear your slippers or sandals when you're out of the house. Do you understand?"

"Yes, Mother."

I held the door open and said hello to Sister Priscilla, then tried to avoid her gaze and brush away the fear that resurfaced as soon as I saw her.

In the refectory, at the head of the table as we sat for tea, Mother seemed to sag. "What's next?" she asked Sister Priscilla.

"Mother, we're going to the contemplatives. Sister Nirmala is waiting for us."

"*Ah cha.* And adoration?"

"We can have adoration there, Mother."

Mother pressed her lips together and looked down. It was obvious to me she would have preferred a few more minutes with us before racing off.

"Very well," Mother said. "But I want to tell you all one thing before we go, and I want you to listen to Mother well. There is a new disease," she said again. "It has already killed men in San Francisco and in New York. It may be a new kind of cancer, but no one is sure, and no one knows how it travels. So no bare feet outside the house. Understood?"

"Yes, Mother," we said. I would miss the feel of fresh grass against my feet. I wished someone had discovered a new disease when I was a novice walking on those gravel walkways in Tor Fiscale.

Sister Leonard and I accompanied Mother and Sister Priscilla to the contemplatives' house. As Sandy backed the car out of the driveway, Mother began prayers. In the middle of a Hail Mary while driving down Martin Luther King, Jr. Boulevard, Mother paused to ask, "What is all that?" The small trim lots of our residential neighborhood had given way to rolling green lawns and stately brick buildings behind a high fence.

Since Sister Leonard remained silent yet again, I said, "That's St. Elizabeth's Hospital, Mother. For the mentally ill."

"All that?" Mother asked, shaking her head.

"Yes, Mother."

"They should get some sheep. Animals are good for mental people." Mother was smiling again. Her eyes had regained some of their sparkle.

After a few more Hail Marys, Mother concluded the prayer and proclaimed, "Praised be Jesus Christ," signaling freedom to talk. Still Sister Leonard just sat fingering her rosary, though prayers were over. I had never made small talk with Mother. I considered mentioning a woman we'd visited at St. Elizabeth's. She'd heard Jesus' advice in the Gospel, "If your right hand causes you to sin, cut it off," and had proceeded to chop off her right leg with an axe—to prevent herself from wandering into bad neighborhoods. Rejecting that story as too gruesome, I asked Mother, in the politest MC English I knew, "What will Mother be doing while Mother is here?"

Mother looked back, smiled, and said, "I don't know." She looked over at Sister Priscilla and said, "Sister has arranged all that." I was surprised. Surely Mother knew about her trips the next day. Wouldn't she need to prepare her addresses at Georgetown and Niagara, and the one scheduled for Harvard the next weekend? When Mother turned to face forward, Sister Priscilla tapped my knee, put a finger to her mouth, and narrowed her eyes. With Mother and Sister in town not even two hours, I'd blundered already.

Later, back at home, we waited for Mother and Sister to return, while dark clouds covered the sun. Before long, rain hammered so hard that raindrops ricocheted off the lawn. Lighting flashed and thunder shook the windows. We hadn't expected rain, and Mother and Sister didn't have umbrellas.

I was portress that week, responsible for answering both the door and the phone. After dinner, during recreation, I stood near the window with my mending, two umbrellas close so that I could rush outside when I saw Sandy's car in the driveway. As the rain continued to pelt the lawn, the phone rang, and I left my post. When I picked up, headlights shone through the window.

The voice asked for information. The headlights drew closer. If I didn't act quickly, Mother and Sister would get soaked.

"I'll call my superior," I said, dropping the receiver so that it dangled on the cord. I raced to the refectory, telling Sister Leonard, "Sister, the phone." I grabbed the umbrellas and rushed through the rain. I managed to have one umbrella ready just as Mother opened the car door, then passed the other umbrella to Sister Priscilla in the back. I'd made it!

I was holding the umbrella over Mother, walking to the house, rain beating all around, when Mother stopped.

"Sister," she said, shouting at me over the storm, "I told you not to come out of the house barefoot."

"Sorry, Mother," I said, stopping in order to keep Mother covered.

"I don't need that," Mother said, looking at the umbrella, anger in her voice. "You should have your slippers on." She looked straight in my eyes. "I told you twice." Then she walked deliberately outside the umbrella's protection. As I reached to cover her again, she moved to the other side and said, "Mother doesn't need *tamasha*. Mother needs sisters who obey her."

These words hit hard—I'd been trying all year to be obedient, but Mother thought I was just putting on a show, creating commotion. Mother dashed to the house, while I trailed behind. By the time she reached the door, Mother was dripping wet. I was humiliated, wet, and annoyed. On the way in, I passed my plastic slippers, right by the front door—in my haste I'd forgotten them. I went to bed that evening even more nervous than I had been. Everything I did disappointed someone.

In our small chapel the next morning, the sound of Mother's voice, resonant and strong, anointed Morning Prayers. When Mother said, *O Jesus, through the Most Pure Heart of Mary, I offer you all the prayers, works, joys, and sufferings of this day*, it was as if she saw Jesus and Mary in front of her, accepting her offering with a smile. When I prayed, God seemed far away, silent and waiting for me to do better.

After breakfast, Mother asked to "see the house"—inspection time. Sister Priscilla motioned Sister Leonard and me to follow Mother. In the refectory, Mother stood in front of the windows. She held one hand against her hip while the other pointed to the curtains. Mother wrinkled her forehead and asked, "What do you need these curtains for? Such long curtains, such fine cloth?"

I waited for Sister Leonard to answer Mother—as she had answered me—but she said nothing.

Mother turned to me, "Why, Sister?"

I repeated Sister Leonard's answer to me: "For the privacy, Mother."

"What do you need privacy for? What do you do here?" Mother asked.

"We eat, and have spiritual reading and recreation," Sister Leonard said.

"And confession, too," I added, which had been the one justification which had seemed almost reasonable.

"Do you think people don't know that you eat and read and that you sin?" Mother raised her palms in what looked like frustration. Her eyes had grown hard. "People should know that you go to confession. There is no shame in that."

I began to feel justified—not perhaps to Mother, but to myself.

We took the stairs into the basement. "Curtains here, too?" Exasperation filled Mother's voice. "So much waste, so much time spent uselessly when you could be serving the poor."

Mother looked around, obviously waiting for a response. Sister Leonard said nothing. I said, "Sorry, Mother." Why should I bear the brunt of Mother's scolding when Sister Leonard had been the one who'd insisted on the curtains?

When Mother and Sister Priscilla left for the graduations, I asked Sister Leonard if she wanted me to take the curtains down. Sister didn't turn toward me. Nor did she answer.

"Sorry, Sister," I repeated. "Should I take the curtains down?"

Spinning on her heel, Sister Leonard looked me straight in the eyes. Her upper lip trembled, trying to keep the anger I saw in her eyes from spilling out of her mouth. "That's a stupid question." She paused. She swallowed. "Today is Sunday, and you can't sew on Sunday. If you take the curtains down now, what are we going to put in their place?"

"I'm afraid Mother will be upset when she comes home and finds the curtains still up," I said. "Maybe we could at least take down the basement curtains?"

"Don't touch the curtains today." Sister spit out each word deliberately. "I will tell you when to touch the curtains."

"Yes, Sister. Sorry, Sister."

When Mother and Sister returned that evening, late from the graduations, I opened the porch door for them. Mother walked quickly inside and genuflected vigorously as Sister Priscilla dragged herself up the stairs. Mother was already in the refectory when I closed the door behind Sister Priscilla.

"Sister, Sister—*Sister*." Mother's call was more emphatic each time. I rushed into the refectory, where Mother stood in front of the windows, looking at the curtains. "Sister," she said to me, anger and disappointment filling her eyes and voice, "I thought Mother told you to take those down."

"Yes, Mother," I said, "but today is Sunday, and we couldn't fix them on a Sunday, so we waited."

"Sister," Mother said, turning until she looked directly at me, her face an entreaty. "Sister, MCs do not question. MCs obey promptly, cheerfully, blindly."

I looked at the floor. I wanted to say, *I've only done what I've been told*, but I remembered Jesus before Pilate, and I remained silent.

As Mother turned to head down the hall, she said, "Sister, take those curtains down."

My hands trembled with anger and confusion as I slipped the curtains off their rods. I folded the curtains, asking God to make my heart meek and humble like His, and to put some sense into my superior's head. As I replaced the empty rod in its brackets, I heard footsteps behind me. "What are you doing?" Sister Leonard hissed.

"Mother told me to," I whispered.

Sister headed toward the end of the room, picked up the hand bell, and knelt to ring the De Profundis. When Mother and the other sisters appeared, we sat down to a late dinner. Mother glanced at the bare windows and nodded. She even smiled a little. Mother talked about the private plane Sandy's father had supplied. "You see how God spoils us—a whole plane all to ourselves."

Sister Fran asked, "How did it go at the schools, Mother?"

"Thank God, Sister, very well." Mother looked pleased with herself, smiling and nodding. "So many people. And they were all so kind."

I put the soup dish on the table, and Mother ladled a generous portion into her bowl. She continued, "They wanted me to give a talk, to the young people who had finished their college. I told them that now they have finished, the best gift they can give each other is a virgin body on their wedding day."

I nearly dropped the bread dish. *No, really? At Georgetown? And will she say the same thing at Harvard?*

"What did they say then, Mother?" asked Sister Fran, whose Filipino sensibilities were probably closest to mine.

"You know, afterward many of them came up and told me, 'Thank you, Mother Teresa, for saying that.' "

Of course they said thank you, I thought. *You're a highly regarded world figure. They'd just given you an honorary doctorate.*

"Someone just needs to tell these young people," Mother said. "Then they will be all right."

I felt the blood drain from my face. I could picture students gathered at a local bar imitating the short, wrinkled nun who presumed to advise them on preserving their nonexistent virginity. I put my spoon down and forgot my soup. I wasn't just embarrassed. I was disappointed. Mother had missed an opportunity. I had imagined the class of 1982 telling their grandchildren that they'd been inspired to increase agricultural yield in sub-Saharan Africa, to form women's cooperatives in Indonesia, to litigate for civil rights in their hometowns by Mother Teresa, who had spoken at their graduation.

Donata, slow down, I told myself. *You're going into overload—rational, logical debate mode. Where is your faith? Where is your humility? You're a junior sister, you don't know anything, and you're judging a Saint. Mother has already told you twice in two days that she needs obedient sisters. Criticizing will only get you into trouble.*

Okay, I told myself. *I won't say anything. I will be a good sister. I'll eat soup, drink water, and keep my mouth shut. Mother knows what she is doing.*

Sister Reginald kicked me under the table and nodded toward the soup dish. I picked it up and headed to the top of the table to pass it a second time.

As I placed the ladle in front of Mother, the silence that was expected of me felt more like cowardice than virtue, but I knew it wasn't my place to speak. If Mother thought talking about virginity to college grads was more important than talking about social justice, that was her call. If I could silence the anger within, maybe I would understand what was really important, as Mother did.

The next two days we hardly saw Mother as she was whisked from appointment to appointment. After breakfast the last morning of her visit, Sister Reginald led Mother on a tour of the garden. I wished I had something other than pride and mistakes to show Mother.

As I watched Mother and Sister Reginald from the window, Sister Priscilla approached me. "You're doing a good job," she said with her little half smile. "Just keep helping Sister Leonard. The sisters are still getting used to the States. They need you."

"Sister, sometimes I get confused," I said.

"You're doing fine, and you can always write me if there are problems," she said. "You don't write enough. I should be kept informed. I'm counting on you to keep this house running properly. Now, could you get me a cup of tea?"

I set the tea on the table, then let myself out the back door. I didn't want to talk with Sister Priscilla. I wanted a moment alone with Mother. I ambled toward the vegetable garden, where Sister Reginald was showing Mother her tomatoes. I lingered near the green beans, and when Sister Reginald was through, I told Mother, "Thank you for coming, Mother."

"*Ah cha,*" she said, walking toward the house. "Is it time to go?"

"Not yet, Mother. Sister is having tea and Sandy is not yet here." I still didn't know how to talk to Mother. Why couldn't I just tell her how confused I was, how much I wanted to do what was right, but didn't seem able?

Mother stopped walking and looked at me for a moment. "Sister," she said.

"Yes, Mother?"

"Sister, do you know what your problem is?"

I took a deep breath. My heart raced. I wanted to hear it, even if it would be hard. Mother could tell me what was keeping me from God.

"Your problem," Mother said, her eyes pinning me down, "is that you like to be consulted."

I wanted to melt into the earth. Mother had seen me, and it wasn't pretty.

Mother's eyes turned softer, kinder. "Sister, listen to Mother. You want to be holy. You need just one thing: Let Jesus use you without consulting you. Then you will become holy. It's simple."

Deep inside, I knew Mother was right. I'd wanted Sister Leonard to listen to me about the curtains. I wanted Mother to ask what I thought about the commencement address. I thought I had useful things to say. I was proud.

"Thank you, Mother," I said, just as Sister Leonard shuffled toward us, calling that Sandy had come with the car.

In the chapel as Mother led the prayers before a journey, all I could hear were her words, just for me: *Let Jesus use you without consulting you.*

Mother was truly great, but she didn't have the battles I did with pride. Mother called herself "a pencil in God's hand." A pencil didn't offer suggestions; a pencil's only contribution was to be available. Mother's patron saint, St. Thérèse of Lisieux, had called herself Jesus' plaything, a ball content to be tossed or left in the corner. I had to become a pencil, a ball, a tool without will or opinion of my own. Mother had given me a prescription for my soul.

13

PARADISE LOST

SUMMER TO FALL 1982
WASHINGTON, D.C.

"Those children of yours are wild." Sister Fran lifted the end of her sari and looked at me through a large tear in the sari's bottom edge.

We were having recreation after the first week of our second summer camp, and it seemed best to let Sister Fran vent. Sixty kids had signed up, so all four of us worked at camp, instead of just Sister Reginald and me. Even with the extra help Sandy had corralled from Mater Dei School (the exclusive prep school in Bethesda run by the conservative Catholic organization *Opus Dei*), we were all tired.

"Joey grabbed Derrick's hot dog," Sister Fran continued loudly, "so Derrick chased him around the table." She narrowed her eyes to thread a needle. "I tried to catch them, but all I caught was my sari on the bench. Those children are wild, I tell you," she repeated.

"Sister Fran," Sister Leonard scolded, shaking a finger while barely suppressing a grin, "you're worse than the children." Sister bent over the refectory table and slipped a knife into the folded edge of a brown paper bag, slashing the paper to use as a cover for her prayer book. "You must be strict, have discipline."

Sister Fran sighed, glanced up at the picture of the Sacred Heart that hung above Sister Leonard's place at table, then silently returned to stitching her sari.

Sister Leonard looked at me. "You must not allow them to fight," she said, "especially that Joey."

"You know," Sister Reginald said, "in Calcutta one sister can easily manage fifty children in a slum school. Children there know to respect and obey."

Even if that were true, it's not fair to expect docility from a kid like Joey, whose mom is on heroin and whose dad is in jail. I kept my mouth shut. Accepting sixty children had probably been a mistake. I had enough trouble with my group of fifteen; my sisters still had a hard time with the local lingo and found the children's behavior literally incredible. *Sorry* and *excuse me* just weren't part of these kids' vocabularies, and *please, Sister* was reserved for asking for seconds on desserts.

Please and *thank you* were some of the first words I'd learned as a child. My peace-loving father had forbidden his seven children to play cowboys and Indians or cops and robbers. When we engaged in the inevitable sibling squabbles, we had to apologize and shake hands before we could leave the room. One of my earliest memories was of carrying a candle beside my dad to protest the Vietnam War.

"I've got an idea," I announced. "We could try to teach the kids to settle their differences peacefully, make it like a theme for the camp." Sister Leonard looked at me blankly. "I could explain nonviolence at the morning sing-alongs, then when we divide into groups, you could each help your kids. We could talk about Martin Luther King, Jr., and maybe you all could tell them about Gandhi. If we all work together on this"—the words rushed out as my excitement grew—"we could have a real impact on these kids."

"Just so long as they stop tearing my sari," Sister Fran said.

"Tell them not to run," Sister Reginald added.

Sister Leonard shrugged, excused herself, told me she wanted to talk to Father Reid, and asked me to dial his number.

I resolved not to let my sisters dampen my excitement. Once they understood the good that we could do, they would be as excited as I was.

Monday morning after a few traditional camp songs, guitar strap still around my neck, I took a deep breath and asked, "Who's ever been in a fight?" Sixty hands shot up.

"Have you ever been in a fight somebody else started?" All hands up again, higher, swinging.

"And what do you do when someone else picks a fight?"

"Kick their ass," a boy in front shouted.

"Send them knocking," Shakeesha said, standing and punching the air.

"And who knows what Jesus said about fighting?" All faces went blank. "Doesn't anybody know?" After a moment, I continued, "Jesus said, 'When someone slaps you on the right cheek, turn the left.' "

"Jesus was a sissy," Jerome hissed. Sister Leonard walked to Jerome and whispered something in his ear, then she put her hand over his mouth.

"Do you really think Jesus was a sissy?" I asked. "Don't you think it takes a lot of courage to stand still while somebody's trying to pick a fight with you?"

"That's why Jesus ended up on the cross," Derrick mumbled, loud enough that we could all hear.

I hadn't wanted to go there, but Derrick saw straight through to the consequences. "Do you think Jesus could have avoided the cross if He wanted to?" I asked.

"Sure, He worked all those miracles," Derrick said. "He's got more power than the Hulk."

"That's right," I said slowly, wanting to make sure they understood, "but Jesus chose not to fight back. Even though He was the Son of God, and perfectly innocent, Jesus let the soldiers tie His hands and lead Him away to be crucified, so that we could all live forever."

"Sister," Derrick said, "there's got to be other better ways to live forever without getting yourself stuck on no cross."

"Jesus had to die to save us from our sins, isn't that right?" I asked.

"That's what the preacher says at Sunday school," Shakeesha answered. Shakeesha attended the Temple Missionary Baptist Church. "It's written in the Bible."

"That's okay for Jesus, then," Derrick said, "just so long as I don't have to get up on no cross."

"Derrick," I replied, "no one is going to put any of us on crosses, but if we're going to be like Jesus, then we have to be peacemakers, even when it's hard. The point is, if somebody's mean to us, we don't fight back and make it worse."

Derrick looked at me as though I were crazy. Most of the little kids looked blank. They would need time to digest this.

The second day of my nonviolence program, we sang "We Shall Overcome," and I asked the kids to tell me everything they knew about Dr. Martin Luther King, Jr., which proved to be quite a lot, and they all agreed that Dr. King was no sissy. On the third day, I taught them "I'm Gonna Lay Down My Sword and Shield," and we talked about King Solomon and the two mothers claiming one baby, and how the real mother's love wouldn't allow any harm, even if it meant giving up her own child. Derrick Porter raised his hand and interrupted, "But you see, Sister, that king had to threaten them with that sword cutting them babies in two before he could get them to shut up." I had chosen the wrong example.

On the fourth day, during breakfast, Joey deliberately threw milk in Sister Fran's face. Joey ducked under the table, and Sister Fran licked her lips and said, "Very tasty." Another boy offered her a napkin, and Sister Fran said, "Joey, here's my other cheek. Have you got more milk?" The boys giggled, and one of them kicked Joey under the table. We weren't quite there yet, but we were moving in the right direction.

A few days later, I noticed Sister Leonard's group at the picnic table under the apple tree, with crayons and coloring books, but I didn't see Sister anywhere. The boys seemed fine, and Mike from Opus Dei was with them, so I didn't pay much attention. Sister must have stepped out for a second.

After I returned from a game of Swinging Statues on the back lawn, Mike was still alone with the boys. "Mike, where's Sister Leonard?" I asked.

"She's inside with Joey," Mike said. "He didn't want to color and started throwing crayons at one of the kids."

"At me," Jerome Porter said, "but I didn't throw any back." He sat up proudly. "I told him like you said, Sister, 'Please stop that,' and then I turned the other cheek."

"Good boy, Jerome," I said, patting him on the back. Out of the corner of my eye, I saw Joey emerge from the kitchen door, rubbing his arm, and Sister Leonard behind him, a thin branch in her hand.

Don't jump to conclusions, Donata, I told myself.

I faked extreme interest in the boys' coloring project. I told myself, *Innocent until proven guilty*. When Sister reached the table, she was smiling, and still holding the stick. "Joey and I had a little talk," she said, tapping the stick in her left palm, "and he's not going to be bad anymore, are you, Joey?"

Joey turned his back.

"None of you boys are going to be bad anymore, are you?" she asked, tapping the shoulders of the two boys nearest her with her branch. The boys looked down and continued to color.

"They're all very good boys," I said. "Aren't you?" No response but the sound of crayons on paper. The only one looking at us was Mike, and when he saw that I saw him, he looked away, too.

As Sister Leonard put her prayer books back on the shelf after adoration that evening, I asked to speak to her. She raised her eyebrows and pressed her lips tightly together before nodding. We walked down the corridor to the office, and I prayed for the right words. Sister Leonard was my superior. I expected Sister to sit when she got to the office, but she didn't, so we both remained standing. She looked at me without saying a word.

"Sister, I was just wondering, did you have any trouble with the boys today?" I asked.

"Those aren't boys—they're uncontrollable monsters."

"No, Sister. They're boys. I know they can be difficult—I had trouble in the beginning, too. They come from troubled families in a violent neighborhood."

"They don't listen, and they don't even speak English, just a lot of strange expressions."

"Yes, their English is very particular. If there's something you don't understand, maybe Mike could help you."

She looked out the window.

"Excuse me, Sister, but did you hit Joey with that stick today?"

"I told you—they're uncontrollable. They don't listen."

"But, Sister, we can't hit kids," I said. "It doesn't do any good in the long run, and it diminishes their respect for you. Besides, it's against the *Constitutions*, which specifically say we use no corporal punishment with any of our people."

"I've read the *Constitutions*."

"Sister, it's against the law. If one of the parents reported you, the police would come."

"Children have to be taught to behave."

"Yes, Sister, but not like that. It takes a lot of patience."

"Don't lecture me on patience."

"Sorry, Sister."

"I've handled children before. I know what they need."

Sister looked away, and the conversation was over. We were supposed to love the children, not beat them. I hadn't imagined that my first big opportunity to let Jesus use me would involve standing in opposition to my superior.

That night, when the other sisters were in bed, I went to the basement and crouched under the stairs. I hugged my knees and cried as quietly as I could. I'd never felt so alone.

Much of the joy of summer camp disappeared under the stress of trying to keep an eye on Sister Leonard's group while also fighting the exhaustion caused by my excessive bleeding. I wanted to be patient—Sandy's doctor had said the hormones he prescribed would need time to work—but the medication seemed to drag me down and make fighting melancholy even more difficult. Sister spoke less and less at mealtimes and very rarely asked me for anything the way she had before, except to dial the phone. I often saw a stick in her hand, but I had no evidence that she'd used it as anything but a scare tactic since the incident with Joey.

I stopped propagandizing for nonviolent problem solving. I didn't want to confuse the kids by singing "I'm Gonna Lay Down My Sword and Shield" while the superior swung a stick around. I tried to remain calm and settle the inevitable grievances by dialogue, compromise, and forgiveness. Some of the kids seemed to be learning. Archie Moore came up to me one day and said, "I wanted to punch Shakeesha when she called my mother a cow-headed bitch, but I just told her that my mother may be big, but she never uses words like that. She looked at me and walked away. I thought that was pretty cool."

I thought it was cool, too, and I tried to keep those little triumphs in mind, but the sight of the stick, never far from Sister Leonard's hand, made it impossible to savor any satisfaction.

When it happened again, on a field trip, I sat the boy next to me on the bus home. Arm around his shoulder, I tried to comfort him and calm myself. I tried considering Sister Leonard's position. I knew that physical discipline of children wasn't uncommon in India, though I had no way of knowing if she'd been beaten as a child. I could imagine that Sister had looked forward to being superior, and expected that she would be treated with respect. Instead, she lived with a junior sister who thought she knew better and worked with kids who ran around her table and made faces when they didn't understand her English. Empathizing with Sister Leonard took some of the anger away, but it couldn't excuse hitting the kids.

When we got home and I closed the office door behind me, I didn't even wait to see if Sister would sit or not. "Sister," I said, "I'm sorry. I know the boys can really be very difficult, but—did you hit Archie Moore today?"

"You don't need to worry about what I do."

"I know you're doing what you think is best for the children, but hitting the kids isn't going to help."

"I don't see you teaching the children how to behave," she said.

"I talk to the kids, I correct them. If they misbehave, I suspend them."

"But you don't know how to make them obey, and somebody has to teach them."

"Sister, what you're doing is against the *Constitutions*, and it's against the law. If you do it again, I'll have to tell Sister Priscilla."

"You do what you want. I know what I need to do."

I knew what I needed to do, too. I only hoped I wouldn't have to do it.

The very next day, I saw Sister slap Keith Monroe after he threw his Kool-Aid against the apple tree.

I hated myself for what I was about to do. I'd always been respectful of my superiors, or at least tried to be so. Though Sister Leonard and I had disagreed before, I had never yet spoken against my superior. I doubted Sister Leonard would forgive me, but I didn't know any other way.

The Rules allowed every sister access to higher superiors, but they did not permit access to the means of access. Using the phone or writing a letter always required permission. If I requested permission to call, Sister Leonard would hover as I spoke, and I didn't trust myself to speak clearly while she listened. Phoning without permission was impractical. Calling the Bronx always required multiple attempts, sometimes over days, because that phone was nearly always occupied. And no matter what time of day I might choose, closing the door of the small dormitory that doubled as office would arouse suspicion. Speaking without closing the door would invite being caught, and I couldn't think of a way to phone elsewhere since we never left the convent without a partner.

I should have asked for paper, but I knew where Sister kept the key—in the small matchbox in the back of the office desk drawer. I unlocked the cupboard and took out two sheets of paper, an envelope, and a stamp. During the next three days, whenever I could manage to disappear for a few minutes, I went to the bathroom, where I closed the door and wrote a few sentences. In this way, my letter grew, and my conviction that I must speak up solidified. So did my self-loathing: The letter was proof that I hadn't been able to manage.

Ten days had passed since I'd slipped the letter into the mailbox, hidden among thank-you notes and utility payments. Sister still carried the stick, but I hadn't seen her use it. Then one evening, as we knelt in front of the Blessed Sacrament at adoration, the phone rang. Sister Leonard left to answer it. As she went, I heard a very distinct voice deep within myself.

Are you willing to suffer anything for the sake of My Kingdom? The voice was calm and deliberate, and was clearly waiting for an answer. I hadn't heard God so distinctly for months. He hadn't asked me permission before.

Yes, Lord, I am willing. I spoke those words in my soul, my eyes fixed on the Eucharist. As I spoke the silent words, strength and courage enclosed me—a rooted peace, a mountain of peace. I would accept whatever consequences my defense of the children required.

At dinner, Sister Leonard did not speak, nor did she eat. Sister Fran made Sister Reginald and me laugh with a story about a man who had shown up dressed in an American flag. The man claimed to be Jesus, and spoke to heaven through a radio in his backpack. During the entire story, Sister Leonard never cracked a smile.

After dinner, Sister called me to her office.

"Did you tell Sister Priscilla that I beat the children?" she asked.

"Yes, Sister, I had to," I said.

"Did you call her?"

"No, Sister. I wrote."

"Without permission?"

"Yes, Sister, without permission. I told you that if you didn't stop, I would have to tell Sister."

"Get out of here."

I turned, but before I moved toward the door, she added, "Sister says I have to apologize to the sisters and to the children, and that she is going to ask if I have done it when she comes. So I'm apologizing, you understand?"

I nodded.

"And I'm never coming to your summer camp again. You manage your own children."

It took four days before Sister spoke again at meals. It took a week before she spoke to me. Normally such silence would have caused me internal contortions. Though Sister's silence was uncomfortable, I was neither worried nor upset. *For the sake of the Kingdom. For the children.*

About a week had passed since I'd told the Lord I was willing. I was walking Sandy to her car, carrying some bread for her to drop at the contemplatives'. "Sandy, I'll see you tomorrow, around ten," I said. "Right?"

"I'm sorry—remind me. What's tomorrow?"

"My appointment with Dr. Bradley," I said. "Remember?"

"Sister Leonard told me to cancel that appointment. She said you're better now."

When I heard this, I tried not to change my expression.

"You are better, aren't you, Sister?" Sandy asked.

"Oh, yeah. I still had it marked on the calendar. I guess I just forgot."

"You *are* better, aren't you, Sister?" Sandy repeated, one hand on
the door of her Cadillac, the other palm up in inquiry as she wrinkled her forehead.

"Yes, sure," I said. I wasn't better, but I couldn't speak against my
superior, and I certainly couldn't go to the doctor without permission.

Sandy looked concerned. "Let me know if you want me to make
another appointment, okay?"

"Yeah. Thanks, Sandy. Tell the kids hi."

As Sandy backed out of the driveway, I was unable to hold back
my tears. I'd had extraordinarily heavy menstrual bleeding, and Sister Leonard knew that. I decided not to say anything, at least not
yet. I was too angry, too depressed, too frightened of what else Sister might do. God would take care of me, with or without a doctor.
Jesus had to be free to use me without consulting me.

Early the next morning, we all lugged heavy bags of clothing from
the basement of the soup kitchen to the basement of the convent, in
preparation for work on the floor of our new clothing distribution
center. We'd been collecting clothes for months. After more than an
hour of carrying, on my way to fetch the next bag, Sandy stopped
me. She wanted to know if Sister Leonard could reschedule a shopping expedition. So I made a quick about-face and ran back to the
convent, where I'd last seen Sister Leonard talking on the phone.

As I rounded a corner in the basement, I nearly bumped into Sister, coming from the opposite direction. "Sorry, Sister," I said.
"Sandy needs to leave and wants to know if she could take you shopping tomorrow."

The look of hatred in Sister's eyes astounded me.

"How dare you come here with empty hands?" she seethed.
"Can't you see how we're struggling? You are the laziest, most in-
considerate sister I have ever seen. Get back to work. I'll talk to
Sandy myself." She slammed the door.

I strode to the basement bathroom, trying to hide my tears and my rage. When I sat, a river of blood flowed into the toilet bowl. The doctor had told me not to carry heavy things. But Sister had said all I needed was faith and generosity, not special treatment. I stayed in the bathroom a few minutes, allowing the blood to flow as I grew both dizzy and rageful. When I came out, Sister was waiting outside the bathroom door.

"So you're waiting inside until all the work is done?" She stepped close, inches in front of my face. The fury in her eyes seemed to drill holes through my head. "Or you've gone to have your little pity party, to cry tears for yourself in the bathroom?"

In one quick motion I put my arms around Sister Leonard's thin waist, lifted her off the floor, and shook her.

The look on her face changed to one of total fear. Still hoisting her high, I murmured, "Sorry, Sister, sorry, sorry." Gently I set her down. She ran out of the basement.

Did I really just pick up my superior and shake her? As I stood in front of the bathroom, trying to come to terms with what I'd done, the basement door opened and Sister Reginald appeared with a bag of clothes. Quickly I opened the bathroom door and locked myself in.

I sat, face in hands. *I lifted my superior and shook her? I didn't mean to, I didn't want to. I don't know how to make her listen. And I was so scared by all the blood, and it is all so unfair, and—*

When I came to, I was on the floor of the bathroom. How long had I lain there? I didn't know. I hoped it hadn't been long. I should have been carrying clothes. I got up, checked my habit for blood, and readjusted my apron to cover the spots. I headed back, a little dizzy, very ashamed. In the basement, I reached for a bag, and Sister Leonard looked at me as though I were a snake, which was exactly how I felt.

Father Reid came for confession that afternoon. Never had I felt a greater need for the sacrament.

I knelt and said, "Bless me, Father, for I have sinned. It is one week since my last confession, and today I picked up my superior and shook her. I didn't mean to do it—I was just so angry and so tired, and . . . it just happened. I've already apologized to her, but I ask God's forgiveness for my anger and for having hurt my sister."

A long, silent pause from the other side of the screen.

"Sister, I don't know if I heard you correctly. Did you say you picked up your superior and shook her?"

"Yes, Father."

"Sister, you can't do that."

"I know, Father, but I did. I guess I was almost hysterical. I feel myself under so much pressure these days, and I couldn't take any more."

"And you apologized to your superior?"

"Yes, Father, immediately."

"Have you gone back to her again?"

"Not yet. It just happened this morning."

"Did anyone else see you?"

"No one, Father."

"Sister, your superior already suffers so much."

"I know that, Father." Sister Leonard was lonely and lacked self-confidence—but I was suffering, too, even if no one knew that.

"Have you no compassion? You have all the advantages here. You're intelligent; you're in your own country. You must be a support to your community."

I know what I've done is indefensible. "I'm sorry, Father. I'm trying."

"For your penance, say three rosaries, beg for the grace to control your anger, and be sure to apologize to your superior again. And next time I want to hear what you've done about all this."

"Yes, Father."

As he said the words of absolution, my head spun, both from weakness and confusion. I didn't know how long I knelt there, but I suddenly realized that Father Reid had finished and I needed to get up. I leaned on the confessional's shelf and tried to press my weight into my hands to lever my knees off the hard wooden kneeler, but my arms shook. Eventually I managed to get up and find my way back to the chapel.

I dipped my trembling hand in the holy water and traced the Father, Son, and Holy Spirit over my heart. *Please, please, don't let me get angry again,* I prayed. I realized—with a clarity I hadn't experienced since that day in the novitiate when I'd stood in front of Mary's statue—that I was capable of every possible evil. I'd crossed the same line Sister Leonard had crossed. I'd violated my own principles.

Over the next few days, Sister and I said little to each other. When I settled down, I approached the office door. Sister sat at the desk, reading. I knocked. Still looking down at her book, she invited me in.

I closed the door, walked in, and sat on the bed near her desk. "Sister," I said, "I'm really sorry about the other day."

She looked up and said, "So am I."

I wasn't sure how to interpret her words. Was she actually apologizing, or was she telling me she was sorry that I had done what I did?

"I shouldn't have scolded you so much," Sister Leonard said. "You usually work very hard. You all do. If you weren't carrying clothes that day, maybe you had a reason."

"Yes, Sister. I was in a hurry because Sandy said she needed to go, and I just ran over—but still, I shouldn't have picked you up like that. I shouldn't have been so angry. I'm so sorry."

"You said you're sorry. You don't need to say it again."

"Yes, Sister," I said, "but it's not only about having picked you up. I'm guilty of the same things I accused you of. I was upset because I felt you weren't respecting me. I used physical force to get out my frustration and to get your attention. It was probably similar with you and the children. You were frustrated because they didn't listen to you, so when you didn't know what else to do, you took a stick."

"Sister Donata, how is your bleeding?"

"Getting worse, Sister."

"I'll have Sandy make an appointment."

"Thank you, Sister."

"I don't think we need to mention this to Sister Priscilla."

"What?"

"We've apologized to each other. You're sorry. I'm sorry. We're not going to do it again. No one needs to know what happened in that basement."

"Thank you, Sister."

We sat wordlessly for a few seconds. This was one of those moments when I resented the Rule against touching—I just wanted to give her a big hug. This woman had a huge heart, and I'd never known it.

When Sister Priscilla came for a visit a few weeks later, she gathered us all in the refectory. "I know you've been having problems here, problems with the children," she said. "Is everything better now?"

Sister Leonard looked at me. The children were my responsibility. "The children are very difficult, Sister," I said, "even more difficult than the children in the Bronx. But they are getting better."

"You aren't hitting the children, I hope," she asked, looking at each face.

"Sister," Sister Leonard said, her voice quavering, "I did beat the children before, but not now."

"And what about the rest of you?"

"No, Sister," we answered more or less simultaneously.

"No what? No, you're not beating the children, or no, your superior is not beating the children?"

I hated this. "Sister, no one is beating the children now," I said. "There was a problem before, but it's finished now."

"I see. And when there was this problem, I want to know what each one of you did about it." I felt like we were back in the Bronx at Sunday reports—except that this time the matter was serious. Sister looked first at Sister Reginald.

"I didn't do anything, Sister," Sister Reginald said, a look of real confusion on her face.

"Why not?" Sister asked.

"I am only a junior sister."

"But if something is wrong, it's your responsibility to speak up. Each of you is responsible for the wrong the others do if you say nothing." Sister Reginald looked down at the floor. Sister Priscilla turned to Sister Fran. "And what about you, Sister?"

"I was disturbed, Sister. I did not like to see the children being beaten."

"But did you do anything?"

"I spoke with Sister Leonard about it."

Sister Priscilla turned toward Sister Leonard. "Sister, is this true?"

"Yes, Sister."

"And did it stop after that?" Sister Priscilla looked at Sister Fran. Sister Fran put her head down.

"Sister, I asked you a question. Did it stop after that?"

"Not right after that, Sister. It stopped sometime later."

"And why did it stop?"

"I don't know, Sister."

"And you, Sister Donata?"

"I spoke with Sister several times."

"And then?"

"And then I wrote to you, Sister."

Sister Fran and Sister Reginald both twisted their heads quickly in my direction.

"You didn't talk about this among yourselves?" Sister Priscilla asked.

"No, Sister," we replied in chorus.

"I see," Sister Priscilla replied, looking to Sister Leonard. "Sister," she continued, "do you see how much your community cares about you? In many communities the sisters would have talked about their superior behind her back, but your sisters did not do

this. I hope you appreciate that, and"—she turned toward us—
"I hope you all continue such charity. You must not discuss the faults
of your superior among yourselves. But," she said, raising herself up
taller in her chair, "you must always speak to your superior when
you see a Rule being violated. If she does not listen to you, you must
report it to your regional superior. This is your duty in the eyes of
God. Have I made myself clear?"

"Yes, Sister."

"Good, very good. I expect this community to become truly
holy."

That was the end of the gathering, but I was confused. She
hadn't even mentioned the need to be kind to the children.

The next day Sister Priscilla called me alone into the office. She
sat on a stool and I sat on the bed. Her face was expressionless. "Sister Donata," she said, "have you been having any problems?"

"Well, Sister, I was bleeding a lot," I said, "but Sister Leonard sent
me to the doctor, and I'm taking hormones. It's a bit better now."

"I wasn't inquiring about your health," she said, raising her eyebrows and sucking her cheeks in. "Have you been having problems
in community?"

"Nothing big, Sister. It was difficult after that problem with hitting the children, but now everything is all right."

"Sister Donata," Sister Priscilla asked, locking her eyes into
mine, as if trying to reach into my soul, "have you ever been angry
with Sister Leonard?"

"Yes, Sister, many times. I am too proud."

"Sister Donata, did you ever raise a hand to your superior?"

"Yes, Sister, once."

"Did you actually pick her up and shake her?"

"Yes, Sister," I said, looking straight into her eyes, "I did."

"Tell me about it."

After I'd told her everything I could remember about that day,
and about all the circumstances leading up to it, she paused for a
moment and looked very thoughtful.

"Well," she said, "I suppose in your situation I might have done even worse. See that it never happens again, and please, please, let me know as soon as there is some trouble here. I am responsible to Mother for everything that goes on in this region. If you don't tell me, if you don't help me, how am I to know?"

I left the office that day stunned. I didn't want to jump to conclusions. It hurt to imagine that Sister Leonard had gone back on her word about not mentioning that day to Sister Priscilla. I needed to know why she'd changed her mind.

After Sister Priscilla returned to New York, I asked Sister Leonard if I could speak with her. "Sister," I said, "the other day Sister Priscilla asked me if I ever got angry with you."

"That's strange," she said. She looked genuinely surprised.

"I thought so, too. Sister, you know I'm sorry for all that I did before, and I thought we were getting along so well now."

"We are. You're a big help to me, and I told Sister Priscilla so," Sister Leonard said with evident sincerity.

"You did?"

"Yes. It was hard in the beginning, but I think we understand each other now. I'm glad you're here."

"Thank you, Sister," I said. Her reply left only one option.

In the days that remained before our weekly confession, I did the best I could to control my anger. I prayed that my suspicions would prove groundless.

When my turn came for confession, I knelt behind the screen and said, "Bless me, Father, for I have sinned. I've been impatient with the children and I haven't always helped the sisters when I could. I've also been distracted in prayer."

"Sister," Father Reid said, "remember that God loves you, and ask him for the grace to help you be more patient. This is very important. Is there anything else?"

"Yes, Father." I took a big breath. I was a little nervous. "I want to ask God's forgiveness for being suspicious of my confessor."

"Suspicious of your confessor?"

"Sister Priscilla was here the other day, and she asked me if I'd ever shaken my superior. Sister Leonard didn't tell her. You're the only other person who knows."

"Oh," he said.

I waited for him to say more, but he said nothing. After nearly a minute, I asked, "Father, did you tell Sister that I shook Sister Leonard?"

"She needs to know how the community is," Father Reid said, a little louder than his usual confessional murmur. "She often calls and asks. It's important that she know, so that she can help you."

"Father, I think that when I told you I picked up Sister Leonard I was making my confession."

"Sometimes a priest faces very difficult decisions regarding confidentiality," he said.

"It was my confession," I said. I waited for him to explain.

"Sister, there are many things you don't understand."

If he wasn't going to do better than that, I'd have to get out before I shook him, too. No priest had the right to break the seal of confession. If he'd thought me dangerous, he could have found a way to alert Sister Priscilla without telling her what he'd learned from me in confession. If Sister Priscilla had been around, I might have shaken her, too. What was she doing, asking our confessor on a regular basis for details about the community?

I went to the chapel, knelt in front of the crucifix, and cried.

Alone in the chapel after Mass the next day, I opened the closet in the corner. I approached the altar to put the sacred vessels away. I placed the glass cruets in their smooth satin cases. I put the shiny paten in its velvet-lined box, and placed the small wooden crucifix on the shelf. I took the chalice in my hands. I wrapped my fingers around the silver goblet, the cup that had so recently cradled the Blood of Christ, the cup from which the priest had drunk. I felt the metal cold against my palms. Before I knew what my hands were doing, I raised the chalice over my head, leaned back, and pitched it forward. The chalice made a satisfying thunk on the chapel floor.

This time I wasn't saying sorry. This was God's fault. Forget that "suffering for the sake of the Kingdom" stuff. God had betrayed me, and I wanted Him to know I'd noticed.

I didn't want to become bitter. I especially didn't want to feel that I could never trust a priest again. The Rules expected me to confess every week for the rest of my life. I tried to forgive, but all I felt was anger. Sister Leonard had forgiven me, and we got on better than we ever had before. I told myself that I should be able to forgive Father Reid, even if he hadn't asked for forgiveness, even if he hadn't acknowledged any fault. I needed to forgive not just for his sake, but for mine.

I tried to force forgiveness, but every time I thought of Father Reid, anger and bitterness dug in even more firmly. At times the anger seemed to choke me so that I could hardly breathe. Forgiveness was beyond my strength. I needed God. I decided to bombard Him until He gave me what I needed.

Preparing dinner for my sisters, I prayed, *God, I don't want to become bitter. Help me to forgive. Help me to trust again.*

While I stacked cans of tomato sauce on the basement shelves, I prayed, *Priests are weak—they are human beings like me. They make mistakes. Help me to forgive. Help me to trust. Don't let me become bitter.*

Taking the discipline with extra vigor, I prayed, *Please, please, tear this anger from my heart. Give me love and compassion.*

At confession, I knelt and spoke my sins, trying my best to look beyond the man who took the place of Jesus—and Judas. My heart prayed, *My God, my God, why have You abandoned me?*

Walking to the soup kitchen, I prayed, *I'm only asking You for something I know You want to give me. Make my heart big enough to receive the grace to forgive. I don't want to be small.*

As I washed my plate, I prayed, *Make me a channel of Your peace.*

The food bank sent a special delivery. I was left to stack case after case of surplus American cheese against the basement wall. With each case, I prayed, *God, help me to forgive.* There was so much cheese I had to fetch a ladder. *God, help me to forgive.* I placed the last case on top of the pile. *God, help me*— In that moment, bitterness let go of its grasp on my soul. Anger melted and gave way to joy. I could hardly believe it. The sun seemed to shine more brightly through the basement windows. The cheese cartons seemed to glow. I could breathe freely for the first time in weeks.

I would never look at a box of American cheese in the same way again. The bitterness never returned. I would never trust him as I had, but I didn't hate Father Reid anymore.

14

LOVEBOOK

As we began the second year of the after-school program, Sister Reginald refused to cooperate. She routinely sat in the corner while the kids in her group ran through the house. When it was time to help me clean up, she lavished attention instead on the vegetable garden: on the zucchini, the beans, and the vine of bitter gourds she'd grown from seeds given her by an Indian Co-Worker.

Most sisters in my position wouldn't have thought twice about calling Sister Reginald to task, but I was tired of the scolding that characterized MC relations. I tried to talk to her nicely, but she stood silent, refusing to look at me. As the days passed and Sister Reginald smiled with everybody else, joking and making herself useful, I understood that she meant her actions as a slight to me, or a protest, but I couldn't figure out why, or which, and my temper rose.

After my encounter with Sister Leonard in the basement, I knew my anger was dangerous. I turned to the little notebook I'd made as a novice, the book I referred to as my lovebook. In the first pages, I'd copied quotes from books and conferences on love. When I read,

To forgive means to be willing to suffer from someone until your loving kindness heals them, I found my strategy. In the back pages of my lovebook, I wrote: *I will love Sr R into healing*.

It looked simple enough.

With tension escalating between Sister Reginald and me and my pesky responsibility to enforce Sister Priscilla's desires pitting me daily against my superior, I didn't need more trouble. The unusually hot September weekend Sister Fran announced, "Two boys at the door to see Sister Donata," trouble came anyway.

"From the soup kitchen?" Sister Leonard asked.

"No—they said they were volunteers in the Bronx."

Sister Leonard raised her eyebrows. The Rule vigorously discouraged socializing. The appearance of unexpected visitors was irritating, yet exciting.

In the parlor a young man I didn't recognize sat quietly at the table while a tall fellow with brown hair paced, his back to me. The pacing fellow turned, and I called out, "Stan!"

"Sister Donata!"

"So lovely to see you," I said. "What brings you here?"

"I came to visit my friend," Stan said, introducing me to the fellow at the table. Stan said the two of them had worked on a Pueblo reserve in New Mexico that summer, and that his friend studied at a seminary near the National Shrine.

They were both damp with perspiration. I asked if they'd like some water.

"Water would be great," Stan's friend said. "I'm exhausted."

"Somebody gave us the wrong address," Stan explained. "We took a cab from the metro stop, but we ended up at the contemplatives'. The sisters told us it wasn't far, so we walked."

"Not far? It's nearly two miles," I said.

"I wanted to give up," the friend replied, "but he insisted."

I left to get water. I couldn't believe Stan had walked all that way to see me. Despite the sweat, he looked great. In the kitchen, I ran the water until it got reasonably cold, filled a pitcher, and brought it out with glasses and a plate of cookies. I wished we had ice, lemons.

In the parlor, Stan was alone. He said his friend had gone to look around, and he took water and a cookie out to him. When Stan returned, he closed the door and sat opposite me at the table.

"So what are you doing with your life?" I asked.

"Still roaming the universe doing good. People keep trying to make me into a priest, but I don't think that's for me."

"No?" I wondered if anyone had told him that Mother thought he had a vocation.

"I've been around enough priests to know I need something more."

"Oh?"

"Eventually I want to get married."

"Doesn't your friend want to come in?" I asked. We weren't supposed to get this personal.

"I told him I wanted some time." Stan paused and tilted his head toward me. A nervous smile played on his lips. "There's something I've been wanting to do for three years," he said, "and I'll have no peace until I do it."

"What's that?" I asked.

"How many sisters are here?"

"Four. The others have gone to the soup kitchen next door."

"They're not coming back?"

"I can take you to meet them." I stood up and moved toward the door.

"No, that's fine," he said, getting up as well.

"So what is it you want to do?"

"May I?"

"May you what?"

Putting his hands on my shoulders, Stan leaned down and kissed my cheek.

"You don't mind, do you?" His brown eyes glistened.

I couldn't move. I couldn't speak. My entire body tingled, cheek to toes.

"Stan," a voice called through the open window, "we'd better be getting back. Dinner is at five."

"You religious and your schedules." Stan continued to look at me as he spoke to his friend.

His friend knocked, entered, and asked for a cab.

I excused myself and fumbled through the phone directory, eventually connecting with a dispatcher. When I returned, the parlor sparkled. Stan glowed. Until the cab came, I tried to join their small talk, but my head was spinning.

The skin on my cheek tingled. I'd thought people were exaggerating when they talked about never wanting to wash off a kiss.

For a few days after the kiss, I was happy in a way I'd never dreamed of.

When my conscience finally kicked in, I knew I shouldn't have let Stan kiss me. That I hadn't seen it coming diminished my guilt only slightly. What would Sister Priscilla think of me? The cries of Sister Dolorosa that night in the novitiate returned and gave me pause: *I need a man.*

The most alluring thing about Stan's kiss was that he'd meant it just for me. He'd spent three years thinking of kissing me. But of course, Stan's love couldn't be better than God's love. Jesus had loved me so much He'd died for me. God had chosen me to be an MC.

Though I was ashamed to mention anything, especially to Father Reid, the next week I confessed having allowed a Co-Worker to give me an inappropriate sign of affection. I rose from the confessional determined not to think of Stan's kiss again. Back in the chapel, I took out my lovebook and wrote: *My God, I love You. Only You. Forgive me, please.*

Though I tried to be kind to her, though I offered suggestions about activities for the girls, Sister Reginald still refused to speak to me when we were with the children, still escaped as soon as she could, still left all the cleaning for me. It had been months. I was some-times tempted to call her to task, but then I would remember: *To for-give means to be willing to suffer from someone until your loving kindness heals them.* I supposed I hadn't loved hard enough yet.

Sister Leonard spent a lot of time talking to Father Reid. I knew Sister Priscilla wouldn't like it. The Rule warned about overfamil-iarity with priests as a danger to chastity and a waste of time. I wor-ried for other reasons.

I wasn't exactly jealous of Sister's relationship with Father Reid. I didn't want to talk to the priest who had breached the seal of my confession, but I did want to talk to *someone*, wanted it so badly sometimes that it hurt. Sometimes I thought of my old friends, a few years out of college by then. It didn't seem fair that Sister Leonard had a friend, and I—in my own country, competent, intelligent, well-intentioned—had no one.

Sometimes when Sister Leonard spoke with Father Reid on the phone or in the parlor, I would imagine what I would say if I had the chance to speak with someone I trusted. I would have started with something safe, maybe current events. Living in the nation's capital and not knowing why Jimmy Carter hadn't been reelected irked me. I would have asked my friend if he or she had read any good books lately, if there'd been any good movies since *One Flew over the Cuckoo's Nest*, the last movie I'd seen, six years before. I would have asked what Simon and Garfunkel were singing.

If I'd had a friend, eventually I would have talked about the kids and about how I didn't always know what to do for them. I would have told my friend about the fourteen-year-old girl and her mother whom we'd visited in the projects. I'd known the daughter as a spunky kid from our first summer camp, but that day she'd sat wrapped in blankets near the TV, her mother complaining that the daughter hadn't left the apartment in months. When the girl reached to turn off the TV, the blankets shifted, revealing a large belly. I asked, "Are you pregnant?" She answered, "Yes." Her mother had nearly fainted. The baby was due in less than a month.

We arranged for doctor visits and baby supplies, but the only thing the sisters said was, "Shame on her."

I might have talked with my friend about how tired I was of the juggling act of trying to obey both Sister Priscilla and Sister Leonard. I might have talked about how much I wanted to be a good sister, but wasn't sure I was able. I might have asked advice about how to love Sister Reginald more. If my friend and I became really close, I might tell her how Stan had walked so far, in such heat, to kiss me, and about how guilty I'd felt, and how fine.

If I'd had a friend, I would have talked about how I still crawled under the stairs sometimes to cry at night. Of course, if I'd had a friend, I might not have needed that dark corner.

Sister Leonard no longer tried to eavesdrop when Sister Priscilla asked to speak to me on the phone, but I hated those conversations with my regional superior. Even more than before, Sister Priscilla insisted I tell her about whatever wasn't right in the community. I usually said that things were fine, but this didn't satisfy her. The way she began to repeat her inquiries, "Are you sure?" and "Is Sister Leonard really keeping all the Rules?" led me to think she had suspicions of her own. Perhaps she knew Sister Leonard and Father Reid spoke often. After all, I knew Sister Priscilla spoke often with Father Reid. It was likely that Father had mentioned that he spoke frequently with Sister Leonard. I became convinced that Sister Priscilla was testing me.

What did God want me to do? God wanted what my superiors wanted—"her known wish as well as her spoken command" was how Mother had phrased it in her *Explanations*. It wasn't important that part of me thought there was nothing really wrong about my superior's conversations with a priest. So one day I said it: "Sister Leonard and Father Reid talk a lot."

"Oh?" Sister Priscilla said, her previously grim voice warming up.

"I don't know what they talk about," I said. "Maybe it is nothing."

"How often?"

I wiped my perspiring palms on my sari. "When Father comes for confession, Sister gives him coffee when he arrives, and they talk ten or fifteen minutes. When he finishes she brings more coffee and they talk for half an hour, sometimes longer."

"I see," she said. "More?"

"Well, they talk on the phone. Three or four times a week, maybe more. I think Father Reid is helping her. Sister always seems happier, more confident after she talks to him."

"How long has this been going on?"

"Awhile."

"Sister Donata?"

"Almost from the beginning," I admitted.

"And it's taken you nearly two years to tell me?" Sister Priscilla's voice was indignant.

"It didn't seem like any of my business. I mean, it's delicate. He's our confessor."

"And you thought she was confessing whenever she talked to him? On the phone?"

"No, Sister, but—"

"You know this is a violation of the Rule," Sister said. "Conversation with priests and seminarians must be limited to whatever is strictly necessary."

"Yes, Sister," I said, thinking of how much time I'd seen Sister Priscilla spend on the phone.

"You were wrong to wait so long to speak up," Sister Priscilla said. "Sister Leonard has given a bad example to the community. It's possible that irreparable harm has been done."

"Sorry, Sister," I said.

"Let me talk to her," she said.

As I called Sister Leonard to the phone, I regretted having mentioned anything. All of a sudden it was clear: Speaking to a priest didn't merit snitching. I'd spoken up out of envy, jealous that Sister Leonard had a friend, and out of a desire to win merit points with Sister Priscilla. Whatever happened next would be my fault.

I didn't know what Sister told Sister Leonard that day. Sister Leonard was a little moody after the call, but she didn't refuse to talk to me the way she had on other occasions. Two weeks later, Sister Priscilla phoned again. She asked me if Sister Leonard and Father Reid still talked. I said they did. She asked if they talked any less. I said it didn't seem so. She asked to speak to Sister Leonard. When Sister Leonard returned to the refectory, she told us that our new superior would arrive on Saturday, and that she would take the train to New York on Monday.

The news floored me. I'd felt guilty since reporting on her, but I'd never thought she'd be transferred. Superiors had three-year terms. Sister Leonard had barely finished two. I hadn't even spoken to Sister Leonard about her conversations before mentioning them to Sister Priscilla. I couldn't remember ever having been more ashamed of something I'd done, not even when I'd shaken Sister Leonard. At least then I'd been honest, up-front. Now I was a rat, an informant, and I'd made Sister Leonard a victim of my envy. I wanted to crawl into a hole somewhere.

Our new superior was a good, honest, cheerful person. Though it was also her first assignment as superior and she hadn't been in the States before, either, she was very bright and caught on quickly. She respected the Rules and seemed to have an intuition for doing the right things, the things Sister Priscilla would want done. I could relax a little—except that every time I looked at her I felt guilty for having told on Sister Leonard.

All the while, whatever else went on around me, I'd been working at loving Sister Reginald into healing. I'd hidden her refusal to help with the kids from the other sisters. I'd found Co-Workers to help with the after-school program while she tended her vegetables or sorted donated clothes in the basement.

It was time—past time—for a more direct approach. One sunny spring morning nearly nine months since she'd first become difficult, we were walking home after visiting families when I asked,

"Sister Reginald, what do you think about our work with the children?"

Sister Reginald stopped and spun on her heel to face me. "Why are you asking?" Her eyes shifted in what looked like fear.

"You don't seem happy," I said. "I thought you might have ideas about how we could improve."

"We don't need to be doing this work at all," Sister Reginald said. "So many people need visiting. Or I could teach sewing class, or we could both sort clothes in the basement. Those children are hopeless."

"They're certainly difficult," I said, "but not hopeless. Haven't you seen at least a little improvement?"

"Not much," she said.

"Maybe they'd improve if you'd help them more," I said. This was as close as I'd come to an accusation since Sister Reginald had first retreated from the kids and me.

Sister Reginald looked down at the sidewalk, then straight at me. "I'm afraid," she said, "I will do something wrong and you will tell Sister Priscilla."

"I would never talk to Sister Priscilla without talking to you first," I said. "I wrote to Sister Priscilla only after I'd talked to Sister Leonard several times—it was a last resort." I didn't mention my recent tattling.

Sister Reginald looked at me with a face I couldn't read.

"You don't need to be afraid of me," I said, not knowing if I even believed that myself.

We walked the rest of the way in silence.

The next afternoon Sister Reginald read a story to the little kids. The afternoon after that, she swept and I mopped. I could hardly believe the progress. The afternoon after that, Sister Reginald got a phone call. When she returned to the refectory, she was crying. Eventually she stuttered, "I-I've got a change. Sister Priscilla is sending me to Harlem. I have to leave tomorrow."

I could hardly believe it. I'd put up with Sister Reginald's resis-

tance for nearly nine months. As soon as she'd decided to be helpful, had even smiled at me a couple of times, Sister was taking her
away. I didn't like it, but . . . "Why are you crying?" I asked.

Sister Reginald wiped her nose, then looked at me for a moment.
Shifting her glance so she didn't have to look me in the eye, she said,
"I have never treated anyone so badly, and no one has ever been as
kind to me as you have."

I wanted to take her in my arms, let her cry on my shoulder, pat
her back and tell her everything would be all right. Instead I said,
"I'll miss you, too," and I helped her pack. That day, I wrote in my
lovebook: *I may have loved Sr R into healing. God, couldn't you let her
stay at least a little while?*

When Sister Priscilla next visited us, only Sister Fran and I remained from the original community. The new sisters were both
fine, but I missed my usual, more difficult companions, the sisters
with whom I'd faced the initial struggles of building a community
and an apostolate, the sisters who had come to accept me with my
weaknesses, the sisters I had so regrettably wronged.

Sister Priscilla had opened more new houses, in Chicago and
Little Rock, bringing the total of MC houses in the United States to
eleven. She was pleased with herself, and remarkably pleasant.
Then, at breakfast one morning, Sister nibbled on the chapatti our
new superior had prepared for her, and announced, "Sisters, I am
surprised at you."

No one said anything. We just waited.

"This morning," she continued, speaking out of the side of her
mouth the way she sometimes did when particularly annoyed, "at
Mass—you just joined right in."

I replayed Mass in my mind. Father Jennings was a young priest
from Kentucky, newly assigned to the parish, not given to the sort of
reverent posturing Sister Priscilla enjoyed, but I couldn't recall a serious misstep.

"Holy Mass is not the place for secular greetings," Sister said.
She raised her eyebrows, sipped her coffee, and waited.

Secular greetings? Oh, I know what she means. But she isn't going to make a big deal of that, is she?

Sister Priscilla continued, " 'Good morning, Sisters' is not part of the liturgy. Neither is, 'Good morning, Father.' "

Ah, yes, she is going to make a big deal out of it.

"We must not allow priests to cheapen the sacred rites," Sister Priscilla said, setting her cup daintily on her saucer. "I'm sure that's not the only liberty he takes. It never is. They start with something that looks small, but one infidelity always leads to another." Elbows on the table, knuckles crossed under her chin, a smile playing on her lips, she asked, "What else does this priest change?"

No matter how many times I had seen it before, I was always amazed at how much glee the spotting of priests' liturgical misdemeanors aroused in Sister Priscilla. I sometimes thought that if she spent just a little time visiting the homes of the poor and listening to their stories, she might gain valuable perspective into life's real issues.

Our new superior sat with her hands folded, eyes downcast, difficult to read. Sister Fran's mouth hung slightly open, and I saw excitement in her eyes. This was Sister Fran's first exposure to Sister Priscilla as she caught a priest in the act.

"Sometimes he changes words," Sister Fran said. "Not many. He sometimes says 'The Lord be with you all' instead of 'The Lord be with you.' "

Sister Priscilla looked at me, her appointed guardian of correctness. I knew that in her eyes, I was failing dismally.

"A word or two," I said, "nothing much."

"You must keep your eyes and ears open," Sister Priscilla said, looking at each of us in turn, lingering a little longer on me. "You must let me know exactly what liberties this priest takes with the sacred liturgy—this priest and any other." She took another nibble at her chapatti. She made a little face—the chapatti wasn't soft enough. "And you must not dignify his 'Good morning' with a 'Good morning' of your own. You're allowing him to lead you astray," Sister said, setting the chapatti on her plate, teeth marks evident. "No more 'Good morning, Father' at Mass. Do you understand?"

"Yes, Sister."

"I'm not sure you do," she said, leaning back on her stool to get a good look at all of us together, then zeroing in on me. "The Church in America is very generous, and we are all grateful to them for that," she continued, "but you must realize the grave danger we face. The Church in the United States has strayed far from the Holy Father. Priests celebrate Mass with potato chips and orange soda. Nuns wear secular clothes and parade in picket lines. In some parishes nuns and priests even train girls to be altar servers. The good Catholic people of this country expect more from their religious, and they are entitled to it."

Potato chips and orange soda definitely crossed a line, but I'd grown up in the midst of the reforms of Vatican II, and changing according to times and circumstances seemed natural to me. The parish switched definitively from Latin to the vernacular the year I made my First Communion as a second grader, replacing magic-sounding Latin words with guitar Masses and sermons against the Vietnam War. So many Catholics believed, as Sister Priscilla did, that Vatican II had robbed the Church of something precious.

Sister Priscilla was my superior. An obedient will should sway my mind, should allow me to think as she did. I lacked Sister Priscilla's appreciation for the sacred, was short a vital receptor for the hallowed. I simply—and fatally—failed to grasp the inherent importance of holy, authorized words. If I was truly going to please God, I would have to grow in the refinement and grace that were Sister Priscilla's hallmarks.

I tried telling myself all this. I had no trouble convincing myself that I lacked refinement—that was obvious. It was harder to shake the feeling that the Lord stood far less on ceremony than Sister Priscilla did, that the fuss about the right words and the proper gestures was a huge waste of energy, that the Church had room for both the refined and the common.

A few days after Sister Priscilla returned to the Bronx, Father Jennings showed up for Mass—the moment I'd been dreading.

After the opening hymn, Father stood at the altar and made the sign of the cross. Then he said, "Good morning, Sisters."

The four of us just stood there.

He repeated, "Good morning, Sisters."

I looked down at the rug.

"Good morning, Sisters," he said again, louder this time.

We stood. Father wrinkled his forehead and shook his head, then continued with Mass.

The next time he came, we repeated the same standoff.

And the next time, the same. Except that time he also added a few other words, scattered here and there.

At lunch that day, one of the new sisters said, "Father changed words."

Sister Fran nodded.

"I'll phone Sister," our superior said.

"At Mass on Sunday, in the parish, Father Larry changed some things, too," Sister Fran said.

After Sister spoke with Sister Priscilla, the cogs started moving. Sister and I spoke with Father Kelley, our local pastor, who was the priest immediately in charge of both Father Jennings and Father Larry. Father Kelley said he'd never heard Father Larry or Father Jennings change words. He invited our superior to the rectory the following Sunday. The rectory was connected to the PA system in the church. Sister and Father Kelley could listen together to the whole Mass.

On Sunday, Sister decided to send Sister Fran and me. Sister Fran sat in the next room with a book, while Father Kelley and I sat at the dining room table, listening to Father Larry celebrate Mass in the church across the yard. Father Kelley fingered a cup of coffee. I sat with a pad of paper and a pen, listening for errant words, a spy in the cause of religious orthodoxy. Every now and then Father Kelley looked at me and shrugged or raised an eyebrow. I caught myself doodling, paper and pen damp with perspiration from my nervous hands. The gospel choir sang, but I was too nervous to enjoy the music.

When Father Larry reached "The Mass is ended. Go in peace," I put down my pen. He had recited the liturgy letter-perfect.

We reported back to our superior, who reported to Sister Priscilla, who told us all to be vigilant, because sooner or later those priests were going to show their true colors. When they did, we should tell Father Kelley, and, of course, we should tell her.

Sure enough, the next week my companion and I heard Father Larry change words at Mass. When our superior told Father Kelley, he said he hadn't heard it and wasn't going to mention our complaints to anyone until he heard something with his own ears. My companion told our superior, who told Sister Priscilla, who said that the superior and I had to make an appointment to speak with Archbishop Hickey, who by then had been named a cardinal. Sister Priscilla said we had to make a list of all the times we could remember Father Larry and Father Jennings, and any other priest of the archdiocese, having changed any words or violated liturgical norms in any way.

I dreaded the meeting. I knew that once we got there our superior would clam up and I'd be left to report on the priests, which was exactly what happened. Cardinal Hickey listened attentively to what I considered our silly complaints. He thanked us for coming to him, and told us he'd "see to it."

I'd carried out my orders. I didn't feel holy. I felt ashamed.

The next Thursday, I knelt before God, my soul wrung out. Over the years, I'd luxuriated in our monthly Days of Recollection, soaking my soul in silence and extra prayer the way I imagined other young women might lower themselves into warm bubble baths. But that particular Day of Recollection, the bathwater was tepid and flat.

Religious life was supposed to have been simple. Mother had shaken the Rule book in our faces. She'd used the word *guarantee*— the Rules were "guaranteed" to bring us to God. She'd told us we would never make a mistake if we obeyed. She'd told us the way to enter the Heart of Jesus was by becoming small.

Alone in the chapel, I slid off my knees and grabbed my lovebook. Cross-legged on the chapel floor, I cradled the little book in my hands. It was my most treasured possession, a reminder of the clarity and freedom I'd felt six years earlier when I'd chosen to specialize in love.

I skimmed the first half. Mother's words filled the title page:

LET JESUS USE YOU WITHOUT CONSULTING YOU.

On an inside page:

Renounce and remain empty of any sensory satisfaction that is not purely for the honor and glory of God. Do this out of love for Jesus Christ. In His life He had no satisfaction, nor desired any other, than the fulfillment of His Father's will.

—*St. John of the Cross*

You must make up your mind to follow the way of self-surrender, the Cross on your shoulders, with a smile on your lips and a light in your soul.

—*Josemaría Escrivá*

I cringed when I read an aphorism of my own creation:

God calls no one to mediocrity, but all to holiness.

These words must have been written by someone else. If the words had once inspired me, they did so no longer.

I turned to the back half of my lovebook, to the cryptic pencil scratches that chronicled my attempts to love. I flipped past the idealistic entries of my novitiate, with their little victories of helping a sister with her bucket or smiling at Sister Julia. I wanted to study the past two years, when things had become worse.

Sister Reginald—well, that hadn't gone so badly. In the end, she seemed to have understood my efforts. Perhaps she was happier now.

Stan's kiss—that was even stranger. One of the few times I'd felt good, at least for a few days, yet so clearly wrong, though nothing we had done had hurt anyone.

Reporting on priests to the bishop, tattling on Sister Leonard—it was too painful to look at. Father Jennings hadn't stopped saying "Good morning, Sisters"; instead, he just stopped coming to the convent.

I'd tried to live by the book, by the Rules, by what obedience asked—but now the book felt tainted, the Rules obscure and irrelevant, obedience obscene.

I knelt in the chapel, tears running down my cheeks. I looked at the tabernacle, where Jesus dwelt in the form of bread. *Speak to me*, I said. *Speak to me.*

Then I sat back on my heels and listened.

Slowly, ever so slowly, a firm, gentle peace arrived. Little by little, the peace began to soothe the pain. With peace came love, wrapping itself around me like a lambswool blanket. Deep inside, I knew again that God loved me, and that I had loved others, not perfectly, but well enough. Without reason, I trusted love.

What I didn't trust was the book, the Rules, the things other people said about love. Nor did I trust myself to figure things out. It was foolish to think I could chart a map to a place I'd never been. I would have no map. I would lose myself to find myself.

I took the notebook in my hands—the notebook I'd so carefully prepared, the lovebook with all my good intentions, all my research, all my longings, my goals, my desires, and my assurance that I knew how to reach them. One by one, I tore its pages out. Dismembered pages in hand, I left the chapel and walked to the empty soup kitchen. I lifted the lid off the big trash can in the corner, tore the pages into little pieces, and let the scraps fall one by one into the garbage.

Less than six weeks later, the Washington *Catholic Standard* carried a double-page spread with liturgical norms for the archdiocese—specific instructions on when people should stand, kneel, and sit; an injunction against holding hands during the Lord's Prayer; a directive that the words of the liturgy be preserved in their integrity; rules about every aspect of the Eucharistic liturgy. Cardinal Hickey prefaced the rules with a note about the Eucharistic liturgy's power to bind the Christian community together in love. The Eucharist may have had that power, but no one could convince me the Rules did. I wasn't buying it.

Though we hadn't done anything but talk to the cardinal, Sister Priscilla was proud of the double-page spread in the *Catholic Standard*. She told us we had finally done the right thing. I didn't feel we had, but I didn't argue.

Then the phone call came, the call just for me. Sister Priscilla told me that being assigned to a new foundation was an honor. Soon I would leave for Winnipeg. She said Canada wasn't as cold as people claimed.

15

FOR LIFE

SPRING 1985 TO SPRING 1986
WINNIPEG AND ROME

Winnipeg was frigid, in more ways than one. We survived the subzero winter by pulling on long underwear beneath our habits and wrapping ourselves in down coats and wool scarves until we looked like mummies. Winnipeg was Sister Rochelle's first posting as superior, and six years under Sister Priscilla had sharpened her from the pleasant sister who had welcomed me in the Bronx. I survived her rants by reminding myself frequently that in May I would leave Canada. I would visit my family, go on retreat, and join my tertianship year in Rome, where, together with my group from the novitiate, I would prepare for final vows.

Luckily, Sister Priscilla didn't visit Winnipeg often. When she arrived in March, snow still piled above the eaves, she decided that we should open a shelter for unwed mothers. We told Sister that Winnipeg already had a home for expectant mothers. Winnipeg needed a shelter for homeless men, dozens of whom froze to death on the winter streets each year. She told us, "Open a shelter for women and children, then." Sister bought a half-empty apartment block, nearly a century old and in bad repair. She told us she wanted it ready for Mother's visit in late June.

A lot of the preparation work fell to me, and it grew complicated. The rezoning permit required endless paperwork. Current tenants required alternative housing. The contractor wanted more money than Sister Rochelle wanted to give him. Frightened neighbors circulated a petition against the project. With the house half gutted and Mother's visit and official blessing scheduled in four weeks, Sister Rochelle fired the contractor.

Sister Priscilla told us her brother-in-law would locate free labor. A gentle white-haired father of thirteen children and an ever-increasing number of grandchildren, Lionel Aquin was in charge of maintenance at St. Boniface College and had connections. Despite repeated requests from Sister Priscilla and Sister Rochelle, Lionel didn't locate anyone.

At this point Sister Priscilla phoned again. I expected dates for my home visit at last, the two weeks with my family that the *Constitutions* granted before tertianship. The other sisters in my group would gather in Rome shortly, already having visited their families and completed their annual retreats. If we delayed much longer, I would be late.

On the phone, Sister Priscilla told me not to worry, that I would visit my family eventually, that a retreat could be made at any time, and that nothing much happened the first few weeks of tertianship anyway. Sister Rochelle and Sister Poonam were to come to the Bronx for three weeks of retreat and classes while Sister Jaya and I finished the shelter. And we weren't to pay for materials—we were to beg donations.

I threw myself into the building project, figuring the sooner we finished, the sooner I could see my family. When I told Lionel that Sister Rochelle had gone and we had to finish before she got back, Lionel was at the convent almost immediately. "I wanted to help you," he said, "but I've been around enough nuns to know which ones aren't worth messing with."

Lionel soon connected us with carpenters, plumbers, and electricians—and talked them into reduced rates. He pushed permit applications through and drove me around town and beyond in search of donated linoleum, drywall, paint, pipes, lumber. Sister Jaya and I forfeited our afternoon siestas and evening recreations and worked into the night. I grew to enjoy the work and its urgency, but I couldn't help thinking sometimes of my group sisters visiting their families, going on retreats, and gathering in Rome without me.

Sister Jaya and I walked door-to-door amassing signatures for our own petition, and a whole crew of locals volunteered to help. The father of the largest family on the block started painting the banister at the top of the staircase and took all day to work his way down. When he got to the bottom, he climbed to the top again to apply a second coat, working well into the night. The workman who installed the linoleum was so impressed with our laughter amid the work that he decided to donate his labor, and even stayed to paint. On June 11, at another meeting of the community council, our rezoning application was approved. By the time Sister Rochelle and Sister Poonam returned from the Bronx, days before Mother's scheduled arrival, the house was nearly finished and we were exhausted.

Sister Rochelle began inspection on the top floor, where she wedged a knife between a doorjamb and a wall. "You should have closed this gap," she said. "Roaches will come live in this space." She pointed out several other defects, without even one positive comment. I made my way to the basement and kicked a plastic bucket until my sandaled toes turned red. Unbeknownst to me, Lionel had come down while I was kicking. He put a grandfatherly arm around me and said, "You've done a good job, Sister. Don't let that *bon à rien* tell you otherwise." He looked into my eyes, then went upstairs without another word.

The next day when Mother arrived with Sister Priscilla and Sandy (Sandy's father had again voltunteered his private plane), I ran to receive Mother's blessing. Mother wagged her finger and greeted me with, "You shouldn't be here, Sister."

That really floored me. I had no idea how Mother knew that I was already three weeks late for tertianship in Rome—and was she blaming me for that? "Don't worry, Sister," Mother said, seeming to read my mind. "I know you were only obeying, but I want you to know it wasn't right for Sister to keep you back."

That Mother contradicted Sister Priscilla surprised me even more. I'd never heard anyone criticize Sister Priscilla. Mother's frankness gave me courage to approach her later that afternoon, when I saw her alone in the office.

"What is it, Sister?" Mother put down the papers she'd been leafing through. She looked tired.

"Mother," I said, nervous about criticizing my superior, but wanting clarity, "I'm concerned that we weren't entirely honest when we begged materials for the shelter. People in North America give us lots of money, and I know we share it with the sisters in Africa and India, but we still have plenty in the bank. Sister insisted we beg building materials, so we had to cancel our work with the poor to approach suppliers."

"Sister," Mother said with a smile, "when we beg, we give people the opportunity to show their love for God. We must not deprive people of the joy of giving. Now they, too, will hear Jesus say, 'You did it to me.' "

"But, Mother," I said, hesitating a bit, "the people who worked for us have families to support and we paid them less than their work was worth. We cheated them."

"Sister, they gave freely, and God will bless them." Mother returned to her papers. Our conversation was over.

It was true that the spirit of joyful giving had buoyed up the whole project and benefited everyone, but I still felt dishonest. When people saw our patched saris and flip-flops, they often assumed we had no money. I wondered if the plumbing supply people and the men at the lumberyard would have been as generous if they had seen us open dozens of envelopes stuffed with checks from Canadian donors each day. If I were a donor, I wouldn't want my gift to sit in the bank while sisters begged paint.

When Mother addressed the crowd in the church that afternoon, she told us that the hungry Jesus waited to be fed, and that when we died and went home to God, we would be judged on love. Again, she repeated that God had made us to love and to be loved. Her words pulled me in and silenced my doubts and misgivings, at least for a while.

After the blessing of the shelter, Mother insisted I go immediately to Rome. Sister Priscilla countered that I needed to file the occupancy application after the fire alarms and sprinkler system were installed the following week. Neither Mother nor Sister Priscilla would budge. Sister Priscilla's claims to know Mother's mind looked different as I saw her resist Mother. At this point I mentioned that I had missed my family visit as well. Mother planned to leave the next morning for Lafayette, Louisiana, which wasn't far from my family. Maybe my parents could meet me at the airport, and after a few days I could return to file the application?

Mother turned to Sister Priscilla. "She hasn't had her home visit, either?" Mother asked.

Sister Priscilla pursed her lips. I packed a change of clothes.

The next morning Mother, Sandy, Sister Priscilla, and I entered the private plane. I had never seen a vehicle so comfortable— generously stuffed seats, pillows, a table with a basket of fruit. Mother settled into an armchair and began a few short prayers to Mary, the rest of us joining in. Then Mother pulled out pad and pen and said, "I'm writing a letter to the sisters."

Sister Priscilla leafed through some paperwork, and I stole glances at Mother. Pad and pen before her, Mother closed her eyes. Within moments, a great peace seemed to settle on her—a peace I could feel even from my seat on the other side of the cabin. After several still minutes, Mother opened her eyes and picked up her pen. Mother wrote gently, deliberately, pausing every now and then, but never for long. I had never seen such focus. We deplaned in Chicago, where we spent two hours with our sisters there, then we reboarded and Mother continued writing, seeming to pour her soul onto the paper.

When Mother left her seat to speak to the pilot, I asked Sister Priscilla how Mother had chosen Lafayette for her next new house. Lafayette certainly had its pockets of poverty, but I wouldn't have listed it among the neediest spots in the world. "A priest has done things with young boys and it's become a scandal," Sister Priscilla said. "People are upset. We'll help the bishop rebuild the image of the Church in his diocese."

In Lafayette, Mother took my parents' hands in hers. She smiled and thanked them for having given their daughter to God. She told them, ever so sweetly, that I would have only five days at home, but that she would send me to finish my visit after final vows.

Riding home past rice fields and refineries felt like being on another planet. Mom tried to make small talk, but my mind was full of Mother writing her letter, of the crowds that had come to hear her speak, of the details that still needed attention at the shelter.

When we finally arrived home, I collapsed onto a bed in my father's office, and spent much of the next few days there. I was happy to see my parents, but the family rhythms—once so familiar—felt strange. I had grown up in that house, romping about in jeans and shorts. Now, wrapped in a sari, I walked sleepy-eyed from room to room as though in a strange land without buckets or bells, with television. On Sunday all nine of us, plus Kathy's husband, came together. My sisters teased me, but their teasing felt more tedious than fun. The food was good, but too rich. Nothing felt urgent. Home no longer felt like home, and my longing to return to Winnipeg surprised me.

After five days in Texas, I flew to Winnipeg to file the occupancy application, then to New York. Another sister and I were packing for Rome when Sister Priscilla called us into her office.

Sister made us sit. She looked deeply into my face, then into Sister Christine's. "Thank you," she said. "You've both been pillars of the region."

Sister Christine and I looked at each other. Though I didn't know any details of what the Indian sister sitting next to me had done during her five years in North America, the look on Sister Christine's face convinced me she hadn't anticipated thanks from Sister Priscilla any more than I had—any more than most sisters in her region would have.

"I mean it," Sister said. "I've counted on you both."

I couldn't look at her. Over the years, I'd learned that Sister spoke with attention first not to the truth of her words but to their expediency.

Sister continued, "I asked Mother for this region, you know." That made me sit up. When Sister Priscilla had first arrived in New York she'd made a big fuss about wishing she'd gone to Manila instead of Sister Andrea. "I told Mother that if she gave me a region where I could start from the beginning, a region with mostly young sisters I could train myself, I would give her a region without problems."

Sister Priscilla sighed. "I haven't completely succeeded," she said. "There are a few little problems—but Mother is pleased with us, and now you're both off for tertianship." Sister's thin-lipped smile scared me. "I hope you'll come back here one day. The region can always use hardworking sisters like you."

Sister gave us her blessing, and I left the office dazed. Feeling neglected and disrespected had felt bad; knowing that Sister had used us—not for the needs of the poor, but to deliver a "problem-free" region to Mother so that she would look good—felt even worse.

Though I'd longed for tertianship, when Sister Christine and I left the next day for Rome—even though we were traveling with Mother—I couldn't understand why I was going at all. The conflicts of the past five years seemed to bombard me anew: Sister forcing me to report on priests and encouraging me to report on Sister Leonard; watching my superior slap a child; guilt about a kiss on the cheek; all the energy uselessly wasted on liturgical correctness and the proper length of curtains. Was I really crossing the ocean to bind myself to this group forever?

When my turn came to sit next to Mother, Mother pushed the Indian food they'd served us from one side of the tray to the other. "Too spicy," she said. She looked tired. I thanked Mother for sending me to my family, and told her about the final phases in the Winnipeg shelter project. "*Ah cha,*" Mother said. "Use your tertianship to fall in love with Jesus." As soon as the air hostess removed her tray, Mother nodded off.

I hadn't mentioned my doubts. Mother expected better of me. *God,* I prayed, *You'd better find some way to untangle this mess. You've only given me one life. I don't want to waste it. Show me what to do.*

As I prayed, I sensed Mother held the key to my survival as a Missionary of Charity. If I was to irrevocably vow my life to God in a year, I needed to get as close as I could to the heart and mind of the woman who drooped, head against her chest, in the seat next to me, the woman who had inspired me to leave home in the first place.

The morning after I arrived in our unadorned three-story house on the Via Casilina—originally a fifteenth-century Trappist monastery— Sister Jose Ann let me sleep in; the next morning she sent me out visiting families. The morning after that, I came back with my sari torn and my knee scraped—I'd fallen asleep while climbing the staircase of an apartment complex.

"You did *what*?" Sister Jose Ann asked.

"Sister, there was so much work in Winnipeg," I said. "I'm just so tired."

My tertian mistress gave me a strange look, then let me sleep the next three mornings. Though I felt only slightly less exhausted, Sister Jose Ann sent me back out for morning apostolate. She made it clear that I'd already drawn enough attention to myself by the simple fact of having shown up a month late. From now on, no exceptions would be made for me.

When I looked at my fellow tertians—twenty-eight in my group and eighteen in the group six months ahead of me—I knew that in many ways I'd had it easy. I hadn't been assigned to care for the dying in Haiti without any previous medical training or to teach cat-

echism in Venezuela with only rudimentary Spanish. I'd never
lacked food for myself or the people under my care, as some of the
sisters assigned to Africa had. I certainly hadn't dodged bullets from
guerilla fighters, as a sister in Colombia had. It was hard to justify
even mentioning my struggles with obedience and loneliness in the
land of plenty.

Nonetheless, being among sisters who knew my earlier self—
Sister Maria Lina, Sister Jelka, and the others from my group in the
novitiate—made me feel less alone. Slowly the old sense of cama-
raderie returned. I was once again with sisters who laughed at my
jokes and who harmonized in the chapel. Though none of us spoke
unguardedly, every now and then someone found the courage to
speak from her pain or her longings, and we felt ourselves friends
again.

There were so many of us that Sister Jose Ann had little time to
counsel or to scold any but the most obviously needy sisters. Under
benign neglect, held responsible neither for big projects nor anyone
else's observance of the Rules, I began to breathe more freely. Carrying water and stacking wood in the shade of ancient eucalyptus
trees was hard, honest, lovely work. Scrubbing the worn marble
floors filled me with peace. Hours of quiet prayer in an airy chapel
with high windows slowly brought me back to myself.

Sister Jose Ann's instructions weren't extraordinary, but they
were free of harshness, and that counted for a lot. I found myself
drawn to Jesus' discourses in the Gospel of John, often meditating
on His counsel: *Be not afraid. . . . Lose yourself in me and you will find
yourself. . . . Love one another. . . . No one takes my life from me; I lay it
down freely.*

The afternoon's class schedule included an hour of study, and
Sister Jose Ann left us free to devise our own study plans. The
Casilina library was better stocked than any MC library I'd yet seen,
but those books didn't draw me the way they once might have. All
other interests faded before my need to understand exactly what
Mother intended for the Society and how she kept going. I'd seen

her focus as she'd written on the plane, and I suspected I would find answers in Mother's *Letters*, the only book I would study that year.

I felt ashamed and chastened the day I read one of the early letters: "When you go to Heaven, Our Lord is not going to ask you was your Superior holy, clever, understanding, cheerful, etc., but only one thing: Did you obey Me? What a wasted life is ours if it is so full of self; you spend yourself on your Superior instead of on Him, your Spouse whose place she takes. . . . Obey because you want to prove your love for Jesus. Obey. Obey."

Though I had to admit that my critical mind wasn't part of Mother's vision for a good Missionary of Charity, Mother never wrote—as I had heard Sister Priscilla often say—that a true MC is one who never breaks a Rule. When Mother talked about what it meant to be a Missionary of Charity, she said, "Be kind and merciful. Let no one ever come to you without going away better, happier. . . . In the slums we are the light of God's kindness. You are a Missionary of Charity, a carrier of God's love, a burning light. . . . Loving must be as normal to us as living and breathing day after day until our death."

I could sign on to a vision like that. I wanted nothing more.

That fall, representatives gathered for the General Chapter in Calcutta, as they did every six years. Though Mother had written a letter asking us to elect delegates who would vote for someone to take Mother's place as superior general, no one seemed surprised when Mother was reelected. The Chapter also voted in a new set of councilors—including Sister Priscilla, whose insistence that sisters pass through the Bronx and leave laden with supplies had probably bought her a few votes. I wondered if they knew whom they had really elected.

In November one of the previous councilors arrived in Rome as our new regional superior. Sister Joseph Michael told us about the Chapter—but, more interesting, told us about herself and her hopes. She said she loved working in formation—she had been in charge of all the novices in Mother House for many years. She missed Calcutta and Mother already but was eager to discover Rome, to meet our poor, and—she said—to learn from us about being an MC outside India.

I'd never seen such an unpretentious, approachable regional superior. She smiled freely and almost sounded like a regular sister.

Shortly after Sister Joseph Michael's arrival in Rome I injured my leg while unloading huge containers of donated disinfectant. My ankle swelled to twice its normal size, and my sciatic nerve was so inflamed that I could barely walk. Since I couldn't visit families, Sister Jose Ann told me to continue my study of Mother's *Letters* during apostolate time. She wanted me to type a booklet with the most important points, and make copies to give our seniors when they took their vows on December 8. The more I read Mother's *Letters*, the more I began to regain enthusiasm for my vocation. I was copying quotations one morning when the refectory door opened and Sister Joseph Michael appeared.

"Don't you work?" she asked.

"Yes, Sister, I—"

"Why isn't this sister working?" Sister Joseph Michael turned to Sister Jose Ann, who had just entered the room.

"Welcome, Sister," Sister Jose Ann said. "We weren't expecting you."

"I can see that," Sister Joseph Michael said, tilting her head toward me as I sat, left foot perched on a stool, a binder of Mother's *Letters* in hand, paper and pen on the table. "Don't the junior tertians go out for apostolate in the morning?"

"Yes, Sister, but Sister Donata hurt herself and can't walk, so she's doing some other work until her leg gets better."

"I see," Sister Joseph Michael said, looking at me. "What other work?"

"I've been studying Mother's *Letters*, from the beginning," I said, pulling out a sheaf of papers with references to dates and page numbers. "I'm tracing the development of Mother's thought in relation to events in the Society's history."

"Very interesting," Sister Joseph Michael said, her voice softening as she sat on the bench next to me and looked through the papers. After a few pages, she set them back on the table. "Carry on, Sister, carry on," she said as she got up to leave. "I hope your leg gets better soon."

When Sister left, I took a deep breath. For a moment she had looked like the sort of regional superior I was used to. I didn't want to be disappointed in Sister Joseph Michael.

During my tertianship, my family wrote even less frequently than usual. It had been nearly five months since my last letter, and I worried about them. The first week of December, when Sister Jose Ann read off the names from the most recent mail, I tried to distract myself with some mending.

"Sister Jelka . . . Sister Donata . . ." *There must be some mistake*, I thought. But she called my name again.

I took the postcard from Sister Jose Ann's hand—the Statue of Liberty with her torch, all lit up against the New York skyline.

November 18, 1985

Dearest Mary,

We hope you are well. Everyone here is fine. We miss you and think of you always.

Please keep us in your dear prayers, and know that we always remember you to the Sacred Heart of Jesus, asking Our Lord's blessings upon you and all your sisters there.

With so much love,
Your dear parents

My throat choked up, then the tears came pouring out. The postcard wasn't from Mom and Dad, even though an American stamp had been pasted in the corner. I recognized the handwriting as Sister Tanvi's. I hadn't mentioned my lack of news, but this fellow tertian must have noticed.

Reaching between the folds of my sari for my handkerchief, I looked around the room for Sister Tanvi—in the opposite corner, looking straight at me. Through my tears, I could see her smiling at me, and I smiled back.

I wiped my eyes and blew my nose.

"What's wrong?" Sister Jelka asked. "Bad news?"

I opened my mouth but couldn't get any words out. I shook my head and let the tears fall.

I couldn't stop thinking how Sister Tanvi must have noticed that Sister Jose Ann never called my name at letter-giving time. She must have looked a long time before finding a blank American post-card and a stamp. And from somewhere she discovered my baptismal name, then slipped the postcard in with the letters.

I couldn't get another word out for the rest of recreation. I tried to hold the tears in, but each time I thought of Sister Tanvi's kindness, the tears flowed again.

The next morning I got word that Sister Jose Ann wanted me in her office.

When I sat, Sister began immediately. "You mustn't cry at recreation," she said. "You've upset the sisters. Several of them have mentioned to me that you were crying."

"I'm sorry, Sister."

"Recreation is the time to make your sisters happy. I thought you knew that."

"Yes, Sister."

"You're preparing for final vows. You will have to be an example to your sisters. You must control yourself."

"Sorry, Sister."

"All right. Go then, and I don't want to see you sad and drawing attention to yourself again, do you understand?"

"Yes, Sister." As I rose anger choked my throat. If I had been crying, there must have been a reason, and she didn't ask, didn't care. That card just touched my heart more deeply than I'd been touched in years. That card and Sister Tanvi's love were beautiful.

I made my way to the chapel and vowed that if I were ever in charge, I would never scold a sister without finding out the details of her situation. I would treat my sisters with kindness, as Sister Tanvi had treated me. I didn't care that I had rarely seen a superior treat sisters that way.

We were lucky to have Mother in Rome for much of December. The Holy Father had invited her as an auditor—and one of the few women present—to the extraordinary synod of bishops honoring the twentieth anniversary of the Second Vatican Council. Mother stayed in San Gregorio, but every now and then she gave us an instruction at Casilina.

Ann and Jan Petrie had premiered their documentary about Mother as part of the fortieth anniversary celebrations of the United Nations. Ann and Jan told us that UN secretary general Javier Pérez de Cuellar had introduced Mother as "the most powerful woman in the world." His praise—"She is the United Nations! She is peace in this world!"—affirmed my vocation, as the Nobel Peace Prize had years earlier.

Sister Jose Ann decided we should prepare a play in Mother's honor just after Christmas. We chose the story of the fourth king, an apocryphal tale of the magus who didn't make it to Bethlehem because he stopped along the way to help people in need. I had a bit part as a soldier who carried out Herod's orders to slaughter the innocents. When I raised a butcher knife to a plastic doll's neck, I heard a loud shout from the audience: "Stop, stop." Mother stood and yelled out again, "Stop, Sister, stop." I dropped the butcher knife to my side, confused.

Mother told us all to sit down. She looked genuinely disturbed. "Sisters," Mother said, "did you see how that sister—that soldier— that sister playing that soldier—was killing the babies? Something worse happens in our own day when a mother takes the life of her own child." Mother continued on about abortion and peace and God's love and sin—but all the while I could only hear her cry echoing in my head: *Stop, Sister, stop.* I didn't know what to make of Mother's alarm. I was just a nun draped in a checked bedcover holding a kitchen knife. Was it Mother's holiness that made her so sensitive? I often thought about that day, but Mother remained an enigma to me. Though I didn't understand how I'd done it, I felt responsible for having distressed her.

The day of writing to ask permission for final vows drew close. I wasn't too worried about poverty, nor about chastity, nor about wholehearted and free service. I worried about obedience. I hated fighting with my superiors, and I hated giving in when I thought they were wrong. I worried that from her position of power in Calcutta Sister Priscilla would further distort Mother's vision for the Society, which could make obedience even more troublesome.

I considered it likely that the loneliness that had plagued me in Washington would return, but Mother's words had taught me that loneliness had value. Loneliness united me mystically with Jesus, who had cried, "My God, My God, why have you abandoned me?"

All told, choosing a life of love and service was clearly the best option possible, even if parts of being an MC still scared me. I wanted to be a missionary of love, the way Mother spoke of love. I wanted to so empty myself of selfishness and pride that God could love the world through me. I wanted my life to count for something.

In the chapel, I laid all my cards before God. *Listen, Lord,* I said, *I think we both know I'm not going to be perfect. I can only promise to do my best as a Missionary of Charity according to my understanding. I won't try to live someone else's model again. Are You okay with that?*

I waited awhile. I didn't hear any big objections. I continued. *I want to love You and to love others more and more every day. That's all I ask, okay? And that You don't leave me. And—* I wanted to add some more conditions, but figured I'd come close enough to violating the spirit of total surrender expected of a good Missionary of Charity.

The day we all sat down to write Mother, I wrote with only a little trepidation and a great deal of relief. A few weeks later Mother's reply granted me permission for final vows. I carried the little slip of paper to the chapel and stared at it for a long, long time. I was going to spend the rest of my life as a Missionary of Charity. God wanted it, and so did I.

Weeks later, on the last night of our eight-day retreat, the night before our vows, I said Night Prayer with everyone else. I stood in line to fill my bucket with water, took my bath, pulled my nightdress over my head, and climbed the stairs to the dormitory as my sisters did. I knelt on the cold floor by my bed, stretched out my arms, and prayed the Paters while they did. Then, while they folded back their sheets and slipped between them for the night, I tucked my flip-flops under my bed and headed barefoot down the stairs. As the last bell rang for the night—the bell by which we were all to be in bed— I entered the refectory and took the chapel key from its hook. I snuck past Mother's closed door, then pulled back the latch on the main entrance and walked into the dark compound.

The cool air rustled my nightdress and the cobblestones poked my feet. As quietly as I could, I padded across the compound. Being caught in the chapel when I was supposed to be in bed would merit accusations not only of disobedience but also of considering myself special. I should have managed to prepare for my vows while kneeling among the crowd during retreat, but I wanted—needed—to be alone with God. Tomorrow I would pronounce the words and sign the paper that would seal my life to God and this community forever.

I turned the key in the lock and closed the chapel door behind me. One solitary candle burned in vigil before the tabernacle. I walked across the carpet, knelt, and laid myself before the Blessed Sacrament, prostrating not in the half-kneeling position we took during adoration but with my entire body prone on the floor, legs stretched behind, arms flat above my head.

For several long minutes I lay silent, just breathing. I began to calm myself into a connection with God, emptying my mind, entering my heart. But fear rose instead and took a furious swipe at me. Fear of what the future might bring, fear of my weakness, fear of His demands, fear of my decisions. I looked over fear's shoulder—belly to the ground all the while—and reached for God. *I trust You. I trust You. I trust You.* Fear rose more powerfully. I repeated my words with deeper longing, allowing the phrase and the longing to carry me forward: *I trust You. I trust You. I trust You.* As I centered myself more fully in trust, I felt fear loosen its grip. I repeated more deeply, more slowly: *I trust You. I trust You. I trust You.*

I love You.

I love You.

After a while, I could distinguish neither Him nor me. Only love remained.

The next afternoon, on Trinity Sunday, May 25, 1986, in the Church of San Luca, I vowed to live as a Missionary of Charity *fino alla morte*, until the day I died. Unable to afford travel to Rome, my parents threw a party at home as I joined my sisters to process down the church's long aisle. Finally, standing behind the altar where the priest stood during Mass, the church bells pealing loud and long, my sisters murmuring prayers, the witnessing crowd overflowing the pews, I signed the paper that permanently bound me to Jesus, then handed that paper with my vows to Mother. No more doubts, no more equivocation, no turning back. I was a Missionary of Charity forever.

16

RULES, AGAIN

SUMMER TO FALL 1987
SAN GREGORIO, ROME

Two summers and many assignments had passed since my final vows. I blamed Sister Joseph Michael for my latest and worst assignment: human adding machine. Each morning and each afternoon I sat at the San Gregorio refectory table with a pencil, a razor blade to sharpen the pencil, an eraser, and piles of papers—monthly accounts from every MC community outside India. I was supposed to make sure the sums tallied; more often than not they didn't, and I had to mail the papers back to Papua New Guinea or the Republic of the Congo or wherever for correction. I hated the monotony, but at least this latest assignment didn't terrify me.

Immediately after final vows, Mother had assigned me to be novice mistress in Tor Fiscale. Novice mistresses were supposed to turn out sisters who became Saints. Novice mistresses did this through their own example, through wise counsel, and by correcting the novices. The *Constitutions* required a novice mistress to be at least thirty-five. I was almost twenty-eight, with barely enough wisdom to know when to keep my mouth shut. I was well-intentioned, but no example. Thankfully, someone must have noticed, and after three days with the novices I'd found myself back in Casilina, assignmentless for the moment.

After a few days I heard that Mother and the sisters in charge (whoever they were, in Rome and in Calcutta) were trying to decide what to do with Sister Maria Lina and me. One of us would be sent to the new convent in Cuba, the other to study theology. The thought of Cuba thrilled me—the people were poor, the Church had been restrained and needed renewal, and I would get to learn a new language. As for studying, being considered was an honor. Fewer than one in a hundred Missionaries of Charity were ever sent to study anything. The sister who was selected to study theology would join nuns from all over the world at Regina Mundi, a pontifical institute affiliated with the Gregorian University, blocks from the Vatican. The Gregorian belonged to the Ivy League of ecclesiastical schools and had been founded by St. Ignatius in the sixteenth century. The opportunity to use my mind again and the prestige of such an appointment were alluring. But every MC who had ever studied theology had ultimately been appointed novice mistress—and I didn't want that. I prayed to be sent to Cuba.

When Mother finally returned our assignment papers after nearly two weeks, Sister Maria Lina's read *Havana;* mine said *Regina Mundi.* I worked my way out of panic by returning to my prayer in the dark: *I trust You. I trust You. I trust You.*

I received my assignment in June; school started in mid-October. In the interim, Sister Joseph Michael first appointed me acting postulant mistress in San Gregorio for three weeks, until the new mistress arrived. Postulants were still learning English and the basic Rules, and I could handle that. The group waited excitedly for Mother, whom they hadn't yet met and who—they hoped—would officially receive them and give them saris. Then, just a week before Mother was to arrive, Sister Joseph Michael said she would receive the postulants, and that I should prepare them for the ceremony. Respectfully I asked if we could wait for Mother—and the shouting began: "Who are you to challenge my authority? What do you know about Mother and her where-abouts? Do you know better than I?" She went on. And on. I'd been the recipient of some fairly fierce reprimands in my time, but never anything to equal what I received that day from Sister Joseph Michael.

I staggered into a storage room behind the chapel and tried to breathe. I decided Sister was probably just trying to keep me in my place so that I didn't get any big ideas about myself now that I was finally professed and had been chosen to study. I swallowed hard and splashed some water on my face. Within minutes I was back in front of Sister Joseph Michael, asking with the best smile I could if she had anything she wanted me to do. She looked surprised, then handed me a stack of letters to open, both of us calm, as though nothing unusual had happened.

Once the appointed mistress arrived, Sister Joseph Michael sent me to do odd jobs in Casilina, then back to San Gregorio, then to Primavalle on the outskirts of Rome. I moved from assignment to assignment so often—a dozen times in two months, never enough time to do anything productive—that the sisters took to calling me "Suor Donata dell'Autobus." I dreaded hearing the phone ring, sus-pecting a new assignment with each call.

Toward the end of summer, Sister Joseph Michael called me to Casilina and handed me a folder stuffed with mimeographed sheets: Mother's letters to the superiors. I hadn't even known these letters existed. Only sisters appointed superiors ever saw them. Sister Joseph Michael told me to retype them into a booklet.

Typing Mother's letters was terrifying—and inspiring: these let-ters were filled with Mother's pain. Over and over, Mother spoke of her sorrow at the superiors' harshness. Mother begged superiors to be kind to their sisters, not to call the sisters names, not to humili-ate them in public, not to punish them. Mother pleaded so often and so hard that I began to feel her helplessness. I was relieved. Until

reading the letters I'd always assumed Mother advised the tough-
ness superiors usually dished out; knowing that she wanted superiors to be kind made me less afraid of one day being given
responsibility.

The day I finished typing, Sister Joseph Michael handed me a
box stuffed with photos—head shots of the sisters, suitable for use
on passports. She said, "The little sisters can get overlooked. Each
one is important. Each one has a story. We need a way to remember
our sisters." Together, we assembled a series of folding charts with
passport photos of each sister in the Society. The photos had names
on the back, but Sister Joseph Michael knew all the Indian sisters
and most of the others, nearly two thousand in all.

For our next project, Sister handed me several books on personality types. Sister hoped that certain problems in community could
be eased if sisters understood themselves and each other better. We
detailed two different personality systems in a simple-to-understand
booklet with drawings, so that even sisters with questionable
English skills could begin to grasp the weaknesses and strengths inherent in their own personalities and appreciate the strengths and
weaknesses of others.

I grew to respect Sister Joseph Michael more than any other sister I had ever worked with, and she seemed to respect me, listening
to my suggestions, even when she didn't agree. I came to learn
(though not from her) that Sister Joseph Michael had been elected
general councilor twice and had served many years as secretary general. When the General Chapter had voted for a new superior general, all but one vote had been for Mother; the remaining ballot had
been cast for Sister Joseph Michael, presumably by Mother.

In October, when school finally started, I went to Primavalle and
settled into my studies with five other MC students: three sisters
who'd already been studying for a year and two others in my class.
At Regina Mundi we joined hundreds of sisters and a handful of lay-
women in a three-year course similar to that of seminarians preparing for priesthood—scripture, dogma, moral theology, spirituality,

missiology, sacramental theology, liturgy, history, philosophy. I loved sitting with sisters from around the world, listening to the priests who taught us as we delved into the history and mysteries of the Church. Many of the sisters, especially those for whom English was a second or third language, found the concepts of our philosophy class particularly challenging, so I led tutorials for them after lectures. It felt good to be using the gifts of my mind again, and though a novice mistress' eventual responsibilities still scared me, I knew I would enjoy the teaching aspects of the job, and that I'd be good at that. For the moment I didn't need to worry much about pride. An MC student's life outside the classroom seemed designed to keep us humble: sacrifice of sleep to study during afternoon rest and long after Night Prayer, extra chores on weekends, always staying behind to care for the handicapped children and expectant mothers while the rest of the Primavalle community attended Vatican Masses on holy days.

After weeks of late-night cramming, the day we turned in the blue books from our last exams we six MC students expected a few days of rest, then summer at one of our many missions in Italy. Students before us had spent their summers playing with children by the sea or preparing meals for immigrants. We were enjoying a celebratory lunch when our superior announced that the others would get their rest and their mission work, but that I would spend yet another summer in Rome. The news that Sister Joseph Michael wanted me in San Gregorio immediately after tea made swallowing my pasta impossible. At San Gregorio, Sister brought me an account book and a pencil and told me to correct the math. When she shook my shoulder an hour later, my head was pillowed on the book and the pencil was on the floor, a long black line dragging across the figures.

A week after my arrival in San Gregorio, the superior called the community together in the refectory. When she entered—late— the dozen of us rose together. Sister Stella beat the air with skeletal hands, motioning the community to sit. Physically, Sister Stella often reminded me of a grasshopper, stalking around on thin legs, her chin jutting in and out of her fleshless face as she spoke. Temperamentally, she reminded me of a half-starved mutt, barking and biting at the least provocation, scrounging for attention and food.

"I'm going to the station to meet a new sister," she announced, raking us with piercing black eyes. I looked at the table to avoid her stare. "She's had some problems in her last community." I looked up, searching for clues in Sister Stella's face. "I don't want any of you asking her what those problems were, but I want everyone to be extra kind to her. Do you understand?" she asked, her voice louder and higher.

"Yes, Sister." It seemed simple enough. Don't pry; be kind.

Sister barked at one of the sisters to accompany her to the train station. I went back to the account books.

When the new sister entered the refectory a couple of hours later, her height surprised me. I'd never seen a sister that tall—at least six feet, and looking taller in her sari. Broad-shouldered, self-assured, with olive skin and striking good looks, this new sister filled the room with a presence that derived from more than her size. As she put her bag down on the refectory table, Sister Stella hopped behind.

"Get Sister Niobe something to eat," she snarled.

"Welcome," I said, smiling at the new arrival as I closed the account books.

"Thank you." Her smile was warm and gentle. Lines under her eyes made her look tired.

As I got up from the bench, Sister Stella growled, "Hurry up."

Facing me, Sister Niobe rolled her eyes.

On the way to the kitchen, I realized that I might like this sister. Having a mind of one's own in a group like this was no small feat.

I searched the kitchen for leftovers, substituting some tinned tuna for the pork liver we'd had for lunch (Sister Stella did tell us to be kind). Back in the refectory, Sister Niobe had parked herself on the bench, elbows on the table, chin in her hands. "Thank you," she said.

Hoping to satisfy my curiosity without being too nosy, I sat opposite her and asked, "Where are you coming from?"

"Madrid," she replied as she speared some pasta. "And London before that."

Sister Stella said, "You didn't say grace."

"Sorry, Sister. Bless us, O Lord, and these Thy gifts which of Thy bounty we are about to receive, through Jesus Christ Our Lord. Amen." Sister Niobe didn't bother to stand or to make the sign of the cross.

As the days passed, I enjoyed seeing the way Sister Niobe let Sister Stella's scoldings—usually just petty nonsense—roll off her back. Meanwhile, the summer passed by, one boring account sheet after another. I used a calculator only when the columns were too crooked on the page for me to add the figures quickly. Doing the sums in my head was usually faster, and gave me a sense that I was, after all, doing *something*. The afternoon heat made concentration difficult, and the phone and the gate bell—which I was supposed to answer whenever they rang, some ten to twelve times an hour—were a constant distraction. Sister Joseph Michael had told me to finish the accounts for 1986 within two weeks, so that I could start on 1987. The deadline was nearly impossible, and I spent several hours working every night after Night Prayer, while most of the other sisters slept.

The sister who prepared visas and tickets for the sisters traveling to the missions was often up with me, as was the sister in charge of the adoption of children from our homes in India to families in Italy. We sat around a large table in the office, each with her own stack of papers and half a dozen candle stubs. Our jobs weren't considered "real" jobs, because they didn't involve dealing directly with the poor or getting our hands messy in some cleanup job. The superiors and the sisters who did real work didn't want the pencil pushers to consider themselves above the others. Giving us far more work than could possibly be done in the allotted time guaranteed we'd miss sleep. Exhaustion and stress would keep us in our place.

The following Sunday afternoon, Sister Stella gave us paper to write our monthly letters home, and told us to write wherever we wanted. Thank God she hadn't insisted we remain in the refectory—it must have been over a hundred degrees in that re-modeled chicken house, and my chemise, soaked with perspiration, clung to my back and tangled itself around my knees. Hoping to find a place to be both cool and alone, I headed for the little garden between the convent and the church—not really a garden, more a little patch of land between the long parallel walls of the convent and the basilica, closed at the end nearest the street by a wrought-iron gate and at the other end by another wall of the basilica. Old marble slabs and gravel paved the ground, and the area was open to the sky. No flowers or vegetables—not even grass—grew there. The garden's attraction was the breeze, the relative privacy, and a palm tree near the gate.

As I pulled back the garden latch, I saw Sister Niobe on the only bench, down near the gate, so I turned to look for another spot.

"Sister Donata, come here," Sister Niobe whispered loudly. "There's room for both of us." I hesitated, but realized that if this place was occupied, there wouldn't be another spot where I could be alone anyway.

As I approached, she patted the bench and said softly, "Sit down. I was hoping you would come." She didn't move from her place near the center of the bench, so when I sat down, our hips touched.

"It's so hot," I said. "Can't you move over?"

"Oh, sure." She scooted over a couple of inches, just far enough that we weren't touching anymore. She hadn't stopped looking at me since I'd walked in.

"I wanted to thank you," she said, "for being so nice to me ever since I came here. It's not easy to change communities, you know."

"No, it's not," I agreed, "but you seem to be doing fine."

"Well, there are some decent sisters here," she said, looking at me so intently that I was beginning to get nervous. "Even Sister Stella has been good to me. But you are the best."

A warning bell went off in my head. "Well, I've got my letter to write," I said, lifting the two thin sheets of airmail paper between my thumb and forefinger.

"We all have letters to write," Sister Niobe said. "Never mind."

I looked up blankly.

"I've been waiting so long for a chance to talk to you," she said, and she broke into a beautiful smile—a smile like a child who'd been given ice cream on a warm day.

That she'd been waiting to talk to me was odd. But the smile— the smile was beautiful. "What do you need?" I asked.

"I don't need anything except the chance to know you better, and to let you know me." Her smile deepened.

"We can do that at recreation. I've got to write my letter now." I wrote, *Dear Mom and Dad*.

"So what's your family like?" she asked.

So she's serious about wanting to know me better? And she's still smiling—okay. "Five sisters and a brother, all younger than I am."

"Oh, so lucky. I have only one sister, much younger," she said. "And your mother?"

"She's fine."

"And your father?" Her earnestness was charming, even if we weren't supposed to be talking.

"They're all fine, and they'll want to get my letter." I turned my shoulder slightly and put pen to paper.

"Now put that down," she said, grabbing my hand, still smiling, "and be polite and ask me about my mother." As she dropped my hand her face took on a look of longing. Maybe she needed to talk about her mother. Sister Stella had said she had problems. We were supposed to be kind to her.

"Okay. How's your mother?"

"My mother is not well. She worries too much. And she is always thinking of her home country, but the doctor has forbidden her to travel. Sometimes she cries thinking of it."

"Where's she from?"

"Singapore, but now she lives in Florence. She would have come to see me today, but she phoned and told Sister Stella that she is not feeling well. Her heart." She put her hand on my knee. She must have felt really bad about her mother. "I took her name, you know?"

"Oh?" Many sisters took their mothers' names.

"Yes," she continued, smiling again, "but I took her name only now. I was Marta when I was born, and in the novitiate I was Sister Augustine. You know, Augustine was a sinner, and I still felt far from God." She looked down, then up at me again. "But when I left Madrid, I didn't want a man's name, so on the train I decided to take my mother's name."

"Just like that?" I'd never heard of a sister changing her name after profession.

"I wanted it. Sister Stella told me to write to Calcutta for permission, but I know what I want, so I told her to call me Sister Niobe, and to introduce me to the community like that." I liked Sister Niobe's self-assurance and envied her ability to convince even Sister Stella to take her desires seriously. Most of us were trying to die to ourselves so that we could become holy. She pursued what she wanted, and seemed to get away with it.

Sister Niobe told me that her mother was the daughter of a Greek businessman who'd married a Singaporean secretary. At a party in a hotel overlooking the Strait of Malacca she'd met Sister Niobe's father, a handsome banker from Spain. The family had moved a lot and Sister Niobe had spent most of her childhood in a boarding school run by nuns in Florence, the city to which her mother had returned after her father's death when Sister Niobe was about to finish school.

When the air cooled and the bell for dinner finally rang, my two sheets of letter paper still read only, *Dear Mom and Dad.*

. . .

I'd been on accounts for three weeks when Sister Agnel, superior of the newly opened house in the Vatican, arrived with a change of clothes. That was odd. Odder yet, she spent three grim days locked morning and evening behind closed doors with Sister Joseph Michael. Sister Agnel was normally a cheerful sister, friendly and smart. I'd heard how well she handled the Church dignitaries and tourists who showed up every day at the Vatican convent; Sister Agnel's Italian was better than that of any other Indian sister I knew, and far better than mine. But throughout those three days at San Gregorio I hadn't seen Sister Agnel smile once, and she'd been nearly silent at recreations. I couldn't imagine what she could have been discussing with Sister Joseph Michael for three full days.

Then something shifted, and while sipping tea that July afternoon of the fourth day, Sister Agnel told funny stories about the women who had accompanied the sisters to the Vatican, stories about Flavia and Agnese and Rita and Sonia, who had helped me in the kitchen when I'd been a postulant. Before getting up from tea, Sister Joseph Michael announced that Sister Agnel would return to the Vatican that afternoon. Sister Agnel smiled.

Sister Niobe, sitting next to me, tapped my shin with her foot and leaned close. She whispered, "Like a prisoner being set free."

As we got up to say grace after meals, Sister Joseph Michael eyed me curiously. Had she seen Sister Niobe whispering to me? Had she heard what she'd said? I hoped not.

Later that afternoon, while I was checking accounts, Sister Joseph Michael entered the refectory. She stood a few moments near the door, watching me. Her eyes on the back of my head made me nervous.

"Sister Donata, would you come to the office for a moment?"

I hoped this wasn't about Sister Niobe's whispering. I hoped even harder that she wasn't going to give me more work.

As I followed Sister into the office, she asked me to close the door and sit down, but she remained standing, and began to pace back and forth. The office—not even four yards square, and filled with Mother's bed, a desk, two stools, and a large pile of cardboard boxes packed with rosaries and Miraculous Medals—didn't sport much pacing room. Sister Joseph Michael covered every inch.

"Sister Donata," she began, continuing to pace, "Mother has entrusted me with some work. I need someone to help me, and I thought I could count on Sister Agnel, but she has so much to do at Dono di Maria." Sister Joseph Michael paused to look at me before continuing to pace. "And she can't really concentrate on this work. It's not the kind of work that interests her, but she is a senior sister, and I thought—" Sister stopped pacing, folded her arms across her chest, looked straight at me, and said, "I want you to help me."

Sister was obviously uncomfortable asking me, and I was uncomfortable being asked, especially since she hadn't given me any clue about the job. For a long time I'd been trying to make myself genuinely available to the needs of others, so there was really only one possible answer.

"If I can help you, Sister," I said, "I will."

"Well, yes, but you see, it's very special work."

I was silent. If she wanted me to help her, she'd have to tell me what it was about eventually.

She began slowly, tentatively, unlike any Sister Joseph Michael I'd seen before. "Now that the new Code of Canon Law has been issued," she began, "the *Constitutions* of all religious congregations have to be revised in accordance with the new code, and Mother wants a draft done before October. She wants to give it to a few priests to review before it is eventually considered by the next General Chapter. Will you help me?"

Now I understood her hesitation. I was just one year finally professed and she was asking me to help revise the fundamental document of the congregation, the book that Mother always held up and said, "If you live by this book, it will make you holy." A book so full of grammatical errors that I'd often been ashamed to look at its pages. The book by which all Missionaries of Charity lived, the book Mother had written on her knees before I was born. *I should not be the one to do this job. I want to do this job. I should not even consider doing this job.*

"Sister Donata, will you help me?"

"I don't know what to say, Sister."

"I can't think of anyone else."

"I haven't studied canon law yet," I said. "We do that next semester. The second-years have all studied canon law already."

"I am asking you." Authority had returned to her voice.

"Sister, would this mean that I could help make the wording grammatical? I mean, I've always wanted to do that. Some of it is—"

"Yes, I know, some of it is embarrassing. We can fix the grammar, but it will mean much more than that."

"Sister, of course I'm willing to help. I'm honored to help. But I have to ask you one thing."

She raised her eyebrows.

"I wouldn't want anyone to know that I was helping with this. They should think it is all your work. If sisters knew I was helping, the *Constitutions* might lose credibility, and, well, some people would resent it."

"I'm glad you understand," Sister Joseph Michael said. I could see her shoulders relax. "This work needs to be done very confidentially. You can work in the garden. I'll tell everyone not to bother you, and if anyone asks what you're doing, just tell them you're helping me."

"And the accounts?"

"Don't worry about the accounts. And don't answer the gate and the phone, either. I need you to concentrate on this work." She reached across the desk and placed a copy of the new Code of Canon Law in my hands. "Start by reading this and taking notes. We'll talk more tomorrow."

As I felt the weight of the book in my hands, I said, "Thank you, Sister," and bowed for a blessing. Sister's hands were warm on my head, and she let them linger.

When she lifted her hands she said, "Thank you," then sank onto the stool I had just vacated.

Every morning after the prayer near Our Lady's statue, I hauled a small wooden table, a stack of books, and a German manual typewriter (inconvenient because I could never remember where they put the *y*) into the garden.

It took some time to recover from the shock of being asked to work on the *Constitutions*. Whenever I'd had a question about what was expected of me as a Missionary of Charity, I had turned first to the *Constitutions*. Now I was reading the *Constitutions* not with an eye to living them but with an eye to changing them.

Sister Joseph Michael made it clear that we were actually changing nothing, and that was fine with me. Together, we would suggest changes as the new code required, but ultimately any changes to the *Constitutions* had to be ratified by the General Chapter. Our first task was a sorting job. The Code of Canon Law stipulated that the *Constitutions* should contain the basic principles of the Society. Practical applications of these basic principles were to be housed in separate documents. The first day we sat next to each other on the bench in the garden, going through each paragraph, marking what should stay in the *Constitutions* and what should be transferred to another document. I took notes on the backs of discarded papers I'd stapled into a notebook of sorts.

After a day or two working side by side, Sister Joseph Michael told me she had other things she needed to see to, and that I should carry on. She came to check on me an hour later, made a couple of corrections, and left me to continue. As the days passed and I got the feel of the work, her visits became less frequent, just once or twice a day. If Sister Joseph Michael didn't come and I had a question, I would go find her in the convent, but never without covering my work first with my apron, pinning down the apron's corners with a few stones. I didn't change so much as a comma without Sister Joseph Michael's approval. When we'd agreed on all the changes, I typed up each chapter as it would appear in the new draft—a challenge of a different sort. My typing had never been all that good, and this draft had to be perfect.

I loved my spot in the garden, where I could be alone, and where the air was much cooler than in the house. A monastery of Augustinian nuns on the opposite hill rang bells on the hour, and the Italian army band practiced at their installment near the tram line, their precise drumbeats a fitting counterpoint to the *click-clack* of my typewriter. Early in the morning, Sister Niobe often peeked in at the convent end of the garden, offering a cheery "Have a good day" before she left to work in the Men's Home. She never asked what I was doing, never came to look over my shoulder. I appreciated that. Instead, she waved from the door and went on her way. Sometimes she winked. I began to look forward to seeing her at the door every morning.

As I typed beside the Basilica of St. Gregory the Great, I imagined medieval monks in that very monastery with their quills and parchment, layering tints extracted from leaves or berries or roots to their illuminated Gospels. Meanwhile, I searched the typewriter for the *y* and reached for the correction fluid, happy to make my own small contribution to the generations of Missionaries of Charity who would follow.

I worked all day and continued to work after Night Prayer in a corner of the office where I hoped no one could see what I was doing. After a few nights, Sister Joseph Michael told me to go to bed with the regular community sisters. I didn't know if she was motivated by a desire to safeguard the work's confidentiality or to let me rest, but I was grateful. I began to love my new routine.

One morning before Mass I lugged my bucket of wet clothes to the lines. The early light played on the gravel, the clotheslines, the open air. I had always been partial to the quiet morning beauty of the San Gregorio washing place. As I pulled my wet sari from my bucket, Sister Niobe approached. She leaned over my bucket and hoisted my wet habit to the line. As she passed my head on her way up, she whispered in my ear, "Sister Donata, I love you."

The clothespin fell from my hand to the ground.

The words bounced around in my head. *Does she mean she loves me the way we are supposed to love everyone? No, I don't think so. She couldn't mean . . . I've waited all my life to hear those words. I never thought . . . I like her.*

I smiled. I knew I shouldn't have, but I smiled anyway.

She picked up the clothespin I'd dropped, her strong, warm arm brushing against mine, and I felt something like an electric charge travel from my arm through my whole body.

I folded my sari and threw it over the line, meeting Sister Niobe's eyes above the dripping clothes. She raised her eyebrows, expecting a reply. I felt the blood rush to my face, and I nodded. Her eyes penetrated mine as she pinned the last clothespin to the line.

All day long, the sky above the garden was bluer than usual. The military band that played near the tram line switched from marches to arias, and a sparrow pecked the garden gravel. I'd never felt so happy.

During the next few days, Sister Niobe distanced herself a bit, not paying much attention to me at meals, not speaking to me out of time, not whispering anything, but smiling every now and then in the corridor. I took this as a really good sign. She wasn't going to make a big deal about anything. We were sisters, after all, and her distance left me free to savor her words without worrying about consequences.

The only change in routine was that before Night Prayer, Sister Niobe began to linger in the corridor, slowly removing her slippers or looking around. Then, when I entered the chapel, she followed quickly and knelt next to me. It felt good to have her close, to hear her voice mingle with mine and with everyone's as we prayed together. As we recited the standard words, my heart sang, *Thank You, God, for such a gift of Your love.* When we sat for the meditation point, Sister Niobe reached for her Bible and smiled at me.

That smile stayed with me, cheering me as I worked in the garden alone, correcting the grammar, reorganizing the text, contemplating options. The code mandated the creation of councils to advise each superior, and the idea of more collegial government excited me. Superiors wouldn't need to be so lonely in their decision making, and the added input could lead to better decisions. Everyone could feel more respected, though ultimate responsibility would still rest with the superior.

The *Constitutions* seemed alive with new possibilities. Our General Chapters, which elected the superior general and her councilors for six-year terms and which were supposed to discuss and make decisions on matters vital to the Society, had never achieved their potential as sources of renewal. Sisters who were members of the Chapter because of appointment to office were all beholden to the people who had appointed them. All appointments were technically made by Mother, but in practice one or two of the councilors came to exercise this power regularly. The more appointed members of the Chapter there were, the less truly representative the Chapter was, and the more invested in the status quo.

So one day I drew together my courage. "Sister," I asked as Sister Joseph Michael sat next to me on the bench, "if the General Chapter is to be truly representative, shouldn't it have more elected than appointed members?"

Sister Joseph Michael sat quietly for a moment, taking the idea in. I could see its appeal growing. "What does canon law say?" she asked.

"Not much. Canon law is rather vague on chapters: 'The general chapter . . . is to be composed in such a way that, representing the entire institute, it becomes a true sign of its unity in charity.' "

She took the book from me. " 'Representing the entire institute,' " she mumbled, " 'unity in charity.' Let me think about this." Sister Joseph Michael took the book with her as she left the garden.

Sister Joseph Michael came back clearly energized the next day. "If the Chapter is going to represent the entire institute," she said, "it should be more international. The sisters nearly always elect the most senior sisters—all Indians." I grew more and more excited as we tossed ideas back and forth for a few days. I also wondered if, in our enthusiasm, we were perhaps exceeding the instruction to make no real changes beyond those necessitated by changes in the code. Eventually the same thought occurred to Sister. In the end she shook her head and said, "We can't go too quickly." We wrote up a clause that required the number of elected delegates to exceed the number of appointed delegates "by a few units," giving discretion to the superior general about how that was to be done. It wasn't all I had hoped for, but it was a start.

The next day I was typing up all these changes when I glanced up from my typewriter to see Sister Niobe just a few steps in front of me.

"What are you doing here?" I whispered. She was definitely not supposed to be in the garden while I was working.

"Don't get excited," Sister Niobe said, smiling again. "No one's at home. Sister Joseph Michael took Sister Stella to see somebody in the hospital." She walked closer. I stood and took a few steps toward her, so that she wouldn't see what I was working on.

"I just wanted to tell you," she said, putting one hand on my shoulder as she looked down at me, "I'm so happy you haven't run away from me."

"Where would I go?"

"I mean, it was a big risk, telling you that I love you. Some sisters wouldn't know how to take it." She gripped my shoulder more strongly and searched my eyes. "You don't know how special you are."

As I looked into her eyes, I felt as though someone had finally seen me for who I was and really appreciated me—valued me not for the things I could do but simply for being me. I knew she wasn't supposed to touch me, but I liked it.

"You're special, too," I said, hoping she could feel it as much as I did.

"I've never loved anyone the way I love you, Donata."

Confused and elated at once, I took a step backward. "I've got to get back to my work."

"Never forget that I love you." She smiled, then backed away, continuing to look at me as she headed down the garden, then disappeared through the door.

She'd called me Donata. Not Sister Donata, just Donata. I'd never felt so special.

Sister Joseph Michael and I were alone in the office one afternoon. She was sorting papers, and I was gathering my things to return to the garden.

"Mother knows you," she said.

"Well," I said, "I've seen Mother every year since I joined. That's more than most sisters get."

"No," Sister Joseph Michael said, "I mean Mother *knows* you." When Sister Joseph Michael didn't want to be explicit, she could be cryptic in a way few sisters had mastered.

I just stood, waiting. I got the idea that she had already said more than she thought necessary.

"She told me to show you things," Sister Joseph Michael said. Then she looked down at her papers again. I carried my stool out to the garden, left to wonder when Mother had said that, what she could have meant, and why Sister Joseph Michael had chosen to tell me, in her own oblique way.

As the days passed, what was becoming clearer was that Niobe knew me. The next letter-writing Sunday, we talked in the little storage room behind the parlor. She told me about her sister and her sister's fiancé, a carpenter—very cute, quite responsible. Niobe was especially fond of mozzarella, and she was thirty-nine years old. I liked apricots and was twenty-nine. She'd joined in 1981, I in 1977. We both loved the hymns of Marco Frisina, a priest-composer at San Giovanni. Our friendship made me feel that I belonged to the Society in an entirely new way. Suddenly I could bring all of who I was into my life as a sister, because someone wanted to know what I'd done before, because someone cared.

I tried not to pay any attention to the fact that Niobe seemed to like to brush up against me. I'd seen the sisters at school from other congregations, even Indian ones. They embraced a sister they hadn't seen in a while, or someone who deserved congratulations. When talking with a sister in a friendly sort of way one might grasp the wrist or fingers of another, and no one thought anything of it. It all looked so natural. Even in the midst of all the prohibitions, the *Constitutions* recognized that "true friendship . . . helps one lead a life of holiness."

The Code of Canon Law devoted a profusion of paragraphs to the process for leaving a religious community through transfer, departure, or dismissal. Since there had always been significant confusion about this, Sister Joseph Michael thought it best to copy all the applicable sections of the code into the *Constitutions,* to help familiarize sisters with the process. This required an extensive rewrite and a particularly long discussion on how to begin the chapter "Separation of Members from the Institute." Sister insisted on an impassioned excerpt from one of Mother's letters: *God is a jealous lover. . . . Our vocation is God's gift to us. We either choose to be faithful and to die for it, or we give it up. Let us be afraid for ourselves.* Sister pointed the passage out to me from the little booklet of excerpts from Mother's letters I'd prepared as a tertian. To me, this particularly vehement quote didn't fit the intent of canon law or of our rewritten chapter. Canon law recognized many reasons a sister might leave, and most of them weren't tied to a sister's infidelity. It was even possible that God could call a sister out of the Society. Hadn't Mother left the Loreto Sisters to found the MCs?

I looked up Mother's letter in its original context, and what I read stopped me cold: "The plain fact is that what has happened is the result of particular friendship. If Eve had not played with the snake, we would not have had original sin. If we do not play with our hearts we shall not have to face such spiritual accidents." Though I'd been downplaying my involvement, it seemed as though Mother might have been writing about Niobe and me. I looked at the date again: 1965. The letter referred to two unnamed sisters who had fallen into particular friendship and had been dismissed from the

Society. The letter gave no details about what precisely the sisters had done. Perhaps their relationship had begun with kind words and winks, with sitting next to each other in the chapel, with saying "I love you."

Mother wrote, "What has happened is a big humiliation for the Society, but it is also a grace in disguise, for it should lead us to be more faithful. . . . Be sincere with yourself. When you see that habitually you are disobedient, you are breaking the rule of touch, you have temptations against faith, against chastity, against poverty, speak in time; that is the golden rule for safeguarding your vocation."

That afternoon in the garden, I sat with the book of Mother's letters open on my lap for a long time, just trying to breathe. I didn't have any temptations against faith or poverty. Niobe made me happier than ever to be an MC, and she'd brought me closer to God—I could feel it. She often tried to sit close to me, and I did like it sometimes—but I hadn't touched her in return and didn't seek her out. Still, she sometimes left notes in my prayer book, and I sometimes thought more about her than about God during times of prayer. We had broken rules of silence and were fonder of each other than chastity allowed. I might spend most of my day rephrasing the Rules on a German typewriter, but that didn't give me the liberty to rewrite the Rules in my life, no matter how good breaking them sometimes felt. I wondered if Niobe experienced the same qualms. I would have to talk to her, to let her know that we needed to stop making exceptions for ourselves.

When Sister Joseph Michael came back to the garden just before dinner, she said, "It's true that the chapter deals with more than leaving because of infidelity. But if we're going to give sisters seventeen paragraphs on how to leave the Society, we'd better give them at least one strong paragraph on why they shouldn't." I didn't have any argument with that.

I spent my meditation the next morning trying to find the right words for Niobe. I would thank her for loving me. I would tell her I loved her, but that I loved Jesus more. During Mass I begged God for an opportunity to talk to her as soon as possible, and to help her understand.

That morning Niobe entered the garden a little after nine. She was frowning. As I got up, she took only one small step forward. It seemed the moment to tell her I was backing away had arrived sooner that I had expected. When I drew closer, she whispered, "I'm going to Napoli today."

"To Napoli?" I took a step back.

"Sister Hilda has to have surgery, and they have no one to drive the van. So Sister told me to go this afternoon, right after lunch."

"When will you come back?"

"Sister told me to take all my things." Niobe wasn't coming back? She smiled and said, "Don't worry. Napoli's not that far. I'm sure we'll see each other sometime. I've got to pack."

Niobe was leaving? I didn't even need to tell her about my decision to create some distance? God was good, taking care of all my problems. At the same time, I would miss her terribly. "Can I help you pack?" I asked as I followed her out.

"No." She stopped at the garden gate. "Sister told me not to tell anyone."

"But you can't go now." She walked out and I followed her, even though I knew I shouldn't and I'd left my work uncovered in the garden.

She pulled me into the parlor and shut the door, taking my hands in hers. "Never forget our secret. No one can take that away. I love you."

Why was I crying? Her transfer was the will of God and a relief. There was obviously something very wrong with me.

"And I love you, too," I said.

Weeks later, I finally slipped copies of the entire new draft of the *Constitutions* into extra-large manila envelopes—to send to Mother, the councilors, and a few select priests. It was a morning of quiet satisfaction, even though no one but Sister Joseph Michael and I knew that a huge task had been completed. There weren't as many substantive changes as I had hoped for, but Sister Joseph Michael agreed to circulate my suggestions as a sort of appendix listing issues the Chapter might want to consider.

I wished for a moment that Niobe could see the look of satisfaction that I assumed illuminated my face. Life was lonelier without her voice in chapel, her notes in my prayer book, her stories on letter-writing Sundays. Niobe had taught me about my own goodness, and about the joys of tenderness. I was grateful.

17

HOLD ME

The second day of our second year of study, I stood at the front of the main lecture hall of the English section at Regina Mundi, watching as a short man, no more than five foot three, strode confidently through the doors at the back. Hands in the pockets of his black dress pants, wearing a white shirt and red pullover sweater, he never broke stride as he sauntered down the side aisle through the room of 180 chatting nuns toward the desk on the platform at the end of the room, nuns' bodies pulling back from the aisle into the rows of desks like the Red Sea rolling back before Moses. On his way, he nodded a hello to this one or that.

Roman sunshine flooded the lecture hall, the rays glinting off the man's black hair as he neared the platform. "I thought he would be taller," whispered the Filipina sister in the gray habit standing next to me, and I nodded. The two of us had the best vantage point in the hall, on the side of the platform, guitar slung over her shoulder, microphone in front of me.

"So you two are this year's singers, are you?" He smiled as he climbed the platform, a touch of gray at his temples, his elegant accent sounding British but not quite. "Nothing better than a good song with which to begin class. What do we have this morning?"

" 'Praise to the Lord,' " Sister Dolores answered, pushing the mike stand nervously forward with her foot.

" 'The Almighty,' " he replied. "Just so."

The bell rang. Sisters moved toward their seats, continuing to chat. He put his hands on the desk and leaned forward, gazing straight ahead. Slowly, the chatting subsided, and he spoke.

"I'm Mark Attard, a Carmelite priest, and you are the students of Special Moral Theology. This semester we shall focus on social ethics, the ethics of justice. But first, a song."

I switched on the overhead, projecting lyrics onto the front wall, and my companion strummed the first chords. Following my lead, song soon filled the room. Father Attard added a very pleasant tenor.

As we returned to our seats, Father Attard said, "Thank you, Sisters. Thank you, indeed. Very nice. Now, shall we get started?" He spoke with incredible speed.

"The study of social ethics is based on the principles of justice, how we human beings treat each other, as individuals and as groups. Take notes if you can, but, as usual, printed notes will be available after class for those who desire them, at the cost of fifty lire a page. I believe someone has been appointed to see to the photocopying?" A Nigerian sister in a bright blue habit raised her hand. "Very well, Sister. You and I will need to have a little chat at the break."

He spoke with conviction, his words elegant and precise, with many references to the Scriptures, to papal encyclicals, and to the Documents of the Second Vatican Council. His passion for his subject was contagious.

In addition to being an excellent teacher, Father Attard was quirky, which endeared him to me, though others were less pleased with his lack of religious dress and title. " 'Call no man on earth your father, for you have one Father who is in heaven.' It's in the Gospel, Sisters. Those are the words of Jesus." We MCs continued to call him Father anyway.

Behind his iconoclasm, Father Attard was a man of prayer. He was the only priest I ever saw in the school chapel outside Mass time. He never missed an all-school Mass, though fewer than half the professors ever showed up for one.

Mark Attard was the rock star of Regina Mundi professors, and many sisters tittered in his wake. I was not immune to his appeal, but Niobe was the one who still occupied my heart, though I hadn't seen her for months. It wasn't that I thought of her all the time—my studies occupied most of my attention—but in all sorts of human moments, moments like Mark Attard's playful banter with the sisters, I would think of Niobe's smile. I missed her cocky confidence, her sassy wink, the way she used to tell me I was special. I even missed—though I didn't want to admit it, even to myself most of the time—the guilty thrill of her hand on my knee, her bare feet on mine under the refectory table.

When we weren't in school, we students lived and worked in Primavalle, an old school on Vatican property that the Pope had given Mother. She turned the school's basement into a convent, where MC students joined a community of four sisters who cared for expectant and recently delivered mothers and their babies. The mothers and babies lived on the two main floors, where we also housed three disabled girls—abandoned children of an inbred family in Sicily.

Navigating life as a student in Primavalle proved tricky. We had to keep up with our schoolwork as well as our duties at home, and to deal with the friction that always seemed to arise whenever one part of the community wasn't engaged in "real work." Each student had night duty once a week, which meant that we checked on the women before going to bed and saw to emergencies—a woman in labor who needed to be accompanied to the hospital, a woman who arrived late, police checking on mothers under house arrest. It was a rare night when the night duty buzzer didn't ring at least once.

I was on duty one January night and was studying for an exam in Scripture the next morning. Sister Dominica had told me to expect a new woman from Zaire, named Monique. Normally new women arrived between four and six, but Sister said this woman sounded desperate on the phone, and she'd agreed to a late arrival.

Sure enough, a little before ten o'clock, the gate bell rang. A young black woman, slighter than most of the African women I knew, stood in a shapeless navy shift, two or three sizes too big for her, grasping the bars of the gate with one hand, clutching a small overnight case with the other. A scar about two inches long ran down her right cheek, near her ear.

"*Buona sera,*" I said, still climbing the stairs. "*Si chiama Monique?*"

"*Sí, suora. Per favore, lasciammi entrare?*" Her voice shook with this plea to enter, and as I opened the gate and she released her grasp of its bars, I saw that her hands were shaking, too. Her Italian betrayed a thick French accent.

I took Monique upstairs, glancing on the way at the poster of Mother that hung near the entrance, with Mother's words: *Being unwanted is the greatest poverty.* Most of the women in the dormitory were already asleep, but one called out, "Don't you have exams tomorrow, Sister?"

"Yes," I replied, "the Gospel of John and the Book of Revelation."

"I'll take care of her. I can't sleep anyway."

I thanked her and turned to Monique, who still stood behind me, looking mostly at the floor with an occasional glance up, and then quickly down again. I asked, "Is there anything you need? Toothpaste, towel?"

"Sister, I have nothing." Her bag had seemed incredibly light. I unlocked the go-down and handed her towels, soap, a toothbrush and toothpaste, a nightdress. "If you need anything else, ask the sisters in the morning."

"Yes. Thank you." Reaching out, she repeated, "Thank you." Her hand was soft and still trembled. I looked into her eyes, so full of fear, and was touched by her gratitude.

As I walked downstairs to the study room and my books, all I could see was the fear in her eyes. The question of the authorship of John's Gospel suddenly seemed to matter very little.

One evening while we were having recreation, the gate bell rang. When the sister who was portress that week returned to the refectory half out of breath from running up and down the stairs, she reported, "Sisters have come from Napoli."

"At this hour?" Sister Dominica looked up at the clock. It was 8:55, five minutes before Night Prayer.

"Here we are." The Napoli superior smiled at the refectory door, lifting five long pepperoni sausages, tied together on a string, hanging down like wind chimes.

"Welcome," Sister Dominica said, and we echoed, "Welcome."

"There's more up in the van, and pasta and *torrone* and milk and tinned tomatoes. A big warehouse closed, and they gave us everything. Take what you want. We've already been to San Gregorio, and when we finish here we're going back to Napoli."

Putting down our mending, we ran to get our aprons. As I climbed the stairs to the van, my heart beat more quickly—only because of the stairs, I tried telling myself, not because I suspected that perhaps more than milk and *torrone* were waiting for me. It had been five months since I'd seen her.

"Do you want flour?" a husky voice could be heard in the dark. It was her voice.

Using the darkness and the sister in front of me as cover, I managed to sneak behind the tall figure with the husky voice and to slide my hands over her eyes.

"Guess who?" I whispered.

"Donata!" The pleasure in her voice raised goose bumps under my habit sleeves. She lifted my hands from her eyes and gave a big, warm smile. I pulled her around to the side of the house, down the far stairs, and into the students' room.

"How've you been?" I asked.

"Longing to see you." She smiled and took my hands in hers.

"We don't have much time."

"I know. Sister Lorraine wasn't even going to come, but I told her, 'Think of the sisters in Primavalle. They are so far away. No one brings them things.' But what I really wanted was to see you."

"I've been thinking . . ." I hesitated. Oh, I'd been feeling. It had been growing inside until I thought it might explode.

"You must do a lot of thinking here in this room, with these books." Niobe waved her hands at the shelves.

"No, I— I want to ask you something."

"Then ask me."

"Will you hold me?"

"Will I hold you?" That warm smile, the smile I remembered so well, spread across her face.

"Yes, in your arms," I said, "just for a minute. I want you to hold me."

"Of course." She smiled. "I'll hold you. But . . ." She looked at all the windows.

"Just a minute." I quickly closed the blinds on the south and east sides, and she closed the ones on the west. Putting her hands on my shoulders, she led me close to the door, planting herself just in front of it, so that no one could enter. Then she opened her arms, and I stepped in.

As she wrapped her arms around my shoulders, I sank into her soft body and rested my head on her chest. Her heartbeat sounded in my ears, my head, my whole body. I folded my arms around her waist. Down the corridor, the bell rang for Night Prayer. She pulled me closer. I felt so steady and secure, enveloped in her arms. I wanted to stay there forever. Then she leaned forward slightly and kissed me, slowly, lingeringly, on the top of my sari-covered head. This was everything I'd hoped for, and more. I gave her a quick squeeze, she dropped her arms, and I stepped back.

She opened the door, and headed upstairs. "When will you be back?" I asked.

"As soon as I can."

. . .

The second semester Father Mark Attard taught bioethics: cloning
and euthanasia, in vitro fertilization, eugenics, abortion, and the issues surrounding the beginning of human life. The stack of notes,
always referred to by its Italian name, *dispense*, was larger than that
of any other course, and the science involved left some of the sisters
baffled, though Father Attard did an excellent job of explaining double helices, cell replication, and the differences between prolonging
life through usual and unusual means. He often referred to new
Church documents that hadn't yet made it into the *dispense*, the
same notes he'd been passing out for years. "The science in the
study of life issues is currently evolving at a tremendous rate," he
said speedily, "and this is one area in which the Church is doing a remarkable job of keeping pace with new developments. I refer you to
recent documents of the Congregation for the Doctrine of the
Faith.

"As you know, the proposal to legalize abortion in Italy is one of
the major issues on the next national ballot," he continued, pacing the
platform. "I propose two special events to focus on this most important issue. The first is a screening of a film depicting an actual abortion, entitled *The Silent Scream*. I have already made arrangements to
screen this film on a free afternoon in your schedule. No student will
be required to attend the film, but the fact that I'll be taking some of
my personal time to show the film should show you how important I
think it is." I'd heard of the film, but I'd never seen it.

"My second proposal is a challenge to the class." He walked
from one side of the platform to the other, arms across his blue-
sweatered chest, using dramatic pause to good effect. Then he
turned to look straight at me. "I propose a debate in which two
teams, composed of however many sisters desire to participate,
would argue both sides of the legalized abortion issue. You would
organize this among yourselves, and I am willing to set aside regular class time for this debate. Participants will receive extra credit
toward their examination marks." He knew I didn't need extra

credit, but his gaze was an attempt to entice me—he wanted me to organize this. "We've had a debate in past years, and it's always proved highly instructional, but it would never be more timely than at this moment." He was still looking at me. "Talk about it among yourselves, and let me know."

As he proceeded to discuss Aristotle and Aquinas' concept of the infusion of the soul—at forty-four days for a boy, eighty-eight days for a girl—the idea of a debate drew me. In high school I'd earned five or six times as many debating trophies as I currently had sets of clothes. I would enjoy the chance to think and speak publicly on my feet again, could already savor the sense of power that came from a well-presented argument.

One Sunday afternoon I was upstairs feeding the three disabled girls biscotti soaked in apple juice when the gate bell rang. Monique stood inside the gate, asking to be let out. She'd been with us more than a month, and according to Sister Dominica, Monique hadn't said three full sentences to anyone yet. At Mass she'd stood in the back for a few minutes, then left in a hurry.

"*Dove vai?*" I asked her. "Where are you going?"

"I have a visitor," Monique replied, looking at the ground.

Across the street a tall man in a black suit and Roman collar stood looking at us. "A friend?"

"He is studying here—a seminarian. A friend of my family in Zaire." Monique still didn't smile. Perhaps she was ashamed to have a family friend see her pregnant. I hadn't known that to be a problem for other African women who'd stayed with us, though some of the Italians found the stigma unbearable. I opened the gate, and as I locked it behind her she crossed the street slowly, her head down. I went back upstairs to feed the children, hoping Monique's friend could cheer her up.

One of the sisters in community reminded me a bit of Niobe—about her same height and age, with some of her devil-may-care attitude, though with less confidence. Sister Timothy didn't have the smile, either, but she had begun to pay attention to me in community, offering to help mend my sari when it tore, to cover my books even before the brown paper had worn too thin. I'd heard she'd led a wild life before she joined—drugs, boys. Perhaps she sensed my hunger. We never talked much, but we had a connection I could feel.

One evening Sister Timothy and I happened to find ourselves in the little room where we stored medicine and other supplies. She looked at me and smiled. She took my hand in hers. I felt heat run through my whole body. She never said a word.

She kissed me, on the lips. No one had ever kissed me on the lips before. We hardly knew each other, but I didn't care. Her lips were luscious, her tongue magical. I had no idea how she knew I wanted this, how she knew that I would not object, would never report her. I would never even ask her what she thought. I thrilled at the way she made me feel—loved and alive. And wanting more.

During the ten-minute break between two consecutive class hours, Mark Attard stepped around chatting sisters in the aisle, headed— I thought—to the lounge, where he could get a cup of coffee. Lately I'd avoided him, staying at my desk to write or read during break. That day, out of the corner of my eye, I saw him dart around a group of sisters, push through a row of desks and chairs, and plant himself directly in front of me.

"Hey, Donata, why don't you do it?" He leaned on the chair behind him, his arms crossed over his chest, while nearby sisters turned their heads to watch, and to listen. "No lame excuses, please."

He looked so eager, so determined. I would have liked to please him—and to have shown off my brilliance.

"Father, I've found some sisters willing to participate"—as I said this he raised his eyebrows and smiled—"but nobody wants to argue in favor of legalization."

"Oh, Donata," he said, flinging his arms down and planting his hands on my desk, his face inches away from mine, "this is a debate." He shook his head. He was very close to condescension. "You take a side not because you believe in it but simply to help everyone understand all aspects of the issue."

"Yes, Father, I know that"—I looked him straight in the eye—"and I've explained it to everyone, but still no one will agree to argue for legalization."

"Well, then, you could argue legalization, and get one or two sisters to oppose it." It was so sensible. But this was Pandora's box.

"I have a particular problem with that."

"What?" I read exasperation in his tone of voice, in the way he threw his head down and rounded it up again.

"Father, it's because of where I live." He waited silently for me to continue. "I live in the same building as twenty-two young mothers, some of whom have newborn babies, and others who are still expecting. I understand all the fine distinctions we're making, but I'm not sure they would. What might happen if one of them heard, and they started discussing among themselves, 'Sister Donata spoke at school today in favor of abortion'? Do you see what I mean?"

"Well, yes. I guess I do." He paused for a moment. "No debate, then?"

"Sorry, Father."

"All right, quite all right." He headed for the lounge, and I determined not to think of it again. I'd told the truth, sort of.

The whole truth included the fact that I was a coward. I wasn't afraid of losing the debate. I was afraid of winning it. The maxim Mother repeated every time she spoke in public should have ended all argument: *The greatest enemy of peace is abortion, because if a mother can kill her own child, what is left to keep us from killing each other?* But the words that chased each other inside my brain were the words printed on the poster outside the women's refectory, also Mother's words: *Being unwanted is the greatest poverty.* Add overpopulation, the future of the planet, the exploitation of women—where

would that lead me? The Church proclaimed that abortion was always wrong, so it was. Sterilization, birth control—they were all
wrong. No need for debate. No need to think. Thinking would
only get me in trouble.

One day I followed Sister Timothy as she carried a basket of wet
sheets up to the roof to dry. I'd been waiting for a moment like this,
aching for it. I was new to lust and let it lead me.

When she put the basket down, I pulled her between the sheets
that were drying in the wind, and I wrapped my arms around her.
She kissed me again. I could hardly bear how good I felt, how my
entire body pulsed. *Heaven*, I thought. *Heaven must feel like this*.

The Wednesday afternoon Mark Attard showed *The Silent Scream*, he
began with a warning: "The pictures I am about to show you are very
graphic, so prepare yourselves, Sisters. I know of no more effective
tool than this film for convincing a woman that the child in her womb
is a true human person, thereby dissuading her from abortion."

The images on the screen showed an embryo, twelve weeks after
conception, with human form, snuggled in the palm of someone's
hand. I felt myself calming down, filled with the wonder of life, the
same wonder I felt looking at a starry sky or standing near the ocean.
The measured voice of the narrator filled the hall: "We are going to
watch a child being torn apart, dismembered, disarticulated, crushed,
and destroyed by the unfeeling, steel instruments of the abortionist."

The doctor on the screen displayed the medical implements:
"The instrument then will come into direct contact with the child
and with a pressure of approximately fifty-five or so millimeters of
mercury . . . the suction tip will then begin to tear the child apart.
The pieces of the body are torn away one by one until finally all that
remains are the shards of the body and the head itself. . . . The abortionist will then attempt to grasp the free-floating head of the child
in the uterus between the rings of this instrument. The head is then
crushed, the contents of the head removed, and finally the bones of

the head, and—" I put my hands over my ears and closed my eyes. A few minutes passed before I felt strong enough to look and listen again.

"The child's mouth is now open. . . . We can see the tip of the lethal instrument move back and forth as the abortionist seeks the child's body. Once again we can see the child's wide mouth open in a silent scream." I felt like I couldn't breathe. *O God, God, deliver us.*

At the end of the film, Mark Attard led a discussion, but I could concentrate only on the memory of those images. Why would anyone do this? That was the missing piece in this discussion. I couldn't imagine anyone having an abortion lightly. There were reasons women did this. Perhaps not good reasons, but certainly desperate ones. I was glad, in my very small way, to be doing something so that fewer women would turn to such an awful solution.

"Have you seen Monique's son?" Sister Philomene asked at lunch one bright May day. "He's so big, with puffy cheeks and a high forehead. His hair is soft and curly—he looks like an African prince."

"Wonderful," I said, eager to see the child. "And how's Monique?" Always quiet, Monique had grown visibly tense and withdrawn as her delivery drew closer. Sister Dominica had asked her several times if she wanted to give the baby up for adoption, and Monique had always replied that she wanted the baby.

"She's quiet and scared," Sister Philomene said. "She doesn't want to nurse the child, either. Sometimes she won't even look at him. I hope she doesn't start to shout and cry and push the baby like Stefania did. It's so sad when social services takes a child away."

We all nodded. More than one mother in our home had entered the darkness of postpartum depression. Later that afternoon, I took the steps to the top floor where the new mothers slept. As I climbed, I heard a baby's howls. When I entered her room, I saw Monique curled up in bed while her son bawled in a cradle.

"Monique, let me see your baby," I said, grabbing her blanketed feet and shaking them. "I hear he's gorgeous."

"He's there." Monique rolled to the other side. "Look if you want."

I took the crying baby in my arms and sat on Monique's bed. "He's lovely—such a cute little nose, and chubby cheeks. What's his name?"

"Figlio."

"Figlio?" Son? I put two fingers in his Pampers. "Look, his diaper is wet. Come, help me change him." She followed as I carried the howling Figlio to the little changing room next door.

"Why do you call him Figlio?" I asked as I removed the wet diaper.

"I had to give him a name before they'd give me the paper to take him home, but I didn't have a name, so I called him Figlio." I could hardly hear her above the baby's cries.

"Oh." I nodded toward the baby wipes, and Monique handed me one. "No, you do it," I said. "Figlio will be happier if his mamma cleans him up." Dropping the wipe on the floor, Monique backed into the corner of the room, tears streaming down her face. I changed Figlio quickly, then carried him to her. When she looked up, she looked not at the baby, but through the window.

"Look, *suora*," she said. "Someone has come." I watched as Monique's seminarian crossed the courtyard of the housing project and looked up at her window. Strange how he never rang the bell— it was always Monique who saw him and asked to be let out. He was Monique's only visitor, and they never went beyond the housing project compound.

"I'm sure he'll be happy to see Figlio." I wrapped him in a blanket and put a little blue cap on his head. But as I laid the child in his mother's arms, she shook, and the boy cried even more loudly.

"Take him, *suora*," she said, thrusting the child back. I cradled Figlio with one arm and Monique with the other as we walked downstairs. Figlio finally stopped crying when I returned him to his mother and opened the gate. For the first time, the seminarian crossed the street—smiling, with a long confident stride, puffy cheeks, and a high forehead, looking like a prince.

When Monique rang the bell to come back in, she smiled at the baby and told me, "His name is Pierre."

One night I wanted to be with Timothy so badly I could have burst. I would not seek her out, though. Except for that time on the roof, neither of us had deliberately sought the other. We never even tried to sit next to each other at meals or recreation. I was sure no one in the community suspected anything. We'd never spoken alone together. But if we happened upon each other in a secluded place, we touched, we kissed. Already four times our eager bodies had found each other.

That night I entered an empty, extra dormitory. The blinds were drawn. The room was so dark that I could not see my own hands, my feet. I bumped my shin on a bed near the door, sat on the bed, and began to pray. *God, You know how much I want Timothy right now. How everything in me wants her close, how my flesh hungers for her. I can't hide that from You. You know how much I want You, too, how I feel Your love when she holds me close. Please, please, can't You give me those feelings without her? You should be enough for me. Let me feel Your love, God. Let me feel Your love.*

As I sat on the bed, head in hands, someone cracked the door open. I couldn't tell who it was. I just sat quietly in the dark. Whoever it was didn't turn the light on, but closed the door and moved in my direction. Soon she was sitting beside me.

"Donata?"

"Timothy?"

"What do you want?" she asked.

"You."

She stretched me out on the bed, my back to the mattress. Fully clothed, she lay on top of me. She did not move. I did not move. I felt the weight of her body on mine, felt her breath on my cheek. She did not kiss me, did not stroke me, just lay there breathing.

I felt her heart beat against mine.

I had never felt anything so comforting, so all-enveloping. I lost all sense of time or place. I was just there with her, only her.

After a bit, I reached under her sari, near her heart. I opened the placket of her habit. I unlaced her bodice. Through the cloth of her chemise, I cupped her breast in my hand. She unfastened her chemise, pulled the front down, and dangled her breast before my mouth. When I'd had my fill, I readjusted her chemise, laced her bodice, and snapped her placket shut.

Still, I lay beneath her. Eventually she rose and left. From the moment she stretched me out on the bed, neither of us had spoken a word.

Nothing had ever, ever felt as good as that.

Four babies were to be baptized on a Sunday afternoon in May. The other three mothers were helping prepare for the party after the baptism. When I found Monique in the dormitory, Pierre was sleeping on one end of the bed, and she was sitting on the other, looking at something in her hands.

"Monique," I said, "we're decorating the refectory—balloons and streamers. Why don't you come down? We're having fun."

No response.

"Monique, you've got to be careful. Pierre could fall off like this. Give me your pillows." I placed one on either side of the sleeping child, then sat next to Monique, my hand on her knee. The object in her hands was a frameless photo of the seminarian.

"Monique," I asked, "is that seminarian who comes to see you good to you?"

"*Sí, suora,*" she said, averting her eyes.

"He seems to like the child."

"*Sí, suora.*" Monique put the photo in her skirt pocket.

"Monique, do you have any plans for when you leave here? Do you need help finding a job or a place?"

"*Suora,*" she whispered, her voice cracking, "I need God to forgive me."

I put my arm around her shoulder. "If you are sorry, God will always forgive you."

"*Suora*, for what I've done, there is no forgiveness."

"God always forgives. Do you want to go to confession?"

"It will do no good." She looked away, and her body began to shake with sobs. "I cannot forgive myself."

"We all make mistakes."

"I have thrown my life away."

"Is it the baby?"

She nodded.

"Monique, forgive me if I'm saying something that I shouldn't, but Pierre looks so much like that seminarian who comes to see you."

"*Sì, suora.*"

"Is it because the child's father is a seminarian that you think God won't forgive you?"

"*Suora*, there is more."

"What?"

"I cannot tell you."

"Monique, did that seminarian treat you badly? Did he rape you?"

"*Suora*, I did not want . . ."

"Then it is not your fault. God has nothing to forgive because you did nothing wrong."

"I should have known."

"Monique, you can't blame yourself. He is so much stronger. He is wrong, not you. Why do you even see him?"

"I have no one else."

"We'll help you. I'll talk to Sister Dominica."

"No, Sister. He will help me."

"Help you? He hurt you."

"He is a good man, Sister. I have no one else."

That afternoon, in the parish church several blocks away, I watched Monique's face as she responded to the priest's questions: "Do you reject Satan? . . . And all his empty promises? . . . Do you believe in God?"

Monique said "I do" in all the right places, but sadness had folded itself in creases on her face, and she never looked at Pierre, even when the priest poured the water on his head and he cried. The seminarian wasn't in the church, which angered me. At least he could have shown up, could have stood in the back of the church if he didn't want to take his proper place next to Monique. Sister Dominica had arranged for two Co-Workers to be Pierre's godparents, and the godmother had knit Pierre's white baptismal jumper, with little booties and a matching cap that had to be removed for the ceremony.

After the baptisms, Co-Workers packed mothers, babies, and sisters into their cars. Pierre's godparents drove Monique, Pierre, Sister Philomene, and me back to the convent. They'd brought gifts for the child, boxes wrapped in white paper with big white bows and silver glitter, which Sister Philomene and I held on our laps. That morning they'd dropped off a big white cake at the convent, with *Dio ti benedica, Pierre* written on the top in blue icing, blue frosting roses around the edges.

When the time came to cut the cake, Monique and Pierre weren't in the refectory. Sister Dominica sent me to look for them, but they weren't in the dormitory, the bathrooms, or the garden, nor had any of the ladies I asked seen her. Finally Sister Philomene told me that the seminarian had come and that all three of them had gone out together. The thought that he'd spoiled the party for them made me so angry that I had to run up and down the back staircase three times before I could go back in to tell Sister Dominica.

"What to do?" she said. "They'll come back. I'll keep some cake for them."

Monique and Pierre never came back. After a fortnight, Sister Philomene opened the white boxes with the silver glitter and put Pierre's gifts in the go-down for some other child. I fed the stale cake to the birds.

Of course, once I got over feeling good about the night with Timothy, I felt really bad. I was too ashamed of this sin to approach our regular confessor, who surely would have recognized me. Instead, I asked one of the students to leave school early one day. I told her exactly what I wanted—to go to confession in St. Peter's.

When we entered the massive basilica, I walked down the aisle of confessionals until I found one with *English* above the door. I knelt, told the priest I was a nun, and confessed that I had sinned sexually with one of my sisters. I told him I was sorry, that I wanted to keep my vow of chastity, that I never wanted to commit this sin again.

He gave me absolution and told me to say three rosaries for my sin. He said nothing more. I got up, found my companion, left the church, and got on the bus to go home.

At home I found Sister Timothy. I told her I couldn't do this anymore.

She nodded.

I asked, "How did you know to come to the dormitory that night?"

She said, "I just knew."

We said nothing more.

Near the semester's end, I was coming down the stairs at school, caught in the press of women in black, gray, white, blue, and even saffron-colored habits, veils framing faces from every continent, chattering in Spanish, French, Swahili, Italian, English, Malayalam, Tagalog, German, most of them heading back to their convents throughout the city for lunch. To avoid getting pulled into answering the gate or helping prepare dinner at home, we MCs shared a sack lunch in the basement lunchroom, then studied in the school library. As I headed for the basement, I spotted a tall African with a Roman collar—Monique's seminarian—speaking with sisters from the French section. Before he saw me, I ducked into the chapel.

I thought of walking right up and saying something, but I was still so mad that I was afraid I might hit him. I shouldn't make a scene. Mother always said everyone was entitled to a good name.

But I wanted to know where Monique and Pierre were, and he shouldn't have been hanging around school. *My God, help me know what to do.* I stepped out of the chapel, but he was gone. I ran down the entrance and into the street—not there. Useless to search the maze of side streets. Still inside?

I pushed against the crush of still descending sisters and asked the receptionist, *"Giorgio, hai visto un seminarista Africano quá?"*

"Sí, suora. He's gone."

Sister Elizabeth would know what to do, I thought. I ran up and knocked at the office of the sister in charge of the English section.

"Yes?" Sister Elizabeth looked up, her eyes kind and intelligent, as always.

"Sister, I need to talk to you about something."

"Sure," she said, indicating a chair at the side of her desk.

"Sister, could I close the door?"

"Of course."

"I don't know how to say this, but there was someone hanging around downstairs whom I don't trust."

She raised her eyebrows and put her hands in her lap, waiting for me to continue.

"An African seminarian was talking with some of the sisters from the French section. I know him from another situation, and I don't think it's a good idea for him to hang around here."

Sister Elizabeth looked at me. I hadn't given her much to go on.

"He was speaking with the sisters from the French section?" she asked.

"Yes, Sister, I think he's from Zaire."

"I suppose Giorgio saw him."

"Yes, he did, but the seminarian was wearing a Roman collar and standing just near the steps. I don't suppose he looked suspicious, so I don't think Giorgio even talked to him."

"Well, then, you should probably go speak to Soeur Elise in the French section. If you're still concerned after talking with her, let me know."

I took the flight of stairs up to the second floor slowly. In my three years at Regina Mundi, I'd never had reason to go up to the floor that housed the French and Italian sections. I'd seen Soeur Elise at all-school Masses. She was an older sister, short and squat, without a veil, with thin gray hair and round glasses.

When I reached the top of the stairs the corridor was empty, except for a short sister who was locking a door. "Soeur Elise?" My high school French was miserable. "Excuse me, but do you speak English?"

"A little," she said, tilting her head as she looked at me.

"I need to talk to you for just a second."

"Ah, but of course. Come in."

Her office had no pictures on the walls, but two large shelves full of books, a window that looked over the Tevere, and, on a small shelf in the corner, a wooden statue of an African Virgin with the Child in her arms. Soeur Elise pushed out a chair from behind the pine desk in the center of the room and rolled it next to a chair against the wall, which she indicated for me.

"Sister, I'm from the English section—"

"Yes, yes, I've seen you."

"Well, I have a concern that Sister Elizabeth thought I should share with you."

She leaned forward in her chair and nodded.

"Downstairs, just a few minutes ago, I saw a seminarian speaking with some of the sisters from the French section. I don't trust this man."

"*Ah non?*"

"Sister, my community cares for many single mothers and their babies. I believe that this seminarian is the father of the baby of a woman from Zaire who was staying with us, and I don't think he should be allowed to hang around school."

"I see." She squinted a bit and took off her glasses, tapping her hand with them. "A woman from Zaire, you say?"

"Yes, Sister."

"She was not, by chance," Soeur Elise said, wrinkling her upper lip and gesturing aimlessly with her glasses, "a thin woman, with a scar on her cheek?"

"Why, yes, she was."

"Was she called Georgette?"

"No, her name was Monique."

"Well, she could call herself anything." Soeur Elise tapped her hand with her glasses some more, then placed the glasses back on her nose. "Did she come to you in January, around the time of the exams?"

"Yes, Sister, she did."

"Is she still with you?"

"No, she left unexpectedly, about a month ago, with a little baby boy."

"Ah, Georgette, Georgette . . ." Soeur Elise spoke softly and looked out the window. "We wondered. . . . She disappeared. No sisters here knew where she was gone, nor the Italian sisters with whom she was boarding, and to speak the truth, they did not wish to be bothered much. We contacted her congregation, in Zaire, and they had no news of her, either." Looking at me and taking off her glasses again, she said, "Now we know."

"She was studying here?"

"Yes, doing very well. She was a fine girl, intelligent, sympathetic, always laughing. Now we know." She looked down at her lap and then up at me again. "Did she leave an address?"

"We don't know where she is."

"Ah, so sad." Then, with determination, "You need not worry about the seminarian here. I shall speak to Giorgio. He has surely seen him."

"Thank you, Sister." I got up to leave.

"Tell me," she said, still seated, "was the baby well?"

"Yes, healthy and strong."

"Good. I am glad."

"He was baptized the day they left us."

"And Georgette?"

"She seemed very strained. We never knew any of this."

"One never knows for sure, does one?" She stood to shake my hand, then turned again, looking first at the Virgin and then out through the window, across the Tevere.

I took the steps down very slowly. This new information dazed me. Monique, a sister? Finally I understood why she had been so depressed: She had lost what was most precious to her, her vocation, and she was convinced that God would not forgive. The seminarian—had he raped her as I'd assumed, or had they been friends, lovers? She must have been so lonely, boarding with Italian sisters who weren't even bothered when she disappeared. Maybe she'd needed someone to hold her.

And what about him? Had I judged him too harshly? Had he been lonely, too? Was he really a good man, as Monique said he was? Perhaps he'd made arrangements for her, found someone to take her in. If only I knew where he stayed, or at least his name. But if I started to inquire, people would get curious, and I had no right to cast suspicion on him. Maybe his sin was no greater than mine for what I had done with Timothy. Perhaps he and Monique had just gone further than they meant to one day.

I should have done more for Monique while she'd been with us, could have gone to see her and the baby more often, could have, perhaps, coaxed her into speaking. At least I could have let her know more surely that I cared.

As I took the steps to the basement, I asked myself if I should say anything to the sisters. Monique deserved her good name, too. If I told them, there would be endless talk at dinner, endless shaking of ·heads, more judging when no one knew what had really happened. If she'd wanted us to know, Monique would have told us. If I were in her place, I didn't think I'd want anyone to know.

During the days that followed, I carried the secret heavily, thinking of Monique, Pierre, and the seminarian as I rode the bus to school, as I fed the disabled children, as I sat in class—a floor below the room in which Monique had studied the things of God and had come to be known as a sister who laughed a lot. Her secret brought us close, somehow, even though she didn't know it. No matter what the full story was, I knew she felt guilty, and mourned what she'd lost. Bearing Pierre had required tremendous courage. I wondered what other options she'd had—a pregnant African nun alone in Rome.

In adoration, I knelt and cried quiet tears. I asked God to show them His love, to hold them all close. The more I prayed, the more I was sure God wanted only happiness for Monique and Pierre, and even for the seminarian. I imagined God embracing them, protecting them, waiting for Monique to realize He was there, waiting for her to break through her shame, waiting for the seminarian to turn to Him. I imagined God holding Pierre when Monique could not. God heard this baby's screams. God would wipe every tear away. That's what He'd promised, and I was going to hold Him to it.

18

EXPLOSION

SPRING 1989
ROME

Zzkkkwwwwwgrrrrrrrrrhhh. The noise jolted me awake and angry.

The din roared from the kitchen, just next to the dormitory, and echoed off the cement walls and high ceilings of the Primavalle convent. Whoever was working the blender hadn't even bothered to close the kitchen door. This was siesta time, not the moment to prepare *merenda* for the disabled girls. The noise of the blender sliced through what little remained of my defenses.

Eventually the bell rang, calling us from rest to tea. At table, teacup before me, I cried.

One by one, they saw me. One turned away, others looked down. Everyone grew silent. MCs didn't cry, especially not in public, but I didn't have the strength to hold the tears back any longer.

Finally, from the head of the table, Sister Dominica asked, "Sister Donata, what's the matter?"

I tried to calm myself but couldn't manage that, either. I spit the words out: "Aren't we entitled to sleep? We students get rest time only twice a week. Why does anyone have to make noise in the kitchen during rest?"

Sister Vincent turned toward me, smiling, and asked sweetly, "Did I disturb you? I didn't mean to disturb you."

"Of course you disturbed me. Who can sleep with all that noise?"

The rest of tea passed in the silence that I had wished for during rest time. I was ashamed of my outburst, but sickness and fatigue had sapped my resistance. I'd worn a knitted navy scarf for the past two months to hide the fact that I could no longer close the buttons on my collar. The glands in my neck weren't as big as oranges anymore, but more like tangerines. The doctor had advised rest as the only cure for mononucleosis, but, as the sisters said, nobody died of mono. I wasn't really sick. I'd taken an extra hour of rest that afternoon back in February when my fever had hit 103°, but no extra rest in the following two months. The fever had gradually subsided until all that remained was the constant pain in my neck, the ever-increasing fatigue, and the sore throat that made it difficult to swallow and sometimes even to speak.

On two different occasions, long before I'd gotten sick, I'd overheard Sister Joseph Michael state that American sisters always exaggerated sickness—and I knew she'd meant me to hear those words. Sister Dominica dragged her arthritic legs up and down the stairs dozens of times a day, and she did it with a smile and a good word for everyone. Before an example like that, resting would look self-obsessed. Besides, this was the last semester of our studies: in addition to regular schoolwork, we were preparing for the *de universa* exam, a thirty-minute oral exam before four professors who could ask us anything from our three years of studies. My days began at 4:40 A.M. and rarely ended before 11:00 P.M. There was no time to rest.

I wanted to be a good Missionary of Charity. I kept up with my schoolwork and housework and I took three buses across town every Sunday for choir practice at Tor Fiscale. I always said yes when Sister Joseph Michael asked me for some special work. The previous semester I'd written a long research paper: "The Presence of Jesus in the Eucharist and in the Poor in the Life of the Missionaries of Charity." In the process, I'd fallen in love once again with the heart of Mother's vision.

Yet while I'd been trying to live the words of the prayer we said each day—*to understand rather than to be understood, to love rather than to be loved*—lately I'd wanted someone to understand and love me, too. I hadn't been unfaithful to my vows since confessing my experience with Sister Timothy a year earlier. Still, a longing for intimacy left me feeling guilty and confused. I wanted someone to see me and say, "You're special." I wanted to be held. I wanted to kiss. These desires struck unpredictably. I'd be mopping the floor or studying the origins of the Eucharistic liturgy, and suddenly find myself longing for Niobe's smile. Father Attard had taught sexual ethics that fall. On the school library shelves, I'd found a sex education book—with pictures. I'd never seen a man and woman coupling before, and I couldn't get the images out of my head. Mononucleosis was commonly known as "the kissing disease," and I wondered if God was trying to tell me something.

Most of the time when I went to pray, the words hung dry in my mouth as I struggled to surrender to their rhythm. I was used to aridity in prayer. Mother and my confessors always said it didn't matter what a sister felt when she prayed; what was important was to persevere, to reach beyond the feelings for the love that resided in the will. I didn't know if I had any love left. These days I mostly struggled to stay awake at prayer. During midnight adoration on the eve of First Fridays, I often found myself staring at the Host wondering what I was doing in a dark chapel in the middle of the night kneeling before a piece of bread. My doubts frightened me. Jesus in the Eucharist was the center of my life, my source of strength, my true love.

In just over a month school would be over. Mother would charge us with training young novices to keep the vows, and I was scared. When Sister Dominica announced at dinner one evening that she would be on retreat during Holy Week, I saw an opportunity to get my soul in order. We didn't have school during Holy Week. I had to make that retreat.

Sisters made retreat once a year, when our superiors told us to. The timing wasn't good. MC students were expected to spend Holy Week packing Easter food parcels for families, organizing days of prayer for neighborhood groups, doing convent spring cleaning, and studying for the *de universa*.

When I asked Sister Dominica if I could join the retreat, she graciously acknowledged, to my embarrassment, that "anyone can see you're tired," then she said I'd have to ask Sister Joseph Michael and the other students. Though my absence would mean more work when they needed to study, Sister Dinah and Sister Christine both generously consented. When I phoned Sister Joseph Michael, her first question was, "What's wrong?" In all the time we'd worked together, I'd never phoned Sister Joseph Michael, had never asked for anything special.

Sister told me the retreat was just for superiors and sisters preparing for vows. I knew I was putting her in a tough spot. Giving the sister who worked with her special treatment would leave her open to charges of favoritism. She asked if I didn't need to study, and I said, "Sister, what I really need is to pray." I wondered if she noticed the crack in my voice.

Sister Joseph Michael asked to talk with Sister Dominica. When Sister Dominica eventually emerged from the office, she smiled and said, "We'll leave on Friday, when your school finishes."

Jesus had heard my prayer.

On the bus to Casilina, I looked out on a city beginning to blossom—myrtle, roses, oleander slowly waking up. After we finished the rosary, Sister Dominica told me that Sister Joseph Michael was very excited about this retreat priest, though he hadn't been ordained a year yet and this would be the first retreat he'd ever preached. Sometimes newly ordained priests said silly things, thinking they knew everything, the oil of ordination still damp on their foreheads. I didn't know what Sister Joseph Michael saw in this priest, but I didn't really care. If he was no good, I could just tune him out.

Instead, as I settled into the retreat I found myself waiting eagerly for Father Tom Hughes' talks. When this prematurely bald priest with the easy smile (who at a little over forty was relatively old for a new priest) spoke, I felt as though he was revealing Jesus' heart to me—not a heart crowned with thorns and flame, but a human heart that cared about the sufferings of others and took concrete action to heal them. Father Tom really got into the scenes where Jesus denounced the lawyers and Pharisees, almost as though he shared Jesus' indignation about hypocrisy, and I liked that, too.

During the retreat's extra prayer time, I found myself drawing closer to Jesus, and I felt this as Niobe and Timothy's gift to me. After my experiences with them, I'd begun to understand that at least part of my early failure to get close to Jesus had stemmed from His humanity. Until then, people hadn't been all that good to me, so how could Jesus, who was human, be good to me?

I now enjoyed holding Jesus in my mind and heart while I meditated, placing myself in the crowd as He preached the Sermon on the Mount, walking with Him through the Galilean hills. During prayer, I even stood with Mary, His Mother, at the foot of the cross. The Eucharist wasn't bread but Jesus, loving me up close and personal. Though others claimed my lack of feeling had been a blessing sent to make me strong, a test to prove my love for God, now it seemed God wanted to prove His love for me. As I reviewed the previous few years, I realized that being close to Niobe and Timothy had felt the way being close to God during deep prayer felt. How could God disapprove my forbidden love when He seemed to dwell there? These relationships had made me feel so much more alive, and we hadn't hurt anyone. Sorting it all out was confusing, but I couldn't deny that I'd broken my vows, and the desires I still felt were dangerous.

I decided to confess—and begin again. With God's help, I would find a way to dwell in His love that didn't involve breaking my vows.

Purple stole around his neck, Father Tom sat on his side of the confessional. I knelt and made the sign of the cross. "Bless me, Father, for I have sinned." Behind the screen I saw him lean closer. A general confession of the previous year's sins was traditional during retreat, and I decided to reach a little farther back in time to the sins with whose aftereffects I struggled most. A general confession didn't require detail, which made coming clean a little easier. "It is one week since my last confession, and today I want to ask God's forgiveness for all the times during the past few years when I've thought more about my own needs than the needs of others, when I've felt sorry for myself, when I haven't served with a generous heart, for the times I've been impatient with my sisters, and for the times I've bent the Rules, especially by showing affection in inappropriate ways. For these and all my sins, I ask God's forgiveness and the grace to begin again."

He paused. I imagined him trying to make sense of that last phrase—"shown affection in inappropriate ways." I wanted to crawl under the confessional.

"God looks at your heart, Sister, and He can't help but be pleased with your desire to serve Him." His voice was gentle, thoughtful. "You've got to be careful, though, to balance the love of others that Jesus talks about in the Gospel with the love of self. Doesn't He say, 'Love your neighbor as yourself'? It's not one or the other. We've got to do both." He'd completely ignored the Rule bending and the inappropriate displays of affection and gone straight to the crack in my soul—to the place where I didn't love myself. He waited for me to say something. "Sister?"

"Father, I'm not sure about that loving myself part."

"Well, you said you've thought about your own needs more than those of others. When you've thought about your needs, have you done anything to meet them?"

"Not much, though I did ask to come for this retreat."

"Then that was loving yourself. You're just as worthy of having your needs met as anyone else is." No one had ever spoken to me like that, not even Niobe.

"But the whole MC life is to serve others," I said. "I've been working on forgetting myself for years."

"Yes, that's the way most religious communities speak, but it's not what Jesus said, is it?" Now he was looking straight through the screen at me.

"Sometimes I do wonder about the way they interpret Jesus' words."

"In those moments when religious life is based more on control than on the Gospel, is it Christian?"

"I'll try to work on the loving myself part, Father."

"Good. Is there anything else?"

I shook my head.

"Then for your penance, ask God to show you how much He loves you."

Oh, if only I could feel God's love more and more. That would make everything so much easier.

"Now I absolve you of your sins in the name of the Father and of the Son, and of the Holy Spirit."

"Amen."

I got up from the kneeler, leaned over to his side of the confessional, and said, "Thank you, Father. I'm enjoying the retreat."

"Are you?" he said, throwing up his hands with a shrug. "I'm glad. I don't really know what I'm doing." He removed the purple stole. We both stood.

"You're a natural," I said.

"Do I detect an Irish accent?"

"No, Father, though a lot of people make that mistake. Some think I'm German or Dutch. Actually, I'm from Texas."

"Certainly had me fooled."

"When I first came to Rome as a postulant, many of the sisters couldn't understand me, so I tried to make it easier for them—pure vowel sounds, clear consonants." He chuckled, and I added, "You're from Australia, aren't you?"

"Yes," he said with a nod. "But I studied in Chicago. I loved America. Are you the only American on retreat?"

"Yes, Father. In fact, I'm the only American MC in Italy at the moment."

"Really? How does that feel?"

"A little strange sometimes. I miss not having someone around who really understands what I'm talking about when I speak of home—you know?"

"I'm the only Australian priest at my house. It can be kind of lonely," he said, then pulled out a list from his notebook. "Are you one of the superiors?" he asked. The list had three columns: superiors, tertians, and novices, with an extra name down at the bottom.

"No, Father, I'm the uncategorized." Pointing to my name, I said, "Sister Donata. I asked special permission to make this retreat, and I'm glad I did."

"So am I," he said.

His words made me feel oddly light-headed.

A few weeks after retreat, just before our exams, as Sister Dominica ladled soup into her bowl, she announced, "Mother is sending Sister Joseph Michael back to Calcutta to be in charge of the novitiate there."

She said more—something about Sister Agnel taking over as regional superior—but the rest passed over my head. *Sister Joseph Michael, going?*

"Sister Donata?" Sister Dinah poked me with her elbow. "Sister is asking if you're going to miss Sister Joseph Michael."

"Well, yes, of course. We worked together a lot."

"No more phone calls," Sister Philomene said. " 'Sister Donata, come here. Sister Donata, go there.' " Her Sister Joseph Michael imitation was too high-pitched. "Your life will be easier now, won't it?"

"Less exciting, anyway."

"Do you mean," Sister Vincent asked, shaking her head, "that you're actually going to miss her? She worked you like a horse."

I didn't answer. How were they going to understand? I hardly understood myself. Sister Joseph Michael had been terribly demanding, but she had believed in me. We'd worked together like partners. She'd recognized not only the part of me that loved being an MC but also the part that liked to think, the part that loved to give, the part that was energized by a challenge. In her own way she'd loved me, and I'd loved her.

When the day of the *de universa* exam arrived, I was nervous but felt prepared. I delivered my essay on the primacy of moral conscience before two professors and answered their questions for fifteen minutes. Then another two professors drilled me for fifteen minutes, free to ask any question from any course over the last three years. When I left the room, I felt fairly confident.

A few days later we dropped by school for the last time. Over the coffee table, Sister Elizabeth handed the three of us our diplomas—neither a bachelor's nor a master's degree, but a certificate of studies on stiff ivory paper, in beautiful calligraphy. Before we left, Sister Elizabeth brushed away a tear as she hugged us good-bye. Riding the bus down Via Nazionale toward San Gregorio, we were particularly silent, our thoughts focused not on the diplomas, so carefully protected in heavy folders and tissue paper, but on the little slips we'd soon receive from Mother—our new assignments.

Every MC who had studied at Regina Mundi, beginning with Sister Fatima and Sister Martin long before I'd joined the sisters, had been assigned to formation work. We had novitiates in six cities: Calcutta, Rome, Nairobi, Manila, San Francisco, and Warsaw. I longed for something different and exciting—not Rome. The novitiate in Tor Fiscale had become stiff since Sister Marie Therese had taken over as superior. Staying in Rome would also keep me in proximity to Niobe, and I didn't need that.

Walking from the bus stop past the Colosseum and up the steps of the basilica, I remembered the first time I'd climbed those steps more than ten years earlier as a postulant, eager to give my life to God. Now, at age thirty-one, as a finally professed sister, I was climbing those stairs to accept a mission from Mother to help other sisters give their lives to God. For a moment I let myself hope that Mother wouldn't assign me formation work after all—I was still four years short of the *Constitutions'* required age for novice mistress. *Give me the strength, Lord, to accept whatever You have planned for me, and to do it as it should be done. My heart, my will—it's all Yours.*

"Well, are we ready?" Sister Dinah forced a smile before ringing the gate bell.

The sister who opened the gate told us that Mother was alone and expecting us. After a short prayer in the chapel, the portress led us to Mother's room.

"*Ah cha.*" Mother's eyes gleamed as she blessed each of us. She seemed energetic, bright, without any trace of tiredness or concern. "I hear you've finished your studies," she said, smiling.

"Yes, Mother," Sister Christine said. "We just received our diplomas."

"Very good. Let Mother see." Mother opened the envelopes carefully, removed the cardboard cases, and examined each diploma. She seemed pleased and took her time. As each moment passed, I felt my heart beating faster. Sister Christine seemed to be having trouble breathing, and the color had completely drained from Sister Dinah's face. All we really wanted was to know where we were going.

"Summa cum laude," Mother said, pointing to my diploma. "What does that mean?"

Mother had been headmistress of the Loreto school in Calcutta. She knew what summa cum laude meant. "It means I did well on my exams, Mother."

"*Ah cha,*" she said, with a twinkle in her eyes. "Give me all those papers, too." She nodded at the large envelopes, embossed with the

Regina Mundi emblem, that poked over the tops of our bags. Mother noticed everything. As we handed over our transcripts, our student IDs, and the *tessere* with our photos and the scores of all our exams, Mother said, "I'll take them to Calcutta."

I winced. I hoped Mother hadn't noticed. I'd assumed we would keep our diplomas. We hadn't even shown them to the sisters in community yet. I tried to smile at Mother, recalling that any MC worth her name should be relieved to be finished with books and papers so she could get back to work.

"Now Mother has something for you." Her eyes glinted with the mischievous look she reserved for passing out assignments. We knelt, but there wasn't much floor space around Mother's stool, and I couldn't find anywhere to put my right knee, so I balanced on my left in the doorway, right knee dangling in the air above the step that led into Mother's office. For support, I grabbed the back of Sister Christine's sari. Mother opened the drawer of her desk and took out three papers, each a quarter the size of a normal sheet of paper, with a sketch of a child nestled in the hand of God. Turning the first paper over, Mother looked up and said, "Sister Dinah?"

Raising a finger, Sister Dinah replied, "That's me, Mother." Her face was even whiter than usual.

Mother looked Sister Dinah straight in the eyes, looked down at the paper again, and announced, "Mother is sending you to Manila." Smiling broadly, Sister Dinah took the paper from Mother's hand and bent her head for a blessing.

"Sister Christine?"

"I, Mother."

Mother lingered over the paper for a moment, then smiled softly. "Mother is sending you to Nairobi."

Sister Christine's hand shook as she took the paper, but her face relaxed. "Thank you, Mother." When Sister Christine shifted to bow, I lost my grip on her sari and teetered toward the step.

"And Sister Donata?" I looked up, trying to regain my balance. I recognized the very particular expression then on Mother's face. I'd seen it countless times during assignment ceremonies, where she first got very serious, wrinkling her brow and pursing her lips, and then grinned widely, so I already knew which words would come next, and my heart sank. "Mother is sending you very far." I tried to smile. "To Tor Fiscale!" I took the paper and bowed my head in one quick motion, not wanting Mother to see my tears.

"Thank you, Mother," I said. She blessed me, then shooed the three of us out of her office with an "*Ah cha*, Sisters."

On the bus home, I stared at the paper. Though I tried to keep them in, tears smeared Mother's words. Why did everything always have to be so hard?

19

MISTRESS

"Sister Bertram," I said, trying to remain calm before the spindly Croatian teenager who had—without any significant competition at all—quickly established herself as my most difficult novice. Just before we'd gotten up from lunch, she had told her fellow novices that the hospital hadn't allowed her to visit the sick that morning. "Sister Bertram," I repeated, "I told you to go to the night shelter at Via Carlo Cattaneo to wash sheets. Why did you go to the hospital?"

"Oh, no, but Sister, surely you make a mistake." Sister Bertram smiled as she said this. "I thought it was strange, you telling me to go to the hospital like that, in the morning," Sister Bertram continued in a high-pitched singsong, "but I am obedient, and I do not question, so I took my partner and I went."

Other novices began to return to the refectory with their clean plates. I beckoned Sister Bertram into the dormitory. "First," I said, hearing my voice rise and trying to lower it again, "you know very well that I did not tell you to go to the hospital. I told you to go to

Carlo Cattaneo. Second, you know we never go hospital visiting in the morning. Third, if you thought it was strange, you should have asked."

"But Sister Marie Therese says we must never ask. Obedience is blind." Sister Bertram smiled, tilting her head to the left, to the right. Sister Bertram had come to the community by personal decree of the Blessed Virgin of Medjugorje. The teenage visionaries in her hometown delivered messages from Our Lady to hundreds of pilgrims each day. These four girls and two boys, some of them classmates of hers, had told Sister Bertram that the Blessed Virgin had specially chosen her to wear the sari of the Missionaries of Charity.

In the dormitory, this young apostle of Mary shook her finger at me and said, "Sister, you have surely made a mistake."

"Sister Bertram, you have been disobedient." An accusation like that would have silenced most novices. I was waiting for Sister Bertram's "Thank you, Sister. Sorry, Sister."

"Oh, no, Sister," she said instead. "I only did what you told me to. You very clearly said, 'Go to the hospital.' "

I didn't have the heart to continue. "Tomorrow you will go to Carlo Cattaneo," I said, shaking my finger at her, hoping I looked stern.

"Yes, Sister. Anything you say." Sister Bertram swung her skinny hips behind her as she walked away.

I had handled that badly. Any other novice mistress would have found a way to make Sister Bertram understand. At that first impudent reply Sister Marie Therese would have delivered a twelve-minute scolding, complete with steely eyes and quotations from Mother, and then she would have assigned her double penance. Sister Bertram was playing me, and I didn't know how to call her out. Since I'd studied, sisters often assumed that I had particular insight into how to form the sisters, but I'd studied theology, not behavior modification.

· · ·

Each month when I approached Sister Marie Therese to renew my permissions, I kissed the floor in front of her feet and spoke my fault. I asked forgiveness for not giving good example to the novices, for not always being with them during manual work and recreation, for not having found enough time to prepare my classes well.

After she gave me my penance, renewed my general permission, and told me to rise, Sister Marie Therese began each month by telling me, "You don't correct them enough. Today's novices are more hardheaded, more worldly, more stubborn than those in the past, and they must be broken."

Like Sister Nirmala in the Bronx, Sister Marie Therese was a convert from Brahmin Hinduism with the reputation for holiness that always accompanied such a conversion story, but her attitude angered me. The first month, I'd responded, "Sister, I understand the novices must be taught." I swallowed, trying to gauge how far I could press this. "And I probably don't correct them enough, but—" She sat impassive on her stool, posture perfect, face expressionless. "But is breaking them what they really need? So many of them come from difficult family situations and are insecure anyway, and—"

"And that's why they need to be corrected, put in their place. Their parents haven't taught them and they have too many problems. You must be firm with them. It is the only way." Sister Marie Therese's novices were well behaved, but they lived in fear. I could see it on their solemn faces, hear it in their self-conscious laughter.

Before too long, Sister Marie Therese started in on specifics. Sister Phoebe must not be allowed to sleep during meditation. If she continued to doze, I was to take her to the kitchen, slice an onion, and have her apply the juice to her eyes. Sister Marie Therese had done this with one of her novices, and it had worked wonders. I had had long talks with Sister Phoebe about prayer and sleep but never felt negligent for failing to mention onion juice in the eyes.

Sister Marie Therese had noticed that another novice avoided heavy work—never carrying or stacking boxes on begging day, but always washing the fruit and vegetables instead. I explained that this novice suffered severe back pain when lifting. Sister Marie Therese was unmoved by my assertions that this sister was always among the first to volunteer for extra work that didn't involve lifting and that even when in pain she was cheerful and obedient. "If she can't do what everyone else does," Sister Marie Therese replied, "she can't be an MC."

Demanding that everyone be able to do everything sounded silly, but Sister Marie Therese had a point. In community when the same sisters were left with the heavy work all the time, they often grew to resent it, making community life difficult. MC life seemed posited on the assumption that we should all be treated exactly the same in everything. But why couldn't we teach the physically strong compassion and cooperation, instead of demanding from the physically weak what their bodies were unable to deliver?

I knew Sister Marie Therese waited for me each month to speak my fault for being too soft with the novices. I knew that I never would.

Sister Marie Therese did do one thing for which I was particularly grateful: that first month she let me sleep an hour extra each morning, and in Tor Fiscale I rarely needed to stay up at night. Over the weeks my glands shrank almost back to normal.

In early August sisters from across Rome gathered to celebrate Sister Dominica's feast day. We were downing whole-wheat chapattis and spicy egg bhaji, talking loudly with sisters we hadn't seen for a while, when Mother rapped the table with the butt of her knife, then spoke into the immediate silence. "Tomorrow Mother is going to Sweden," she said. No news here. Mother traveled a lot. And Sweden wasn't one of her more exciting destinations. We didn't even have sisters there yet.

Sister Agnel, who seemed to be doing tolerably well as our new regional superior, leaned over her plate and added, "Mother will be attending a gathering of all the different Christian religions." She paused a moment. "And Sister May will accompany Mother."

Sister Marie Therese's eyebrows rose. Postulants didn't accompany Mother. As I looked for Sister May, I realized that, of course, she wasn't there. Postulants didn't even rate breakfast with Mother. Sister Agnel explained, "The meeting is in Sister May's hometown, and the people there have asked for her."

Dumbfounded silence followed. We never knew whom Mother would choose as a traveling companion—most often it would be the regional superior, but sometimes a different sister would accompany Mother, usually a senior sister, nearly always a sister with final vows, never a postulant or a novice. Even though sending Sister May (an amiable, mature sister who had been a doctor before joining) might inspire other Swedish women to join, the news was still stupefying.

From the far end of the table I decided to break the silence, saying the first thing that came to mind. "My sister lives in Sweden, Mother."

"*Ah cha,*" Mother said, turning to Sister Agnel.

"I didn't know your sister was in Sweden," Sister Marie Therese said, looking piqued that I had a piece of information she didn't.

"Dorothy's a computer programmer for a Swedish telecommunications company. She's been in Stockholm two years now." I chewed slowly on my chapatti, and Sister Marie Therese continued to stare at me. "She'll probably go back to Dallas next year," I added. Sister Marie Therese lifted her chin and turned to the sister on the other side of her.

Before long, Mother rapped on the table once more, looked straight at me and said, "Sister, Mother is taking you to Sweden."

"Excuse me, Mother?" I hadn't expected that at all.

"Phone your sister and tell her to meet us at the airport," Mother said. Then, turning to Sister Agnel but speaking loudly enough for everyone to hear, she added, "The other sister is too young." Sister May and I were probably pretty close in age, but I wasn't going to argue my good fortune. I was going to travel with Mother. I'd be close to her, alone with her. Maybe I'd get a chance to ask her advice about my novices. Perhaps I could even be helpful to the woman who had shown me how to please God.

That evening in the airport's VIP lounge as we awaited boarding,

Sister Agnel pulled me aside and opened my bag. "Take these," she whispered, stuffing two bricklike boxes into my bag. "Make sure you always have them with you." The weight pulled my arm down.

"What's that?" I asked.

"Miraculous Medals. Make sure you don't run out." I should have known. Mother loved to give people these medals, which Our Lady had asked St. Catherine Labouré in 1830 to have cast and distributed throughout the world. Many people experienced cures after wearing Miraculous Medals.

"And take this, too." Sister Agnel poked me in the side with a small rectangular plastic box with several compartments. "Mother's medicine. Make sure she takes it on time, but be discreet. Mother doesn't like to take it because it reminds her that she's sick." I nodded. A handwritten schedule was taped to the top of the box: *Blue pill, 6 a.m. and 6 p.m. Green capsule with lunch. Two white pills 10 p.m.* Since her third heart attack two years earlier, Mother's energy had steadily declined, and her ankles were often swollen. Even so, she did more than any seventy-eight-year-old I'd ever met.

We were the last passengers to board. They settled us in the first-class seats to which airlines always upgraded Mother, hoping to avoid the hubbub that would inevitably follow upon the knowledge that Mother Teresa was seated in coach. One by one, the flight attendants came to speak with Mother. One begged prayers for a daughter who had left the Church; another told Mother that her life had been changed after feeding babies in Shishu Bhavan in Calcutta; a third asked for a "small note for my mother, who is very sick," to which Mother immediately responded by writing on a little card from her bag, *Jesus loves you very much. Suffering is the kiss of Jesus. God bless you, Mother Teresa.* Each time, Mother turned to me and asked, "Medals, Sister?" and I placed a few Miraculous Medals on her outstretched palm. Before giving the medals out, Mother kissed each one.

As the plane taxied, Mother reached into the seat pocket in front of her and took out the *International Herald Tribune* they'd offered us when we boarded. I hadn't seen a current newspaper up close in years.

"Another flood in Bangladesh," Mother said, shaking her head.

"And still that war and famine in Ethiopia." She opened the paper more widely, offering me one end to hold, and pointed to a picture of a child with a distended stomach. "People are suffering so much. The sisters will have plenty to do." The picture resembled the photo of the child in the article in which I had first read the name Mother Teresa.

"Mother," I said, "that picture reminds me of—"

"Of so many poor in the world, Sister, so many poor." I kept quiet as Mother folded the paper and reached under the seat for her bag. She removed some letters, a pad, and a pen. Mother had work to do. I would talk later.

Inside my bag I found a book underneath the medals and medicine. Sister Marie Therese had given me *Sharing the Darkness* to see if it was suitable for the novitiate library, and I was about half through. The book was written by a doctor named Sheila Cassidy who had worked in Chile, where she had been imprisoned and tortured for having treated a wounded revolutionary. After her release from prison, she entered a cloistered monastery for several years, then left religious life to work with the hospice movement. In her book, she tempered the austerities of religious life with humanity and common sense. Toward the end of a chapter in which she wrote about her experience of exhaustion, depression, and burnout, I read,

> Is it *really* the will of God that we should deny our humanity and work ourselves into the ground? I suspect not. . . . The world longs for its Mother Teresa figures because it can put them safely on a pedestal and admire them, but it feels quite differently about nurses (who do the same work) belonging to a trade union and protesting about their salaries!

I closed the book and shoved it in my bag, realizing how often I'd thought something similar. Mother never stopped working, and neither did we. Mother always rushed to be first in the chapel for Morning Prayer, then she often slept during meditation. I'd often thought that we might serve the poor better and with less irritation if we weren't dragging ourselves around.

During a quick meal of gnocchi and pork, Mother listened to a middle-aged Italian man across the aisle tell her about his son's drug problem. When the flight attendant swept in to take the trays, Mother leaned forward, close to the attendant's face. "I need your help," Mother said.

The attendant quickly replied, "Oh, yes, Mother Teresa, anything."

"All the leftover food, the food that people haven't opened but that you will have to throw away anyway," Mother explained, opening her hands wide, "please could you tell the people in the plane to collect it, and I will give it to the hungry?" Mother made this request each time she traveled by air. I'd met Mother at Fiumicino many times when she'd arrived with boxes and bags filled with mini candy bars, apples, crackers and cheese, little packets of instant cream, of sugar and salt.

But this time, the flight attendant tried a diplomatic refusal. "I'm sorry," she said, "our rules don't allow it." Mother's appreciation for rules was unique in my experience. Mother adhered absolutely to the *Constitutions* of the Missionaries of Charity, but the laws of nations, cities, towns, and airlines held no sway—especially when Mother could finagle something for the poor.

Mother sat back in her seat, widened her smile, and sharpened the twinkle in her eye. "Just tell them that Mother Teresa is on board and that she has asked this favor for those who have no food." Continuing to smile, Mother locked the flight attendant's eyes with a penetrating gaze. "It's just a little thing," she said, "and anyone can do it."

The flight attendant turned to her companion, who had overheard the conversation. They raised their eyebrows at each other. Until now, they'd guarded the fact of Mother's presence, hoping to avoid commotion. But they didn't want to refuse Mother Teresa, and it was clear that Mother was going to persist until she got what she wanted.

Soon one attendant stationed herself at the curtain between

business and coach and remained there throughout the flight. People in business class who had overheard the discussion brought their extra food directly to Mother, and she gave each of them a medal. She told me to ask a flight attendant for a trash bag. Meanwhile, another attendant wandered through coach, asking for donations.

When we landed in Stockholm, the Catholic bishop, a Salvation Army major, a Lutheran pastor, a Catholic priest, several photographers, and Dorothy were all waiting for us. Dorothy looked a lot like I did before I joined, except better: Her hair was very well trimmed, and she wore a little makeup and a very nice suit.

Amid popping flashbulbs and rounds of handshaking, which Mother tried to avoid by folding her hands to her chest in the prayerful Indian style of greeting, Dorothy and I spoke.

"When I asked for time off at work because my sister was coming to Sweden with Mother Teresa, they asked me why I didn't just ask for an extra day at the lake, and couldn't I think of a better excuse, because they know I don't go to church," Dorothy said, a sparkle in her eyes.

At this moment a flight attendant carrying three trash bags approached Mother.

Mother told her, "God bless you," then turned to the Salvation Army major. "I'm sure you could use this. Don't you feed the poor?" The major, who had no idea what was happening, accepted the trash bags from the flight attendant. It didn't matter to Mother that the little packets of salt and the handful of candy bars wouldn't alleviate world hunger. What was important was that nothing go to waste, especially not an opportunity to remind people of the poor.

Meanwhile, the bishop approached me. "We'll be going now," he said. "I'm so sorry that I haven't found a convent for you and Mother as she requested, but the convent nearest Örebro is more than two hours away, so you'll stay with the Lutheran pastor and his family."

I was beginning to understand my role. I was like the secretary of an important person. Practical questions, which people didn't want to address to the important person, were addressed to the secretary, who spoke to and for the important person. This made the secretary something of an important person, too.

I whispered, "Mother, it's time to go."

"*Ah cha*," she said with a nod, then spotted Dorothy. "You must be the sister."

Dorothy extended her hand, and Mother accepted it.

"So we are ready to go now. Come along," Mother said.

"Come along?" Dorothy echoed.

"Of course. You'll be coming with us." Mother turned and headed out, not waiting for a response.

"I didn't know I was going with you," Dorothy whispered to me. "Why didn't—"

"Come along now," Mother repeated as she turned around.

Dorothy shrugged, and the Salvation Army major, hauling two trash bags, led the way out, followed by the priest, who carried the third.

During the first few miles in a large van, Mother nodded off several times, even in the middle of her own sentences. I wanted to speak with Dorothy, whom I hadn't seen in four years, but we were all trying to be quiet so Mother could rest. Still, Mother woke and asked, "Are we reaching yet?" The bishop answered something about how beautiful the countryside was. When Mother woke again she repeated, "Are we reaching yet?" The Salvation Army major told her how happy people would be to see Mother the next day. She dozed off again, head on my shoulder, and everyone kept very quiet. Eventually Dorothy leaned over and whispered in my ear, "Is it real? Pinch me."

I pinched, and she pinched back. Mother snoring on my shoulder, a ride in a van through the forests of Sweden still light at nearly midnight in August, my sister at the airport, VIP lounges, alone with Mother—it was a dream, wasn't it?

When we pulled into the dark driveway of the Lutheran pastor's home in Örebro after two and a half hours of driving, I asked the

Salvation Army major the time, and he told me it was 12:20. The pastor's wife, two grown sons, and a daughter came to the van to greet us, all of them as tall and thin as birch trees grown too close together. All I could think of was bed, but Mother seemed to have regained her energy. After the priest said he'd be back in the morning at eight to pick us up, the pastor's wife asked if we'd like something to eat, and Mother said yes.

Inside, I watched Mother smile as the pastor's wife removed a tray from the refrigerator and placed it gently on the brick island in the middle of the kitchen. Then Mother's face drooped. On the tray were ten delicately stacked open-faced finger sandwiches, each about an inch and a half square, some with cheese, others with smoked salmon. Mother wouldn't have asked to eat unless she was really hungry, and now I saw her calculating the division of the ten delicacies among the eight of us.

The pastor asked Mother for a prayer, but she deferred to him, and after everyone had a few bites, Mother watched as the pastor's wife put the tray and its two remaining sandwiches back in the refrigerator.

I leaned close to Mother's ear. "If Mother is still hungry—"

"No, Sister."

The pastor took Dorothy off to the study, and his wife led Mother and me to a medium-size room with delicately flowered wallpaper and twin beds with pink chenille bedspreads.

"I hope this will do," she said.

"Thank you very much," Mother said, folding her hands at her chest and bowing. "Thank you. God bless you."

The pastor's wife shut the door, and I put our bags down on the armchairs while Mother set a lamp on the floor and began pushing the nightstand.

"Mother, may I help you?"

"A chapel, Sister. We must have a chapel." We dragged the nightstand to the center of the room, and Mother asked for her handbag. Reaching inside, she pulled out a plastic statue of Mary, about four inches high, the greenish yellow kind that glows in the dark. Mother kissed the statue, then placed it gently at the center of the nightstand. "Do you have a candle, Sister?"

"No, Mother, but I saw flowers in the living room."

"Bring one."

In the kitchen I filled two glasses with water, then picked out a bright red zinnia from the arrangement on the coffee table and put it in one of the glasses. Back in the room, I handed the makeshift vase and flower to Mother.

"*Ah cha*, very good, Sister."

I took the medicine box from my bag. Mother's last dose had been scheduled for ten, and I could have given it to her if I had remembered, but I'd been too excited and distracted. Taking out the appropriate pills, I offered them to Mother with the other glass of water.

"Not now, Sister. After Night Prayer."

"But, Mother, it's already so late."

Mother knelt in front of the nightstand. "In the name of the Father and of the Son and of the Holy Spirit." I put the glass and the medicine on top of the other nightstand, then knelt down next to Mother. There was something strangely sweet and weirdly intimate about kneeling in front of a nightstand with a fluorescent Mary between twin beds with pink bedspreads in the house of a Lutheran pastor at one in the morning. Mother led the prayers and I answered. Just Mother and me and Our Lady.

When we finished our prayers, I offered Mother the medicine again, and she took it. In the meantime, I turned down Mother's bedspread and set her nightdress on the pillow. When I turned around, Mother was examining a digital clock on the remaining nightstand, turning it over in her hands.

"Sister," she said, "please set the alarm." This was a simple clock, like the one I'd had near my bed before I joined the sisters, but all MC clocks were still the windup kind, and Mother was obviously confused by all the buttons.

"Yes, Mother. What time shall we get up?"

"Father is coming at eight, so we should have breakfast by seven-thirty." Mother counted on her fingers. "Before that we need to finish our Morning Prayer and meditation, and also spiritual reading, which means," she concluded, looking up at me, "that we should start prayers at six. We'll also need to make the beds, so we should get up at five-thirty."

"But, Mother, it's nearly one-thirty now."

"Yes, Sister." She dug in her bag again and handed me a small bottle of holy water. I blessed the beds. After saying her prayers by the side of the bed, Mother began to snore moments after her head hit the pillow. I set the alarm for 6:40. *May God forgive me.*

When the clock sounded some five hours later, Mother's "Let us bless the Lord" was nearly simultaneous with the clock's electric buzz.

"Thanks be to God," I answered, rolling out of bed and onto the pink shag.

Mother led the prayers in a loud voice, with her usual conviction, and I answered, very groggy.

Mother finished dressing before I did and went off to the bathroom. While she was gone, I quickly made her bed, then mine. When I turned around Mother was already kneeling in front of the "chapel," her hands folded and head bowed in front of our Swedish altar. As I hurried to the bathroom, Mother looked up and pointed to the clock. "Sister, it's late."

"Yes, Mother," I said. I grabbed my toothbrush, dashed to the bathroom, rounded the corner in the hall, and rammed into Dorothy.

"What's happening?" she whispered, eyes barely open, standing just outside the study door. "Isn't it very early?"

"We're going to say our prayers. Mother wants to have breakfast about seven-thirty."

"Uhhh," she groaned. Dorothy had always been the late sleeper in our family. She closed the study door behind her.

In the bathroom I remembered Mother's medicine, so I stopped in the kitchen to get a glass of water. When I returned to the bedroom, Mother knelt on the carpet, already halfway through Morning Prayer. "Where have you been? It's late."

"Sorry, Mother," I said, reaching for the pill container. "I just went to get some water for your medicine."

Mother took the medicine and water, and I looked down to Mother's open prayer book, the place marked by a small card with a picture of Jesus' face, crowned with thorns. At the bottom of the card, Mother had written in her own round script, *Jesus, I love You so much*. I was embarrassed to have stumbled across something so intimate. I also felt privileged. The card confirmed what I already knew—that Mother's love for Jesus animated everything she did, that it was the source of all her energy—and seeing it written in her own hand made my heart beat faster.

"Sister?" Mother handed me the empty glass, then we continued the prayers where she had left off.

When we reached the point where Mother should have begun the Prayer Before Meditation, she sat back on her heels, turned to me, and said, "We should have spiritual reading now. We can make meditation quietly in the car."

I nodded.

"You read," Mother said, handing me her book. "First from mine, then from yours."

Aloud, from mine? Why couldn't we have silent spiritual reading, each from her own book, like usual? I supposed Mother was tired—it would be easier for her if I read aloud, but how in heaven's name was I going to read Sheila Cassidy's criticisms to Mother? I supposed I could start at the beginning—there was no overt criticism of Mother there—but Cassidy's *Sharing the Darkness* was an undeniably modern book on every page, not the sort Mother would approve. And what if she told me to start where I had left off?

I opened the book Mother passed to me, a collection of the writings of St. Peter Julian Eymard, a nineteenth-century French priest.

Mother slumped on the rug next to me and closed her eyes. I read slowly, carefully: "'Belong entirely to God through love, entirely to your neighbor through a gracious charity, entirely to the divine Eucharist by the offering and sacrifice of your whole self.'" I'd avoided what I secretly termed devotional drivel ever since my first profession, when I'd been allowed to choose my own books. But Peter Julian was speaking Mother's language of simple love for Jesus, and it fit this morning. I silently begged, *Please, Mother, let me read this book to you all morning. Forget about my book.*

"'Be the apostle of the divine Eucharist, like a flame which enlightens and warms, like the Angel of His heart who will encourage those who love Him and are suffering.'" I read even more slowly, and Mother's head began to nod. "'Please pray that, like the bread of the sacrifice, I may lose my life, my substance, my personality, to be changed into the spirit and life of Jesus, retaining only a human appearance, humiliation and poverty.'" I was beginning to lose patience with Peter Julian. I wondered what Sheila Cassidy might say to him. I droned on, and soon Mother's chin was on her chest.

A nagging voice inside me asked, *Why are you reading books that you can't read in front of Mother anyway?* My excuse was that I hadn't chosen it—Sister Marie Therese had given it to me. *But you agree with it, don't you?* I just swallowed and tried to keep my voice even, continuing to pray that Mother not wake up. At seven-thirty I just stopped.

Mother looked up. "Keep reading, Sister."

"Mother, it's time," I said, nodding toward the clock.

"But what about your book?" she asked.

As I reached for it, she shook her head and said a concluding Hail Mary. Never was I happier to repeat, "Holy Mary, Mother of God, pray for us sinners."

That morning we had Mass in the little Catholic church. Mother gave out Miraculous Medals to everyone we met—all the people at Mass, people on the street, everyone who crowded around. Dorothy carried half the medals in her bag to make the weight tolerable, and when I ran out she restocked me.

Back at the house, after a lunch of light soup, Mother returned to our room. There hadn't been much for breakfast, either. I was still hungry, and I was pretty sure Mother was hungry, too. Our hosts must have read the magazine myths about Mother Teresa eating only a slice of bread and a banana for breakfast and a plate of rice for lunch. When no one was looking, I swiped two bananas and an apple from a fruit basket on the living room table.

In the bedroom, Mother looked up, hands in her bag. She nodded at the fruit in my hands and smiled. "*Ah cha*, Sister. Where did you get those?"

"From a basket in the living room."

"You didn't ask for them, did you?"

"No, Mother, they were on the table. They must have left them there for anyone who wants them."

"Very good," she said. Then she drew her hands out of her bag and opened them to reveal several caramels and a couple of peppermints. Reaching in again, she pulled out a few small wrapped chocolates. "Take the apple and some of these to your sister," Mother said.

When I came back, Mother was halfway through a banana, and several crumpled candy wrappers lay on the nightstand next to the digital clock.

That afternoon, after several meetings, Mother asked for a medal for a teenager with a bright purple Mohawk.

"Sorry, Mother, there aren't any more."

"Sister," Mother said, "I need to give him Our Lady." She looked at me with a frown that made me feel two inches tall.

"I'm sorry, Mother."

She just shook her head, then turned to the boy. "God bless you," Mother told him, and he smiled.

That evening, Mother looked so small behind the podium, which came to the middle of her neck. Though thousands of people gazed on her from every corner of the stadium, applauding ever more loudly, Mother was still looking down when the archbishop raised his hand for silence. Then Mother began. "The poor people are great people. Once someone told me about a Muslim family who had no food. So I took a bag full of rice to them, and the mother thanked me, and then I watched as she divided the bag in two. I asked her what she was doing, and she told me, 'They are hungry, too.' A Hindu family, next door. They were hungry, too."

Dorothy, hands in her lap, leaned forward, eyes fixed on Mother. No one in the crowd moved. I'd heard this story countless times, but each time it still moved me. Would I have that kind of generosity if my family were starving?

"All people hunger for love, whether they are Christian or Muslim, Hindu or atheist. As Christians, we are all called to be a sign of God's love to everyone we meet. Then we will radiate Christ to the world." That was the whole reason I had joined, the reason I was sitting beside Mother, to bring love to the world. I experienced an enormous surge of goodwill, as though all the people in the stadium and all those watching on television were being moved to loving action because of Mother. The world was a better place because of Mother and what she did, because of what we did.

At the reception after the prayer meeting, Mother kept repeating the same stories to the same people—and most of them involved numbers: five thousand people fed in Calcutta every day, more than two hundred MC tabernacles throughout the world. The way she repeated herself was embarrassing; Mother was obviously exhausted. The archbishop arranged for a private plane to return us to Stockholm. Onboard, Mother slept and Dorothy and I talked in whispers, trying to squeeze four years of news into a half-hour flight. My parents had sent her a photocopy of one of my recent letters, and she asked me what novices were and why I was their "mistress," curling her nose a little at the word. I knew I should ask her why she didn't go to church anymore, but I didn't feel like it. Dorothy looked happy when we hugged in the airport. She thanked Mother and gave her a hug, too, which Mother didn't refuse, though she didn't hug back, either.

From Stockholm to Rome, Mother spoke again to each flight attendant and to everyone in first class. Again she asked for a collection of food. Again there was no time to talk to Mother about my novices and their troubles.

Mother returned the next day to Calcutta, and everyone asked me about the trip. I told them Mother was tired but never wanted to slow down, that she kept giving and giving and giving. I told them how everyone in the stadium had listened to Mother so attentively, how she had told them the story of the Muslim family who shared with the Hindus. I didn't say a word about the intimate card in Mother's prayer book, though I thought of it often.

Three days later Sister Agnel phoned.

"Mother's had another heart attack," she said, her voice shaking. "She's in the hospital in Calcutta."

Immediately I remembered the pills I hadn't given Mother on time. I should have been able to find a way to give her more rest. I'd caused her stress when the medals ran out. I should have found her more food. Perhaps if Sister May, the doctor, had accompanied Mother, this heart attack could have been avoided. That entire day, and for several days after, I walked around in a daze.

Mother was later transferred to Forest Grove Nursing Home in Calcutta, where she stayed for three weeks. They said that she would never be able to travel again, never be able to address large crowds.

I asked special permission to write to Dorothy, and I spoke to Sister Marie Therese and to Sister Agnel. I told them I was grateful for the opportunity I'd had—perhaps the last opportunity anyone would have to travel with Mother. I asked forgiveness for my negligence. Dorothy wrote back that it wasn't my fault. Sister Marie Therese scolded me and told everyone in the novitiate that I'd been irresponsible and that Mother's heart attack was payment for my ineptitude. Sister Agnel said it was impossible to take care of Mother, that Mother would work no matter what, that she wanted to die on her feet, giving all to Jesus, and that I shouldn't blame myself.

I wrote to Mother, thanking her for letting me accompany her, telling her how sorry I was that she was ill. I assured her of my prayers, and thanked her for letting Dorothy come along. I also told her I wanted to help the novices become good MCs but so often didn't know how.

I never received an answer to that letter.

When Mother was released from the nursing home, she wrote to the Pope, asking permission for a special General Chapter to elect a sister to take her place as superior general. The news surprised and saddened many sisters. It saddened me, too, though I thought it sensible. Perhaps Mother had finally recognized the need to take a break, not to overextend herself. She probably knew the transition to a new superior general would be difficult for many sisters, and wanted to be around to facilitate the change. The Pope gave permission for the special election, and we began yearlong preparations for the Chapter and the election of Mother's successor.

In a few months I would have to recommend which novices should take vows, which needed more time in the novitiate, and which should be sent home. The prospect terrified me.

I continued to feel lost with the novices and regretted not having asked Mother's advice about how best to deal with them. It was obvious to me, and understandable, that a few of the novices were still looking for a mother. Others wanted a friend, a companion, a confidante. They complained that they missed me at recreations when I left them for other work. Sister Joseph Michael had asked me to prepare a simplified, illustrated version of my Regina Mundi thesis, "The Eucharist and the Poor." I really didn't have time to do it during the day, but it wasn't just for the sake of the work that I skipped recreations. Limiting my time with the novices would help keep them at a proper distance.

The novices' affectionate enthusiasm pained me. When I saw them laughing and singing, I imagined them overworked in the mission houses, misunderstood in community, frustrated in their apostolates. Their earnestness reminded me of the enthusiasm I'd once felt. I mourned what I had lost, and what they might lose, too.

When they came to see me individually, the novices began to open their hearts. They spoke of troubles at home—an abusive, alcoholic father, an absent mother. They talked of their longing for God and of the joys and difficulties of prayer. They told me things they said they'd never told anyone else. Sometimes they cried. I once sat on my hands to avoid embracing a tearful novice. I couldn't play with the Rules anymore. Sometimes I prayed with a novice, guiding her in a meditation in which I helped her picture a painful memory, then invite Jesus to enter and heal that memory, a technique I'd read about. I didn't mention my approach to Sister Marie Therese, who probably would have recommended doubling a troubled novice's use of the discipline and chains.

One December day Sister Marie Therese stood in the compound while the novices rushed about preparing to leave for the apostolate. "My group tells me," she said, looking at me rather impassively, "that your sisters enjoy Scripture class."

"Yes, Sister, thank you," I said. This was the first good word Sister Marie Therese had had for me since I'd arrived nearly six months earlier. "We all enjoy it," I explained. "St. John is so deep, and the sisters all share their insights in—"

"Sister Donata," Sister Marie Therese interrupted, raising her eyebrows and holding her elbow in her hand as she shook her index finger at me, "novices are not meant to enjoy Scripture class. Scripture class means you talk and they listen, and they should not leave the room feeling anything but compunction. Do you understand?"

"Yes, Sister," I said.

"Sister Phoebe still sleeps during meditation."

"But not as often, Sister. She is really try—"

"She still sleeps during meditation."

"Yes, Sister." I looked down, hoping to hide my annoyance and frustration. *I really should say something, for the sake of her novices.*

"And Sister Bertram—"

I looked up.

"Sister Bertram is your just reward," Sister Marie Therese said, smiling for the first time in the conversation.

A few days later, Sister Marie Therese and I were in her little office, settling the details of the upcoming Christmas party for the children, when the telephone rang.

"Chi parla?" Sister Marie Therese listened, then looked at me sideways, spoke a bit more, then handed the receiver to me. "Marta, asking for you," she said.

I shrugged. I didn't know any Marta.

"Sister Donata," the voice on the other end of the receiver said, "I love you." *Oh, yes, I do know a Marta,* I thought. Niobe's baptismal name was Marta.

"Aaa, sí?" I stumbled.

"Of course, you know I love you."

Sister Marie Therese hadn't taken her eyes off mine, and her gaze bore more deeply with every passing second.

"I want you in my arms," the voice on the phone continued. "Next year I'll come to Rome and we'll be in the same city again."

"Ooo, no." I looked down, trying to avoid Sister Marie Therese's stare.

"Somebody in the room with you?"

"Sí, esattamente."

"I'll call later." Her voice was pitiful.

I didn't want her to call at all. I'd been successfully shielding myself from bothersome longings since I'd been with the novices. Besides, Sister Marie Therese could sniff trouble even before it entered a person's subconscious. *"Penso di no,"* I said. *"Arrivederci."* As I put the receiver back, Sister Marie Therese's eyebrows peaked like arrows on her forehead.

"Just somebody I knew from Primavalle," I said, "wanting to know how I was."

"You shouldn't receive calls," Sister Marie Therese said, her arms folded very definitively across her chest. "It's a bad example for the novices."

After the call, I wasn't able to get Niobe out of my mind. I'd been so happy to be free of her all this time. But she didn't know that. The last time I'd seen her had been the night of the hug. And she mentioned coming to Rome—she would be a tertian in June. I certainly didn't want to think of seeing her at choir practices and gatherings. At least, I hadn't wanted it for some time now. I had things under control.

Mother began to mend. We heard that she'd started traveling in India. We thanked God for such an astounding recovery.

Meanwhile, it was January, time to write reports. I took a notebook to the chapel, wrote each sister's name at the top of a page, and prayed for guidance. I tried to be as objective as possible. As I wrote, I found it wasn't as difficult as I had anticipated, that I actually had a fairly good sense of where each sister stood. When I got to Sister Bertram's page, I felt as though I were writing a report on myself and my failures. I hadn't helped her overcome her lack of sincerity, her laziness, her basic immaturity. I didn't consider it necessary to send her home, at least not yet. She was young, and with more time, lots of grace, and a real desire to change—something that a postponement might give her—I hoped she could outgrow most of her weaknesses.

I read each sister's report aloud and we talked. No one had any real objection to what I'd written, but once or twice, after listening to a sister, I realized that I'd misinterpreted her, so I changed a detail or two. The meetings went well, until Sister Bertram.

"Sister," she told me, "you cannot say that I am not ready for my vows. I have done nothing wrong, and Our Lady has sent me here."

"Sister, Our Lady may have sent you, but that doesn't mean you're ready. You won't be going home. I'm just giving you the time you need to prepare yourself better."

"Sister," she said, locking her eyes into mine, "I am ready."

"Do you know," I asked, hoping my gaze would drill through her stubborn resistance, "how to obey when it goes against your will?"

"Behold the handmaid of the Lord," Sister Bertram said, drawing her lips into a determined line. "I always obey God's will."

"So many times you haven't done what I've told you."

"Only when you are not listening to God, like now." She folded her arms across her chest, convinced that she had won.

"Sister Bertram, I can't change my report. You're not ready. In your letter to Mother you are free to write whatever you sincerely believe."

After our meetings, the sisters all brought me the first drafts of their letters so I could check for spelling and grammar mistakes. The third paragraph of Sister Bertram's letter read, *My mistress thinks I am not ready for my vows. She does not like me and does not try even to understand me. She persecutes me every day. It is my privilege to suffer for the Gospel. Our Blessed Mother has chosen me to do great things. May God forgive my mistress' soul.*

I was pleased with Sister Bertram's paragraph. If the council needed any proof of her unfitness for profession, she had just supplied it.

Not long after I'd sent the reports, on an early spring afternoon under a bright Roman sky, I walked into the chapel, genuflected, and did a quick double take. A tall, bald priest sat at a table near the altar, a sheaf of papers in hand. Father Tom looked up at me and smiled. I felt my face flush as I made my way to the back of the chapel. Sister Marie Therese had said someone new was coming to give talks and hear confessions of the first-years. I hadn't imagined it would be Father Tom.

He spoke honestly about community and its difficulties, distinguishing humility from allowing others to treat you as a doormat. When he finished his talk, I left the chapel with a little more hope, just for having seen him. Father Tom returned several times that spring, each time giving an excellent, practical talk. I could have joined the queue of novices waiting for confession, but I chose not to. I liked him too much, and was happy to enjoy him from a distance, without any possibility of complication.

Excitement ran high during the weeks leading to profession. We chose the songs for the ceremony and doubled choir practices. We washed and boiled their blue par saris. During extra prayer time, we begged God's grace. Each day the novices asked me, "Sister, have our answers come yet?"

When I said, "No, not yet," their faces fell, they talked about other things, and the underlying tension grew. Sister Bertram, however, remained remarkably calm. "I'm not worried," she said when other sisters asked if answers had arrived. "Our Lady is taking care of me. Mother knows the truth." I hated to think how she'd feel when the answers came, and began to fear postponement might push her into a breakdown.

Finally, in early April, Sister Marie Therese called all the novice mistresses into the office. "I've just been to San Gregorio," she said. "Sister Agnel has received the answers from Calcutta."

My heart skipped several beats. I hadn't realized I was as nervous as the novices about receiving the replies.

"The good news," Sister Marie Therese continued, "is that Mother will come for professions."

"Thank God," we said, hardly able to believe it. We'd prayed hard for Mother's recovery but had resigned ourselves to her absence.

"The other news is that the entire group will be taking vows," Sister Marie Therese announced, looking straight at me.

"All?" I gasped. "What about Sister Bertram?"

"The council has given her permission."

"But she's not ready. I made that clear."

"This once I agree with you. She is not ready, but she is taking vows. That's why I've called all of you here." She looked intently at the two first-year mistresses. "You must know that how you train these sisters may be all they ever receive. You cannot expect they will get another chance. If you do not do your job—" She looked at me, pausing significantly. "Then the sisters may never get formed." She pulled herself up even straighter on the stool. "The entire Society suffers when sisters leave your hands unprepared because you have neglected your duty. Each novice under me has always been ready. I make sure of that."

The other two mistresses looked at their hands. Everyone knew Sister Bertram was particularly difficult, and it was obvious that Sister Marie Therese meant to humiliate me.

"Sister Agnel will come tomorrow to give the sisters their permissions," Sister Marie Therese announced, almost triumphantly. "You may go."

I went straight to the chapel. *Jesus,* I prayed, *did the councilors believe Sister Bertram when she said that I persecuted her? Why would they trust her word over mine? Wouldn't they have asked me if they had questions? Surely it's not because she said Our Lady called her.*

Something had to be done. I decided to talk to Sister Agnel.

When Sister arrived, she looked quite solemn. She called me into the office. "The decision of the councilors is final," Sister Agnel told me. "You wrote your report. Sister Bertram wrote her letter. You have to accept."

"But, Sister, you know she's not ready to go to a mission house."

"Yes, I know that," Sister Agnel said with a sigh.

"Then how can we send her?"

"We're not sending her. The council is sending her. Mother is sending her." Sister Agnel sighed again, then looked me straight in the eye. "You need faith. God will take care of it. You did your part, now don't worry about it anymore."

When Sister Bertram emerged from the office after having received her permission paper from Sister Agnel, she smiled and waved the paper wordlessly in my face.

Sister Agnel returned to Tor Fiscale a few days before we entered the profession retreat. The more I got to know Sister Agnel, the more I liked and trusted her. She was intelligent and kind, never overly pious. I never saw her flustered or impatient with the sisters. With outsiders she was both friendly and—a word I had never thought of in connection with an MC before—professional, with her ever-excellent Italian and warm smile.

Sister Agnel had received a packet from Calcutta containing the future assignments of my novices. She said that these assignments didn't always come early, but they had this time. She wanted to know if I saw anything that ought to be changed. "We can't ask for a lot of changes, but if there is a sister who you know can't bear the heat and she's been assigned to Yemen, it would be better to get that changed now."

Looking at the assignments made me a little queasy. I couldn't find anything that needed obvious adjustment, but seeing those names paired with missions across the globe made me regret again that I hadn't done a better job for the sisters.

Sister Agnel cleared her throat and said, "Sister Donata, you don't seem happy here. You don't smile and laugh the way you used to. Everybody notices it. Sister Dominica tells me she's never seen you so sad."

I'd been struggling, but I never thought it showed so much that sisters would notice. It was touching to know they did. "It's hard working with the novices," I said. "They're so young, so enthusiastic, so affectionate. Some of them seem to want me to be their mother, but I don't want them to get attached to me or dependent, and I can't just be rude to them. It makes me nervous to sit in front of twelve adoring faces." I paused to gauge Sister Agnel's reaction. She nodded thoughtfully.

"Everything's so basic, here, Sister. I have to spend my time teaching them how to get the stains out of their serviettes, and when to keep silence, and all those other things Sister Marie Therese thinks are so important, but I'd like to give them more. Then when I teach Scripture class, they like it too much, and Sister Marie Therese tells me I have to be stricter. But I can't be like her—"

"She's a saint, isn't she?" Sister Agnel said, interrupting before I might say something I would regret. "We were in the same group. Our mistresses were always telling us to look at Sister Marie Therese. She is holy."

I felt like shouting, but the obvious fact that I'd failed my own novices so miserably kept me quiet.

"Not everyone is meant to work with the young sisters," Sister Agnel continued. "I was thinking . . . I need a new tertian mistress, but you are still quite young. Do you think you could handle the tertians?"

"I don't know, Sister." The suggestion seemed to have fallen from a far distant planet where things were even stranger than they were in Tor Fiscale.

"Tertians aren't affectionate and enthusiastic like the novices," Sister Agnel said. "Tertians come back as though they've been living in war zones, bruised and discouraged. They need someone who will understand them. . . . I don't know, though."

"The tertians?" My mind raced. Niobe would be in the next group of tertians. "I don't know, either, Sister." *I can't be Niobe's mistress. I want to be Niobe's mistress. I've got to get out of here. I can't be Niobe's mistress.* "Sister, half of them will be older than I am. I don't think this is a good idea."

"You may be young, but you have more experience as an MC, and that's what counts," Sister Agnel said. "You could teach Scripture class and spiritual life. I need someone to do it, and I think it would be good for you." She reminded me of Sister Joseph Michael, needing help and not knowing where to turn.

"If you need me, Sister, I will try," I said. I doubted the councilors would approve me, anyway. I still wasn't even technically old enough to be novice mistress, and surely Sister Marie Therese would let them know what a mess I'd made of that.

"I don't make the final decision," Sister Agnel said, "but I will send recommendations to Calcutta soon."

"I'll do whatever you need me to," I said.

When my twelve novices took their vows in Mother's hands, they shone with excitement. I was happy for them, and frightened at the same time. They were now the spouses of Jesus Crucified, as God had called them to be. When Mother announced their assignments and gave them the little card of God holding the child in the palm of His hand, I begged Him to make up for all that I had been unable to give them.

I received my new assignment the next day: tertian mistress at Casilina. Sister Marie Therese seemed surprised. She told me,

"We'll miss you here. You know that the novitiate is the most im-portant part of formation. 'What a sister is in the novitiate, she will be all her life.' " Sister Marie Therese had a rare smile on her face as she quoted those words from *Mother's Instructions*. "You can't do much with a sister by the time she's a tertian," she continued. "They have to be formed when they're young. But not everyone's able to do that, I suppose."

"I'll miss you, too, Sister," I said. It wasn't a lie. I'd definitely no-tice the absence of that constant tension I experienced when she was around.

I wasn't at all sure that living with Niobe again wouldn't be even worse, in an entirely different way. I begged God to save me from myself.

20

ROSES FROM HEAVEN

SPRING TO SUMMER 1990
CASILINA, ROME

Two tertians stood in line ahead of me, outside the parlor, under the eaves. The late May air was bright, not yet muggy the way Rome always got later in the summer. A breeze tickled eucalyptus musk from the trees that towered along the path. Casilina's pleasantness mitigated my anxiety about my new assignment—twenty-eight tertians, half of them older than I, two of them in their sixties, and I was supposed to prepare them all for final vows. Just thinking about it made me dizzy. I knew Niobe would be coming, but I didn't know when, and I didn't ask.

The parlor door opened and closed again, making me next in line. The group didn't have a regular confessor yet, and the Casilina superior had called Father Tom. I remembered the advice he'd given the only other time I'd confessed to him, more than a year earlier: *Learn to love yourself.* I still had a lot to learn.

I didn't feel like hiding behind a screen. I needed to face this new assignment and myself head-on. When the parlor door opened, I walked in and shut the door, took a chair from behind the table, and asked, "Do you mind?"

"It's entirely up to you," Father Tom said.

I put the chair a couple of feet in front of him and sat down. I looked at his face, but that didn't seem right. I looked past his ear, but that wasn't comfortable, either. I looked at the floor.

"Bless me, Father, for I have sinned. It's a few days since my last confession, and I've been appointed mistress of a new group of tertians." I took a deep breath. "I don't want to repeat the same mistakes I made when I was novice mistress. I couldn't agree with the Tor Fiscale superior's philosophy of formation, but I never had the courage to tell her so. I was always torn between what I was expected to do and what I believed was right. I didn't have any confidence, and I didn't do a very good job training the novices. Deep inside, I knew God was calling me to stand up for what I believed and to challenge the system, but I preferred to be a conformist, not to rock the boat. I failed."

Now, take responsibility. Look up.

His eyes were a clear green, his chin both firm and gentle. "If women could be priests," he said, "you'd be the one I'd make my confession to."

"What are you talking about?"

"Sister, you're dealing with real issues, not superficialities."

I looked down again.

He continued, "Despite what you might think, it's not often that a priest gets to deal with real issues in the confessional, with someone who struggles to do what's right and who's willing to learn and to change."

"Father," I said, looking into his eyes, "how does anyone know what's right? They always say the superior speaks the will of God, but I'm not sure anymore."

"In most religious communities nowadays obedience is more nuanced. My congregation takes obedience very seriously when it comes to mission assignments, but our superiors make those decisions only after dialogue with us, and they don't dictate every aspect of our lives. This business of superiors who speak for God sounds scary to me. Thousands of people were tortured and killed during the Inquisition in the name of God."

"But if I believe it's God's will for me to be an MC—and I do believe that, I know it through and through—then God wants me to live the vows the way the MCs interpret them, not the way anyone else does, or the way I think it should be done, right?"

"Well, it's true that you can't live in an MC community without following MC Rules, but that doesn't mean the Rules can't be changed. They're not written in stone. If you think God is asking you to stand up for what you believe, He may be calling you to challenge the MC way of thinking."

Well, that is what I just said in my confession, and what I've been feeling—and even what I'd hoped to do in my work with Sister Joseph Michael on the Constitutions—*but I didn't imagine overthrowing the whole "voice of God in the superior" concept; I just want to be kinder to the sisters.* "The others are so sure they're right, Father, and I'm not sure at all. I'm full of questions, and they have all the answers."

"Keep asking the questions, Sister. Eventually you'll find answers that will be right for you, and then you may be called to share your thoughts with others."

As he raised his hand just above my head and spoke the words of absolution, I felt a soft, tingling heat flow through my head and travel my entire body. When he finished, I couldn't move for several seconds. When I finally got up to leave, I turned to thank him once more and realized he'd skipped something.

"Father, what about my penance?"

"Sister, for your penance, I suggest you stop thinking about your transfer as a sign of failure. Moving from the novices to the tertians looks like a promotion to me. Your higher superiors must trust you, otherwise they wouldn't have given you this position. Remembering that will be your penance."

I'd never received such an unusual and useful penance, had never left the confessional feeling better than I did that day.

· · ·

All twenty-eight of my tertians were supposed to have arrived by June 6, and we'd started the program that day, but two weeks later we were still expecting three more. Sister Elsitta and I were in the office, settling the division of household duties while the sisters were on morning apostolate. Casilina housed two communities of tertians—Sister Elsitta had the seniors, who had already been in Casilina for six months and were scheduled to take vows in December, and I had the juniors, who were just beginning their year of tertianship. Sister Elsitta was pleasant enough, but I couldn't say I trusted her. This Indian sister, about a decade older than I, seemed superficial, flighty, overly concerned about the whiteness of her sari. When Sister Elsitta and I had nearly finished organizing the housework, we heard a knock at the office door.

"*Ciao*, Sisters," a deep voice announced, and the door swung open. There she stood, tall and bright. I wanted to jump into Niobe's arms; I wanted to send her away. I wanted to lean into her ear and whisper "I love you"; I wanted to frown and tell her to pretend we'd never met.

"Sister Niobe," Sister Elsitta said, "we expected you long ago. You're the one coming from closest, and you're nearly the last to arrive!"

"Well, you know, Sister, my mother has not been well, and my sister got married, and I had a very bad, bad cold, and so Sister Agnel gave me permission to stay at home a little longer, but"—she opened her arms very widely—"here I am now." She smiled, then bowed for Sister's blessing. Niobe turned to me and said, "And so, Sister Donata, you are going to be my mistress?"

"It looks that way, doesn't it?" I avoided her eyes and helped her lug her box into the refectory. If anyone else had been around, I'd have asked her to help settle Niobe's things. In the refectory, she tapped my shoulder, but I didn't turn. *I have to be strong*, I told myself.

"What is this, not even a smile for your old friend?" The pleading in her voice pulled me around, and I attempted a smile.

"Welcome," I said.

"Doesn't look like it," she said.

"You're number twenty-six. Hand me your books and I'll put them on the shelf."

"What's this all about? I'm not twenty-six—I'm Niobe, remember?"

"Yes, I remember," I said as she handed me her books. "But things can't be like they were before."

"What do you mean?" she said, laying her sari on the clothes shelf.

"We need to talk." I tried to make my voice firm and strong, but heard a quaver at the end.

"Okay, let's talk." She spread her arms open again and tossed her head back, as if examining me from afar.

"Not here," I said, reaching for her plates and stacking them on the shelf. "Let's go upstairs and I'll help you make your bed."

"Okay," she murmured, half to herself, "so you're going to help me make my bed. Is that supposed to make me happy? You don't even look at me, as if I don't exist."

"Bring your sheets," I said, heading up the stairs quickly.

When she entered the dormitory, Niobe closed the door behind her, dropped her sheets on the nearest bed, and wrapped her arms around me.

I stiffened my muscles, arms at my side. She let go, and I looked straight into her eyes, trying to make mine impenetrable. "Things can't be like they were before," I said.

"Calm down," she said. "I'm not going to bite. Let's talk peacefully. What's changed? You're still you and I'm still me. We still love each other, don't we?"

"Yes, but now I'm responsible for your formation. We'll have to create some distance. I won't be able to treat you any differently from the others. Sometimes I'll have to tell you things you don't want to hear."

"I like everything that comes from your mouth."

"You don't know what I'm—"

"Take it easy." She put her arm around my shoulder. I lifted it off.

"Niobe, what we did was against the Rules."

"You liked it, didn't you?"

"That's not the point. You're getting ready for your final vows."

"And you're going to help me. Why can't we be friends?"

"Do you know how jealousy can destroy a group?"

"Listen, we just have to be clever about it. Don't think that I'm so stupid as to let everyone see. Trust me." She looked very deeply into my eyes.

Laying down the law wasn't going to work, not then. The last time we'd seen each other I'd begged her to hold me. When she settled into the group and got over her disappointment that things couldn't be as they had been, then she would listen. I was sure.

The tertians and I settled into a routine: apostolate in the morning after breakfast, then class and prayer all afternoon. During personal prayer time and manual work in the evening, sisters could come see me to talk and to renew permissions. When they queued up in front of me, every morning and evening, I tried to pour love into my hands as I blessed them. Sometimes I felt something I could only describe as energy radiate from my palms to my bowing sisters.

Sister Agnel had certainly been right: the tertians were different from the novices. These sisters came knowing their need for prayer in a very existential way—I didn't need to convince any of them that survival as an MC depended on developing a deep relationship with God. Instead, I had to help them find the way to do it—which was tricky because they'd been trying for at least eight years and needed new ideas. I was thankful for my studies and taught classes on ways to personalize the Psalms and on methods of meditation.

Rule Class made me nervous. These sisters had real questions about situations they'd encountered in the missions: work so demanding it had left them frustrated and dismayed, superiors who'd asked them to do questionable things, people they'd hoped to bring to God but couldn't quite reach. Many of them had confronted challenges far more difficult than anything I'd faced. One had worked among unfriendly Muslims in Sudan. Another—a smart, tough Indian sister with little training—had been put in charge of an orphanage of fifty small children in Egypt. Two sisters had served under superiors who, from the stories they told, seemed seriously unhinged. Just four years earlier I'd been a tertian myself— I couldn't pretend to any sort of authority in front of these sisters.

During class they often seemed dazed. Sometimes they looked as though they wanted to say something or ask something but didn't yet know if they could trust me. I told them we all had problems, that I wouldn't judge them. But even I didn't know if I could be trusted to give good answers.

In July we received news that Sister Dominica and Sister Elsitta had been elected to the General Chapter. The Chapter sisters would gather in Calcutta at the end of August, and the election of the new superior general was set for September 8, the Blessed Virgin Mary's birthday.

Though the upcoming election was pivotal to the Society's future, we weren't supposed to talk about it, even among ourselves. Gossip and speculation could interfere with the Holy Spirit's work. Still, I devoured the clippings priests and Co-Workers brought us, the media hot with conjecture, especially in India. Even *Time* ran a piece on the upcoming election: Would the sisters choose Sister Frederick, previously second-in-command, or was she too harsh a disciplinarian? Sister Priscilla, currently responsible for sisters' mission assignments, was a powerful contender. As the first to join, Sister Agnes was a sentimental favorite, but perhaps not ambitious enough.

I thought Sister Joseph Michael would be a good choice, though there wasn't much talk of her and I knew she didn't want the job. It had pained me to sometimes see Sister shudder when she mentioned current and former councilors bickering for power and position, neglecting the needs of the sisters and the poor. Though she'd objected, Sister Joseph Michael hadn't been able to keep Sister Frederick and Sister Priscilla from pulling the Society further and further to the right.

I knew I wasn't supposed to worry, that I should leave the election to the Holy Spirit, but I'd realized for some time that the Holy Spirit had a difficult job making His way past our human fears and the MC reverence for authority—to say nothing of the power lust of Sisters Frederick and Priscilla. Sister Frederick was currently circumnavigating the globe, propagating the catechism program she'd developed with the help of Father John Hardon, S.J., the white-headed priest whose classes we had attended when we were aspirants. When Sister Frederick claimed to promote and defend the Church, she always meant the Pope and bishops and official teaching, never the faithful—a stance that distorted the same magisterium she claimed to revere. To me, her program's emphasis on doctrine and laws seemed a far cry from Mother's Scripture-based spirituality of the heart.

While I fretted about elections, I also hoped the Chapter's discussions of the new *Constitutions* might bear fruit in more humane policies. As she had promised, Sister Joseph Michael would circulate a list of my suggestions. I begged God to give the Chapter wisdom and courage, and I waited to see what the Holy Spirit might be able to accomplish because and in spite of us all.

After Rule Class one day, Niobe followed me into the office and shut the door before I even noticed she was there. "That was great," she said. "I've never had a Rule Class like that. They're usually so boring. But the way you talk, you make me see that MC life is something beautiful."

What was beautiful was the smile on her face. It warmed me every time I saw it. Niobe had been mostly good since she'd arrived. She'd sat near me at the head of the table several times, but it was normal for a sister to sit near the mistress when she first arrived, and she hadn't overdone it. She looked intently at me during class, but I couldn't really fault her on that. On the other hand, when she came to renew her permissions, kneeling in front of me, bending that big, confident body of hers to kiss the floor, she'd announced the shortest list of faults I'd ever heard. When I indicated the bed opposite me, she sat next to me, her leg pressing against mine, so I had to scoot over a bit. But mostly she'd been good.

"Thanks for the encouragement," I told her. "Giving class to tertians is kind of scary. They deserve something more than the novices, and I think they expect it."

"You're a natural," she said, again with that beautiful smile. "I just want to give you a big hug," she said, and opened her arms wide.

"No," I said. "I really don't think we should, though I appreciate the gesture."

"It's not a gesture," she said, "it's a hug," and she wrapped her arms around me.

As I had when she arrived, I kept my arms to my sides. "Sister Niobe," I said, "we can't do this."

"All right, all right already," she said, letting me go. "Just don't call me Sister. Hearing you call me that hurts."

I was frightened of that part of me that still wanted her arms around me. That evening, I took the discipline with more force than usual. The next morning when I fastened the chains around my arm and waist, I pulled them tight.

Niobe was lax not only in chastity but also in silence, punctuality, and obedience. Her life before joining the sisters had been difficult in many ways, so it was only natural that her problems would be different from the problems of other sisters. Perhaps I could help her continue her conversion. Being close to God was the most exciting adventure in the world, and I wanted her to know that, too. Helping her draw near God in prayer, as I'd been able to help a few of my novices, would be the best way to show her my love. We could belong to God together, without taking back anything for ourselves.

I called Niobe to the dormitory and told her I wanted to try something. She nodded. "I want to give you a series of meditations.

It will be like your own private mini-retreat, except that you won't keep silence—you'll do everything with the group, but whenever you pray, you'll meditate on the texts I'll give you."

"Okay. I'm ready." She sat opposite me, hands in her lap. That gave me hope.

Following the *Spiritual Exercises* of St. Ignatius, I started her with a meditation on the first chapter of Genesis, the creation of the world and its wonders from chaos. I told her to come back the next evening to tell me what she'd discovered, and to get the next day's meditation point.

She bent her head for a blessing, and on the way up she let her shoulder brush against mine. Her hand grazed my right breast. I couldn't tell if the touch was deliberate or not. If I confronted her, I felt sure she would deny it, and I'd be left looking like a suspicious grouch.

During personal prayer time, I watched as Niobe tucked her Bible under her arm and walked up and down the garden. I didn't see her open the Bible, but perhaps she'd read the passage earlier. The garden, of course, was not a bad place to meditate on the first chapter of Genesis. I hoped that was what she was doing.

The following day she sat near me on the bed. "How was your meditation?" I asked.

"Wonderful," she said, slipping her hand over my knee, her brown eyes looking straight into mine. "I thought about all the beautiful things God made, and told him how grateful I was for all His gifts, especially you."

"Well, that's a good start," I said, brushing her hand off my knee. "Tomorrow, start with how God created *you*." Her eyes never broke contact, even for an instant. "And please, I'd prefer it if you didn't touch me, okay? Now is the time to concentrate on God."

"Oh, sure. Sorry." She placed both hands flat on the bed.

The fifth of August, shortly after Niobe had begun her mini-retreat, the tertians were in a tizzy. It was the Feast of the Dedication of the

Basilica of Santa Maria Maggiore, and we were going to attend the solemn chanting of Vespers in the basilica. Niobe volunteered to stay in Casilina to give dinner to the refugee ladies in the home. She didn't like crowds. I was pleased—she'd been demanding a lot of attention lately, and I needed a little breathing room.

The church was packed, the celebration grand—a big choir, dozens of priests, lots of flowers and incense. Toward the end of the service, the choir intoned the Magnificat. As the familiar strains of Mary's hymn filled the basilica, people pointed toward the gilded ceiling, their oohs and aahs audible over the organ music. A cloud of red, white, and pink appeared above the main altar, widening as currents of air caught and scattered what vaguely resembled colored snow. The rose petals floated throughout the church, eventually falling on the heads and shoulders of the worshippers, on statues, on the altar, on the floor.

I knew what to look for, and saw how the end of one of the gilded panels had been lifted. Every now and then I caught a glimpse of a broom, sometimes a hand, pushing the petals out. Most of my tertians hadn't noticed the broom or the hands yet. They stood open-mouthed, faces tilted back so far that their necks must have hurt, gasping in wonder with the crowd.

I loved to watch my sisters, especially the innocent, unjaded ones, who hadn't yet seen the hands, who might never see the hands, who believed the petals fell from heaven. Their faces lit with joy as they ran to gather the holy relics, plucking them from one another's saris, picking them off the floor before anyone could step on them. They would be disappointed at dinner, when their more observant sisters would tell them about the lifted panel and the hands. They would deny it at first: "No, no. These are Our Lady's flowers." Then their faces would darken as the aura of the miracle wore thin. Still, they'd press the petals in their Bibles. They would send them in little packets of folded wax paper to loving parents, to ailing grandparents, to uncles whose harvests were failing, to aunties praying to become pregnant, to siblings about to be wed, to newly baptized nieces and nephews. They would write, *These are the holy petals from the Mother of God.*

But we were not yet home, and while some sisters gathered petals, I visited the chapel to the left of the main altar, where the Blessed Sacrament was often exposed beneath an ancient icon of Mary with the child Jesus in her arms. The icon, attributed to the evangelist Luke, portrayed a sturdy, powerful Mary, with no trace of fluff in her. I liked that Mary. After a prayer, as I walked down the steps out of the chapel, I spotted some tertians in busy conversation with a tall man, his back to the side chapel. I overheard a few words: "—with your sisters . . . South Bronx . . . Sister Donata and Sister Priscilla."

One of the tertians giggled, and another called to me in a stage whisper, "Sister, Sister."

From the steps leading into the main body of the basilica, I looked over the heads of the sisters, and into Stan's eyes. The same deep brown, over an amazed smile.

"Sister Donata," he said.

The tertians separated to make a path for me, and I put my outstretched hand into Stan's. His hand was warm, his grip firm, his gaze steady.

"I never expected to meet you here," he said. "I just saw the sisters and started talking. I was hoping, but I never thought—"

"Yes, it's a great surprise," I said. "Did you fall from heaven with the rose petals?"

"Not really. Actually—" He looked down, shuffled his feet a bit, and then looked straight into my eyes. "I'm here to get married."

"Married?" That was a surprise. I wondered what Mother would think. She'd been so sure Stan had a vocation.

"Yes, to an Italian girl. I came to meet her family, and we're getting married on the fourteenth."

"Congratulations. That's great news." His smile had disappeared, his eyes were blank.

We talked for a while. He'd met his fiancée at church while she was finishing graduate studies at the University of Wisconsin. Stan had tried the seminary for a couple of years, but that hadn't worked out.

"Where's the wedding?" I asked.

"Her family lives near St. Luke's Church."

"San Luca? Off the Via Casilina?" That was hard to believe.

"Yes. Do you know it?"

"I made my final vows there. It's a ten-minute walk from our house."

Stan invited me to the wedding, and I explained that the Rules didn't allow time off for personal things such as the marriage of a friend. Even if he'd been my own brother, I wouldn't have been able to attend. Stan shook his head a little and said he'd still love to see me. I wrote our phone number on a slip of paper and told him to call.

"Great." He put a hand on my shoulder. "I can't tell you how happy I am to see you." He slipped the paper into his pocket. "I'll be out most of today, but I'll call tomorrow."

"Good," I said, taking one last look into his eyes before I led the tertians to the next chapel.

The following day Niobe walked behind me into the dormitory after class. "What's all this humming in the washing place, joking at lunch?" she asked as she shut the door. "You look very happy today."

"I met a friend of mine yesterday at Maria Maggiore," I said. "He's going to call today."

"He?" Niobe turned her head and looked sideways at me.

"He was a volunteer in New York. He helped with summer camp."

"Do you always get this happy when you're expecting a phone call from someone you worked with ten years ago?"

"He's special."

"What do you mean?" Niobe scooted toward me, bending forward and turning her face so that she could look me in the eyes. "How special?"

"You promise you won't tell anyone?"

"What are friends for?"

"He gave me my first kiss."

"Ah, very special," she said, nodding. "So you knew him before?"

"No."

"He kissed you in New York?"

"No. He came to see me in Washington, walked two miles, said he'd been wanting to do something for three years, and then he bent down and kissed me."

"*Mamma mia*. Just like that?"

"Just like that."

"Nothing more?" Niobe asked, eyebrows raised.

"No, nothing more. He just kissed me and left. I didn't see him again until yesterday."

"Now I understand—humming, singing. When are you going to start dancing, put on your best sari, a little lipstick?"

"Don't be silly. He's just calling, and he's just a friend, and he's come to Rome to get married."

"To get married? Too bad. Probably means not many more kisses for you." Then she cocked her head to one side and raised her eyebrows. "Unless you'd like one from me."

"Niobe, don't be silly," I said.

"I've been wanting to kiss you for more than three years. Ever since the first day I met you."

"How can you think of such things?" Of course, I realized very well that she could think of such things. And seeing Stan had reminded me how good such things could be.

"How did you think that you wanted to be hugged, in Primavalle? Remember?"

"Sure I remember. My body just wanted it. I wanted to feel your arms around me, to be surrounded by you, to get lost in you. I wanted it for months and months." I paused. "I wanted it even in San Gregorio."

"You did?"

"Yes, but not at first. It was something that grew slowly." I looked into her brown eyes, then saw her lips, soft, round. "Since the time you told me you loved me—that's when the desire started and began to grow."

"I do love you. And I want to kiss you."

"Niobe, we can't." I shook my head, tried to convey a firmness I did not altogether feel. I'd never told Niobe about Timothy, but I remembered Timothy, and I remembered Stan. And I remembered my vows and that I was her tertian mistress and—

Niobe leaned over and pressed her lips against mine, then began to lick my lips with her tongue. Even as I knew I shouldn't allow her, I started to tingle all over. Niobe teased her tongue into my mouth and ran it along my gums until I felt like I wanted to faint.

"Don't you kiss back?" she asked, winking.

"I . . . I don't know how. I've never been kissed like that." Those words were entirely true.

"This time," she said, "just let your lips and your tongue play with me, let them reach for me, the way I'm reaching for you."

She pressed her lips against mine again, and my tongue hesitated. My lips stiffened until the touch of her lips, the play of her tongue melted life into mine. I pressed back, and her tongue caressed my tongue like a wave rolling onto the sand, taking the sand back into itself, carrying the sand out to sea, then lapping again, surging, cresting, her arms around my shoulders, my hands on her back, chest to chest, mouth breathing life into mouth, until the shore disappeared.

I was still tingling from Niobe's kiss when Sister Emelda took a seat on the bed in front of me. She sat for a moment, not saying anything, her chin firm, the skin drawn tight over her forehead. She was pouting.

"Sister Emelda?" I asked.

She remained silent for a few moments more, then blurted out, "Sister, I've been waiting over a week to see you. You have no time for me, but you always seem to have time for others. Why is that?"

Well, that was direct. I waited a moment and took a deep breath.

"I'm sorry, Sister Emelda," I said. "You really shouldn't have to wait. But there are twenty-eight of you, and some need more help than others. I'll try to do better next time. What did you want to talk about?"

"Now I'm just so mad that I've had to wait so long while others can see you anytime they want that I'm just angry about that."

"Are you jealous, then?"

"It's not right, Sister. You have something special with Sister Niobe. She's more important to you than the rest of us are."

"You're all important to me." I hated to see that pained look on her face. In the beginning spending time with Niobe hadn't mattered so much, because other sisters weren't yet eager to see me. Now many of them had decided to risk opening up, and I hadn't been available. "You're right," I said. "I do spend more time with Sister Niobe. Sometimes I have to decide which sisters need more help."

Sister Emelda said nothing. Her hand gripped the edges of the stool as she looked at the floor. I didn't know what she needed from me, and I might have destroyed my chance of ever knowing.

"I'm sorry, really I am," I said. "You're right to complain. I'll try to do better. Please forgive me, and tell me again when you need something. I won't make you wait so long, I promise."

She still didn't look up.

"And please pray for me, that I may know the right thing to do."

"Oh, yes, Sister, I am praying for you." Sister Emelda bowed her head for a blessing, then got up and left.

Stan never phoned. I told myself it was better that way. On the day of his wedding, we were having adoration when the bells of San Luca rang and rang and rang. An ostinato, steady under the rosary's rhythmic exchange, formed the counterpoint to my wandering thoughts. I prayed that Stan and his new wife would be happy, that they would love each other well. Then I thanked God for His love for me.

I thanked Him for Niobe, then I apologized about Niobe. I'd limited Niobe's reports on her mini-retreat to every third day, giving more time for other sisters. Still, she'd kissed me again. She said I looked like a newborn thing, just hatched and full of wonder. She called me her "little *pulcino*," her baby chick. Those kisses surprised me—first because they existed at all, and then because each one felt better than the last. What surprised me most, though, was how they felt so much like the best moments I'd felt in prayer, and the passion I'd felt as a teenager in Austin, when I'd known without any doubt that God loved me.

As I knelt there before the Blessed Sacrament, I knew what Niobe and I were doing was objectively sinful. Why, then, did I find myself happier than I had ever been? Ordinary things seemed to glow—the plates in the refectory, hymn books at Mass, my sisters' saris. I'd always heard lust described as a dreadful sin, a violent sin, a sin in which one cared nothing for the good of others but only sought greedy pleasure for oneself. Yet when I spoke to the other tertians I did so with more confidence and compassion than I'd known before. In chapel now and most days, I did not tire of remaining on my knees—giving myself seemed easy.

I'd read St. Bernard, St. John of the Cross, St. Aelred of Rievaulx—they all spoke of the soul's relationship with God as that of two lovers. Their writing was passionate, sensual, and approved by the Church. The Song of Songs spoke longingly of God: *May he kiss me with the kisses of his mouth! For your love is better than wine.* Jesus had considered love the most important commandment. St. John even said, "God is love." I didn't want to be the kind of sister who was more concerned with keeping the Rules than with the love of God.

I needed advice, but I struggled to open myself to the occasional, often odd, English-speaking priests we'd found in Rome that summer. I'd confessed "inappropriate expressions of affection for my sisters" without elaborating, and no one had asked me to clarify. Until the universities opened in the fall, finding a suitable confessor for the group—an empathetic, mature priest, comfortable with his own humanity, acquainted with religious life, fluent in English, willing to prepare and deliver a half-hour talk and then hear the confessions of twenty-nine nuns every Thursday afternoon—seemed unlikely. I considered asking Father Tom but knew I couldn't. Though he would be good for the sisters, I didn't trust myself anymore with people I liked. I would wait and do as Mother always said: *Take whatever God gives you, and give whatever He takes, with a big smile.*

That evening, with Stan's wedding over and my contemplation of love continuing, I took the discipline in my hands and beat my thighs until they stung bright red. I pulled the chains tighter in the morning, until their points dug into my flesh. I wanted answers.

Days before the sisters were scheduled to leave for the General Chapter in Calcutta, I sat at the desk in the office, preparing a class on John 4, the story of the Samaritan woman at the well. Jesus asked the woman to bring her husband, and she said she couldn't do that, and Jesus said that was right because she'd had five and the man she was living with at the moment was not her husband. That hit close to home. The woman I loved was not my husband. Jesus was.

Sister Elsitta opened the door halfway and asked, "Would you like to join my group for the talk this afternoon? I've asked Father Hugh because Father Paul is sick." She was bubbly. "Father Hugh gives really good talks. He's coming at three."

"Sure," I said, turning a page. Jesus told the Samaritan woman, *Whoever drinks the water I give will never be thirsty; no, the water I give shall become a fountain within, springing up to eternal life.* Though Niobe had sometimes seemed like cool water, she was not a fountain within. Lately my attraction for her felt more like quicksand.

"I'll send my group," I said, "but I don't think I'm coming." I had to find that spring of eternal life within, and I had to do it by myself.

When the group entered the refectory later, I asked them about Father Hugh's talk.

"He's really good," Sister Patrick said. Sister Patrick was an Irish sister, athletic in her former life, a sturdy and eager leader.

"Down-to-earth," another tertian added.

"I like that he talks from the Scriptures," someone else said.

Niobe nodded. "He was okay."

Maybe I should have gone for the talk, I thought. I hadn't found that interior fountain. Every time I looked up from my Bible, I saw Niobe gazing at me, an adoring smile on her face.

When I finished telling the sisters how Jesus satisfies every thirst, Sister Elsitta knocked at the refectory door and peeked in. "Sister Donata," she said, signaling me out with her eyebrows. In the hall she practically sparkled as she said, "I've found a confessor for your group."

"Really?"

"Yes, and he's agreed to come. I have everything arranged."

"Oh?" *At least she could have asked me first.* "Who is it?"

"Father Hugh. He's still here and would like to talk to you."

As we walked to the parlor I tried to quiet my irritation. Maybe this Father Hugh would be fine; after all, the sisters had liked his talk.

I followed Sister Elsitta into the parlor and saw a tall bald priest behind the table. "Sister Donata," he said, rising. "It's good to see you again."

"Father Tom?"

"I'm glad you remembered my name."

"Sister Elsitta told me—ah, yes, of course. You are Father Tom Hughes."

"Look at that," Father Tom said, smiling at Sister Elsitta. "She remembered my whole name."

I was so glad I hadn't asked for him. Through Sister Elsitta, God had chosen. I was just taking whatever Jesus gave and giving whatever Jesus took, with a big smile.

I didn't like the fact that my first confession to Father Tom as my regular confessor would have the extreme excesses of particular friendship as its subject, but I couldn't avoid it. I needed help, and I needed it badly.

I entered the sacristy, pulled out a chair, and took a deep breath. "Bless me, Father, for I have sinned. I have a special attraction to one of the sisters in my group, and I give in to my feelings for her. Actually, we've been friends for several years, and I never imagined I'd be her tertian mistress one day, and now it's very hard."

"Sister, God gives us friends to help us, to support us. There's nothing wrong in having a friend."

"But, you see, I spend a lot of time thinking about her, even during times when I should be praying, and—" *Come on, say it.* "We've sometimes expressed affection for each other in inappropriate ways."

"Inappropriate ways?"

I took a deep breath. *Get it out, Donata.* "It started with her trying to sit close to me. Then it was hugs and—we kiss. I know I shouldn't behave like this, but I feel so much better when she's around, and she encourages me, and I'm happy with her, but we're breaking our vows and I'm giving her wrong ideas about chastity, and I spend so much time with her that I don't always have time for others."

He paused for a moment, as if weighing what to say next, but all he said was, "Is there anything more, Sister?"

"No, that's all, Father."

"Then keep listening to God. I feel sure He'll help you sort this out. God understands your struggles."

He hadn't said much, but when he absolved me, I felt a burden lift from my shoulders. I left the confessional sure that God had forgiven me and would give me grace to fight my inclinations.

21

I CAN'T

I nearly dropped the phone when the sister from San Gregorio announced that Mother had been reelected superior general. How could the Chapter spurn the request of an old woman for a little rest and the opportunity to train someone to take her place? And why hadn't Mother refused the election? The sister on the phone also reported that since the *Constitutions* allowed only two consecutive terms to a superior general, the Chapter had petitioned the Holy See, and within hours the Curia had granted the exemption.

I held my breath as the sister announced the new roster of councilors: Sister Frederick first, then Sisters Joseph Michael, Priscilla, and Monica. I wondered if Sister Joseph Michael could count on support from Sister Monica, a sister who'd impressed me as more motherly than political.

The sister also said the Holy Father had called Mother to Rome. She was to address the synod of bishops, and would arrive in just a few days. I wondered if Mother was as devastated by most of this news as I was.

. . .

I was still reeling when Niobe followed me into the office and shut the door. As she reached for me, I looked firmly into her eyes and told her, "I really don't want to today."

"Just one kiss," she said, moving closer.

"No, please, I can't do this anymore." I took several paces backward. "It's not right."

"You don't like it?" she asked, putting her right arm around my left shoulder.

"It's not a question of whether I like it or not." I stepped back. "It's not right. We have vows." I took her arm off my shoulder. "Niobe," I said, "I'm sorry. I should have said no long ago. What we're doing is wrong."

"But we love each other. How can it be wrong if we love each other? Just one kiss." Niobe moved closer, grabbing me around the waist.

"No."

She pushed me against the wall, both hands pressing on my chest. I tried to push back, but I couldn't budge her. She brought her face closer to mine, pressed her lips against my lips, and tried to ram her tongue through my clenched teeth.

When she finally let me loose, I ran to the chapel. *My God*, I prayed, *I am so sorry. Deliver me from my mistakes. Please, please forgive me.*

The next time Niobe came to talk about her meditation, she tried to kiss me again. I pulled away.

She looked disappointed but didn't try to force anything. She sat down on the bed next to me and put her hand on my knee.

I removed her hand and asked, "So how did your meditation go today?"

"I looked at the trees and the sky, and saw how beautifully God has made everything."

"You didn't meditate on the Beatitudes, as we talked about last time?"

"No—I can't pray like that. Words are not important to me. I want to experience beauty. That's what brings me close to God."

"Do you ever feel God asking you to change anything?"

"Change anything?"

"Yes, in your life. To become more generous or honest, or anything like that."

"I'm all right with God. God hasn't asked me to change anything since I entered."

"How can that be? How about when you're with me and you ask me to do things I don't want and I tell you no and you do it anyway?"

"Are you making this about us? I thought we were talking about God."

"You can't talk about God separate from your neighbor."

"I don't give in to you for your own good. You don't know what it's like to be loved. How will you ever know if you push me away? I just want to be a beautiful sign of God's love for you. What could be wrong with that?"

I was exhausted. She had been a beautiful sign of God's love for me. But it no longer felt like love. It felt like something else, and I didn't like it.

"Niobe," I said, "I'm telling you I need a break. If you love me, you will respect this. Let's just behave like normal sisters."

"For how long do you want this 'break'?"

"Until I say otherwise."

"Okay." She shrugged, then bowed for a blessing.

A couple of days after I'd announced the break and before we'd had another mini-retreat meeting, I felt a shove from behind as I entered the bathroom. Niobe pushed me in and closed the door behind us.

"Niobe," I whispered, "what are you doing?"

"I love you," she said. "I want you." She pushed me against the wall with both hands. "I need you. No more break."

"Niobe, let me go," I said.

"You can't say that you don't love me. I know you do."

I heard the sound of footsteps in the hall. Her hands against my chest hurt.

"Niobe," I whispered, "let go." She eased the pressure a little but did not remove her hands. "I love you," I said, "but I'm not going to express that love in a physical way anymore. I can't do it."

"Why not?" she said.

"It's not right," I said. "Now let me go."

She pressed more firmly into my chest with one hand and began caressing my face with the other. "My little *pulcino*," she said, "you don't know what you want." She kissed me on the forehead, paused to listen for footsteps in the corridor, then opened the door and went out.

The next day Niobe followed me into the office. Before she could pin me down, I stepped on her foot.

Incredulous, she looked at me. I pointed to the bed. She sat and I stood by the door, leaving it open just a crack.

"Niobe, do you know that we have both taken vows of chastity?" I asked.

"Are you trying to make me feel guilty?" she said. "I told you, I don't experience God the way other people do, with words and books and Rules. God doesn't live in books. He lives in people."

"Then don't you think God would want you to respect the wishes of other people?"

"You don't know what you want." Her tone was vicious.

"What I want is for you to stop touching me," I said. "And we're going to stop this special retreat of yours, too."

"But I need your help, and I'm learning so much, and you told me you loved me. How can you not have time for your friend?" She'd switched from anger to pleading so quickly that I felt dizzy.

"It's useless, Niobe. You're not improving—you're not even trying."

"Of course I'm trying. How can you say that? Who are you to judge me?"

"Come back and see me when it's time to renew your general permission, not before. Not in the office, not in the dormitory, not anywhere."

"Suit yourself," she said. She got up and slammed the door behind her.

Niobe did not appear for dinner that night. Sister Patrick went to call her at the end of the garden, thinking she hadn't heard the bell, but when she returned, Sister Patrick whispered in my ear, "Sister, she says she's not coming."

"Let her be," I said. She didn't show up for recreation, either, nor for the blessing before Night Prayer, nor for Night Prayer. By the time I got to the dormitory, she was already in bed, sleeping with her back to my bed a few spaces down.

I hardly slept that night. I asked myself a thousand times if I was doing the right thing. Each time I answered yes. I still felt something very tender for Niobe, but if she couldn't respect my request to keep her hands off me for three days, this was not love.

In the morning Niobe got up with the community and came to the chapel for Morning Prayer and Mass but didn't show up for breakfast. The sister who went to the garden to call her came back with a frown. "She's says she's not coming. I think she wants you to go get her."

I was tired of giving in. I was on my way to San Gregorio for lunch with Mother. Niobe would come round sooner or later.

As Mother led grace before lunch in San Gregorio, her voice sounded flat and weak, and she moved more slowly than usual to her stool at the end of the table. Since all the "big" sisters of the region were in Calcutta at the Chapter, I took a place just two seats down from Mother. I hoped she wouldn't see the strain of the past few days on my face, but Mother hardly looked up. She seemed completely drained.

Even with my concerns about Niobe, I still found plenty of energy to be angry at the Pope. Why had he called this ailing woman away from a moment of real importance to her and to her sisters? No one left the Chapter during deliberations, especially not the foundress and superior general.

Mother's eyelids drooped. She pushed the pasta from one side of the plate to the other, occasionally rounding up a *radiatore* or two on a spoon and placing them in her mouth for a long chew before swallowing. Everyone felt awkward: We couldn't ask Mother about the Chapter because the members were all sworn to secrecy, and we'd already asked her about the synod, and all she'd said was, "The Holy Father looks very tired." If Sister Joseph Michael had been around, she would have told a funny story—she knew how to help Mother out of herself. Then I remembered.

"Mother," I said, "last week I got a letter from my grandfather, who's ten years older than you are—he was born in 1900." Mother nodded slowly, without looking up from her plate. "He told me that he didn't understand how Mother could keep going around the world at her age, and he said that when I see you I should tell you that he thinks you should rest."

Looking straight at me, Mother shouted: "I can't!" Her eyes piercing me, she shouted even more loudly, her voice quavering: "It is God's will!" After a moment, Mother looked down at her plate again, and I looked at mine, fork trembling.

For several seconds no one at the table moved. Slowly forks began scraping enamel bowls again, and quietly, at the far end of the table, conversation resumed.

My God, what did I do? Would it have been possible to choose a worse story to tell Mother? Probably not. What was I thinking? I wasn't thinking. I was just trying to fill a silence.

I realized I was still angry at Mother—not for shouting at me, but for having given in to the sisters. I was a continual witness to my own failure to stand firm when someone wanted something from me, but somehow I'd assumed Mother knew how to insist, how to make others do what she saw was right.

Mother had spun a web of beliefs about God's will, and now she was caught in it. Until then, Mother had sometimes seemed a demure Saint, hands folded, always repeating the words of Our Lady: "Be it done to me according to your will." At that lunch in San Gregorio she cried out like Jesus on the cross: "My God, my God, why have you abandoned me?"

When I returned to Casilina, I taught class. Niobe did not come. I told the sisters Mother was tired. All the time I talked to them about methods of meditation, I was thinking of Mother and her pain, and of Niobe, alone in the garden. How long was she going to stay there? What was she thinking, feeling? How many people had I angered that day?

Before recreation, Sister Patrick told me, "Sister Niobe can't just stay in the garden like this. I went to convince her to come back, but she says she's not coming unless you come to her first." I could have sent a message with Sister Patrick, but I didn't want to involve other sisters in this.

Moonlight shone on the path, casting eerie shadows through the eucalyptus branches as I walked toward the end of the garden. *My God, help me.* Should I be angry and demand that she return? That wasn't likely to be effective. Should I ask forgiveness? I didn't see that I'd done anything wrong—at least not the things she would think were wrong. I had to find a way to make her come back without giving in to her.

As my feet crunched on the gravel, I saw a form at the end of the garden move even closer to the wall. Her back was turned to me. I stopped about five feet behind her.

"Niobe, please come back," I said.

Only crickets broke the silence. Finally she spoke. "You don't care that I've been out here for more than a day, alone, crying, hearing those words of yours in my head, 'You're not trying.' How can you say I'm not trying?"

"If you were trying, you would be with the community, wouldn't you?"

"How can I?" Her back still faced me. "You said such ugly things to me."

"I didn't mean to hurt you."

She said nothing, just picked up stones and threw them at the wall.

I couldn't bear the silence. I had to see her face. "I really do miss you, you know?"

Still she did not speak, did not turn around. A train passed just behind the wall, blowing its whistle and making the ground shake. The moon hid behind clouds. I heard more stones against the wall.

I heard her take a few steps—toward me, I hoped. "I think you owe me an apology," she said.

"An apology? For what?"

"For judging me. I've been trying very hard. You don't know how difficult it is for me. You think I'm taking advantage of you, but my heart is pure. All I want is to come closer to Jesus."

"If you want to come closer to Jesus, why didn't you come for adoration?"

"I prayed here, and when you were out in the morning, then I went to the chapel."

"Niobe—"

"You can't judge me. I love you."

"I love you, too." I didn't want to say that. I had been determined not to say anything vaguely resembling that. "Now, please come back."

"Is that an apology?"

"Come back, Niobe. I miss you."

She turned around. "If you're really sorry, give me a big hug." I moved forward into her arms, and she entered mine. Entering her embrace was strange and right and wrong and beautiful and very, very dangerous. My mind knew that. The rest of me didn't seem to care.

22

NIGHTS

FALL 1990
CASILINA, ROME

One particular autumn night I was up late, finishing letters to send with sisters leaving for Ethiopia. Sisters in the missions had it hard, and letters eased their loneliness. At the dormitory door, I slipped my plastic slippers off and carried them in my hand, careful not to disturb my sleeping sisters. A sliver of light shone through a single shutter near my bed, probably left open by Niobe. When we'd changed beds at the beginning of the month—as we did every month, rotating spots on the clothes shelves and bookshelves and plate shelves as well, to avoid becoming attached to any particular space—Niobe had begged me to assign her a bed near mine. She hadn't asked any favors for a while, hadn't cornered me in the office or bathroom since her self-exile to the garden. When she'd pleaded, "Pleeeease," just like a kid, I decided it couldn't hurt. Besides, having her sleep near me would be a safe way to be close.

The light from the shutter guided me through the long, narrow aisles between the beds. At my bed, I removed the crucifix from my side, kissed it, and placed it on top of the blanket. Jesus' bronze body glinted in the moonlight. I unpinned my sari, folded it, and placed it under the pillow as I simultaneously pulled out my nightdress, a smooth motion honed by years of repetition.

Kneeling by the bed, I kissed the floor, then stretched my arms in the form of a cross. Fatigued, I rushed the five Our Fathers and five Hail Marys that had been my bedtime prayer for the last fourteen years, trusting Jesus wouldn't mind. After a concluding Glory Be, I kissed the floor again. Still kneeling, I clasped my crucifix and bent to kiss the wounds of my Crucified Spouse, renewing my vow of poverty as I kissed His right hand, chastity on the left, obedience on the right foot, service on the left, begging grace to persevere as I kissed His side.

I slid my nightdress over my head while wiggling out of habit, bodice, and chemise in the intricate dance at which I had eventually, after years of entanglement in sleeves and straps, become quite deft. As my day clothes fell to the floor on which I still knelt, I pushed my arms through the sleeves of my nightdress, fastened the snaps in the front, and rose. I folded my habit and undergarments, then lay them on top of my sari, under the pillow. Finally I reached to close the shutter. In pitch darkness I folded the blanket back, crawled between the sheets, and set my glasses under the bed.

I closed my eyes and turned my head slowly, then rolled my shoulders to release the ache of hours bent over paperwork. The steady snores of a sister at the far end of the dormitory alternated with the occasional groans of another. I was trying to recall the morning's Gospel passage when I felt something warm—a hand, on my left arm. I jerked my head. No one stood beside my bed.

God, what's happening to me?

The hand moved slowly up my arm, toward my shoulder.

I shook my arm, but the hand did not stop. First one inch, then another, the hand slid up my arm.

I twisted my head in the darkness but still saw no one. *No, I'm not crazy. I really feel a hand on my arm.*

When it reached my shoulder, the hand rested there. Its size, its weight, its musky smell—Niobe, in the bed next to mine. My body seized. I didn't want her touching me again—and in the dormitory someone might see us.

I reached to dislodge her hand, but as I shifted, her hand vanished. Hours passed before thoughts of that creeping hand finally gave way to restless sleep.

Niobe didn't come to see me the next day, which was fine with me. I didn't want to think about that hand. There were plenty of other things to worry about—tertians to talk with, classes to teach.

That night I was again last to the dormitory, and so tired I didn't even think of the hand. I was nearly asleep when I felt the hand gently massage my shoulder. This time it didn't feel creepy. After a minute or two it felt good. That firm hand kneaded fear and resistance out, and I relaxed into a deep sleep.

Again she didn't come to see me that day. I was so relieved not to deal with Niobe during the day—not to have to talk her into distance, not to fear what she might do behind closed doors—that I started to look forward to the nights, the relative safety of the shoulder massage amid the snores of the dark dormitory. The nightly massage felt caring and didn't steal time that belonged to others. I'd missed the part of Niobe's attention that was kind.

Yet I worried. I dreamed of the two of us standing before Mother and Jesus. Jesus accused us with impassioned words: *You hypocrites, wearing the white robes of chastity by day, partaking of fleshly pleasures by night. We damn you to eternal fire.* Mother pointed toward the steaming pit. This was really unusual. I never dreamed of hell, never thought much of hell. I hardly believed in hell.

I worried that someone in the next bed over, or across the aisle, would see us or hear us. This sister would report us, and before going to hell, I would be sent to Siberia and Niobe to Freetown or Papua New Guinea.

When Niobe stretched over one night and began to unbutton my nightdress, I pushed her hand away. Shoulder rub, yes; groping, no. Her hand returned. I wrapped my fingers around her wrist and pulled up hard but could not dislodge her. She resisted so firmly, so surely, that I couldn't even feel the resistance, only a stubborn weight planted on my chest. A whisper was dangerous, but I breathed out a solid "No" anyway. For a moment neither of us moved. Then the fingers slipped under my nightdress and marched across my torso. When the fingers reached my breast, I was so absolutely still that my breath stopped. As the hand cupped my soft flesh, resistance melted, and we seemed to float above every snoring sister in the dormitory.

After the Chapter, Sister Martin de Porres took Sister Elsitta's place as superior of Casilina. I felt confident with this short, plump, intelligent sister from north India, with a cross tattoo on her forehead like Sister Sajani's. Sister Martin and Sister Fatima had been the first MCs to study at Regina Mundi, when I wasn't even in junior high.

Each Thursday I continued to sit opposite Father Tom for confession, trying to take responsibility for my sins. I avoided his eyes; I didn't deserve the compassion I found there. I was particularly ashamed of my repeated struggles with Niobe. What we were doing was obviously wrong. I should have been able to put an end to it, but Thursday after Thursday, I confessed the same sins.

One Thursday I looked at my hands, then at the ceiling, then into Father Tom's eyes, then quickly to the floor. "I know what I'm doing with this sister is wrong," I said, "but sometimes it feels so good. Even God seems closer, and I start to feel that He really loves me again. I can't understand. I want to be faithful to my vows, and I want to be with her all the time, and I don't want to neglect the other sisters, and I end up all confused."

"Sister," he said, leaning close, "life can get very complicated. God knows your goodwill, your desires. The experience of human love can be very healing."

"Sometimes I feel that I'm being healed, freed, and at other times I feel like I'm in a trap or a cage and I can't get out."

"What is that cage made of?" His eyes were concerned, inviting.

"Sometimes the cage is my vows, because I want so much to be with her and I feel God so present when I'm with her, but my vows say I shouldn't. At other times my desires for her are my cage, because I want to be faithful to my vows but don't seem able. Sometimes she seems like the cage, because she doesn't listen to me. Sometimes my confusion is the cage, because I have all these different desires at war in me and I can't figure out what God wants."

"Honest questions can be more important than answers. Just keep asking the questions, and continue to be honest with yourself. I know it's difficult to be in a place of uncertainty, but keep searching, without getting too uptight. You'll find your own way. Listen to God in your heart."

Before I left that day, Father Tom added, "If you need me anytime, during the week, whenever, just call me. We can talk. If I'm free, I'll come down. You don't have to go through this alone."

Such a generous offer. I knew I wouldn't phone—phoning required asking permission, which would raise questions. If a priest arrived at the gate unexpectedly, asking for me, there would be even more suspicion. But the thought that he was willing comforted me.

Niobe followed me into the dormitory one day. "That was a great class," she said, shutting the door behind her. "Really great."

I put my Bible on the desk, relieved that she wanted to talk about class, and asked, "What did you get out of it?"

She grabbed my arm and pulled me close. She pushed back my sari and reached one hand inside my habit, clutching for my breast. I tried to push myself away, but her grip held me fast. This was the first time she'd tried anything during the day since she'd banished herself to the garden.

"You can't do this," I said.

"I love you. I want you." She whispered, "I need you," and began untying my bodice.

"Niobe, stop."

"No. I need you."

I kicked her shin, and she loosened her grip, though she didn't let me go.

Her face was blank. "You can't do this to me," she said, rubbing her shin with one hand.

"You can't do this to *me*," I said, tying my bodice.

"Don't you know I love you?"

"I love you, too, but not like this." I tried to make my voice firm, authoritative. I tried to imagine I was Sister Marie Therese, delivering an ultimatum.

"You don't know what real love is. You've never felt it, skin against skin, one body inside another." She stopped rubbing her shin and looked at me, her brown eyes searching me. "You don't know that feeling."

"I've chosen not to know it. I've given it up. I belong to God."

She shook her head. "You never had a chance. You don't know what you've given up. How can you give a gift without knowing what it is?"

"Niobe—"

She held my shoulders in her hands and shook me a little. "You need to experience real love," she said. "I will show you. Just give me one night, and then I won't ask anymore."

"You don't ask now. You just take."

Her eyes registered hurt, like that night when she'd complained that I'd told her she wasn't trying. She turned her face away.

I cradled her chin in one hand and guided her gaze back to me. "No more pushing me against the wall?" I asked. "No following me into the office?"

"No. I promise," she said. "Let me give you just one night, then I will stop. Let me show you how much I love you, and let yourself feel it."

It was tempting, but what she was suggesting was so clearly sinful that I shouldn't even consider it. "Niobe, I don't need to feel it."

"You don't know what you need."

"Niobe, leave me alone."

"I love you. You don't know how much I love you."

Picking up my Bible again, I walked in front of her and out the door, to the chapel, heart thumping in my chest, skin tingling with forbidden thoughts.

As the days passed and I busied myself with supervising the tertians and explicating the Gospel of John, curiosity over Niobe's proposal returned. I found myself remembering Bernini's marvelous statue of Teresa of Avila in the Church of Santa Maria della Vittoria—the art history book I'd read at school said the statue was erotic, that the artist had depicted Teresa in orgasm. She looked as though she'd been carried outside herself, into something greater, into God. How could that be wrong?

A willful violation of my vows was obviously wrong. Even thinking these thoughts was sinful, and I was tired of it all. Niobe promised to leave me alone if I gave her one night. Then we could be normal, peaceful. She would stop paying attention to me, and I could stop my sinful curiosity. It was tempting.

I thought about it all the time.

The marble under my bare feet was cold that night, the shutters, save the one near my bed, drawn. Only the deep breathing of the sisters and the creak of springs as someone tossed on her mattress disturbed the dormitory's quiet.

I pulled the final shutter gently closed and leaned over her bed. In the darkness I could not see her form, but I knew where her shoulder was, and I touched it gently.

"Tonight," I whispered in her ear. "I want it tonight."

She rolled over and grunted. "Not tonight. I'm tired."

All this time she's been after me to do this, and now she's tired? "Now or never. I'm ready."

She rolled over. She grunted. "Tomorrow."

I did not move.

She turned in bed and whispered, "Do you really want it?"

I paused, but I did not hesitate. The pause was for emphasis. "Yes."

"Go upstairs—the empty room, in the middle. I will come." I nodded, even as she pulled the sheet over her head. At the door I turned back to look. No one seemed to be paying any attention.

I met no one on the stairs. I prayed for a deep sleep for my sisters. *God, I dare to ask Your assistance, even tonight.* At the top of the stairs I paused in the shadow cast by a nearly full moon against a half-open shutter. A sister snored in the dormitory on the right. I turned left. The beds were empty in the three small, unused rooms that lined the corridor between the top of the stairs and the bathroom. I entered the middle room and pulled the door silently behind me, leaving it narrowly cracked.

What am I about to do? Better not to think about it. I have decided, and I will do it, and tomorrow I will confess. I will not think. I will look out the window and wait. Beyond the fence, I saw the street, trees, buildings with lights on. The breeze rustled my nightdress. Would she lift it when she came? Footsteps approached, then passed the door and continued on. *Dear God, please don't let anyone come looking for me.* I held my breath and my chest tightened until I heard the toilet flush. The footsteps passed the door again, and I sat on a bed. *Should I be standing or sitting when she comes? Or lying on the bed?* Then the door opened, and she was there. I never heard her coming.

"Are you sure?" she whispered, her breath warm against my cheek. "Yes."

She turned the doorknob carefully and closed the door. With both hands, she grabbed one end of a bed and nodded me toward the other. We lifted the bed quietly and placed it against the door, blocking the entrance. Niobe unfolded herself, upright, still.

"You are so beautiful," she said. She held out her arms, and I entered. She smelled like woodsmoke and soap, and I felt safe. She invited me onto a bed in the corner, and I sat, looking into her eyes. She lifted my legs onto the bed, her arms strong yet gentle. At first she sat beside me, caressing my face with her fingers, kissing my eyelids. Then she nudged me onto my back, and I pulled her down with me. She stretched her body on top of mine, face to face, limb to limb. Her weight comforted. She pulled back my headpiece and ran her fingers across the nubs of hair, kissing the top of my head. She kissed my forehead, my cheeks, my lips, and all the while her weight pressed down, her body mirroring my own. Her lips, sun-rough, traced paths down my arms.

"I love you," she whispered. "I want you. I need you."

The next morning I made my confession behind the screen. I could hear Father Tom breathing on the other side. "I did something really wrong," I said. "I mean, I had the most marvelous experience last night—the Church says it is a sin—but I never imagined anything so wonderful." He pressed his head closer to the screen. My heart beat very fast. "You know, with that sister I've felt close to. I know I wasn't supposed to, but it felt like a real experience of God's love. I don't know if you understand—"

"Yes, Sister, I understand." His gentle voice did not judge me.

"Like I said, I know it was wrong. I won't do it again—that was part of the reason I did it. She said she would stop if I let her have one night. I suppose I must have offended God, and I'm sorry for that, but I don't know how God could honestly be offended by something so wonderful. Didn't God make us like this, after all? Except of course I promised Him I wouldn't do it, and now—" I took a deep breath, trying to draw shame out of my heart, but exuberance bubbled up instead. "I never knew my body was capable of that. But God knew, and God called me here, and I won't do it again." I clutched the ledge of the confessional.

"Sister, I hardly know what to say."

"Just give me a penance, Father."

"A penance? A penance for something like this?" He almost sounded happy for me. But I'd just committed a mortal sin. He must have been looking for a penance big enough.

"Sister, I want you to meditate on the first chapter of Genesis, the part where it says that God made man and woman in his own image and likeness. Will you do that?"

"Yes, Father."

"Good."

"Father, the absolution?"

"You want absolution?"

"Yes, Father, I'm really sorry."

"I absolve you in the name of the Father and of the Son and of the Holy Spirit."

"Amen."

I was so glad that was over. Niobe and I could go back to normal. I wouldn't have to think about those things anymore.

That afternoon Niobe followed me into the dormitory to renew her general permissions. As she closed the door with one hand, she grabbed me with the other and pushed me against the door.

Her upper body pressed against me while her hand reached under my sari. She was not gentle.

"Niobe, don't. I gave you what you wanted. Now you've promised to leave me alone."

"Your body is so beautiful."

"Niobe, now I've experienced my body, and I want to give it back to Jesus." She flattened me more firmly against the door. "Niobe—stop. You promised."

"How can you stop now?" She pulled down my underpants. I kicked her shin, but she continued. "You are so beautiful." The tingling between my legs felt so good. It shouldn't feel good. This was sinful. "You are so beautiful."

"You're greedy, and we both have vows of chastity."

"I want to make you feel good." Footsteps in the hall. Niobe immediately straightened, dropped my sari, and stepped back slightly, leaving her hands on the door at my shoulders, like a cage. The footsteps continued toward the bathroom. She pressed herself against me again.

She pressed herself against me in the dormitory that day, she pulled me into the office when Sister Martin wasn't there, she followed me into go-downs and bathrooms. I pushed back. I kicked. I stepped on her feet. She pushed harder and longer. I confessed my inability to stop, my confusion, my intolerance, my desire. I moved my bed away from hers. I told her never to touch me again. She told me she knew what was best for me and what I really wanted. I hated it. I loved it. I wanted it to be over.

23

SUBTERFUGE

FALL 1990 TO SPRING 1991
CASILINA, ROME

About a week after the night that should have ended every-thing, Sister Agnel came for a visit. She said she wanted to see me privately. She looked very serious. I was sure someone had told her something about Niobe and me. As frightening as that was on one level, on another I was almost relieved.

"I shouldn't be telling you this," Sister Agnel said as she sat on Mother's bed, indicating a stool for me. "At the General Chapter we took an oath not to reveal anything we discussed. But I've thought about it a lot, and there's something you need to know." Maybe this wasn't about Niobe and me after all.

"At the beginning of the Chapter," Sister continued, "the coun-cilors read all the letters that the sisters from the mission houses had written. At a certain point they got to a particular letter, and Mother became very angry." Sister Agnel looked down, then up at me, seeming unsure whether she should continue.

"You don't have to tell me, Sister."

"I wish I didn't have to tell you, but I think I do. Mother was angry because the letter talked about a sister who touched another sister. And it was very explicit—not nice to listen to. A senior sister said that a junior sister in her community wanted special attention, and that the junior sister touched the senior sister, forcing her, and the letter said exactly where she touched her, and how often. The letter also said that as a novice this junior sister had done the same things to other novices, and that her novice mistresses knew, but allowed her to take her vows anyway. As the councilor read the letter, we could all see Mother becoming very angry. Before the letter was finished, Mother stood up and said the letter shouldn't have been read. She said it was a serious matter and told us to forget that we had ever heard it. She told us never to mention it again. Then she said that the regional superior of the sister who wrote the letter and the regional of the sister the letter mentioned should see Mother right away." Sister Agnel shook her head. I wasn't sure I wanted to know what happened next.

"I never saw Mother so angry," Sister said. "She said the Chapter had no right to spoil a sister's name. But no names had been read, and I didn't know who the letter was from, nor who it was talking about.

"The next day several sisters came to me quietly and asked, 'How did it go with Mother?' I told them I hadn't seen Mother, and they looked at me strangely and went away. Then after lunch one of the regionals told me, 'I know the sisters in that letter. It happened in my region, and now one of those sisters is in your region.' She told me I'd better go see Mother.

"Well, I still didn't know who it was, but I went to Mother and she was still upset. She asked me why I took so long to come, and I told her that I didn't know who the letter was talking about, and that I still didn't know, but that someone had told me she was in my region.

"Mother didn't believe at first that I didn't know, but afterward she told me. Mother kept repeating that the sister's name had been spoiled, that the Chapter had no right to talk about things which were a matter for confession, not for public discussion." Sister Agnel sighed, like she didn't want to continue.

"Mother must have been upset," I said, "that the sister had been allowed to take vows and was forcing the other sister like that."

"No." Sister Agnel shook her head. "Mother was upset because the senior sister had written the letter, and Mother said that the senior sister must be at fault, because no junior sister can force a senior sister to do anything, and the senior sister should have known better and should have had the decency to keep such things to herself and not write to the Chapter about them.

"The reason I'm telling you all this"—she took a big breath in—"is because that sister is in your group now, and I want you to keep an eye on her." She paused, then said the inevitable. "That sister is Sister Niobe." Another long pause as Sister Agnel looked at the ground, then straight into my eyes. "You can't tell her any of what I've told you, but you must watch her, and if you see that she is getting close to any sister, you must separate them immediately. When the time comes, you'll write your report, but it can't look like I've told you anything. You'll have to see it with your own eyes."

"I won't tell anyone," I said, shaking my head. "Thank you for telling me, though. I'll watch her."

"Mother was so angry. I've never seen Mother angry like that."

I left the office stunned. How many other sisters had Niobe told "I love you"? How many had she convinced? How many had she pushed against walls, shoved into corners? Sister Agnel said that she'd started when she was a novice—and then there'd been that mysterious "trouble" she'd had in Madrid, the problems we weren't supposed to ask about.

Mother's position flabbergasted me. Mother didn't care that Niobe abused and manipulated other sisters—she was upset because others were spoiling Niobe's name by talking about it? Of course Mother blamed the senior sister. Oh, Niobe was clever. She wasn't choosing novices any longer—she chose sisters who were supposed

to know better, sisters who would be held responsible. I was responsible more than most—I was her tertian mistress.

Niobe had a problem. That was obvious now. I had a problem,
too.

Using the clues in Sister Agnel's story, I was able to identify the
sister who had written the letter: a Westerner, intelligent and hardworking, but overweight and an outsider socially, probably someone
who had never heard the words "I love you" before, though she
hadn't been able to stop longing for those words. Someone who
had—like me, I thought—wanted to hear those words so badly that
she'd clung to them like a life raft when, in fact, they were a lead
weight pulling her under.

When the time came to write reports, I started with the easy ones,
each sister's name at the head of a new page in a little notebook.
Twenty-eight pages with twenty-eight names. *Sister Tobit Paul: generous, cheerful, hardworking, deep faith and personal relationship with
God, can improve in punctuality. Sister Emelda: serious, committed, hardworking, can be judgmental. Sister Ilario: simple, cheerful, stubborn if op-
posed. Sister Patrick: strong sense of duty, deep desire for prayer, tries her
best to make her sisters happy, needs to relax a bit more. Sister Josefa:
cheerful, prayerful, withdraws when upset; suffers from severe asthma, so
should not be given hard physical labor or be exposed to dust.*

After completing these short notes, I would add other observa-
tions, form complete sentences, a paragraph or two. At the end of
each report I had to make a recommendation. This was the last
chance for the Society to send someone home. Once a sister took
final vows, canon law forbade the Society to dismiss her unless she
did something really serious, such as run away with lots of money,
get married, or publicly support abortion clinics. Not uncommonly,
someone who had appeared zealous as a junior sister relaxed into
incredible laziness after final vows, or a sister who had obeyed un-
questioningly refused assignments or started arguing. My recommendations were important.

With the tertians I had more options than I'd had with the novices. If a sister needed to strengthen her prayer life, I could suggest that she be given another six months in tertianship, in which case she would remain in Casilina and join Sister Martin's group. If she needed to be tested regarding community living or the apostolate, she could be given additional time in a mission house. The easiest thing for everyone was for a sister who wasn't ready for vows to realize it herself and ask for additional time in her letter to Mother. That way she showed humility and avoided the stigma of having been "postponed."

I felt fairly confident in recommending most of the sisters in that group for final vows. They'd been eager to learn, united, hardworking and serious, without lacking in good humor. I didn't expect much trouble when the time came for me to read each sister her report before sending the reports to Calcutta—except for Niobe.

Why did Niobe even want to take final vows? She would have been happier in the world, I thought, marrying somebody rich, traveling in style. I knew Niobe didn't want to be postponed. She'd been postponed before first vows and often had remarked that it hadn't done her any good. I knew Niobe should go home, but I didn't have the strength to tell her so. She would complain that I didn't love her. She would banish herself to the garden once more. I hadn't been able to convince her not to touch me; how could I convince her to go home? She needed someone else to help her leave in peace.

Sister Niobe: doubtful sincerity, avoids hard work, weak prayer life, difficulties with chastity, seeks special treatment. Not ready for final vows. Should go to Calcutta for further testing.

When sisters arriving from Calcutta brought the permissions, Sister Agnel told me that Sister Niobe had been postponed for six months.

"Good," I said. "Here or in Calcutta?"

"Here."

"She should go to Calcutta."

"The council wants her here," Sister Agnel said. "She is our problem."

"When will you give the permissions?"

"I won't," Sister Agnel said. "Mother's coming in a week, to prepare for the house in Albania."

When Mother came, the sisters in line outside her room shifted from one foot to another, looking up, down, left, right. From my seat near the open refectory door I searched for a smile on the face of at least one, but all I saw were wrinkled foreheads, tight cheeks, closed eyes. Most of the sisters clutched a copy of the *Constitutions* or *Mother's Instructions*, in which they'd stashed several holy cards they would ask Mother to autograph for their families. Many of these sisters hadn't seen Mother since their first professions, but I knew that most of them could think only of the little slips of paper that waited behind that closed door.

As sisters emerged from Mother's room, some smiled, others cried. Sister Patrick wiped her forehead and looked for me, waved her paper and nodded. Another emerged as though she'd run a marathon, panting, "My God, I made it, I made it."

Niobe was nowhere to be seen. There was nothing too unusual about that. Mother would take a good while to see twenty-eight sisters individually, each of whom would enter, kneel down, kiss the floor, speak her faults and ask pardon, receive her paper and a blessing from Mother, and then speak with Mother for a while, usually still on her knees. Each sister took her place in line when she felt ready. Some sisters waited in the chapel, others paced the garden.

Finally, when nearly everyone had already been through the line, Niobe joined the queue outside Mother's door. She leaned against the bookshelves in the corridor, a copy of *Mother's General Letters to the Sisters* cradled in her arms. Smiling at the sisters in line, she said, "Loosen up a little. Mother's not going to kill you." No one responded. "Come on now—what are you so nervous about?"

"Be quiet," Sister Tobit Paul snapped, staring Niobe down.

As the sisters entered and exited, Niobe continued to lean

against the bookshelves, leaving a gap in line. Sister Emelda, behind her, whispered, "Move up," and Niobe turned to look down at her for a moment, then remained rooted in place. Though Niobe knew I hadn't recommended her for profession, she was the only nonchalant sister around. She must have been at least a little nervous, but it was like her to put up a strong front. I worried that, in her fury when she received her postponement, she'd accuse me of not caring for her, even walk out of the house, and I, in my weakness, would run after her.

Finally the door opened again and Niobe slid in. I wondered, now that she was in front of Mother, if she would finally speak her faults sincerely. Would she accept her postponement with humility, or would she rant and accuse me of having written lies? *Why is she taking so long? Is she telling Mother all her personal history? Is Mother being taken in by the sincerity Niobe can exude with so much heartfelt duplicity?* I tapped my fingers on the refectory table. *This is taking—*

The door opened, and Niobe smiled, but not at me. She turned sharply through the door, and sauntered to the garden.

When the bell rang for lunch, everyone went to the compound. Mother began grace, then sat on the little stool prepared for her while the rest of us settled on the carpets spread over the ancient Roman cobblestones. Mother never used to use a stool, but her legs were so swollen that she accepted the stool gratefully.

Sister Agnel took her place next to Mother, and Sister Martin sat on Mother's other side. I sat next to Sister Agnel. One of the tertians brought food for the four of us, while the tertians served themselves buffet style from a table at the back. Soon several sisters sat near me, telling me how relieved they were to finally have permission, how Mother signed the cards for their parents, how she looked so tired . . . and then Niobe elbowed her way into a space that didn't exist, so that she could sit close enough that we could hear each other, but not close enough that we would speak with each other.

"I'm so happy it's over," I heard Sister Patrick tell Niobe.

"Yes, well, it's not quite over for me," Niobe replied.

"No?"

"No, I asked for another year, so Mother is sending me to a mission house."

I dropped a fork full of pasta, leaving a trail of tomato sauce down my sari. *She asked for a year? What in heaven's name could she be talking about?* Then it crystallized. Mother must have told Niobe that she'd have six months more in tertianship. Niobe then told Mother that she had realized she needed more time, that she wasn't ready, and could she please have another year instead of just six months, because six months wasn't enough time to conquer her faults. What it really meant was that she wouldn't have to live with the stigma of being postponed, but with the distinction of having had the humility to "ask for more time"—and that when her year was up, she'd return to Casilina in *my* group, not someone else's.

I was still fuming when Mother began talking, with great pride, about the house she would open in Albania. This was the moment for which we'd prayed so long. For the past several years, whenever Mother arrived in Rome, she'd asked for an appointment with the Albanian ambassador, the ambassador of the only legally atheistic nation in the world, a nation where hundreds of priests and religious had been imprisoned, where making the sign of the cross was a criminal offense. The ambassador always told Mother that her request for a convent was impossible. Mother had continued to insist. She was the world's most famous Albanian, and they finally yielded. Albania changed its laws, and Mother was bringing her sisters to open a convent. Though Albania would be a difficult assignment, it had become one of the most coveted as well. The sisters going to Albania were special, and we applauded as Mother announced their names: Sister Ancilla, Sister Geralda, Sister Nellie Rose—Sister Niobe.

The furious applause was nothing compared to the roar within me. Sister Niobe? To Albania? Had she asked for that, too, or was it

some weird twist of fate? It was not unusual for a sister with problems to be strengthened and tried in a particularly challenging mission, or to be sent to a particularly "honorable" mission, to show her
that the Society still trusted her—but this was almost too much to
believe. The only good thing about this was that, at least for a while,
Niobe wouldn't be in Casilina with me.

24

VIRGIN

"Work on the dissertation has been slow," Father Tom said, stirring his coffee one Thursday afternoon in late June, "so when Sister Agnel asked me to go to Albania last weekend, I jumped at the chance."

I always waited to make my confession until the tertians had finished, so that Father Tom and I could segue naturally into these late Thursday afternoon coffee breaks, where he drank coffee and we both talked. Though being with Father Tom often excited me, nothing had made my heart race as much as this mere mention of Albania. I cursed myself. I was over Niobe, relieved that she'd been gone nearly three months—wasn't I? I offered Father Tom the plate of cookies, and he took two.

"The sisters hadn't had anyone to hear their confessions in English for a while," he continued, "and Sister Agnel wanted me to give them a talk. Things are really tough there—everything is so poor, and people ask for things all the time—the bell at that gate rings constantly." Father Tom took another sip of coffee.

I knew Albania was poor. What I wanted to know was if he'd seen Niobe. I was sure he knew that. Though I'd never shared my lover's name with Father Tom, Niobe's identity had become obvious when she hadn't taken vows that May.

Finally he said, "Sister Niobe drove to the airport to pick me up."

I pictured Father Tom next to Niobe in the front seat. I wanted so badly to have been in that seat.

"She drove me from place to place all weekend," he said, licking a cookie crumb from the corner of his mouth. "Those Albanian roads are hardly roads at all, but she handled the van like a pro, and we kept up a lively conversation. I can see why you like her. She's one of the most interesting sisters I've met." He paused and stirred his coffee. "Apart from you, of course."

I tried not to respond. Life was already complicated enough.

After a few more sips of coffee, he said, "You look quite low these days. Is something more than the usual bothering you?"

I was touched that he'd noticed. None of the sisters had asked—especially not Sister Dorothy, our new superior and senior tertian mistress. Sister Dorothy had been one of Mother's students in Calcutta and was among the first sisters to have joined. She enjoyed her status as a senior sister, and was too busy calling me useless and negligent in front of my tertians to have noticed that I hadn't been well. The specifics of my situation were embarrassing, but Father Tom had heard worse from me. "I've got menorrhagia," I said. "I lose a lot of blood every month. The doctor put me on hormones." I sighed a little. "You can imagine how I felt in the pharmacy, a nun with a prescription for birth control pills. They haven't had much effect on my bleeding, but they depress me. I feel like crying, and there's nobody to talk with. Sister Dorothy is impossible. Sister Agnel is good, but she's always busy."

"Yeah, I know what you mean. Not being able to talk is the worst part of religious life for me. We're supposed to be brothers in the Lord, but we're frightened to be honest, because you don't know who will repeat things to whom. The priests I live with are so old that most of them can't relate to what I have to say, anyway. To make things worse, my Italian isn't good enough to get all the nuances I'd like into a conversation. There are plenty of English-speaking priests in Rome, but only a handful at the house where I live."

He sighed, then added, "Weird things have been happening lately. Someone cut wires the other night, and we lost electricity in an entire wing. I suspect an older priest who seems to be suffering from Alzheimer's, but he refuses to see a doctor." He put his cup down and shook his head. "We've caught him piling rubbish outside the bedroom doors of other priests."

"I didn't know you priests were so interesting." I smiled at him, but he frowned and threw up his hands.

"Interesting? Lonely and frustrated, and if I try to talk about spiritual things, they look at me as though I'm crazy. They want to talk about soccer scores. The other night I tried discussing politics, and two of the priests from Sicily started a fistfight—one broke the other's glasses, and I couldn't understand a thing they said, but apparently they were cursing each other in Sicilian." He looked down, defeated.

"Why do you stay, Father?" I asked.

He looked into my eyes again. "I like being a priest," he said. "Spiritual life is important to me. I feel I have something to offer people, and I love to teach."

"You're good at it, too."

Father Tom smiled and rested his hand on my arm. "Why do you stay?" he asked. His hand felt good on my arm. He lifted it too soon.

"I feel God wants me here. I gave Him my word, and I'm not going to take it back," I said. "I love serving the poor, living like Jesus did, quiet prayer. So many of the sisters are wonderful—even Sister Dorothy has some redeeming qualities."

Father Tom smiled.

I continued, "I have something to offer, too. When I shared my thesis on the Eucharist and the poor, the novices drank my words in. I also did a workshop for the senior sisters in Belgium, and we got into some really honest discussions. I think I can make a difference."

"Good for you," he said. "I don't have much hope of making a difference in my community—we're centuries old, and I'm the new bloke on the block, but I know I can help others. Coming to you sisters makes my week."

We sat just looking at each other. It was nice, for a few minutes, not to feel alone.

I knelt in the chapel for adoration, seeking peace. In Casilina we prayed where Trappists, with their vow of silence, had chanted the Psalms for centuries. During air raids in the Second World War, the Servants of Divine Mercy had prayed in the tunnel under the chapel. Now we Missionaries of Charity knelt, fingering our rosaries.

I wondered if, over those many centuries, any of these people vowed to God had struggled with problems like mine. I'd recently received letters from Niobe. She'd asked for mozzarella and chocolate—a violation in itself since only superiors were supposed to request supplies, and then only from the regional superior. Then she'd gone on to ask for another night with me, a night in the small dormitory upstairs. I knew Niobe had asked Mother for time in a mission house so she could come back to my group, but I couldn't live with Niobe again.

Days earlier, when Mother had returned from Albania, I'd begged her to send Niobe to Calcutta to finish tertianship. I told Mother that I'd received disturbing letters, that Niobe liked me too much. I hadn't gone into specifics—from what Sister Agnel had told me, I understood that Mother wouldn't have wanted specifics even if I'd had the courage to give them—but I thought Mother would have understood enough when I told her Niobe liked me. Instead, Mother told me, "You are the best one to help her. Just keep her in her place."

That particular November afternoon, I told the Lord that I wanted to be faithful but that I was weak and scared. I gazed into the Host: Jesus present in the form of bread, so simple, so poor, so pure. *My God, I love You. I love You.* The words came easily and sincerely.

God loved me, too, just as I was. I rested silently in His presence, and confidence filled me. There were so many things I couldn't handle, but God could handle them all. I hadn't had many moments of trust like that recently, but this moment was so sweet that it seemed to put all my worries to rest. He would have to help me maintain that confidence when Niobe returned.

I tried to forget about Niobe and concentrate on the tertians in front of me, who were opening up. They talked about problems in their mission houses, problems at home, difficulties with prayer and self-acceptance and patience and humility. I wanted to help, but I was never sure if I was doing it "right," and I found myself emotionally drained. I told Father Tom, and he smuggled me a book of pop psychology written by John Bradshaw, a former seminarian. Bradshaw talked a lot about pain caused by "holes in our hearts." Bradshaw said a person suffering from toxic shame needed to tell her story and find acceptance in the eyes of another person. He talked about the healing power of touch and hugs. That might have been good advice outside the convent, but my experiences had taught me that touch could be a double-edged sword.

The Bradshaw book didn't address maintaining a proper distance while helping others. Bradshaw seemed to assume the helper and helpee met for an hour or two a week—not that they prayed, ate, and slept together day after day. I needed advice, but I couldn't expect Sister Dorothy, or even Sister Agnel, to understand why I thought talking to the sisters about their pain was necessary. We'd all been taught that pain was something to offer up, and our lives before joining were something to forget. The Bradshaw book would have intrigued Sister Joseph Michael, but I still needed it, and worried what might happen if on its way to Calcutta the book fell into disapproving hands. I remained guarded even with Father Tom, careful not to violate the confidentiality of sisters we both knew so well. I told myself that the good I might accomplish was worth taking risks, and I begged God to guide me.

Meanwhile, I continued to grow physically weaker. The menor-rhagia worsened so that I had to wear incontinence diapers several times a month. The pitch and frequency of Sister Dorothy's scold-ings continued to wear me down, the tertians' needs to drain me, the medication to depress me. Prayer was difficult, and I wondered where I'd find the strength to go on.

During confession one Thursday, after I'd listed my sins, I found myself wiping tears away with the back of my hand and cursing my lack of restraint. I closed my eyes and turned away.

A good minute or two passed in silence while I waited for Father Tom to say something. Eventually I opened my eyes and met his, di-rectly in front of me.

"You're doing your best." His voice was gentle and sweet, so un-like those I'd grown accustomed to. "You've got too much on your plate right now. You don't need to try so hard. Concentrate on what's important and let the rest slide." He said more, but I couldn't listen, and couldn't stop the tears that coursed down my face.

When he raised his hands to absolve me, he reached close and placed his hands not near my head but on my head. As his palms touched my headpiece, warmth spread downward, through my head, through my chest, through my belly, down my legs to my toes. As he pronounced the words of absolution, I felt as though I were melting away.

I couldn't move. He looked at me. His eyes lingered, but he said nothing. I got up to leave. At the door I said, "Thank you."

All that week, I felt Father Tom's hands on my head. Every morning and every evening for fifteen years, my superiors had laid their hands on my head. I could remember times when Sister Joseph Michael's hands had communicated something approaching friend-ship, when Sister Leonard's hands had transmitted fear, when Sister Priscilla's hands had conveyed contempt; never could I remember hands that felt like his.

Father Tom's hands weren't like Niobe's, either. There was no taking in his hands. They were all-giving. Father Tom's hands communicated a love that knew me and still found me good, a love that reached inside and smoothed the wrinkles away.

The next Thursday, after I'd finished confession, I said, "Father, I have something more to tell you."

"Yes?" His eyes were so green, so deep, so serene.

I stared at my hands, at my feet. "Well, I want to tell you, but I don't know if I can."

"Tell me later if you want," he said, "when you feel ready."

I nodded. I wasn't ready. I was scared. I was lonely. I wasn't sure.

I'd always felt something in Father Tom's presence, an electricity that I was sure the voltmeter in my father's shop would have registered as dangerously high. Father Tom had sometimes said things that made me think he felt something, too—like how Niobe was interesting but not as interesting as I was, like how if women could be priests, I'd be the one to whom he'd confess. I'd never told him how I felt in his presence. I didn't want to spoil things.

I felt safe with Father Tom, free to be myself, content. Maybe I didn't need to be afraid. He was a priest, and he took his priesthood seriously. We saw each other only on Thursdays. Surely our vows and the time restrictions would insulate against the electricity.

The next Thursday I swallowed hard and looked him in the eyes. "Father, I just want to say that if you ever feel like laying hands on me when you give me absolution again, like you did a couple of weeks ago, you don't have to wait until I'm crying."

"Okay."

"You can do it whenever you want. It felt good."

"Yes," he said. "I'd like that, too."

Sister Dorothy told us she was going to give the tertians a seminar on the vows, and that she was going to start with chastity. She went on to say that she had a liberal understanding of the vows and that we were in for a treat. Sister Dorothy was obviously intelligent. I tried to listen with an open mind.

Some of the things Sister Dorothy said were indeed more enlightened than things I'd heard from other MCs. She said that it was normal to feel temptation, that we were human, and that if we felt attracted to someone, we should talk about it with a sister we trusted. She didn't give any indication of how we could manage the privacy necessary to talk to a peer—there were no mechanisms in place for speaking to anyone but the superior. The more she talked, the more it seemed she hoped sisters would come to her with their problems with chastity. I even began to wonder if that was the whole point of this seminar—to present herself as an authority so she could receive the sexual confidences of her sisters.

When Sister Dorothy talked about masturbation, she turned bright red—Sister Dorothy could turn redder than any Indian sister I'd yet met—and said that while masturbation was a sin, it was a normal human thing, not something we should get too worked up about. I had never heard a Missionary of Charity use the word *masturbation* before. Mother sometimes said that we mustn't touch ourselves, and that if it was necessary to clean ourselves up at certain times of the month, it wasn't a sin, but we should avoid cleaning ourselves there at other times. When we were postulants, Sister Dolorosa had emphasized that we should never use our bare hands when washing ourselves, but should use a washcloth. She added that baths should be taken while wearing our chemises—we should soap up the washcloth, rub the cloth over ourselves (we could pull up the chemise to rub our chests, bellies, and upper legs, but should always keep it on and avert our eyes), then after we were sufficiently soaped, we should pour the water over ourselves without removing the chemise. We could remove the chemise to quickly dry ourselves. I'd given the chemise bath a few awkward tries before abandoning it as clumsy, inefficient, and clammy.

So the fact that Sister Dorothy said the *m*-word and thought sexual temptation human rather than depraved was refreshing. One of my former tertians had once confessed to me that she pleasured herself every afternoon during siesta—quite a feat in a dormitory with twenty other sisters. Recently I had tried a couple of times but always stopped early, figuring it was less sinful that way, even though I knew there were no gradations in sins against chastity.

Not too long after Sister Dorothy had concluded her seminar, a group including novice mistresses and superiors had gathered, and Sister Dorothy told this story: "When I was with the novices in Australia, I entered the novices' dormitory one afternoon. One of the novices was moving about under the covers, putting herself into strange positions. When I asked her what she was doing, she told me she was doing exercises. I asked her, 'Exercises for what?' She told me these exercises let her feel what married people feel when they are together." Sister Dorothy blushed as she told us this.

"Then what happened?" asked one of the novice mistresses.

"Why, we had to send her home, of course." Sister Dorothy stood there matter-of-factly shaking her head.

No one said anything after that, though a novice mistress from Germany winked at me, stifling a laugh. It was impossible to reconcile Sister Dorothy's matter-of-fact "we had to send her home" with her earlier claim that masturbation wasn't something to get worked up about. I was left with the inevitable conclusion that during the twenty minutes Sister Dorothy had pontificated about masturbation to a room of sixty sisters, this liberal nun in her sixties had had no idea what she was talking about.

On Thursdays, when I confessed, I found myself looking more and more deeply into Father Tom's eyes. In his eyes I found respect, concern, love.

When Father Tom laid his hands on my head to give me absolution, deep peace enveloped me. I wanted to give some of that back to him. One day I stood behind his chair and laid my hand on his shoulder. I channeled all my love into that hand, and hoped he felt it. When I lifted my hand, I went to the table and poured his coffee.

Sunday mornings were my most peaceful time at Via Casilina. After Mass, the tertians of both groups left the house quickly, off to gather children for Mass, visit prisoners, bring Communion to the shut-ins. At home, one tertian cooked and minded the gate, and I prepared classes or did work that Sister Joseph Michael continued to send me from Calcutta. One particular Sunday morning, Sister Dorothy snapped her fingers at the refectory door, face bright red.

I followed her to the kitchen go-down. "Do you see this?" She pointed to several stacks of long-lasting UHT milk, in liter cartons.

"Yes, Sister."

"Which boxes should be used first?"

"The ones with the earliest expiration date."

She marched into the compound, shawl swaying behind her, and pointed to the trash can. "Which milk did your tertians use for breakfast this morning?"

"The newer ones, Sister. I'm sorry."

"Sorry is not enough. You must train the sisters to responsibility. You must see everything they do. Everything. You are the most negligent mistress I have ever seen. Even the servants in my father's house would never have done such a thing, and here *your* sisters do it. They will turn out even worse than you, and it will be *your* fault." Her eyes popped as though they might burst from her head.

When she finally finished, I said, "Sorry, Sister," and watched as she marched away. Strange as it might seem, I felt pity. Sister Dorothy was one of the loneliest people I'd ever met, and I wasn't even sure she knew that.

After tea that day, I explained how to read the expiration date, with the Italian system of stamping day first, then month, then year.

As soon as she finished washing her teacup, Sister Reena approached me. "Sister, I don't understand. I was cooking this morning. I heard the way Sister scolded you." She wrinkled her little nose and looked up at me. "How can you keep so calm after all those things she said to you?"

"Sister Reena," I said, "have most of your mistresses and superiors scolded you, shouted at you?"

"Yes, Sister, all of them, except you."

"Did you learn any more from them than you learn from me?"

"I was frightened of them, and I learned to keep my place."

"Why do you think I didn't shout today?" She shrugged. "Think hard."

"You want us to see that when we become superiors we can teach our sisters without making them feel bad."

"St. Francis de Sales said, 'Nothing is so strong as gentleness; nothing so gentle as real strength.' Why should you raise your blood pressure over four liters of milk? Aren't there more important things to worry about?"

Four times in the next three days, sisters mentioned the milk speech to me and said they'd learned something. One of them told me that Sister Reena had been repeating the story to everyone in the group. Maybe I wasn't doing everything wrong.

Sometimes the tertians cried when they told me things they said they'd never told anyone. I felt privileged to listen, though problems recurred: Some sisters grew jealous of the time I spent with others; sisters became dependent on me, and I wasn't always able to help them outgrow the dependency; there were even a couple of sisters I found myself attracted to, and I struggled hard to keep my hands to myself.

Mother had always said that if we lived by the *Constitutions*, we were guaranteed sanctity. But the *Constitutions* didn't seem to understand the pain my sisters talked about, and doing things the way they'd always been done didn't help the sisters much. If I was going to make a difference, I would have to step outside the lines drawn by Rules and customs. Outside the lines, there were no guarantees. When I listened to sisters' pains, when I asked them to consider patterns in their lives, when I prayed with them, the healing seemed worth the risks, but only time would tell.

One particular winter day, a tall, gentle Indian sister came to the dormitory to renew her general permissions. I told her I'd noticed that she'd been particularly quiet at recreation and seemed distracted in chapel. I asked if something bothered her.

She looked out the window, biting her lip. I waited.

"Sister," she said finally, "Sister Niobe is coming from Albania soon, isn't she?"

"Yes, next month."

"Sister, I'm frightened."

"Oh?"

"We were in the novitiate together. She was second-year and I was first-year, but she always tried to sit near me when we had common meals or recreation, and she came to look for me during housework, and she left notes in my prayer book, and—"

"And you feel uncomfortable that she's coming to our community?"

"Sister, I'm terrified." She looked down at her hands, then up at me again. "I don't want to judge her. Perhaps she has changed. But she . . . she can be very insistent."

"Well, she won't be with us very long, just a few months." This sister had been more courageous with me than I'd been with Mother, and I admired her for that. "If Sister Niobe gives you any trouble at all, just tell me," I said.

"You know she changed her name, Sister?"

"Yes." Niobe had taken her mother's name the year I met her.

"She wants everyone to forget what she did in the past. In the novitiate, in the mission houses. So many sisters know Sister Augustine had problems. She thinks if she calls herself Niobe people will forget about Sister Augustine, but I can never forget."

She looked out the window again. I was just as scared as she was.

Sister Joseph Michael arrived in Rome for a week in late January, to get me started on a manual for sisters in charge of formation. As we reviewed the first pages of our *Formation Directory*, Sister Joseph Michael said, "I hope you don't mind." She continued looking at the pages on the desk, not at me, as she said, "At the Chapter, sisters kept thanking me for the new *Constitutions*. At a certain point it felt dishonest. I told them you had done most of it. No one objected— they could see the work for themselves—but . . ." Sister Joseph Michael slumped, shook her head once and looked away.

"Sister Frederick?" I asked.

Sister Joseph Michael sighed. "Not happy. And more unhappy when Mother sent me here to work on this with you." She shook her head again. "We've got to make sure to emphasize the catechism. If we don't give her that . . ." Sister Joseph Michael winced.

I would carry through with my plan to show Sister the Bradshaw book, but I knew that references to forming the sisters' humanity would need to be asides in the new *Directory*, not emphases. I also decided not to mention Niobe to Sister Joseph Michael. Sister had enough troubles, and I didn't want to disappoint her. Niobe was my problem.

One morning I left Sister skimming the Code of Canon Law while I went for another checkup. My doctor admitted the hormones hadn't worked and suggested a dilation and curettage, minor surgery to scrape the lining of my uterus. Before she returned to Calcutta, Sister Joseph Michael told me that doctors had once suggested a D&C to Mother, but that Mother had refused to compromise her consecrated virginity.

That floored me: first with shame at the knowledge that Mother had once had medical problems like mine yet surely never allowed herself to get depressed, then with pity for Mother and her overly literal understanding of consecrated virginity. To scrape the uterus, a physician had to insert instruments through a woman's vagina, but puncturing the hymen surgically wouldn't have altered the gift of her sexuality to God—Jesus wouldn't have loved Mother any less without her hymen.

Virginity as a concept had never held as much power over me as it had over some sisters. I'd been amazed by stories the Indian sisters told about examinations village girls were forced to undergo before marriage, how when the women appointed to perform those examinations deemed some girls ineligible, the elders exiled those girls from their villages. I hadn't grown up with stories of Santa Lucia, the girl with the lovely eyes who, in order to repel suitors and so maintain her virginity, had plucked her eyes from their sockets. Lucia always appeared in Christian art with her eyes on a silver plat-

ter. When, as a postulant, I heard the story of how eleven-year-old
Maria Goretti told her attempted rapist in 1902 that she preferred
to die than be raped since rape was a mortal sin, I blamed the eleven
stab wounds from which she died the next day on whoever made this
girl think that rape was a sin for the one being raped, and that
changing a potential rapist into a murderer was somehow an improvement. I understood my vow of chastity as the gift of my sexual
powers to God, but for me, the physical fact of my virginity was
mostly a reminder that no man had found me attractive enough to
bother with. Technically, I figured I wasn't a virgin anymore anyway,
not after that night with Niobe: even if my hymen was intact, I had
tasted forbidden fruit.

Mother had her reasons for refusing surgery, but I wanted my
energy back. I wanted to feel like myself again—and to stop wearing
those huge diapers that made me rustle when I walked.

My doctor scheduled the surgery at a hospital in Ostia, near the
sea. Early on the appointed morning two sisters left me in a room
with five other women, palm trees outside the windows. I unwound
my sari and climbed into bed in my habit and headpiece. My doctor
checked on me later that morning. He said I'd have surgery the next
day.

I was surprised by how much I enjoyed those few hours in the
hospital near the sea, breathing in the fresh salt air, with no bells, no
crowds, no Rules.

One of my roommates hadn't seen me when I'd arrived, and she
wanted to know why I covered my head. My explanation that I was
a nun didn't satisfy her; she knew nuns who didn't cover their heads.
I lifted the corner of my headpiece, revealing my nubs of hair. She
gasped and turned away.

The doctor returned before dinner. "Good afternoon," he said
without a smile, which was odd not only because he'd smiled more
than any doctor I'd known, but also because whenever we'd talked
we'd always spoken Italian. "I have some papers for you, Sister.
They say that you give consent to the operation." I nodded. He low-

ered his voice. "You must sign that you allow that this surgery will remove signs of your virginity." He paused and looked at me. "You know that, Sister, don't you?" His eyes looked sad.

I nodded. Why was everyone making such a big deal about this? It was clear that he'd spoken English not just to make sure I understood—my Italian was fine by then—but to give me privacy with what he considered a delicate question.

I signed the papers, and he said, "Thank you." I hadn't felt sad about the surgery until then, but the regret in the doctor's eyes dispirited me. I wondered if performing this surgery on someone with an intact hymen was unusual for him, if this was the first time he would surgically remove evidence of a woman's virginity. I looked at the women in the beds around me, four of them older than I, one younger. I assumed that each of them had, on some day in the past, lain with a man. The only sheets my blood would stain would line a surgical table.

I told myself it didn't matter, that God loved me, that—despite the complications—Niobe had loved me, that I'd received more love than I had the right to expect. Still, that night the young woman in the bed opposite mine asked, "*Suora*, why do you look so sad?"

The next morning, a nurse handed me a gown and told me to take off all my clothes. She repeated, "*Tutti.*" Even my underwear. No curtains separated the beds, but years of removing clothing while surrounded by others had prepared me to slip into this gown without exposing myself. After several minutes, two male orderlies arrived with a gurney. They told me to remove the gown. I told them I'd take it off when I was under the sheets on the gurney, but they said, "*Suora*, we've seen it all," and one of them undid the bow at the back. I lurched between bed and gurney, slipping my bare body between the sheets as quickly as possible.

The orderlies pushed my gurney through the hospital corridors, joking as they went. As I watched the lights and ceiling tiles glide by, I knew it wasn't losing that flap of flesh that was making me sad—it was losing it all alone, in a hospital. I remembered Sister Dolorosa's shouts of "I need a man."

I tried telling myself that I wasn't really losing anything that was mine. My body belonged to Jesus. I'd given away my virginity—and the opportunity to lose it with another person—long before. Losing one's virginity before marriage was sinful anyway, but I imagined sometimes that sort of sin was beautiful. And sometimes not. I thought of the village girls who had been exiled for having failed their premarital exams. I thought of Lucia's eyes on the platter, of Maria Goretti's screams. I thought of Mother, refusing medical help so she could keep her hymen. I thought of Mary, pregnant by the Holy Spirit, Mother of God, Virgin of Virgins, miraculously pre- served a virgin even after the birth of Jesus, Queen of Virgins, Holy Virgin, ever Virgin, closet locked, morning star, garden enclosed.

I thought of the incontinence diapers and the hormones and told myself that health was all I wanted.

When the orderlies pushed me through the doors of the operat- ing room, I prayed as I always did when I felt myself in trouble: *Jesus, I am Yours. I give You everything.* When the anesthesiologist told me to count, my mouth said, "*Dieci, nove, otto,*" but my heart said, *Jesus, I am Yours. I give You everything.*

When I woke, even in my grogginess, what I felt was not so much the physical pain, which was minimal, but that the sadness had deepened.

Back in the room, the other women didn't speak to me. I slid be- tween the sheets and pulled the blanket over my head. Where could I find a doctor who would excise that part of me that still longed to be known and loved by another? I pulled the sheets more tightly and tried to still my sobs. Eventually, gratefully, I fell asleep.

After a while I felt a tapping at my shoulder, then a shake. I pulled back the sheets and opened my eyes. The room seemed skewed, my mind still foggy. "Sister," I heard, "Sister Donata, I'm here."

I looked around. Two sisters stood at my bedside. I reached

under the pillow for my glasses. One of Sister Dorothy's tertians had come, and who was that? . . . No, it couldn't be.

"Sister Donata, I'm here," she repeated, and Niobe put her hand on my shoulder. I shrugged, hoping to dislodge her, but her hand didn't move. "I heard you were going to the hospital. I've come for you."

She smiled, that warm smile of hers, that smile I didn't want to see. She said something, the other sister said something. My head spun. The other sister left the room. Niobe put her arm around me and planted a kiss on my forehead. "My *pulcino*," she said. "I'm back. You don't need to worry anymore."

25

WORD OF HONOR

Barely a week after I returned from the hospital, I helped guard the Casilina gate. Hordes of paparazzi stood on one side of the gate, excited nuns and British Secret Service agents on the other, Niobe next to the agent in charge. That blustery February afternoon we expected a princess.

I'd been the first person in Casilina to learn that Diana might be coming—but I hadn't believed it. The day before, when a man in a spiffy suit had told me that he and the others inside the big black limo were from the British embassy, come to inspect the premises in advance of Princess Diana's visit, his story had impressed me as clearly bogus. Mother had undergone heart surgery in San Diego six weeks earlier, then she battled pneumonia. She'd recovered enough to travel to Rome, but was again in the hospital.

I let the front man inside the gate, just to be polite, but I made the car wait outside while I looked for Sister Dorothy.

Sister Dorothy phoned Sister Agnel, asking about the princess story. The side of the conversation I heard included Sister Dorothy shouting into the phone, "What *tamasha*! You don't tell us anything and Sister Donata has left the Brits locked outside the gate!" I ran down and, through the limo's window, apologized to Britain's ambassador to the Holy See.

When the ambassador emerged from the limo, he tugged self-importantly at his tie and asked to see where Mother and Diana would meet. I led him into Mother's room, which, in her absence, Sister Dorothy had appropriated for herself. The tin of water perched atop the wood-burning stove hissed as the ambassador and two secret service agents examined the windows and peered into the bathroom. The three men nearly filled the tiny room. I wondered what they would have to find for us to fail inspection. Suddenly Sister Dorothy pulled a clothespin off the line near the stove and stuffed a pair of half-dry underwear between the folds of her sari, the ambassador and his companion turning to take it all in. While the inspection continued, the chauffeur practiced driving the limo through the gate and into the compound, stopping just before the steps, repeating this simple maneuver three times until he was sure of the approach.

Mother arrived for dinner that evening, straight from the hospital. She looked better than I'd seen her in several years. The surgery and rest had obviously been good for her.

At recreation that evening I asked one of the tertians who'd been stationed in London to tell me about Diana. I remembered that some of the Co-Workers in Washington had talked about a big Cinderella wedding, but I didn't know more than that. "Oh, Sister," she said, "Princess Diana gives the queen a lot of trouble. The people love her, mostly, but she's always embarrassing everyone. Her picture is in the newspapers almost every day." The sister looked around a bit, leaned forward, and said, half under her breath, "Prince Charles chose her because he couldn't find anyone else who was a virgin. The future queen has to be a virgin when she gets married." My stay in the hospital fresh in my mind, I flinched a little at the virgin reference. The sister lowered her voice further. "She hasn't always been faithful," she whispered.

A mischievous princess who didn't mind flouting the rules and whose chief attribute was no longer virginity—I liked that. I went to bed eager for the next day's visit, conscious that two of the world's most admired women were going to meet at our house.

When we filed into chapel at five for Morning Prayer, I was surprised to see people at the gate in the near-dark. When they saw us, they started ringing the bell. We turned a light on and saw multiple cameras hanging from the necks of our visitors. Sister Dorothy, up with the rest of us for once, leaned toward me and said, "You're in charge of the newspaper people. Keep them out and make sure they behave."

The wind whipped my sari as I made my way to the gate. "We're praying now," I told the men armed with cameras and microphones.

"We need to stake out our places," one of them told me.

"This visit is private," I said, relishing my power. "You're not getting in, not now or later. This is a convent."

"Princess Di is coming. When Di comes nothing is private."

They began to speak at once—English, Italian, French, Spanish, something that sounded like Dutch or German or Swedish. Someone asked for coffee, another for the rest room. I pointed to the bar across the street and headed back to the chapel, leaving them behind the locked gate. Throughout the morning new press people rang the bell, and we repeated the same volley of requests and refusals. Their determination to get photos of the princess reminded me of the way people often behaved at professions: shoving and shouting, staking out positions at the end of aisles, bruising themselves and Mother in their efforts to touch the living Saint.

The agent got updates on an earpiece. At a quarter past two I went down with him to the gate, bringing along the tallest and strongest sisters, which of course included Niobe, the tallest of them all. On the way to the gate she managed to whisper in my ear, "Why all this fuss for a princess? You are my queen."

I pretended I hadn't heard, and told Niobe she was in charge of opening the gate on the agent's signal. After more crackling on his earpiece, the agent announced, "Three minutes," then "Two minutes," then "Sixty seconds," though we still couldn't see anyone approaching. When he said, "Five seconds," Niobe threw open the gate, and the sisters made a human chain to hold back the photographers. The limo appeared and slid through the gate.

When Diana stepped out, we all began singing and clapping. One of the sisters reached over Diana's head and ringed her with a garland made of pink and white net flowers. The princess accepted our garland and our song with a shy smile, as though she was eager for the fuss to be over.

Diana looked like most people did when waiting to see Mother—eager, hopeful, not knowing quite what to expect. Though we'd given Diana all our attention, it was obvious that in Diana's eyes, Mother was the queen of this show.

Mother reached out and took Diana's hands in hers. Diana smiled and leaned down to speak to Mother. The shortness of her skirt made the leaning a bit awkward, and I wondered what she could have been thinking when she'd dressed that morning. I remembered what Mother had once told a girl in a mini at the National Shrine in Washington. The girl had said, "So nice to see you, Mother Teresa." Without batting an eye, Mother had replied, "It's nice to see you, too, but Mother doesn't want to see as much of you next time." After a bit, Mother took Diana's hand and led her into her room. I envied the princess, not so much for her long legs sheathed in black stockings or her ability to travel as she pleased but for her uninterrupted time with Mother.

While Mother and Diana talked, I went to the chapel. I hoped Mother wouldn't disappoint Diana. I hoped Mother would listen to Diana, that she wouldn't just tell her, "Be only all for Jesus through Mary." When the sisters in Beirut found themselves under fire and called Mother to share their difficulties, Mother asked them, "Are you dead yet? Call me when you are dead." Simply put, good martyrs didn't complain, nor did they waste money on phone calls. I wondered whether Mother would urge Diana to embrace her suffering, if she would give her any comfort, if sometimes those were the same thing. Surely Mother would tell Diana, "I will pray for you." Mother was likely to give Diana a Miraculous Medal. What would a princess do with a stamped aluminum orb—wear it around her neck, put it under her pillow at night?

I was fairly certain Diana would understand me, that she felt the longings I felt—to be understood, to be held, to be loved, to be appreciated for who she was as a person, not just for what she could do for others. Mother gave no evidence of ever having experienced these longings. Surely millions of people throughout the world loved Mother, appreciated her, wanted her close, but had Mother ever longed to rest her head on the shoulder of someone who understood her?

I heard footsteps and voices behind me and saw Mother and Diana in the compound. They'd been inside for about half an hour. I went to see if they needed anything. Diana glowed. Mother looked young. Mother said, "I'm taking Diana to the chapel, Sister. Please see that no one disturbs us."

Mother took Diana's hand. At the chapel door, Mother stooped to unbuckle her sandals. Diana slipped off her pumps and followed Mother right up to the tabernacle, where they both knelt. Some sisters approached the chapel; I told them Mother wanted privacy. Soon a crowd of sisters gathered outside the chapel. The ambassador and secret service men stood in the compound, the chauffeur at the door of the limo. The photographers on neighbors' balconies fiddled with their lenses.

I looked at the shoes outside the door—Mother's ragged, repeatedly mended sandals next to Diana's shiny black pumps. I looked through the open chapel door at the world's two most admired women kneeling before Jesus, the wrinkled Saint of the poor and the privileged, gorgeous woman reputed to be a sinner. Two women with big hearts, women to whom love was central, though in very different ways. In the end, just two women, kneeling before God. The photographers, the ambassador, the sisters—we all knelt before God, whether we knew it or not.

When Mother and Diana came out of the chapel, Diana thanked Mother, then thanked all of us. She looked just as shy as she had when she'd arrived. We thanked her and sang another song, then Diana folded herself into the black limousine. At just the right moment we opened the gate, and she left. Together with Mother, we entered the chapel for adoration.

Dealing with an international phalanx of paparazzi was a walk in the park compared to dealing with Niobe. Shortly after Mother left, Niobe found me in Mother's room alone. She reached to hug me, but I stepped on her foot. When she came to renew her permissions, I indicated a seat opposite me. Ignoring that, she parked herself next to me. When she edged closer, I stood. When she left the room, I cried. I'd hoped that when she returned from Albania, after having spent so much time with Mother, she would understand that things had to be different. I'd hoped that distancing myself wouldn't hurt as much as it did.

I assigned the sister who'd told me she was frightened of Niobe's return to a bed near mine, and I assigned Niobe a bed in a dormitory down the hall. I worried what she might do far from my sight, but I figured that, at least for a little while, I was in greater danger than the other sisters. Besides, I knew that if I let Niobe seduce me, I would be of no help to them.

In the refectory, I sat at the head of the table, and when she set her plate near mine during lunch or dinner, I barely spoke to her. When under the table at breakfast one day she put her hand on my knee, I reached down and pinched her wrist. She didn't wince, but she didn't try that again, either.

When she came to renew her permission, she complained that I was being uncharitable. I told her that I was being chaste and that she'd better get used to it. She said I'd become hard. I said yes, I had. She asked me if I still loved her. I said love didn't matter. I could hardly believe I said that.

I kept track of where she knelt in the chapel, next to which sister she set her soup bowl at dinner, with whom she shared the bench during class. She seemed to choose places at random, just as the Rule required, favoring no sister over another. No matter where she sat, she found ways to look at me. At first her eyes spoke of love, then of yearning. Her eyes accused, ignored, chastised. Finally her eyes grew hard. Her shoulders drooped, and she shuffled from place to place. Gone was the tall, confident sister who had sauntered into the refectory at San Gregorio and enchanted me.

When time came to write reports, I wrote that Niobe should be sent home, that she seemed incapable of living a life of chastity. I knew it was the right thing to do.

In late March, a group of sisters arrived from Calcutta. I suspected they brought answers about who would take vows, but Sister Agnel told me no. Instead she handed me a letter addressed to Sister Niobe. The handwriting on the envelope was Mother's. I hoped, I prayed, that Mother was telling Niobe to go home.

When I gave the envelope to Niobe, she smiled. "Ah, Mother," she said, then turned her back and walked away.

A few hours later Niobe asked to see me. "Mother has asked me to write a letter," Niobe said. "I need to do it right away, and I want to write it in the chapel."

"Fine," I said. "You don't need to attend class or do manual work this evening. Take all the time you need." Niobe had always spent as little time as possible in the chapel. I wondered what Mother could have said, what Mother might have asked, that Niobe felt the need to respond in the chapel. If I'd asked her, she might have told me, but I didn't want to share special secrets with Niobe anymore. Nor did I trust her to tell me the truth.

Niobe continued, an earnest expression on her face, "I want to write it all alone, just me and Jesus, in the chapel."

"I can't ask the other sisters to stay out of the chapel."

Finally she said she wanted to write it at night, and she wanted me to pray while she wrote, but she didn't want me in the chapel—

I could pray anywhere else. Her eyes pleaded. "It's a very important letter," she said.

After the final bell rang that evening and everyone else was in bed, I opened the shutter on the back chapel window and stood outside, watching while Niobe dragged a table from the sacristy into the chapel and set it in front of the tabernacle. How naïve of me to assume that Niobe would sit on the floor, as any other sister would have done. She pulled a chair behind the table. She stoked the stove, turned around and winked at me, then started writing. It was cold outside. I went into the refectory and sat on a bench.

God, I prayed, *whatever is going on here, let Niobe be honest. I've asked You so many times to help her be chaste—You must be tired of hearing that prayer. Maybe You could find a better place for her.*

It was a relief not to long for Niobe anymore, not to yearn for her smile, for her words, for her body near mine. But I was not yet entirely free. The more I begged God to make Niobe honest, the more I heard questions within myself, questions about a new dishonesty of my own. What did it mean that I longed for Thursdays, for baring my soul in confession, for Father Tom's hands on my head in absolution? Looking into his eyes brought me pleasure and peace and excitement all at once. Sometimes I let my hand brush his when I offered him coffee. A violation of chastity was a violation of chastity, big or small, realized or fantasized about. I'd promised Jesus everything. I had to back away from Father Tom.

I wandered out to the compound. Through the chapel window I could see Niobe, her back bent at a purposeful angle, her shoulders strong, the pen set firmly between her fingers. I had never seen Niobe doubt. She always seemed sure, definite, stalwart—even now, writing a letter I could only assume would help determine whether she stayed in the community or not. I was rarely sure, even about little things. It was past midnight when Niobe finally lugged the table and chair back into the sacristy and handed me a sealed envelope.

The next Thursday, I faced Father Tom and confessed having allowed my affections to get the best of me. I meant my affections for

him, but I left it unspecific. I squirmed a bit when he gave me absolution, hoping to shake off the warm feeling that came unbidden. I
made sure to keep my hands to myself. I poured his coffee but didn't
say much. I avoided his eyes.

Within ten days, permissions arrived—the regular slips of paper,
and a sealed envelope for Niobe. After Sister Agnel passed them out,
Niobe came to me. "Mother gave me eight months with Sister
Dorothy," she said, smiling. "And I have something precious, too."
She waved an envelope in front of my face.

Eight more months with Niobe in Casilina. I hoped God knew
what He was doing. And I hoped that at the end of the eight
months, Niobe would go home.

The remainder of my group took their vows at the end of May in the
Church of the Gesù. Mother stayed in Calcutta, recouping her
strength. In the brief space between their profession and the arrival
of my next group, I went to the novitiate in Poland to give the
novices a course on the Eucharist and the poor.

Sister Jacqueline Claire, the French sister who had given me my
first and only organ lesson back when we'd both been novices, was
the superior of the novitiate. The other mistresses were also fairly
young. As I listened to the mistresses I noticed that they worked as
a team, with an understanding of each of their novices as individuals. They were strict, but they were also understanding. The novices
seemed to adore them, but I didn't get the idea that any lines had
been crossed. I gathered that each novice mistress spoke with her
novices about their personal lives, that the mistresses were aware of
how past experiences and perceptions could influence present behavior, and that they prayed in private with their novices. Individual,
spontaneous prayers might have gotten them into trouble with Calcutta, but they didn't seem worried about that.

I didn't feel secure enough to ask them questions—whether they
had permission to pray with the novices like that, what sort of problems the novices had, how they helped them, whether they had any

books to recommend. I certainly didn't want them to think that I'd come to investigate them. I didn't share my troubles. They seemed to have everything under control, and I was ashamed of the mess I'd made of my life.

I left Poland knowing it was possible to have good relationships with sisters under one's care, and determined to create those relationships with my next group.

Mother was in and out of Rome a few times that summer, opening another house in Albania. She always glowed when she came back from Albania. One of her latest stories had to do with the Albanian practice of *besa*—the word of honor that must never be taken back, even at harm to oneself. She told us we must love Jesus like that; we had given Him our word, our *besa*, and must never break our honor.

The MC Fathers needed a place in Rome for their seminarians, and Mother gave them our novitiate in Tor Fiscale, which meant that the novices moved in with us. Counting the tertians, the novices, and all the mistresses, we were ninety-two sisters in Casilina. Sister Dorothy became even more difficult and controlling. When my new tertians looked at me, their eyes spoke of need. Father Tom was wonderful, but I had decided to pull back from him. In a house bursting with people, I was lonelier than I had ever been.

One August evening, the sisters were inside watching *Brother Sun, Sister Moon*, the year's film for the Society Feast (also the previous year's film, and the film of two years before that). One of the Co-Workers brought a TV and a VCR, and twice a year sixty of us crowded around the little screen to watch a film. I'd first seen Zeffirelli's *Brother Sun* when I was in high school, and I had loved it. In my favorite scene Francis and Leo haul huge stones to rebuild the church of San Damiano. Shepherds and beggars, barefoot and happy, come to help, and everyone sings: "*Ogni uomo semplice porta in cuore un sogno, con amore ed umiltà potrá costruirlo.*" But that time, when I heard those words about every simple man carrying a dream in his heart, a dream that can be built with love and humility, my throat closed and I could hardly breathe. I decided to take a walk.

I strolled alone in the twilight between the eucalyptus trees. A train rumbled just beyond the wall. Leaves rustled in the breeze. Crickets chirped. The medicinal smell of the eucalyptus teased my throat open again. I strolled past rows of beans and lettuce, walked among the waving artichokes, and headed toward the crucifix, at the far end of the long grape arbor. I wanted to sit on the bench at the foot of the cross, to think and listen and empty myself.

As I neared the end of the arbor, I noticed someone sitting on the bench near the crucifix. I began to turn, then caught myself. Who, I wondered, was sitting there? Normally nobody liked to miss a movie—the others hadn't seen the film four times the way I had. Standing still, I made out two voices speaking softly, laughing gently. Two voices? They must have been sitting very close together.

I couldn't make out who they were, much less whether the sisters were from my group or Sister Dorothy's. I hated playing police-woman. But I did have a responsibility, and these sisters sat very close together. As I stood weighing my options, I'd almost decided to head back to the house and to leave it to their consciences when I recognized one of the voices—Niobe's.

My stomach sank. Whom had Niobe charmed now? I lifted my feet quietly, deliberately, my flip-flops padding softly on the soil. I wanted to catch Niobe off guard. When I got close enough to see her arm around the other sister, who rested her head on Niobe's shoulder, I said, "Hello, Sisters."

They turned, Niobe's companion lifting her head so suddenly that she knocked Niobe's chin. Niobe did not move her arm. "Hello, Sister," she said. "We're talking. Do you care to join us?"

"You're talking awfully close together."

"Yeah, we don't like to shout."

Recognizing this as a reference to my own voice, which I realized was far louder than I had intended it to be, I spoke more softly.

"You should be with the others at the movie."

"I've seen it before," Niobe said, her arm still around her companion's shoulder. The other sister belonged to Sister Dorothy's group. She was a smart, tough, hardworking sister from south India, about my size, and I saw her pull Niobe's elbow in an attempt to get her to move her arm, but Niobe didn't budge.

I looked straight into the eyes of the other sister and said, "Be careful."

Niobe hadn't changed at all.

I had my hands full with the problems of my new tertians, which included the first group of Polish MCs. The sisters from Poland were smart and passionate, better educated than most MCs, and also more inclined to be gloomy. Though she was no longer in my group, I also kept an eye on Niobe. She and the sister from the garden often sat together, though I never saw them doing anything improper. When she wrote her reports, I asked Sister Dorothy what she had recommended for Niobe, but she wouldn't even hint. I hoped Sister Dorothy understood that Niobe's problems made her unfit for convent life. Sister Dorothy was a senior sister; Mother and the councilors would listen to her. I prayed harder than I had yet prayed, begging God to do whatever it took to make sure Niobe would never make her final profession.

When sisters arrived from Calcutta with papers, Sister Dorothy was away from Rome for a few days. Sister Agnel called me to San Gregorio.

"The council has voted," she said.

"And?" I asked, wanting to hear and not wanting to hear at the same time.

"Niobe will take vows," she said, looking me straight in the eye.

"No, Sister. Really?"

"Yes, really." Sister Agnel shook her head a little. I couldn't speak. Sister turned to the stack of other business that had arrived from Calcutta.

I couldn't understand. Mother and the councilors had heard the letter the sister had written to the Chapter, and they knew Niobe had started preying on sisters when she'd been a novice. They'd read my reports and knew she hadn't really changed—unless Sister Dorothy had okayed her. It was possible, I supposed, that Niobe had managed to hide some of her more pernicious failings in the eight months she had been with Sister Dorothy, but it was obvious to everyone that Niobe avoided hard work whenever possible, and it should have been obvious to the sister in charge of her formation that her prayer life was superficial. Of course, these faults alone were not enough to send a sister home, and Niobe had been post-poned twice already.

Others might not see the predator lurking behind the self-assured smile; perhaps even Niobe was blind to the harm she inflicted. Knowledge—and complicity—gave me responsibility. Niobe couldn't be left to take advantage of another sister again, nor to take vows she had no intention of keeping.

"Sister, can you delay giving out those permissions?" I asked.

"I can wait a little," Sister Agnel said, raising an eyebrow at me.

All the way home, my lips moved in response to my companion's Hail Marys, but my mind was racing. I had to act swiftly. I had to do it in writing. I had to be explicit but not graphic. I had to both ac-knowledge my sins and make the councilors understand how dan-gerous Niobe was. I had to make sure word got to Mother. I couldn't let fear of repercussions keep me from doing what was right. I should have come clean long ago.

I sent my letter FedEx to Mother in Calcutta, with a copy for Sister Joseph Michael, since I didn't know if Mother was in Calcutta, and even if she was, I didn't want to risk my letter getting lost on Mother's desk.

Sister Dorothy's group grew more and more nervous by the day, as all groups did while waiting for permission to take their vows. Only Niobe seemed unperturbed.

Thursday came. I didn't look forward to telling Father Tom about my letter. In recent months I'd cycled through several waves of fear I was getting too close to Father Tom, of knowing he was good for me, of feeling guilty because I liked him too much. I had currently suspended doubt and fear in favor of appreciating his support. Father Tom was always ready to listen to my troubles and never judged me. He was wise and loving. I could control myself, and he never did more than put his hands on my head.

"You did *what*?" He looked incredulous, angry, and worried, all at once.

"I was afraid you would react like this," I said. "If I had asked your advice, wouldn't you have told me to keep quiet, that I had done enough already, that I was naïve to imagine the sisters would listen to me? You would have been afraid that I'd suffer uselessly for speaking up."

"Precisely," he said, "and I would have been right. But you—" He shook his head, and some of the anger drained from his face. "You've been brave and honest, and I'm proud of you for that." Father Tom smiled, but his eyes and forehead were definitely still worried. "Do you think Niobe will try to retaliate if they send her home?"

"I don't have anything more to hide. What can she use against me?"

"She's very resourceful," Father Tom said.

I paused and looked at my hands. "You know, the whole thing is so sad. In spite of everything, she can be so good sometimes, and some of the things she did actually helped me. It was"—I looked up—"really wonderful sometimes."

"I know it was," he said with a great deal of tenderness.

"Something went wrong, ugly, manipulative. I still haven't figured out what to do with the part of me that wants to love and to be loved."

Father Tom looked at me and nodded. The more deeply we examined this question, the more we realized there were no easy answers. Just saying no didn't give any clues about what to do with the feelings, the desires, the energy.

"I had to write that letter. If Mother sends me to Siberia, I'll be cold, but at least I'll be able to work with the poor again, which is what I've always wanted anyway."

"But I would miss you terribly. You—you do a good job with the sisters." His face turned slightly pink.

"It's in God's hands," I said. My right hand slid—just for a moment—onto his knee.

Ten days passed since I'd written my letter. News had gotten out that the permissions had been sent—the sisters who had come from Calcutta knew what they'd brought, and had expressed surprise that the permissions hadn't been distributed. A few of Sister Dorothy's tertians grew nervous almost to the point of paranoia. Individually, several of them approached me, asking, "Is it about me? Surely you know, Sister—tell me." I told them not to worry, that everything was going to be fine. Niobe maintained her uncanny calm.

Finally Sister Agnel phoned. She said Sister Frederick had called and that she wasn't happy. Sister Frederick would arrive in San Gregorio that evening, and she wanted to speak to me first thing.

When I heard Sister Frederick stomping down the San Gregorio corridor that evening, I remembered her footfalls echoing down that same corridor the first time I'd seen her, nearly fifteen years earlier. I was determined not to let her intimidate me this time. I knew she wouldn't pass up an opportunity to humiliate me, whatever Mother might have decided.

Sister Frederick sat behind Mother's desk. "Sister," she said, modulating her high-pitched voice so that it sounded softer, almost kind, "do you know that I had to leave the sisters in Germany in the middle of a catechism course to come see you?" She spoke surprisingly slowly, and with gentle eyes. This was a Sister Frederick I had never seen before.

"I'm sorry about that, Sister."

"It's been very disruptive. They are all waiting for me to come back." Sister Frederick's eyes, still fairly gentle, searched me out. I didn't flinch. "Mother tells me that you have an objection to Sister Niobe taking her final vows."

"Yes, Sister," I said. "I believe that Sister Niobe is not capable of living a vow of chastity."

"And I believe you know this because you have not lived your vow, either." She raised her eyebrows. The pitch of her voice reverted to its usual octave.

I swallowed. "Sister, that is true, and I am very sorry for it. The first time Sister Niobe was with me as a tertian, we both did things against our vows, but when she returned after being postponed, I understood many things much better, and I was stronger, and I did not repeat my mistakes. I saw, however, that she continued the same sort of behavior with other sisters."

"Sister, do you know what a serious responsibility you have as tertian mistress?" She'd lowered her voice again, though her words remained intense. "You are to form these sisters to a life of holiness. If you do not live a life of sanctity, how can you expect them to?"

"I'm sorry, Sister, and I've realized my mistake. I've asked forgiveness of God and the Society. What worries me is that Sister Niobe doesn't seem to realize that she's breaking her vows, and that she's not sorry."

"You didn't give her very good example, did you?"

"No, Sister, but afterward I showed her that it's possible to change, and I've told her many times that it's wrong."

"But your actions speak louder than your words, don't they, Sister?"

I kept quiet, without averting my gaze. If she needed to upbraid me over and over again, I would let her do it, but I wanted her to understand about Niobe, too.

"Sister," she continued, "I am sure God forgives you. Jesus forgave even Mary Magdalene, but this is not the way for a sister who has been entrusted with the formation of others to behave. Why didn't you speak up sooner?"

"In my reports, I always said that Sister Niobe had problems with chastity. I made it very clear that unless she had a very strong conversion, she should not be allowed to take her vows. I also spoke to Mother about it when she was here, though I didn't go into all the details. I begged Mother to send Sister Niobe to Calcutta to continue her tertianship, and I asked Sister Agnel the same thing."

"Sister, the Society will have to think very hard about whether you should be allowed to continue in any position of responsibility. You have your final vows. You will not be sent home, but you must understand that you have done wrong."

"I will serve wherever I am sent, as I have always done."

"The Society has given you much, invested three years in your education."

"Sister, I am sure the Society will decide whatever is best for everyone. I am ready to take responsibility for my actions. When I wrote that letter, I knew that Mother would be disappointed and that sisters would question me. I felt it necessary to do everything in my power to avoid having other sisters fall into the same trap I fell into, so I wrote the letter. Sister Niobe can be very persuasive, and I am not the first sister who has fallen prey to her, nor have I been the last. I only pray that there may be no more. I've done my part. Now it is the responsibility of the Society."

"Sister." Sister Frederick sat up straight, in full possession of her customary voice. Her eyes drilled holes into me. "Sister, you do not need to remind the Society of its responsibilities. You must learn to take care of your own." I remained silent, but I did not bow my head.

Two days later Sister Agnel came to Casilina. I didn't see her before she started distributing the permissions. I had received no indication from anyone about whether Mother and the councilors had reconsidered.

After Niobe received her paper, she came to me.

"I'm taking vows," she said.

"I hope you'll keep them," I said, disappointed but not surprised.

"You don't know me," she said, shaking her head, and leaning very close. She whispered in my ear, "Even you, who I love so much, you think you know me, but you don't." She stood a little straighter and continued, "Mother knows me. We became friends in Albania."

"I'm glad Mother knows you so well. Do you know yourself?"

"No need to be uppity. I know you don't want me to take vows, but Mother knows my heart. I wasn't worried like the rest of them. I had this." Niobe opened her Bible and pulled out an envelope.

I didn't ask to see the envelope. I didn't want to play any more games.

Niobe held the envelope out. "Read it," she said. I didn't move. "Go ahead." She shoved the envelope at me and I took it.

On the envelope, I saw Niobe's name—in Mother's handwriting. I remembered that envelope. Niobe had waved it in my face, calling it "something precious." It was Mother's response to the letter Niobe had written in the chapel that night. "You belong to Jesus. You are precious to Him. You must suffer one more humiliation before becoming the Spouse of Jesus Crucified for life, but you have Mother's word that you will be allowed to take final vows after this. Jesus loves you very much."

I folded the paper and returned it to the envelope. "You can fool Mother," I said, "but you can't fool Jesus. Remember that."

I handed her the envelope, and walked away. I had been stupid to think I could change anything. It didn't matter what I'd written or what Sister Dorothy might have recommended. Mother had decided six months earlier. She had given her word—her *besa*.

I tried to excuse Mother, to put her actions down to ignorance— surely Mother's intentions were good, she wanted to forgive as Jesus forgave—but I hadn't been the only one who'd tried to educate her.

The more I thought about it, the more I saw danger in that word *besa*. Keeping one's word was not more important than doing what was right. What looks right one day may not be right the next, and we have to allow ourselves to reconsider.

On December 8, Niobe took her final vows. I couldn't remember ever having felt so powerless.

26

BAD, BAD MISTRESS

SUMMER 1992 TO SPRING 1993
CASILINA, ROME, AND OSTIA

Sister Chandani staggered out of the chapel, holding her side, her face as white as a newly starched altar cloth. This middle-aged tertian leaned on me all the way to the refectory, where I stretched her out on a bench. She writhed so much that I was afraid she might fall. This was the opportunity I'd been waiting for.

In Mother's room, as I lifted the phone, I saw my hand quiver. "Fulvio, can you come right away to take me to Ostia? Sister Chandani had surgery there last week and she's in a lot of pain."

"*Vengo subito.*" I knew he'd come. Fulvio was perfect—always eager to help, never asked questions. The timing was perfect, too. We'd just started the triduum for the Society Feast, three days of silence and prayer. Since no one was supposed to go out unnecessarily during triduum, no one would be suspicious of a tertian mistress who accompanied Sister Chandani instead of sending a tertian—they would see it as a sacrifice I made so they could have their prayer time.

I gathered a change of clothes for Sister Chandani, her night-dress, her toothbrush.

There were empty beach houses near Ostia, and plenty of churches. Ostia was far enough from Rome that the sisters didn't know it well. When I'd been there for my D&C, one of the nurses had taken me to a room where they collected things people had left behind. The room was overflowing, and she'd wanted me to take the extra clothes for the poor.

I scribbled a note on the refectory board, telling the tertians that Sister Chandani and I had gone to the hospital, that they should carry on with the schedule.

I fetched my bag and put in a *gettone*, a token for a phone call. I put in one more, just in case. I was tempted to take a bus pass, but I wasn't sure they were valid in Ostia, and the sisters needed them anyway. In the chapel, where the sisters knelt for adoration, I put my Bible in my bag, then joined them, thanking God for arranging things so well.

Soon the portress whispered that Fulvio had come. I genu-flected, stood, and turned my back.

On the way to the car, I detoured to the parlor, where Father Bob was hearing confessions. I'd known Father Bob when he'd been a seminarian and I'd been a tertian. Now he was superior of the MC Fathers in Rome and confessor to Sister Dorothy's tertians. I sig-naled to the sister at the head of the queue, and when the door opened I walked into the parlor and around to the other side of the confessional. Purple stole around his neck, Father Bob looked up.

"Father, please pray for me that I don't do something stupid." He smiled and nodded. He probably had no idea what I was talking about. I'd been hoping for an opportunity like this, but I still wasn't convinced it was a good thing to do. All I knew was that I couldn't take the pressure anymore. I wanted to breathe again.

I settled Sister Chandani in the back of the car so that she could stretch out if she wanted to, and I took the seat next to Fulvio. Even before I fastened my seat belt, I pulled my rosary out. No wasting time with chitchat today. I told Fulvio, "*Preghiamo*. Let's pray," and he nodded and made the sign of the cross.

"*Ave Maria, piena di grazia . . .*" The sun beat on the nearly empty streets, most Romans having fled to the mountains or the sea, as they did every August. Little beads of perspiration dotted Fulvio's neck. My palms felt clammy, and I shook a bit. I pictured Sister Dorothy's face growing progressively redder when she realized that I'd slipped past her. It would be quite a shame for her to try to live down the talk, but I couldn't feel too sorry about that.

In the back, Sister Chandani sat almost straight against the seat. Her breath came more regularly, though her face was still pale. I gave her a smile, and she nodded back, her left hand clutching her side.

As we got closer to the sea, palm trees appeared on either side of the boulevard, and the breeze from the coast cooled things a bit. At the end of the long driveway, Fulvio pulled in front of the emergency entrance. Out of the car, I turned back to open the door for Sister Chandani, but she was already out.

"How do you feel?" I asked.

"Oh, a little better, but it still hurts plenty."

An old lady and her tiny dog were the waiting room's sole occupants. I walked up to the acceptance window and explained Sister Chandani's case: cysts on her ovaries removed last week by Dr. Genovese, severe pain that had started about three hours earlier, would probably need to stay for treatment and observation.

"*Che fortuna*," the receptionist said. Dr. Genovese happened to be in the hospital and would come check the *suora* himself.

Meanwhile, Fulvio said he was going to get a *caffè*. "Do you want anything?" he asked, knowing full well that the Rule forbade sisters to eat outside the convent.

Automatically I said, "*No, grazie.*" I probably should have said yes. Coffee and a *panino* would have made my getaway a little more comfortable. I was trying to remember the way from the emergency room to the storage room for left-behind clothes when Sister Chandani and Dr. Genovese reappeared.

"*Cosí presto,*" I said, wondering how they could have finished so quickly.

"Nothing serious," the doctor said. "She'll be fine. Just a little gas. I've given her some *digestivo*."

"*Dottore*, are you sure?" I asked. "Sister was in such terrible pain. She could hardly walk just a few minutes ago."

"I've checked her. She's fine."

"But, *dottore*, don't you think she should stay, in case the pain comes back, so that you can keep an eye on her? We live in Rome, you know. It's so far away. It takes over an hour to drive here."

Sister Chandani looked at me with a smile. "No, Sister, really, I'm feeling much better now. I think I'll be fine. I should like to go home."

As I got in the car, I slammed the door. An opportunity like this was unlikely to present itself again soon.

I pulled the rosary from my side and held it in my clenched fist, the beads hard as stones against my palm. Ave Maria after Ave Maria, I spit the words like BBs from a gun, cutting short Sister Chandani's and Fulvio's replies.

As I began the second decade of the rosary, my clenched fingers started to tingle, with a charge like static electricity, but gentler, and warm. I opened my hand. The beads felt soft, like flower petals. The tingling climbed up my arms, through my shoulders, and issued a gentle jolt to my heart.

When we started the third decade, the harsh midafternoon light eased, muting and deepening the bright colors of the oleander, the palm trees, the sky, as though it were dusk, yet the August sun was just slightly west of center.

As I began the Padre Nostro, I perceived a gentle, smiling presence above my left shoulder, above the car. I sensed this presence somehow descending closer, applying a light but firm pressure to my shoulders, as if someone were placing a soft blanket on top of me. I felt cocooned like a baby, my mother cooing over me, singing a lullaby.

Part of me thought this was crazy, but I didn't care, because it just felt so good.

As we cruised the *autostrada*, the presence intensified. Someone was smiling at me. This presence seemed to hover about five feet above my left shoulder, above the roof of the car. I sensed the presence as benevolent, feminine, protective. Though I saw nothing, heard nothing, she offered me wordless comfort. As consolation enveloped me, my agitation seemed to melt. She was above the car, but the car was no obstacle to our communion. An angel, the Blessed Virgin, my imagination, a nervous breakdown?

By the middle of the fourth decade, I realized that I didn't feel angry anymore. It was fine that Sister Chandani had to come back. In fact, it was very good. Everything was going to be all right.

The beads of the rosary slipped through my fingers like silken spheres. The rise and fall of the prayer words, *piena di grazia, il Signore è con te*, caressed my skin. The angular edges of the buildings by the side of the road seemed rounded. Things glowed.

I didn't turn to look at Fulvio or Sister Chandani. I just looked out the window. When we finished with the Salve Regina, not one of us spoke until we pulled through the gate at Casilina.

As we got out of the car, Fulvio shook my hand and said, "*Suora*, that was some rosary, wasn't it?" I nodded and smiled.

The pendulum swings of that Ostia trip were truly dramatic but otherwise typical of my spiritual life that year. At midday I often found myself writing in my examination-of-conscience book some variation on: *I can't bear it any longer.* More than once I wrote, *Trapped, trapped, trapped.* Sometimes, while waiting for the next sister to renew her permissions or before taking off my glasses at siesta, I looked out the dormitory window to a corner in the back of the garden, beyond the artichokes—the precise spot where I planned to dig a hole, crawl in, and cover myself with dirt—except that by evening I'd be writing, *God sent peace today* or *All is well.*

I couldn't blame the mood swings on the hormones—my excessive monthly bleeding had stopped and I wasn't taking them anymore. My work often kept me up late, reducing my sleep to five or six hours a night, but which MC wasn't tired? Sciatic nerve pain and a bone spur made walking difficult—but I didn't have to walk much anyway, and I got permission to use a stool when sitting on the chapel floor became excruciating.

I sometimes stewed under Sister Dorothy's rants, and steamed when she pulled my group out of a much-needed silent day of recollection for a long, chatty lunch with one of her former tertians or kept sisters home from the apostolate to create feast-day decorations. The tertians were needy and I worried about how to help them, but on the whole, when I stood back and looked at things objectively, nothing seemed to merit my schemes to escape.

When I told Father Tom about the trip to Ostia, he shook his head and took my hands in his. "You can't just disappear," he said. "Tell me you wouldn't do that. Tell me you'd call."

He told me, as he had several times before, "Don't wait until it's too much. Call me when you're having a bad day. We can talk."

He said, "I hate to see you in so much pain."

He kissed the top of my sari-covered head.

I liked that.

I avoided Father Bob. I didn't want to tell him what it was I'd asked him to pray for, and sometimes I blamed his prayers for foiling my grand escape, which still seemed like a good idea on my down days.

Instead, I went back to work and waited for the next mood swing, trusting God to rescue me when things got too bad.

My new group opened up quickly, and I'd begun to feel more confident helping them. When the normally cheerful Sister Nolly told me a male relative had abused her as a child, she cried. I told her that Jesus loved her, and she cried some more.

Sister Nolly had a childlike appearance—short, with a gentle face and big eyes—and she seemed to come naturally by the childlike faith we'd been encouraged to cultivate but which had always eluded me. She kept the Rules meticulously, told me that she had never skipped the daily chains or discipline, and that she always said the Paters by her bedside as slowly as she could. When she prayed, she sometimes imagined herself receiving the infant Jesus from Mary, then imagined herself rocking Him to sleep.

Though Sister Nolly had seemed relieved to tell me of her early abuse and consoled when she saw that I hadn't rejected her, within a few weeks this formerly sprightly sister dragged her feet and avoided looking sisters in the eye. She arrived late for class and wouldn't eat. She began speaking in a high-pitched whine of no more than a word or two at a time. Sister Nolly grew gaunt and pale and almost haunted. The transformation was frightening to behold.

When she talked to me privately, Sister Nolly seemed to suck herself in, becoming as small as she could. She whimpered that the world had become dark. She said she was sad all the time. Sometimes she sucked her thumb. She wanted to know where Jesus had gone.

In San Gregorio, I asked Sister Agnel for the name of a good psychiatrist. Sister Agnel told me that MCs didn't see psychiatrists. Mother didn't approve. Cheerfulness was a moral duty for a Missionary of Charity. *In other words,* I thought to myself, *we could give the men and women in our homes Valium or Haldol, but Jesus should be enough for the sisters.*

I told Sister Agnel I'd never seen a sister so depressed, that Sister Nolly needed help. Within the week, Sister Agnel visited us at Casilina. After seeing the dark rings under Sister Nolly's eyes, the way her habit dangled on her ever-tinier frame, and how Sister Nolly hung her head and grew irritable with the sisters (some of whom also grew irritable with her), Sister Agnel passed me a slip of paper with the name of a doctor and a phone number on it. She whispered, "Take her, but don't tell anyone."

On the three buses to the hospital where the doctor had agreed to see us, Sister Nolly leaned on me as we stood in the aisle, put her head on my shoulder when we finally got a seat, then whimpered a little and said, "I'm scared, Sister."

Sister Nolly clinging to my arm, I thought of my own sadness and fears, my inability to deal with the challenges of my own life. I thought of the apostles at sea, terrified in the midst of a storm, and how Jesus calmed the waves and told them, "Do not be afraid." In that moment, a deeper compassion than any I'd yet felt welled up within me. Together—God, the doctor, Sister Nolly, and I—we would find a way to help her heal.

The doctor diagnosed Sister Nolly with depression so severe that it was complicated by age regression. He gave her a prescription, and we made an appointment for the following week.

When a sister took medication—which wasn't often because an illness was a cross to be borne more than a malady to be cured—she kept the medicine on her plate shelf, nestled between her cutlery and her teacup, where anyone could see it. I owed it to both Sister Agnel and Sister Nolly to keep the visit to the doctor a secret, and even if she'd had a place to hide them, I didn't trust Sister Nolly to take the pills on her own. I decided to keep her medication in my desk in the dormitory, and told Sister Nolly to come every evening at the beginning of manual work, an hour I routinely used to talk to individual sisters, and I'd give her the medication.

That evening, while the others chopped wood, hauled water, and cleaned the stove, Sister Nolly was first in line to see me. When she entered, Sister Nolly strode straight to me, wrapped her arms around my waist, and buried her head in my sari. She sobbed. I wrapped my arms around her thin shoulders. I told her that Jesus loved her, that she didn't need to worry. Eventually I handed a pill to her. I told her to take it, then go to the chapel until dinner.

On succeeding evenings, Sister Nolly, eyes still fixed on the floor, often wanted to be held. Though MC Rules forbade it, Jesus never said, *Don't touch.* Jesus' touch was healing, and I'd experienced Father Tom's touch—and even the embraces of Sister Timothy and sometimes of Niobe—as healing. Bradshaw's books and Henri Nouwen's recent writing both recommended that an emotionally wounded person find a safe person to hold him or her. Holding Sister Nolly wasn't sexual for me. I didn't yearn for it, I didn't want more. Holding Sister Nolly felt like being a channel of grace, perhaps a bit like being a mother. Of course, I didn't know what she felt, but since Sister Nolly was operating at the level of a young child—about seven or eight years old, the doctor had said—I didn't worry too much about chastity. I thanked God for having given me a small group this time; even if I had to give five or ten minutes to Sister Nolly every day, there was still time for the others.

The evening before our third trip to the doctor, when Sister Nolly said, "Hold me," her big brown eyes looked up at me. Eye contact! Even while her eyes pleaded, *Take me in—protect me—I need to know that I am not alone*, I could see that she was getting better.

One day Sister Agnel handed me a large bundle of papers wrapped in twine. "From Calcutta," she said. "Read them carefully, and keep them private." I opened the bundle to find the annual reports written by my tertians' previous superiors, something I'd never been sent before. According to the accounts of Sister Nolly's superiors, she had given eight years of eager, competent, joyful service, though two of her superiors also alluded to a stubborn streak. Over the past few weeks, Sister Nolly had begun to make eye contact again with two of her fellow tertians, sisters she trusted. I arranged for her to speak with Father Joseph, who had founded the MC Fathers. Father Joseph was a wise, gentle soul, someone who understood that prayer and willpower were not always enough. He later told me he'd never seen a sister as depressed as Sister Nolly, nor one who clung so tenaciously to Jesus.

I hoped that, given enough time, Sister Nolly would return to joyful service again. In the meantime, I gave her medicine and I held her. Some sisters began dropping resentful comments about the amount of time Sister Nolly spent with me, including the long trips to see the doctor, trips I couldn't explain to them. I talked the sisters' resentment over with Father Bob, to whom I had started making my confession every now and then.

"How much time do you spend with her?" he asked.

"Five or ten minutes a day," I said.

"And they even notice that?"

"We're women," I said. "Women want relationships."

Father Bob looked incredulous, but after a moment his face seemed to register gears clicking into place, as though I'd given him the missing clue in a big puzzle. The next week I saw him with an issue of the theological journal *Concilium* under his arm. This particular issue was dedicated to feminist spirituality. He blushed when he realized I'd seen it.

In my instructions, I reminded the community that every sister was also one of the poor, that our sufferings united us with Jesus, that we all had different needs, and that He had called us together to love one another, even when it was hard. Feisty Sister Lita seemed impervious to my pleas for empathy. Even before Sister Nolly grew ill, Sister Lita had been difficult, complaining almost constantly—about the weather, about the food, about the poor, about her sisters. During her week alone in the kitchen, I found her muttering to the pots. The only time she seemed to have no complaints was when she came to see me privately. "Sister, everything is fine," she would say, smoothing her sari with her hands.

If Sister Lita happened to be close as Sister Nolly retrieved her plates or her books, Sister Lita would hiss, "Hurry up, Nolly." At least twice when I was called away from a meal or recreation, Sister Lita had barraged Sister Nolly with questions—even as the others urged her to stop—demanding that Sister Nolly reveal where she went with me every week, and why she was such a big baby. Finally Sister Nolly had hissed back, "It's none of your business." When other sisters told me about this, they clearly wanted me to do something about Sister Lita, but I sensed they also wanted answers.

Most of them would have understood. I could have educated them about mental illness, without telling them that I took Sister Nolly to a psychiatrist and that she took medicine. But Sister Nolly stubbornly refused to let me say anything. I told her that sisters already knew something was wrong, that her illness was nothing to be ashamed of. Sister Nolly's reply was always the same: "No, no, no."

In the midst of all the tension in the community, my moods still swinging inexplicably, I opened an envelope from one of my former tertians. She had sent me a short, happy letter, and a photo. In the photo, she stood against a clear blue sky. Her hands were clasped behind her back and joy radiated from her face. She looked as though she were leaning forward into life.

I placed her photo in my Bible, marking John 10:10—a passage I meditated on often during those months—where Jesus says, *I came that they may have life, and have it abundantly*. This former tertian was someone who had known plenty of difficulties in her life, someone I'd been able to help a little. Whenever I looked at the photo and pondered the Gospel, she reminded me, *Live life to the fullest. Don't let your troubles get you down. Life is an adventure*.

One day I moved the photo to my prayer book, at the spot in Midday Prayer when we paused to examine our consciences. Each day this joyful sister seemed to ask, *Does God excite you? Have you shared His joy with others? Are you living life to the fullest?* More than once, her questions pulled me from my gloom. Jesus had promised a full life, and together with Him, I would find it. I knew I would.

When I was having a particularly difficult day or week, Thursdays with Father Tom would see me through. Each week, for twenty or thirty minutes after my confession, Father Tom and I talked as friends talk, sharing a joke, the week's events, our hopes, our fears. I thought about him often during the week but didn't feel guilty about that anymore. Father Tom wasn't dividing my love for God; he made God feel closer, and helped me find courage. One Thursday just before Christmas, Tom suggested we drop the titles, and I agreed. It felt good, right, to call him Tom. "Father" didn't fit anymore. When he called me Mary, my heart jumped.

On a particular January morning, Tom was scheduled for Mass. During meditation I'd read, once more, the words of Jesus: *I came*

that they might have life, and have it to the full. That morning, life to
the full had led me to think of Tom, of the way the skin around his
eyes crinkled when he laughed, of the way he always seemed to
know how I was feeling. I thought of things he'd told me over the
nearly four years we'd known each other: *Learn to love yourself. . . . If
women could be priests, you'd be the one I'd confess to. . . . I'd miss you terribly. . . . Call me Tom.*

After meditation, in the washing place, I skipped the second
rinse of my clothes, hurrying to hang them so I'd be in the chapel
before he strode in. I took my usual place in the corner. Tom didn't
see me there behind the organ, scanning his back as he entered the
sacristy, watching as he left the door ajar.

I paused for a moment, taking it all in: the Blessed Virgin on her
pedestal, the red light burning near the tabernacle, the life-size
wooden Jesus on the cross behind the altar, the palm-size crucifix
jabbing my side. I took it in and marched forward anyway, the words
from the morning meditation echoing in my mind: *I came that you
may have life.* I opened the sacristy door and closed it behind me.

He had just set his bag on the sacristy table, and looked up in surprise. "Mary," he said.

"Tom." Before he could say anything else, before I could talk
myself out of it, before anyone knocked on the door, I stepped forward, wrapped my arms around his neck with its Roman collar,
stood on my tiptoes, and kissed him on the lips. After a while, a
good, long while, I eased back onto the soles of my feet, let go, and
walked out without another word.

Just two days after my moment with Tom in the sacristy, I was in
bed, my leg propped up on a pillow while the tertians studied in the
refectory below. I'd sprained my ankle helping carry canned goods
into the go-down, exacerbating the ever-present pain in my leg. I
could have continued teaching, elevating my leg on a stool, ignoring the pain, but I was happy to seize an excuse for a little time
alone.

As I lay there, I prayed quietly, placing myself in God's presence, letting His peace wash over me. After a while I heard a knock at the dormitory door. "Yes?" I called out from my bed at the far end of the room.

Sister Nolly entered, looking tinier than ever. Closing the door behind her, she made her way past the long rows of beds, hunched forward. When she reached my bed, she faced me, silent.

"Sister," I said, "what do you need?"

Still wordless, she sat on my bed, face away from me, her skinny bottom near my waist.

"Sister Nolly?"

She looked over her shoulder and focused her big brown eyes on me. "Please, Sister," she said.

"What do you need?"

She kicked off her slippers, pivoted, and stretched out next to me on the bed, her head near my shoulder. "I'm so scared," she said, voice tiny, body shaking.

"I'm sorry to hear that, Sister Nolly," I said. "Why don't you sit up, on that bed over there, and tell me about it?"

"I'm so scared," she repeated. But instead of sitting on the other bed, she put her hand on my shoulder for leverage, climbed up, and stretched herself on top of me.

Even through the blankets that separated us, I could feel Sister Nolly's heart beating fast. Her breath came in gasps and gulps. She wasn't the only one who was scared.

"Sister," she said, in a tiny voice, "please let me stay here, just for a minute."

I should have said no. I should have insisted that she sit on another bed and tell me what was scaring her. Instead I thought of Sister Nolly's pain. Instead I remembered how healing lying with Sister Timothy had been for me, how wondrous it had felt. I said, "Just for a minute."

I didn't put my arms around her. I didn't touch her in any way. I just let her lie there, her arms at her sides, while I lay beneath, both of us quiet. Using only love, I tried to wrap her in compassion. Slowly I felt her calm down. Her heart beat less quickly, her breath grew more regular. I was happy to help her, but I worried about another knock at the door. She turned her head to place her ear on my heart. Eventually—three minutes later, four, five?—I said, "Sister Nolly, it's time to get up now, don't you think?"

"Just a minute more," she said.

After another minute or two, Sister Nolly sighed, and I said, "Enough?"

The words were barely out of my mouth when the dormitory door opened and I saw Sister Lita. She gave a sharp gasp, said, "Sister, Sister," then took a few steps forward, a few steps back, a few steps forward, then raced back out the open door. I heard her footsteps heavy and fast on the stairs.

I had nudged Sister Nolly with my knee as soon as the door opened, but she still hadn't relinquished her perch on my belly. "Not very polite, was that, Sister?" Sister Nolly said. "She didn't even knock."

When I entered the refectory ten minutes later, all heads turned to look at me. From their expressions, it was obvious that Sister Lita had given a full report.

Before I could say anything, one of the sisters announced loudly, for everyone to hear, "Sister, we don't really know what went on up there, but we trust you. We are sure there is an explanation."

"Thanks for the trust," I said. "That means a lot to me."

They waited for more. What could I tell them?

Another of the sisters spoke up: "Sister Lita told us that you and Sister Nolly were fornicating in the dormitory."

The first sister repeated, "Sister, we believe there is an explanation."

"There was no fornication," I said. Sister Nolly still hadn't given me permission to say anything to anyone about her illness. To the fifteen faces questioning me, I said, "We'll talk about this later." Under my mask of calm, I trembled, cursing my stupidity.

. . .

I felt the eyes of the community on me throughout that day and the next. I could hardly think straight. At Midday Prayer I opened my prayer book hoping for courage from the smiling sister's photo. Instead I saw Jesus—crowned with thorns, covered in blood from having been scourged. The caption at the bottom of the picture read, *I looked for one to comfort me, but found none.*

Someone had replaced my smiling sister with a bloody Jesus looking for sympathy—a dependable consolation stolen from me by a judgmental pilferer of holy cards. Who had taken it—Sister Lita, another tertian, Sister Dorothy?

In Rule Class I emphasized the importance of respecting others' personal belongings, that it was a breach of privacy to look through someone else's Bible or prayer book. I was furious, and though I felt violated, I didn't remove the bloody Jesus—perhaps the holy-card thief was right. Perhaps if I'd spent more time looking at Jesus crucified and less at my sisters I wouldn't have been found with one of my tertians lying on top of me in bed.

Looking at Jesus, mocked as a king, I heard the taunt of the photo thief: *Hail, O mighty tertian mistress. Hail, O holy sister. Look where you are now.*

When I entered the parlor that afternoon, eager for advice and consolation, Tom stopped me before I could open my mouth. "There's something I have to say," he said.

"I want to hear it," I said. From the sound of his voice, I suspected he had issues with that foolish kiss in the sacristy just days earlier, though that seemed like an entirely different lifetime. "Tom," I went on, "I want to hear what you have to say, but I'm not sure I can bear it right now. Something has happened. Could you tell me whatever you have to say next week?"

He nodded.

"I'll be very upset if you don't tell me next week," I said. "I want to hear it, okay?"

"Yes, fine. What's going on?"

I couldn't look into his eyes at first. I called myself stupid and dense and weak. Calmly he told me not to be so hard on myself. I told him about Sister Nolly on top of me in bed, about how Sister Lita told the community we had "fornicated." I told him about the bloody Jesus in my prayer book. I told him I'd broken the Rules one time too many, that I had jeopardized all the good I'd tried to do, that only pride had made me imagine I could help heal the sisters.

He held my hands in his. He told me to look into his eyes.

I told him Sister Nolly refused to let me talk to the group, that I could hardly look the sisters in the face, that I didn't know if Sister Dorothy had heard anything yet.

"This is a sticky situation," he said, "but you're going to come out of it fine." I wasn't sure he believed that. I wasn't sure I believed that, but we both wanted to believe.

I said I wanted his prayers, but I wasn't asking for absolution, that I'd confessed my stupidity already. He said I had to convince Sister Nolly to let me speak to the community about her illness. He said I had to do it soon.

That afternoon I reminded Sister Nolly that I had tried my best to help her, that I had rarely refused any request she'd made, and that allowing me to explain to the others was something she could do for me. Prying consent out of her like that felt dirty, but I knew that in the long run speaking out would be best for everyone, including her.

She relented. I could say what I needed to, but she didn't want to be there when I talked to the community.

I called my tertians together. I explained that Sister Nolly was ill—not crazy, but ill. I explained to them that her depression was partly due to an imbalance of chemicals in her brain, that she had been to a doctor, and that she was getting better. I acknowledged that these months had been difficult for the entire community, and I thanked them for their patience. I told them that Sister Nolly's particular form of depression meant she sometimes behaved like a small child, doing things small children did, and that, in her own way, she saw me as a mother sometimes. I didn't specifically mention the incident in the dormitory, but trusted they would make the connection.

I told the sisters that Sister Nolly had been reluctant to share this information previously, but that she had agreed to allow me to do so now. I invited them to ask questions, and told them I would answer if I could. I was surprised when none of them asked anything.

Over the next few days, a lot of the awkwardness I'd felt after the "fornication" announcement dissipated. Though I could hardly believe it, the sisters' trust in me seemed to increase, as did their patience with Sister Nolly. Even Sister Lita relaxed a bit. What I couldn't know was how far outside my group of tertians the fornication story might have traveled. I knew it wouldn't remain contained forever.

When the next Thursday arrived, I insisted Tom first tell me whatever had been on his mind the previous week.

"That kiss," he said.

"Yes," I said.

"You're very good at that." He looked at me and paused. I felt my whole body tingle. "Believe me, I appreciate it," he continued, "but don't ever do that again before Mass." He threw his hands up in the air. "I can't celebrate Mass like that. I couldn't think of anything else the whole time."

"I apologize. Thank you for telling me. I won't do it again."

"Not before Mass," he said again.

"Not before Mass," I said.

As time drew close for writing reports, I worried about Sister Nolly. Obviously, I couldn't recommend her for final vows. Just as surely, releasing her to Sister Dorothy for certain demolition was out of the question. I suggested she go to the contemplatives for a while, but Sister Nolly refused. I was stumped, and asked Sister Agnel's advice.

"We'll have to do something before you write reports," Sister

Agnel said. "If we leave it to the councilors, she could end up with Sister Dorothy or in Albania. . . . Maybe I could bring her here."

San Gregorio was the furthest thing from a restful house that I could think of; it was more like Grand Central Terminal—sisters on their way to Mozambique or Moscow, a home for more than a hundred men and a soup kitchen near Termini Station for another eighty, sisters interviewing nervous Italian couples hoping to adopt Calcutta orphans, night runs to carry sandwiches to people on the streets—Sister Nolly would get lost in San Gregorio.

Still, Sister Agnel seemed to understand Sister Nolly's problem better than anyone else had, and the busyness might help Sister Nolly get out of herself a little.

"She could come see you on Sundays," Sister Agnel said. "She might need that for a while."

"It's a good plan, Sister," I said.

Convincing Sister Nolly to go to San Gregorio took most of the next day. Finally Sister Agnel came to take her away.

On Thursdays I opened my soul to Tom as I always had, but I began confessing my sins to Father Bob on Wednesdays. I was treading the line between keeping the spirit of the Rule and breaking its letter often enough that I needed a confessor who could give me entirely objective advice.

Besides, I'd read canon law. A priest who absolved his partner in sexual sin incurred a de facto excommunication. The way I saw it, the kiss hadn't been a big sin, but it had been sexual. I never wanted to force Tom to choose between absolving me and remaining in the Church. I also never wanted to hear him call what we had sin.

Whatever slack in tension the community felt at Sister Nolly's departure was soon taken up by another cause for tension: reports. The day Sister Lita showed me her letter to Mother, I wasn't too surprised at the expression of utter confidence in her own goodness. When I read her my report, she disagreed with nearly every clause.

At the end, when I recommended more time in tertianship, she sat back and looked me straight in the eyes.

Coldly, deliberately, she said, "You will not send that report."

"I have to be honest," I said.

"If you try to postpone me, I will tell Mother," she said.

I shrugged. I'd been waiting for this. "Do what you think is right," I said, "and so will I."

She left, a little less cocky than she'd been when she'd walked in.

I knew Sister Lita would make good on her threat. She would tell Mother that I had fornicated with one of my tertians and she would embellish the story. What Sister Lita didn't know was that I had already confessed worse things to Mother. I wasn't sure that Mother would understand how different Sister Nolly and Niobe were. It was likely that Mother would think I'd broken my promise never to get romantically involved with a tertian again.

That night, after everyone else had gone to bed, I went to the chapel. I prostrated myself before the Blessed Sacrament, body flat on the floor. I didn't say much. I wasn't looking for guidance. I was looking for courage.

I lay still for a long time. Then I went to the back of the chapel, pulled my examination-of-conscience book off the shelf, and wrote:

> *Dare to be different.*
>
> *Dare to live by your own convictions, not somebody else's.*
>
> *Dare to believe that you can and should make a difference in the world, that you have a precious contribution to make which no one else can offer.*
>
> *Dare to face your fears and live in the strength of the spirit, unfettered by human respect, a free spirit before the face of your God.*
>
> *Dare to believe that you may really be right, and that even if you're not it is better to have erred in sincerity than never to have dared to live.*

Mother arrived in Rome a few weeks later, bent and tired, but eager to talk to Vatican diplomats about opening MC houses in China,

Vietnam, Burma, Cambodia, and Turkey. She also brought the permission papers with her and was determined to distribute them herself. I knew my day of reckoning was near.

Most of the sisters, even the two who had asked for more time, came out of Mother's room and thanked me. The joy on their faces cheered me, and I knew I'd been able to help several of them in significant ways.

When Sister Lita came out, she walked straight to me. "I warned you," she said. "You never listen. Now Mother knows everything."

As she walked away, I thought, *Dare to be different. Believe in God's voice speaking in your soul.*

Soon Sister Agnel found me. "Mother is upset," she said. "I told Mother not to believe everything sisters say when they are agitated." Despite her ever-calm demeanor, Sister Agnel seemed a little shaken, too.

I knocked at Mother's door, and Sister Agnel walked in behind me. Mother looked up from her desk, her wrinkled face screwed tight. "Sister, what is this Mother hears about you?" she said.

I took a step closer to Mother and remained standing. "I don't know what Mother is hearing."

"Sister, they are telling Mother that one of the tertians was with you in the bed." Mother's face was one huge question mark.

"Mother," I said, taking a deep breath, "I was resting one day. I had hurt my leg. This sister was very depressed and she came and lay down near me." I winced inwardly. *Near*, of course, was not exactly right. She had been on top. I would have preferred to have been completely truthful, but I didn't have it in me to tell Mother she was lying on top of me.

"How could you allow that, Sister?" Pain covered Mother's face.

"Mother, she was so depressed. Very sick. I was under the blanket. It didn't last very long. She's not here anymore, Mother."

"Sister, look at Mother. Did you ever do anything else with this sister?" Mother's eyes searched my soul. I knew I was about to disappoint her and disgrace myself.

"Mother, sometimes I held her." Mother looked down as I said this. She shook her head. "This sister was so sad. She asked me to hold her, and sometimes I put my arms around her. Nothing more."

Mother shook her head again. When she looked up, the disappointment in her eyes pierced my heart. "Sister," she said, "your intentions may have been good, but you cannot do this. You don't know what it will bring up in her, holding a sister like that."

Mother was right, of course. A person could last a long while without touch, but once someone had experienced the comfort, joy, and sheer relief of another human body close, the desire to experience that again was hard to deny. Perhaps no one knew that better than I. "I'm sorry, Mother."

"Sister, promise Mother that you will never touch this sister again."

"I promise, Mother."

She looked—of all things—satisfied.

"Now, what to do with this tertian?" Mother asked, not missing a beat. "She says she doesn't need to be postponed. She says you have not been a good mistress."

"Mother," Sister Agnel interrupted, "the others have told you good things about Sister, haven't they? This sister is upset. Mother can't change the decision just because a sister speaks badly of her mistress."

Mother looked long and hard at Sister Agnel, then she looked at me. I didn't know what she was thinking.

"All right," Mother said. "Call this sister back in here and I'll talk to her. And you," she added, looking at me, "never again."

"Never again, Mother," I said, relieved to have my sins out in the open, and grateful that Mother had chosen to forgive me once more. The way she had immediately moved on made me realize that the ability to forgive made Mother strong. Like Jesus who refused to condemn the woman caught in adultery, Mother set the sins of her sisters aside and let us start again. I wasn't sure that was always wise, but that day I was grateful.

.   .   .

After a few days, I told Sister Agnel that I wanted to work with the poor again. I wasn't a person who could be tertian mistress. Sister Agnel told me to write a letter to Mother and the council, and to give it to her so that she could give it to Mother.

When Mother returned to Calcutta, she took Sister Lita with her. At first Mother had sent Sister Lita to Sister Dorothy's group, but Sister Dorothy had refused to let her in the refectory. "I don't want that kind of trouble," I'd overhead Sister Dorothy tell Mother, a remarkably bold statement of the type only very senior sisters could utter. Sister Lita would finish tertianship in Calcutta. When I watched them board the plane, I knew that Mother also carried my letter, with my hopes for a simpler life. Working with the poor again would be good for me, I knew it. This hope, and Tom's support, carried me through the next months.

When professions and new appointments came at the end of May, there was no change for me. I asked Sister Agnel how this could be. I had been so clear in my letter.

"I didn't send your letter to Calcutta," Sister Agnel told me. "I need you here."

27

SEXAHOLIC

When Sister Agnel told me that I had to spend another year with the tertians, I thought again of running away, but I didn't have the energy for it. Instead, I asked for a retreat. I needed to get right with God. I was looking forward to the silence, but I hadn't expected to end up with twenty sisters from the Russian region in a dingy summer vacation house outside Moscow. The dacha, formerly used by higher-ups in the Communist Party, had been loaned to the Missionaries of Charity for two weeks, on condition that we kept ourselves discreetly inside the house.

As I made my way to the dorm, the buckling linoleum and damp walls seemed haunted by the ghosts of previous unsavory inhabitants. Dejected at the prospect of eight days of confinement in that seedy house, on the verge of an assignment I feared, I sinned that night. Over the months I'd tried my best to avoid touching myself, but that night the desire for those intensely good feelings bested me. Perhaps I also realized that if this retreat accomplished all I hoped, masturbation would be high on the list of things I would swear off forever.

Confessing masturbation wasn't a good way to get started with a new priest, but I couldn't go to Communion with a mortal sin on my soul. The next day, during that first confession of the retreat, a screen separating us, I didn't say much, and neither did Father Gary. I'd known this tall Canadian priest by sight since I'd been a postulant and he'd been a seminarian, coming with Joseph, then a brother, to help out in San Gregorio. I liked Joe, but Gary seemed standoffish, a little arrogant. When Father Joseph had started the Missionaries of Charity Fathers, Father Gary had been the first to sign up. I'd barely seen him over the ensuing decade, but I'd recently heard that Father Gary had a gay brother. This gave me some faint hope that Father Gary might have insight into my problems.

The day after my masturbation confession I entered the dark parlor again, pulled out a chair, and told Father Gary face-to-face that I'd been struggling with sexual desires for six years. I confessed a very complicated relationship with a sister who eventually became my tertian, a short-lived relationship with another sister, feelings of attraction for yet others, and love for a priest, my hand on his shoulder, his hands on my head, a kiss. I told him that though I hadn't felt sexually attracted to a depressed tertian, I had embraced her when she asked me to, and that one day she had crawled up on me while I was in bed. I told Father Gary that over the years I'd repeatedly thought—even during times of prayer—about the people to whom I felt attracted. I told him that during the six years since my first relationship, I often longed to express my love physically, that I had sometimes longed for it so much that I'd felt a stabbing pain in my heart or a weird sort of yearning ache in my bones and muscles. I told him I wanted to be free of sexual desire, that I was ashamed of what I had done, and sorry.

When I finished my confession, I looked down at my hands. I didn't suppose Father Gary heard confessions like this every day, especially not from a nun entrusted with as much responsibility as I'd been given. I'd never heard any sister admit to my sort of troubles. After a few moments, Father Gary said, "Sister, you're a sex addict."

His words startled me. I swallowed hard. A sex addict?

"Only one thing will help you," Father Gary continued. "You need to do the twelve steps of Alcoholics Anonymous, but apply them to sex instead of alcohol."

Father Gary reached for a pencil and paper. My mind began to race. Bradshaw's books had said that people could be addicted to almost anything, but I'd figured my desires were part of a delayed sexual awakening. Though I was thirty-five, I thought of myself as a sexual adolescent, sure that with time I could master my urges and stop breaking my vows. But what did I know? Father Gary had experience with hundreds of souls and was at least a decade older than I.

Father Gary put down the pencil and handed me his list. "When you've finished these three," he said, "I'll give you the next steps." He told me to pray a rosary in reparation for my sins, and he kept his hands close to his chest when he gave me absolution, tracing the sign of the cross with small, stilted gestures.

I took the list to the chapel.

　　1. Admit that you are powerless over lust—that your life has become unmanageable. This was easy. Lust obviously had the upper hand.

　　2. Believe that God can restore you to sanity. I knew not only that God *could* restore me to sanity but also that God *wanted* to help me—after all, He'd been the one who'd called me to chastity in the first place.

　　3. Turn your will and your life over to the care of God. I apologized to God and told Him that I was ready to give up everyone and everything that stood between us. Once again, I offered Him my will and my life, and begged Him to have His way with me.

The next morning I returned to the parlor and asked Father Gary for the next steps. He raised an eyebrow. "Father," I said, "I'm ready to move on. I've got to get this thing under control." I handed him the paper, and he added the next two steps to the list:

4. Make a searching and fearless moral inventory of yourself.

5. Admit to God, to yourself, and to another human being the exact nature of your wrongs.

"Step five isn't just a regular confession," he said, handing the paper back to me. "You've got to go deeper than just listing your deeds. You need to locate the specific defects of character from which your deeds spring. Be very precise about your lack of moral integrity, and don't leave anything out."

This didn't seem too hard, either. In my confessions I'd always tried to get at the root causes of my sinfulness. Over years of confession I'd come to realize that, as with most people, I'd emerged from childhood with a bruised self-image and a longing for love that continued to haunt me. I'd been conceived just a month after my parents' marriage, and by the time I was seven, there were five of us. While other kids my age played hide-and-seek, I scrubbed floors, folded clothes, and boiled macaroni. Still, my mom always seemed overwhelmed. At school my good grades made me popular with the teachers but not with other kids, who taunted me. My classmates never let me forget that I was fat, freckled, four-eyed, and had the shortest hair in class (as did all my sisters—my mom insisted that neither she nor her daughters had time to waste washing and brushing long hair). As I tried to ferret out the causes of my sinfulness, I realized that I'd grown up thinking of myself as unlovable and of my worth as defined by what I could do to help others. I also nurtured more than a little resentment.

For years—both before joining the convent and after I'd entered—my prayer had been, "Let me know that I am loved." Throughout his talks in the chapel, Father Gary spoke of God's love as thirst. God had created human beings because He thirsted to love and to be loved by us. On the cross Jesus' cry of thirst expressed His desire for human love. In recent years God had responded to my painful thirst to experience His love, but He hadn't sent me the mystical interior feelings I'd expected. Instead He'd sent people to love me, and I'd grasped at that love with both hands. I'd wanted it too much and had gone too far.

Back in the chapel, I filled the pages of my notebook with my moral inventory, cataloguing the weaknesses and unholy desires that led me to sin. After two days of work, I showed Father Gary my list. He flipped page after page, then said I hadn't thought about it enough. He said I needed to spend more time in prayer and be really honest. How much more honest could I be? What did he think I was hiding? He told me that when I returned to Rome he would send me a Sexaholics Anonymous book. After I'd read the book, I should finish my inventory and confess my sins to a priest, which would be step five.

I had hoped to get step five out of the way that day, to confess my sins to Father Gary. I needed to get my addiction under control before returning to Rome, where Tom and a new group of tertians awaited me. I spent the next few days trying to be more thorough, but didn't find much to add to my inventory.

The last day of the retreat, Father Gary sent for me. When I entered the parlor, he was sipping his farewell breakfast coffee, bag by his side. He stopped sipping long enough to tell me, "I want to be fully honest with you. You need to know that you are a very seductive person, and that you must change that."

Seductive? That word hadn't yet made it onto my moral inventory.

He put the cup down, licked his lips, and stood. "That's all I have to say. I just couldn't leave without telling you." He half smiled and grabbed his bag. He had a plane to catch.

All through that morning and into lunch, the other sisters laughed and told stories, enjoying the release from our eight days of silence. I laughed, too—nervously—but I couldn't listen to their stories. All I could hear was that one word echoing in my brain: *seductive, seductive, seductive.* I'd never thought of myself as a provocative temptress. I certainly hadn't been trying to seduce Father Gary. I knew that I had to watch myself with people to whom I felt attracted, but Father Gary didn't fall into that category at all.

At lunch, the regional superior announced that Father Gary had suggested further rest for me. She'd gotten permission from Sister Agnel to send me to the sisters in St. Petersburg for a few days. That was incredibly kind. If Father Gary had understood my need for a break, he was probably right about my being seductive, too.

The St. Petersburg sisters took me to the Hermitage Museum and to the Summer Palace of the tsars, but even the masterpieces and the ferryboat rides couldn't drive the word from the back of my mind: *seductive, seductive, seductive.*

When I returned to Rome, I was very careful to keep my distance from the sisters, and I backed away from Tom again. No matter how much rigorous honesty I tried to apply to my analysis, I still couldn't figure out *how* I was being seductive, so I didn't know which specific behaviors to avoid. This, I thought, made me a very dangerous person indeed.

Back in Casilina, I continued to feel drawn to Tom, and saw Father Bob when he came on Wednesdays. When I confessed that I thought I was in love with a priest, Father Bob told me, "When we were in seminary, they told us that *if* we would fall in love was never a question; the only question was *when*." He told me, "Falling in love isn't sinful—it's human." Then he added, "As people who have vowed chastity, what is important is that we never give voice to our love. We may feel it, but we must never say it or show it in any way."

"It's too late for that," I told him.

"That complicates things," he said.

I told him how much this priest had helped me, and how we both wanted to be faithful to our vocations. Father Bob didn't advise me to cut this priest off completely, but he did recommend avoiding time alone with him behind closed doors.

That Thursday I asked Tom if he would mind moving our weekly talk to the garden. As we strolled between the eucalyptus trees, we talked, but I was too ashamed to tell him I'd discovered I was a sex addict.

The next Wednesday after confession, Father Bob nodded at a

package wrapped in brown paper, lying on the parlor table. "Father Gary sent this and asked me to give it to you," he said. "He told me not to give it to Sister Dorothy."

I could see that Father Bob wasn't comfortable going behind my superior's back. To allay his fears, I opened the package in front of him. The book had a plain glossy white cover, without any words or pictures. The interior title page read *Sexaholics Anonymous*.

"Yeah, I guess Sister Dorothy doesn't need to see this," he said.

I read the *Sexaholics* book when I thought no one was looking. The book told of people who'd had dozens, sometimes hundreds of partners. Though my sexual experiences were far more limited, I didn't have much trouble admitting to myself that I was a sexaholic. I thought about sex—sometimes several times a day. I'd never seen porn, but the juicier parts of the Bible sometimes aroused me. Most significantly, I'd allowed my desire for sex to so overtake me that I'd broken my vows.

While I could accept *sexaholic*, coming to terms with *seductive* proved more difficult. The word kept rattling around in my brain, shaming me. I couldn't look Father Bob in the eye the day I told him Father Gary had called me seductive. Father Bob sat silent for a moment, then said he'd never thought of me that way.

"*Seductive* is a word I've heard Father Gary use to describe someone who seeks attention, sexual or not," Father Bob explained. "I don't know what he meant with you, and I don't know what he felt in your presence."

That last phrase stuck in my head: *what he felt in your presence*. Was it possible that Father Gary felt attracted to me, and that he'd chosen to blame that attraction on my seductiveness?

In July, Mother collapsed of exhaustion in Bombay. In August, malaria overtook her in Delhi. In September, heart and lung trouble sent her to the hospital in Calcutta. As the news grew worse and worse, everyone grew anxious. We increased our prayers and doubled our penance. I tried my best to behave as Mother expected of me.

We received news that Father Van Exem, who had been Mother's spiritual director when she received the inspiration to begin the Missionaries of Charity, was also ill. He wrote a letter to Mother, telling her that he had asked God to take his life and to spare hers. When I heard this, I was struck by what sounded to me like romantic devotion. Father Van Exem obviously shared a deep spiritual bond with Mother, but I was sure they had never been anything but chaste. Why couldn't I manage that?

Father Van Exem died the day after he'd offered his life. Mother recovered.

When I finally told Tom that Father Gary had recommended Sexaholics Anonymous to me, he was surprised at first. "I don't think you're an addict," he said, "but the twelve steps use sound spiritual principles—they're good for anyone who's trying to grow." He offered to make the twelve steps the subject of his weekly talks to the tertians, and to smuggle me books on the steps.

Tom said there was power in sharing one's struggles—a power I'd certainly experienced. He said the twelve steps worked best in groups, so I divided my tertians into four groups of six sisters each—"Sinners Anonymous." I wanted the sisters to feel free to speak without having to worry about their mistress and reports, so I didn't join any of the groups.

Instead, Tom and I formed our own little sinners group. Though we shared nothing more than our thoughts, the attraction between us grew so strong that sometimes I had to sit on my hands to keep from reaching for him. I noticed that Tom's palms sometimes glistened with perspiration.

At first the tertians were enthusiastic about learning the steps, a new spiritual tool on the road to holiness. Before long, though, some sisters grew nervous. Candidly admitting inclinations to self-importance, jealousy, or chronic laziness required more honesty than most MCs were accustomed to. Still, many sisters rose to the challenge, and I watched as humble vulnerability seemed to yield better results than previous years of striving for spiritual perfection.

Though I still didn't understand exactly how *seductive* applied to me, I asked Father Bob one Wednesday if he would hear a long confession. It was time to admit to God, to myself, and to another human being the exact nature of my wrongs, time to abandon the thrill of attraction and of breaking the Rules. I hoped my step five confession and my decision to forever reject any sexual expression of love would turn me more surely toward God, the only source of peace. I thought often of St. Augustine's words: *You have made us for Yourself, O Lord, and our hearts are restless until they rest in You.*

Toward the end of my confession I admitted that I still wasn't aware of having seduced or manipulated others, but that I was sorry for whatever sins I had unknowingly committed.

After Father Bob absolved me, I expected to feel clean, unburdened, free. Instead, I left the parlor feeling that things were still unfinished. Though I couldn't have explained why, I was keenly aware that the last word on my life as a human being with a body and desires hadn't yet been spoken.

As I knelt in chapel, reciting my penance, the words of St. Paul to the Romans returned to me: *God makes all things*—even sin, I thought—*work together for good for those who love Him and who are called according to His plan.*

Loving others wasn't always easy for me, and Sister Dorothy was one of my greatest challenges. I would have liked to work with her collaboratively, as I had with Sister Joseph Michael, but Sister Dorothy didn't treat any sister as an equal.

When we received news of the destruction of several churches during ethnic strife in Kosovo, Sister Dorothy told me, "I can understand that they kill the people, but why do they have to destroy such beautiful churches?" I then truly understood there was little chance of Sister Dorothy and I ever seeing eye to eye on anything.

That winter, Sister Dorothy felt particularly cold. The novices lived in the prefabricated building we'd previously used for refugees, and Sister decided to move in with them—they had central heating. I couldn't resist taking advantage of the fact that this left Mother's room—and the telephone—free at nights.

The first night I phoned Tom he was surprised. The second night he was eager. The third night I was late and he was anxious. We couldn't speak for long—like most priests, Tom had a private phone in his own room, but I never knew when someone might walk in on me, or who might be standing outside the door, trying to overhear.

Hearing Tom say "I love you" before I went to bed each night was like retiring to paradise. I felt a little guilty, but not guilty enough to stop.

Sister Agnel called me into her office one day in April. "Sister Dorothy's term will expire next month," she said. "I need to recommend a new superior for Casilina. The European novices need to learn to obey an Indian. I'm thinking of Sister Constancia. What do you think?"

I knew Sister Agnel wasn't really asking my opinion. She was preparing me for the fact that I wasn't going to be appointed superior of Casilina. Since I was assistant superior and had evident leadership abilities, many sisters considered me the obvious choice. While it was true that obeying an Indian sister would give the novices practice living under someone with different cultural sensibilities, Sister Constancia was already senior novice mistress, so appointing her as superior of Casilina—in charge of both novices and tertians—wouldn't change much about how novices learned to obey. Sister Agnel was being kind, but I already knew I'd never be appointed superior of Casilina. At least some of the councilors were aware of my troubles with Niobe, and I'd heard that Sister Lita had been gossiping about me all over Calcutta. I didn't expect to be appointed superior of anything, much less of a formation house with novices and tertians.

"Sister Constancia is a good sister," I said.

Sister Agnel nodded. "There's something else," she said. "The councilors want you taken off formation duty."

"Fine," I said with relief. "You know I want to go back to regular work."

"Not like this," Sister Agnel said.

"What do you mean?"

"Mother is very upset," Sister Agnel said. "Mother wanted to know—again—if the stories about you are true. Sister Lita has told everyone in Calcutta about how you . . ."

"Fornicated," I said.

"Yes, 'fornicated' with Sister Nolly. The councilors are putting a lot of pressure on her to get you out of formation work."

"Sister," I said, "I'd love to go to a mission house."

"Listen," she said. "I have something to tell you. I've had a sister watching you."

"What?"

"One of the tertians in your group. I knew she would notice if anything was going on. I told her to watch you and report to me."

I was flabbergasted. I'd never imagined Sister Agnel would have spies.

"You've had problems in the past." Sister Agnel waited.

I nodded.

"But I don't think you have them now. This sister told me that no one has ever helped her—neither priest nor sister, not even me—as much as you have helped her. She said you don't correct the sisters in public, but that when she comes to renew her permissions, you help her understand herself and you do it with compassion. She told me that you've helped her change things that she's been struggling with for forty years. She says you have no favorites and that you've taught the sisters to pray. The novices and novice mistresses tell me similar things—your classes help them more than anything else."

Sister Agnel sighed. "I can't recommend you for superior, but neither can I lose a tertian mistress like you. The Society needs you, both now and in the future. If you leave Casilina now, everyone in Calcutta will believe those stories and your reputation will never recover. We can't let a few past mistakes and rumors spread by an angry sister deprive the Society of all you have to offer."

Everything Sister said left me dazed, but she had a plan. "I'm going to tell Mother everything I've told you today. She's already upset with me for disagreeing with the councilors, because that makes things difficult for her in Calcutta, but I think she will listen to me. If I can convince Mother, Mother will stand up to the councilors."

"Thank you, Sister," I said. "But I still want to go to a mission house."

"One more year," she said. "And I think you should know that I wasn't planning on telling you all the things that tertian told me about you, but she said she wouldn't tell me anything unless I told you everything I heard from her. You're doing a good job. Thank you."

Sister Agnel laid her hands on my head in blessing, and let them linger a bit. I left the room a little dizzy. How was I going to survive another year?

The weeks that followed brought many new assignments, but not for me. Sister Agnel convinced Mother that I'd learned my lesson and deserved another chance. Sister Constancia replaced Sister Dorothy as superior of Casilina, and Sister Elena replaced Sister Agnel as regional superior of Italy. One of the last things Sister Agnel did while still regional was to send me to Napoli for a week of rest before my new tertians arrived, a rest I deeply appreciated.

After the break, I approached my new group with more confidence than I had with any other. I knew I wasn't as good a sister as Sister Agnel imagined me to be. She knew nothing about Tom and our nightly conversations, how the strength and wisdom I used to serve the sisters were derived at least as much from my relationship with him as from prayer. Still, the validation Sister gave me helped balance the browbeating I'd received from Sister Dorothy, and I was pleased to think that I had actually helped some sisters.

A general letter Mother had written that March particularly touched me: *Only the thirst of Jesus, hearing it, feeling it, answering it with all your heart, will keep the Society alive after Mother leaves you.*

Mother emphasized over and over again the need to draw close to Jesus: *You will hear, you will feel His presence. Let it become as intimate for each of you just as for Mother—this is the greater joy you could give me.*

I recognized Mother's letter as an opportunity to talk to the sisters about intimacy. My excitement grew as I prepared a mini-retreat I titled "Open Your Heart." Of course, I spoke about intimacy with Jesus, but I often drew on my experience with human beings, relationships that had convinced me I was lovable in a way that prayer did only in passing moments. I told the sisters that every relationship required hard work, and I detailed seven steps of intimacy: fascination, trust, honesty, commitment, communion, suffering and service, and joy.

I knew how lonely some of these novices and tertians were. I told them God was eager to let them know He loved them. I told them they didn't need to be afraid of God. When I admitted that for many years I'd struggled to truly feel that God loved me, one sister said, "I thought I was the only one who didn't feel Jesus' love all the time." I watched as sisters throughout the room nodded. I told them we all had an emptiness within that longed to be filled. When I explained how resentment, guilt, and fear could block the experience of love, they asked questions that showed they understood and were ready to grow. When I spoke of the joys of intimacy as a foretaste of heaven, we ached together.

Mother was in Rome all October and part of November, invited by the Holy Father to participate in the bishops' synod on religious life. Though more than 85 percent of religious were women, Mother was one of only a handful of females allowed to witness the Pope and bishops as they discussed consecrated religious life. As priests, bishops had made promises of celibacy and obedience to the bishop, but few of them lived in community as consecrated religious with vows of chastity, poverty, and obedience. Why were bishops issuing detailed directives about the lives of nuns and brothers?

Throughout the synod, Mother stayed at Dono di Maria, just a few steps from the Audience Hall where the synod met, and one afternoon I took the tertians for tea with Mother. Mother looked more rested than she had in a long time, and her eyes twinkled like those of a little girl. She told us the bishops were concerned that some congregations of sisters were straying from poverty and obedience, and she admonished us again to be holy, reminding us of her promise to give Saints to Mother Church. Then Mother sat up particularly straight and said, "Sisters, I think we should all hurry up and die." I'd never heard Mother say anything like that before. She continued, "We should hurry up and die because this Holy Father is canonizing everyone."

She giggled, but it didn't seem to be just a joke to Mother. I'd realized for some time that when Mother talked about becoming a Saint, she didn't mean merely becoming a holy person in union with God—she meant being recognized as a Saint, being canonized by the Church. Becoming a Saint was the one approved ambition for a Missionary of Charity, and in this respect Mother was an ambitious woman. She was doing a lot of good in the world, and she clearly loved Jesus, but I sometimes wondered if her desire for canonization made her more obedient to the hierarchy than a true prophet usually was. In a few days, Mother would become one of the few women to address the synod, and I found myself wishing she were more like Joan of Arc, Catherine of Siena, or Dorothy Day—the kind of saint who spoke truth to power. Mother was perhaps the only woman alive with sufficient moral and popular capital to challenge the Vatican and hope she might be heard. I doubted that Mother understood the implications for the poor and for women when she backed the Pope on birth control, the all-male priesthood, and the primacy of obedience. Standing with the Pope was a reflex for Mother. She was a woman who knew her place, and the Pope called her "my best ambassador." If he lived long enough, Pope John Paul II would surely canonize Mother. Though I continued to love and respect her, the day Mother told us to hurry up and die was the day I ceased needing her approval.

· · ·

In Tom's presence on Thursdays, I could be completely myself. Mother had it right when she said that we were made to love and to be loved. In more than one way, loving and being loved by Tom had advantages over loving and being loved by God. For one thing, I could look into Tom's eyes. For another, Tom didn't exercise power the way God had done since I'd become an MC. When I'd been at home, I'd often felt a sense of partnership with God similar to what I felt with Tom, but once I'd become an MC, God—through the sisters—had exerted dominion over my every thought and action.

Occasionally on Thursdays, in the parlor—behind closed doors despite Father Bob's admonition—I sat opposite Tom and took his hands in mine. My conscience and that corner room with its scantily curtained windows kept me from doing much more than holding his hands. Tom seemed to have an additional brake that never allowed him to reach for my hands unless I extended mine first, to touch my face unless I had first caressed his cheek. I knew his reticence wasn't indifference but respect. Tom had seen me struggle to free myself from Niobe's bullying, and had witnessed the vacillations of my conscience. He was also sensitive to the power difference inherent in the way our relationship had begun and continued—confessor and penitent, older man and younger woman—and he wanted to leave me completely free.

One day Tom told me, "I wish I could say that my feelings for you are entirely platonic, but I can't." I could see that his fondness for me troubled him sometimes—or perhaps it wasn't our feelings but our vows that complicated things. I worried about him, but I didn't ask much about his struggles; I feared his conscience might push me away the way my conscience had at times pushed him.

In our nighttime conversations, safer because of the distance, we sometimes fantasized about marriage. We both loved our vocations and knew that sisters would never be allowed to marry and that permission for priests to marry wouldn't be granted in our lifetimes, but we had our dreams. One night he told me how he longed to walk with me in the park, for everyone to see, me leaning on his arm, the two of us together. I told him I sometimes dreamed of waking up next to him in the morning. I told him I'd like to iron his shirts and rub his back and read with him in front of the fireplace after dinner.

I finished steps six and seven (*Become entirely ready to have God remove all defects of character,* and *Humbly ask Him to remove these shortcomings*) and was working on step eight (*Make a list of all persons you have harmed, and become willing to make amends to them all*) when one Sunday morning I answered the phone in Mother's room.

"*C'é lo nella mia mano,*" the voice on the phone said. "I have it in my hand. Help me! I don't want to anymore." The man's words came out in little jerks. He was breathing quickly. The sisters had mentioned an obscene caller of late. I almost hung up, but the desperation in his voice tugged at me.

"What's your name?" I asked.

"Giovanni," he said.

"Giovanni, God loves you."

"God doesn't love me, *suora,*" he said, still breathing heavily.

"Nonsense, Giovanni. God is love."

"*Suora,* I don't believe you." Giovanni paused for a moment. "I'd like to believe you."

"That's a first step," I said.

Giovanni's breath slowed. I tried not to picture what he was doing. We talked for a while. Giovanni told me he lived alone, that he was thirty-five, that he'd once had a real girlfriend but she'd ditched him, that his sister didn't like him. He told me that he liked hookers and had once done something with a little girl, something shameful.

"I like to talk to you," he said. "The others, they just hang up."

I told him, "You need to change your first line."

I told him he could call again if he wanted to. As I set the receiver in its cradle, I realized I might have just had my first real Sexaholics Anonymous meeting. The thought that God might be making use of my sinfulness to help someone felt very good indeed.

. . .

Giovanni phoned several Sundays in a row, and as he shared his struggles, he seemed to be having fewer of them. Then one Sunday I heard shame in his voice. "*Suora*, I've slipped far," Giovanni said. "I was good. I didn't give myself the saw all week, then I slipped. Yesterday I went out on the street near the market and bought myself a woman for an hour."

In that instant, Giovanni ashamed on the phone and waiting for a response from me, I realized I wasn't a sex addict at all.

Unlike Giovanni, I would never dream of approaching a stranger for sex. Unlike Niobe, I would never demand sexual services from a lover who didn't want to give them. Unlike the people in the *Sexaholics Anonymous* book, I would never haul a stranger I'd just met into a broom closet for a quickie or use my family's grocery money to buy porn.

Though curiosity and the need to feel appreciated had often motivated my lust-driven encounters with Niobe and Sister Timothy, I'd outgrown that. I longed for physical intimacy with Tom not because I was sexually obsessed but because my body sought passionate expression of genuine love. This wasn't perverted; it was natural.

"*Suora?*" Giovanni asked. "*Suora*, are you there?"

I brought myself back and told Giovanni that God understood his frustrations. I told him that he shouldn't worry too much about slipping from time to time. I pointed out that paying a woman for sex was at least better than using his strength to force sex on someone who didn't want it. As I had in the past, I invited him to do something to help others who had problems, to volunteer at a soup kitchen or convalescent home. Giovanni thanked me for listening. I thanked him, too, though I didn't explain why.

Relief and a sense of integrity followed on the knowledge that I was no sexaholic. I was a woman who loved, and whose body wanted to love, too.

Of course, I still had a problem. A woman who longed to bed the priest who used to be her confessor, a woman who called him every night to say she loved him—such a woman, even if she wasn't a sex-aholic, wasn't a good nun, either.

I may not have been a good nun, but I decided my worry about being a seductive sexaholic had sapped too much of my energy. As long as Tom didn't interfere with my duties to my sisters, I would look on our love for each other as a gift from God, who was bigger than the Rules.

The next Thursday I walked into the parlor and settled myself in a seat opposite the man I loved. I looked into his eyes and told Tom that if he ever wanted to take my hands first, that would be fine with me.

He smiled. "I've been waiting for that," he said.

"I know," I said.

28

POLITICS AND SILENCE

Before she would tell me anything, Sister Yvette made me promise that I wouldn't repeat what she was about to say. I never imagined I would regret that promise before I'd even returned the phone to its cradle.

This former tertian of mine had called because a priest had shouted at her. Sister Yvette thought Father Doug's outburst was somehow precipitated by the notes—my moral theology notes—that she'd given him. Though I warned her, she didn't yet appreciate that she was about to enter a theological minefield.

Doug McCarthy had first appeared in the South Bronx convent the summer after my first profession, as a volunteer for summer day camp. A lanky fellow with intense eyes, a short fuse, and little imagination, Doug was not a good match for the kids. But Sister Priscilla liked Doug and took him under her wing. Each morning she personally assigned his daily tasks, and the two often had long talks in the parlor. When Sister Priscilla was elected councilor and Sister Frederick took over in New York, Doug befriended her as well. No one was prouder than Sisters Priscilla and Frederick when Doug was ordained a priest for the Archdiocese of New York.

Cardinal O'Connor sent Father Doug to study in Rome, grooming him to become professor of moral theology for the Archdiocesan Seminary. Between classes, Father Doug said Mass at several MC houses and served as confessor.

My most recent encounter with Father Doug followed Sister Priscilla's request for the notes I used when teaching. She'd said she was looking for ideas for her classes with senior sisters. I'd been flattered and sent her nearly a dozen files. Then one day after Mass, Father Doug accosted me. "You teach the Enneagram," he said.

"Actually, Father, I've never taught the Enneagram."

"That's not true," he said. "You sent the notes to Sister Priscilla."

"Those were notes I helped Sister Joseph Michael prepare," I said, "but I never taught the course. As I understand it, the Enneagram classifies people by the sort of defense systems to which they tend, and I prefer to teach sisters straightforwardly about defenses, without typecasting them."

"You're smart," Father Doug said, "but you have the wrong friends. The Enneagram is a bunch of hooey. Unchristian. You'll never get anywhere like this."

If Father Doug was offering me friends like his, friends who could take me places, he was barking up the wrong tree. The Enneagram had been Sister Joseph Michael's first attempt at helping sisters understand themselves better, and I could only admire her for that. Though some Catholics claimed its system of nine personality types was tainted by occult origins, the Enneagram wasn't sinister. Using theological correctness to cloak ecclesiastic ambition was what looked sinister to me.

Father Doug's mentors, Sisters Frederick and Priscilla, were both daughters of military officers, both accomplished strategists who used intimidation and the judicious granting of appointments to control the sisters and move up the MC hierarchy. Together, Sisters Frederick and Priscilla comprised 50 percent of the council's votes and 90 percent of its ambition.

A good tertian mistress would have hung up on Sister Yvette that day. Protocol demanded that a sister ask advice only of her current superiors, but I heard panic in Sister Yvette's voice. Consistently cheerful and competent when she'd been my tertian three years earlier, Sister Yvette had gone on to so impress the students of Regina Mundi's English section that they'd elected her their representative. Sister Yvette wasn't the type to panic.

After I'd promised confidentiality, Sister Yvette explained that, at Father Doug's request, she'd loaned him Father Mark Attard's moral theology *dispense*, the printed notes professors often distributed to students. This particular bound copy had my name on it. When Sister Yvette asked Father Doug to return the notes, he asked her if she'd read them, particularly the section on abortion. When she said yes, Father Doug shouted, "You simple-headed fool!" and stormed out.

During his next weekly Mass at Primavalle, Father Doug had delivered a rant about defending truth, exposing heretics, and opposing dissidents. After Mass, in the sacristy with Sister Yvette, Father Doug slammed the *dispense* on the table and demanded to know what she thought of them. She murmured thanks for returning the notes, then ran to catch the bus for school.

"Sister Yvette," I told her, "I know you did this innocently, but there could be trouble."

"How?"

"Some sisters have been looking for ways to discredit the school for years." I should perhaps have been more specific, but we MCs were trained to silence regarding a superior's faults. I'd never before talked about Sisters Priscilla and Frederick with anyone but Sister Joseph Michael and Tom. "Sister Yvette, have you noticed that when certain councilors come to Rome they always ask about the school, that they bring the conversation around to whether professors are faithful to the Church and whether they wear religious habits and Roman collars?"

"Sister, Father Attard is an excellent professor. Who cares what he wears?"

"A priest without a collar is just a first step. But if these sisters tell Mother they've caught a priest with questionable teaching about abortion, they might convince her to stop sending sisters to study."

"Sister, Father Attard opposes abortion—you've heard him— and surely the councilors know Regina Mundi is a good school."

I didn't like to shatter Sister Yvette's innocent belief that everyone was like her, doing her best for the common good, but Sister Yvette needed to know what she was up against. "People in power don't always like to share their power."

Sister Yvette was silent for a long minute. I was sure she'd noticed that novices and tertians often preferred the classes taught by sisters who had studied to the rants of superiors more concerned with buttressing their power than teaching. I didn't know if she'd noticed that our popularity was sometimes perceived as a threat to their methods and ideas, as well as to their positions. Already Sister Frederick and Sister Priscilla had narrowed the pool of priests permitted to give talks and hear confessions at Mother House. By granting access only to priests deemed adequately traditional, these councilors limited sisters' exposure to potent notions like accountability, shared responsibility, and personal growth. Regina Mundi was the only theological institute in Rome exclusively for women. No one imagined Mother would ever allow sisters to study with priests and seminarians. If they succeeded in discrediting Regina Mundi, Sisters Frederick and Priscilla could wield exclusive control over every MC's education. I insisted that Sister Yvette alert Sister Dorothy, who was now superior in Primavalle, where Sister Yvette and the five other MC students lived; our new regional superior Sister Elena; and Sister Juliana, currently in charge of the English section at Regina Mundi.

"Sister, I'm not talking to all those people simply because a priest got angry. I only told you because you know Father Doug and you know the school and it was your *dispense*. I thought you would tell me not to worry. I just want to be peaceful again."

"The time for being peaceful is past. Sister Yvette, will you allow me to speak to Sister Elena?"

"Sister, don't speak to anyone. If it gets bigger, then I'll say something."

"How will you know if it gets bigger? Things get bigger in Calcutta long before they get bigger in Primavalle."

"They'll be upset that I talked with you."

"They'll be more upset that I *let* you talk, but we can't worry about that now. Promise me you'll tell me whenever something happens connected with this?"

"I'll call if I think it's important, okay?"

"It's all important."

"Pray for me."

"I've started already."

A fortnight later, Sister Yvette phoned again. Father Doug had continued to shout during his homilies, accusing sisters who didn't stand up for the truth of disappointing Mother and the Holy Father. Then Father Doug had yelled at Sister Yvette in the sacristy about responsibility and moral relativism. He asked if she ever challenged Father Attard in class. When she said no, he told her it was sinful to keep quiet in the face of evil.

"Evil?" I asked. "Did he mention something specific?"

"He said that if I didn't have enough sense of the True Faith to see what was wrong, then I didn't deserve to be studying."

Sister Yvette still hadn't told anyone else about Father Doug's shouting. She told me she didn't want to upset anyone or cast suspicion on Father Attard. "But," she said, "the way Father Doug shouts makes me so nervous that I can't study, I can't pray, and during class I can't look Father Attard in the face."

"Sister Yvette, you have to tell the people who can do something about this."

"But nothing is really wrong."

"If nothing is wrong, why can't you look Father Attard in the face? Why can't you pray?"

Silence.

"Sister Yvette, Father Doug is right about speaking up when it's necessary. Your silence could hurt others."

Sister Yvette told me she didn't want to get Father Doug in trouble, and I asked her if she wanted him to get Father Attard or the school or the students in trouble.

"Sister," she said, "you exaggerate."

Frustrated, I couldn't think of a way to alert Sister Elena or Father Attard without telling them what I'd heard from Sister Yvette. I'd never met the new head of Regina Mundi, Sister Juliana. I couldn't ask Tom's advice even in a veiled way. He knew priests who taught at Regina Mundi, and he knew Sister Juliana; he would be able to connect the dots.

The next time she called, Sister Yvette's voice shook. The stories were similar—angry diatribes at Mass, no details as to Father Doug's specific objections. What had intensified was Sister Yvette's distress. "Sister," she said, "he shouts as I've never heard anyone shout. The way he looks at me scares me."

I volunteered to come to Primavalle, where we could speak together to Sister Elena, who was there for the superiors' retreat. Finally, Sister Yvette agreed.

At the table in the students' room, I searched the *dispense* on abortion while Sister Yvette and two other students studied. I found pages in which Father Attard listed common objections to the teaching that a child's soul was infused at the moment of conception. The most powerful objection dealt with the possibility of twinning. Sometimes, even two weeks after conception, the growing embryo replicated to create identical twins. Since souls don't divide, it wasn't clear if a new soul was created, or if the embryo, a human person, died at that moment, releasing its soul and allowing the creation of two new persons with two new souls. To further complicate the matter, sometimes twins recombined, reverting to one individual. Since souls don't fuse, did the two persons die, so that a single new person, with a new soul, was created? The *dispense* admitted the problem and offered thoughts toward a solution, but no definitive reply. To state that a question hadn't yet been adequately resolved was not to imply that resolution was impossible. Weren't students meant to look at issues, even perplexing ones, honestly?

On another page I found a note I'd scribbled in the margin: *prenatal diagnosis—see class notes*. "Sister Yvette," I whispered across the table. "has Father Attard updated the *dispense*?"

"I'm not sure," Sister Yvette whispered back. "We don't buy new *dispense*. We just use yours. But I don't think he's changed them much. He always mentions in class when he teaches something not in the *dispense*."

A process like that could get a professor in trouble, I supposed, if someone examining the *dispense* hadn't heard the lectures. Did Father Doug object to what was missing?

"So what did you want to see me about?" Sister Elena stood at the study room door, raising her arms in that lovely Italian way of hers. The three of us found seats in a go-down that had been stuffed with beds as a dormitory for retreatants.

I explained that Sister Yvette had called me because of something connected with the school and that I had insisted on this meeting. Sister Elena—not the sort of superior who objected to sisters talking things over—just nodded. After Sister Yvette recounted her conversations with Father Doug, Sister Elena asked, "But does this Father Attard really teach against the Church?"

"Not against the Church," I said. "But Father Attard is a very busy priest. He probably hasn't changed his *dispense* in eight or ten years. Recent encyclicals and proclamations, especially about bioethics and right-to-life issues, don't appear in the notes, though he always mentions new documents in class."

"Sister," Sister Yvette interjected, "Father Attard is a good priest. He's dedicated and prayerful and he cares about the sisters. He even took the trouble to show us a film about abortion after regular hours. Father Attard is pro-life."

"What do you suggest?"

"We need to alert Sister Juliana," I said. "If Father Doug is so angry that he shouts at the sisters during Mass, then I'm sure he's already said something to his friends in Calcutta."

"Does Father Doug have connections in Calcutta?" Sister Elena's voice caught, and dropped just a little.

"He's friendly with both Sister Priscilla and Sister Frederick," I said.

Sister Elena sighed. "Before we do anything, I need to know exactly what Father Attard teaches." Sister Elena took the *dispense*, then said, "If little things are missing, I might not notice."

We decided to take the *dispense* to Father Matthew, a moral theologian we both knew, and whom Mother had called a "holy priest." For years Father Matthew had been Sister Joseph Michael's spiritual director. More recently, Father Matthew told Mother that during prayer he had heard Jesus say, "Tell Mother Teresa I thirst." This had touched Mother, and she frequently mentioned that a "holy priest" had told her this; only a few of us knew this holy priest's identity. Sister Elena said she would make an appointment.

After reading the sections I'd marked and leafing through the notes for another minute or two, Father Matthew handed the *dispense* back to me. "You've studied," he said. "What do you think?"

I was annoyed that we'd come to him for advice and now he was asking me, but Father Matthew knew Sisters Frederick and Priscilla. His caution was understandable.

I told him I thought the *dispense* were basically fine, that though they omitted some of the latest documents the professor always brought students up to date during class.

"It's dangerous not to keep *dispense* up to date," Father Matthew said. "Especially for moral theologians. We teach the most controversial material out there. I understand that we priests get busy, but it's not professional."

"But it's not heresy, either?" Sister Elena asked.

"Not heresy," Father Matthew replied, "but you've got to be

careful around beginning students. I'm not sure he needs to bring up all the distinctions in an intro course."

"Thank you for your help," Sister Elena said. "I'm glad we don't need to worry."

"I didn't say you shouldn't worry. If someone wanted to make a stink about this, they could."

When we left, I could see that Sister Elena felt better, and so did I, at least a little. Now perhaps Sister Elena would be ready to speak to Sister Juliana.

"I'm not sure that's necessary," Sister Elena said. "But I'll think about it."

During those weeks of Father Doug's shouting and Sister Yvette's cowering, I developed a sinus infection that wouldn't go away. After months of headaches and thick green mucus, the sisters sent me to an ear, nose, and throat specialist at Ospedale Gemelli. The doctor took a look, ordered an X ray, then said I needed a sinus operation. The next day I found myself in a bed on the eleventh floor. I tried to push aside worries about Regina Mundi and the machinations I was sure continued in Calcutta. The frustration made my soul feel almost as miserable as the sinus infection made my head feel.

From my bed near the window, I gazed on green hills, sheep, and olive trees. To the south, the dome of St. Peter's dominated the Roman skyline. More urgent surgeries and Italian bureaucracy delayed my operation a full week. I decided to use the time as a private Lenten retreat. I sometimes took the elevator down to the chapel, but I felt closest to God when I was alone in bed, looking on the hills and asking His guidance. The sisters came to see me each day, two at a time, and I renewed their permissions and counseled them, but mostly I enjoyed the rest, the solitude, and the view.

I looked forward to evenings when, in my nightdress at the pay phone, I called Tom. When my roommates saw me foraging in my drawer for another *gettone*, they generously replenished my supply of phone tokens. I loved to listen to Tom talk about his day, joking about what some old priest had said at dinner, keeping me up to date on events of the outside world. I told him how my trust in God was growing, how during days spent watching the trees and the sheep and the hills I'd finally understood that being attentive to God's voice within me was more important than listening to what other people said about God. I told him I could feel God rejoicing in our love.

Though I longed to see him, I asked Tom not to visit. I felt self-conscious in my nightdress and robe, and I never knew when the sisters would arrive. I also knew how much I needed my time alone with God.

One afternoon shortly after my operation, Sister Yvette and a companion appeared at my hospital bed. Sister Yvette had lost weight. Her face was pale, and black bags hung under her eyes.

After preliminaries about my health, Sister Yvette told her companion that she wanted to speak to me alone. She got right to the point, her voice frantic.

"Today Cardinal Laghi came to celebrate Mass at school. You know," she said, "he's in charge of Catholic education. After Mass he met the section representatives. He pulled me aside and said, 'Don't worry, Sister. We're looking into that problem with the priest.' " Sister Yvette gripped my arm. "Sister, how does he know? What does he mean, he's looking into it?"

"I don't know," I said. "Don't you think it's time to mention something to Sister Juliana?"

Sister Yvette looked at the floor.

"Pull yourself together. If the cardinal knows, you have no time to waste."

Sister Yvette stared out my window. Though I could tell she hadn't been sleeping and that Father Doug had probably been yelling again, I didn't feel sorry for her.

"Sister Joseph Michael is coming to town in a few days," I told her. "You should speak to her, too."

"Sister," Sister Yvette looked me in the eyes. "You promised not to say anything."

"Unless you release me from that promise, you're the one who has to start talking."

Sister Yvette hung her head. I cursed myself for my inability to convince either Sister Elena or Sister Yvette to speak up. While their silence frustrated me, I knew the real danger was in whatever was happening in Calcutta and the Vatican.

That evening on the phone I told Tom that people who used God for political ends angered me. He told me he often felt the same, but that he couldn't let those people get him down. "My vocation is bigger than that," he said.

I felt my vocation was bigger, too, but I wasn't content to be a quiet presence of love and acceptance while others commandeered the Society. I wanted the opportunity to speak truth to power.

After two weeks in the hospital, I returned home. The sisters were glad to see me, including Sister Joseph Michael, who had come so the two of us could finish the *Formation Directory*. Though I was still in pain, having Sister in town relieved some of my anxiety about the school. Sister Joseph Michael, Sister Elena, and all the mistresses were catching up on MC news at tea when one of the tertians announced a phone call for me.

As I walked to the main house, I prayed that it was Sister Yvette, calling to tell me she'd spoken to Sister Juliana. "Hello?"

"There's trouble."

"Tom?"

"I'm in Sister Juliana's office. She got a letter from Cardinal Laghi this morning."

"Oh, no."

"Do you know about this?"

"I've been afraid of it," I said. "What does it say?"

"Laghi's letter doesn't say much, but it includes a copy of a letter from Mother accusing Mark Attard of not teaching according to the mind of the Catholic Church. Mother asks the cardinal to investigate, and threatens to remove the sisters from school if the cardinal doesn't act. Sister Juliana can't understand. She says she's never heard the sisters complain about Father Attard. She asked if I knew anything, and I told her I might know someone who did."

"Tom, I don't know anything about this letter, but I know something's been going on. Sister Joseph Michael is here. I'm going to ask her about it. Can you tell Sister Juliana to call in half an hour?"

When I returned to the refectory the other mistresses had gone, and I interrupted Sister Elena and Sister Joseph Michael. "Father Tom says there's trouble at Regina Mundi."

"I was surprised no one mentioned it at tea," Sister Joseph Michael said. "Everyone in Calcutta is talking about it. Sister Frederick and Sister Priscilla are trying to convince Mother that the school isn't faithful to the Church. They enlisted Father Doug to make inquiries. Mother doesn't know what to think."

"Well, she's written a letter," I said, "and sent it to Cardinal Laghi."

Pale, Sister Elena said, "I asked Sister Agnel's advice, and she told me that if there was a problem, the sisters in Calcutta would consult me and I could deal with it then. I never thought they would go straight to the cardinal. We didn't want to say anything about a little shouting—mostly Father Doug has been good to us. We don't want to make him look bad."

"Strange," Sister Joseph Michael said. "In Calcutta they've been speaking of almost nothing else for weeks. Sister Frederick and Sister Priscilla are getting everyone riled up about obedience to Holy Mother Church. They're putting pressure on Mother to withdraw the students." Sister turned to me. "Cardinal Laghi—isn't he Sister Jacinta's uncle?"

"That's right. And years ago he took Mother around when she first arrived in Rome, helped her find a house for the sisters."

Sister Joseph Michael looked at Sister Elena. "Sister Frederick will be here in three days. We ought to see Sister Juliana before she arrives."

When they left, I prayed. I prayed that Sister Yvette would finally tell Sister Juliana everything she knew. I prayed for Father Attard, dreading the moment he would learn that Mother Teresa had called for his investigation. I offered the throbbing in my cheek that things might go easily for him.

Back from Regina Mundi, Sister Joseph Michael said, "I'm optimistic. Sister Juliana is a reasonable sister, but naturally upset that she hadn't heard anything until she got a letter from the cardinal."

When Sister Joseph Michael and Sister Elena returned from the Vatican, Sister Joseph Michael finally looked confident. "Cardinal Laghi doesn't want to make any fuss. He'll investigate—he has to—but he'll do it quietly. I think we'll be able to stop this before it gets too big."

Then, hours before Sister Frederick arrived, Sister Joseph Michael escaped to Napoli. I felt abandoned, but Sister Joseph Michael said the move bought Sister Juliana time to maneuver.

As soon as Sister Frederick deplaned, she summoned Sister Trinidad, Sister Dorothy, and me to San Gregorio. The three of us had, at different times, completed courses at Regina Mundi. As my tram passed the Colosseum, I prayed for calm, sound judgment and for the strength to speak honestly. I didn't want this meeting to be sullied by any personal vendetta on my part. As we waited in the parlor, the calm I felt surprised me, even though I'd prayed for it.

Sister Frederick entered and we stood. She snapped the door behind her and began speaking while we were still adjusting our seats. Her eyebrows were snowy white, her eyes hard. "Come now, Sisters, I have no time to waste." Her voice seemed even higher than usual. "I want to know where each of you stands on this Regina Mundi affair. Sister Trinidad, you will speak first."

"Excuse me, Sister?" Sister Trinidad waited. "Did Sister say something about Regina Mundi?"

"Don't play with me."

"Sister, is something wrong? I don't know—"

"You don't expect me to believe that." Sister Frederick threw her hands up. Her long fingers seemed all bone.

"I'm sorry, Sister, I finished school last year. If there's a problem, I don't know about it." Despite Sister Trinidad's apparent sincerity, Sister Frederick clearly didn't believe her.

"And you, Sister Dorothy?"

"I'm sorry, Sister, I don't know about a problem at Regina Mundi."

"Pretending like this will do you no good. Aren't you superior in Primavalle, and didn't you sit through his classes there?"

"Whose—"

"Sister, they don't know," I interrupted. I had things to say.

"I haven't asked you yet." Sister Frederick glared at me. "I will deal with you later."

"I don't know if Sister is referring to something in particular," Sister Trinidad said in a conciliatory tone, "but Regina Mundi is a good school, with good teachers. What I learned there helps me with the novices. I'm grateful to the Society for sending me there."

Sister Frederick stared furiously at Sister Trinidad. Sister Frederick obviously expected lines to have been drawn. I wondered whether Father Doug's tantrums had been designed to divide the students so that when she arrived Sister Frederick could label them.

"And you, Sister Donata, what do you say for yourself?" Sister Frederick interlaced her fingers, boring holes in me with her eyes.

"Sister, I know there are problems, but Regina Mundi is a good school, and Father Attard is a good priest; I'm sure we can work this out."

"A good school cannot allow someone you call a good priest to teach contrary to our Holy Faith, and I would have expected you to know that. Or perhaps it's not knowledge but courage and conviction that you lack."

Sister Trinidad and Sister Dorothy looked at each other. Sister Dorothy jumped in: "Regina Mundi is very loyal to the Church."

"You were not sent to study to have your eyes blinded," Sister

Frederick exploded. "We expected you all to be discerning and re-sponsible, and to stand up for the truth. People know that the sisters are sent to Regina Mundi, and now they will think the Society ap-proves of disloyal teaching."

"Sister," I said, unable to keep quiet any longer, "there is some-thing I don't understand, and I would like to ask you."

Sister Frederick froze, neither indicating permission to speak nor forbidding it.

"If we thought there was a problem with the school, why didn't we speak first with the people involved instead of going immediately to the cardinal in charge of Catholic education? This could have been solved at a much lower—"

"How dare you question Mother's wisdom?" Sister Frederick's voice rose another half octave, and her face turned red.

I fought to remain calm. "Sister," I said, "you and I both know Mother did not write that letter. Mother signed the letter, but she didn't write it." Of course, I hadn't seen the letter, but I knew its main influences, and I was tired of Sister Frederick and Sister Priscilla hiding behind Mother. "And when Mother signed it, she thought she was signing a letter asking advice about a delicate mat-ter from an old friend who had driven her around Rome to find a house for the sisters twenty years ago. But whoever wrote that letter knew they were writing a letter from the Catholic Church's living Saint to the cardinal in charge of Catholic education for the Univer-sal Church."

"How is it that you seem to know so much while the other sisters pretend to be in the dark?"

This was a tricky question, but Sister would find out sooner or later, and I needed to be completely honest with her. "When Father Doug started giving angry homilies to the sisters, Sister Yvette spoke to me," I said. "She'd been my tertian and wanted advice."

"She is not your tertian anymore. You had no right to talk to her. I am ashamed of you. I am ashamed of all of you. You were chosen by the Society as mature sisters, yet not one of you opened your mouth when this priest who doesn't even dress like a priest spoke against the teaching of the Church."

"Sister, no one—"

"But, Sister—"

"Enough!" Sister Frederick snorted. She paused a moment, drawing herself up taller on her chair. "I forbid you to speak of this again to anyone, even in confession. Do not speak about it among yourselves or to the students. I do not even want to hear you speak about it to me. I will handle this from now on."

I hadn't expected to be slapped with a decree of silence. As a councilor, Sister Frederick didn't have the power to issue commands unless she was speaking in Mother's name, with Mother's express authority, and she never claimed that. Of course, ordering us to silence would leave Sister Frederick free. She obviously wasn't interested in learning the truth about a priest I was fairly sure she had never met; her agenda was different.

When we left, Sister Dorothy refused to look at me. She was Sister Yvette's superior, but Sister Yvette had turned to me.

In the tram, Sister Trinidad asked what it was all about, and I told her, despite Sister Frederick's prohibition. Father Doug was confessor to her novices, and after the way Sister Frederick had treated her, Sister Trinidad deserved an explanation. We all deserved an explanation. Who had authorized Sister Frederick to turn the Missionaries of Charity into Policewomen of Orthodoxy?

After a few days, I returned to the hospital for a checkup. I told the doctor my sinuses seemed worse and that the pain kept me up at night. He barely looked at me before saying, "Everything is normal. A little pain is nothing to worry about."

I returned home to work on the *Formation Directory*, to teach the tertians, and to worry about what Sister Frederick might be doing in San Gregorio. Someone told me that Sister had several long conferences with Father Doug. She also went to see Cardinal Laghi, but didn't go to Regina Mundi. In Primavalle she berated the students for failing to defend the Holy Faith. She offered no opportunity for response or questions. Though most of the sisters still didn't understand what was going on, she forbade them to speak about anything connected with Regina Mundi—not among themselves, not with anyone at school, not in confession, and particularly not with Sister Joseph Michael.

Sister Frederick also interrogated the novices about a retreat Father Matthew had preached. One novice mentioned that Father Matthew had said that if we understood how Jesus dwelt in our sisters, we would genuflect before them as before the Blessed Sacrament. The novice told Sister Frederick she didn't think Jesus was in the sisters and the Blessed Sacrament in the same way. Sister Frederick agreed—despite the obvious fact that Father Matthew's comments had been a rhetorical flourish, not a lesson in dogma. Sister Frederick called Father Matthew an unfaithful priest and gave orders to uninvite him for Mass and confessions and retreats. By smearing Father Matthew, Sister Frederick armed herself against the possibility that Mother might consult him, and she tainted Sister Joseph Michael, who considered Father Matthew her spiritual director.

When Sister Frederick finally left Rome, Sister Joseph Michael returned. I told her everything I knew, hoping she could intervene somehow. Sister told me that when she spoke with the students, they refused to talk, citing Sister Frederick's decree. They would say only that they were concerned and upset, and that they prayed for a quick and peaceful resolution.

No one I talked to knew the precise charges against Father Attard. I supposed Father Doug had written an exposé for Sister Frederick and Sister Priscilla, but all we knew was that Sister Frederick said it was something we should have spotted and objected to. Keeping us in the dark put us on the defensive and made rational discussion impossible; if they had a real case against Father Attard, they would have spelled it out.

Shortly after Sister Frederick returned to Calcutta, Tom told me that Cardinal Laghi had completed his investigation. The cardinal had asked Father Attard to update his *dispense* and to apologize to his students. According to Tom, the matter was closed. As much as I wanted that to be so, I didn't believe Sisters Frederick and Priscilla would agree to a peaceful, reasonable solution. Father Attard's *dispense* were merely the means to an end, and their end hadn't been achieved yet.

29

EASTER

SPRING 1995
POLICLINICO UNIVERSITARIO
AGOSTINO GEMELLI, ROME

After another sleepless week, I returned to the hospital for another follow-up exam, my left cheek swollen like a chipmunk's. The doctor took one look and said, "You're staying. You need another operation." The canal between my left sinus and my nose had completely closed.

The hospital was nearly empty since the medical school was on a two-week spring break, including Holy Week and Easter. Most of the nurses and doctors, among them my surgeon, were on vacation. All the patients who could manage were sent home and were told to come back the Tuesday after Easter, when the staff would return to full strength. I was told to stay, that I'd be called to the operating room as soon as the reduced staff could manage.

In the meantime, I prayed. I felt ashamed to be part of the system that had allowed Sister Frederick to exercise such abusive power, and I feared more damage to come. I had never seen a clearer example of God not speaking through a superior. I offered the pain, which continued to keep me up nights, in reparation for her sins, and I asked God to guide me. When I gazed on the hills outside my window, I knew again that God resided in my heart far more surely than He did in the Rules.

Finally, on Wednesday of Holy Week, the surgeons operated on my sinus, my own personal Passion Week celebration. The next day, though I had trouble standing, I forced myself downstairs to the hospital chapel for Holy Thursday services. Dizziness forced me back before services were half through. On Good Friday I didn't stand through the Passion narrative but sat, conserving my strength for the Veneration of the Cross, when I took my turn to kiss Jesus' wounds on a life-size crucifix. I slept fairly well both nights and felt better on Holy Saturday. I was determined to stay for the entire Easter Vigil— the longest service of the liturgical year—but I managed only through the ceremony of light and the first two readings.

When I returned to the ward, I talked to the sister in charge, then phoned Tom and asked him if he was free Easter morning. If he celebrated Mass in the ward, in the open space in front of the nurses' station not far from my bed, I should be able to stay for the entire celebration. I called Casilina and asked two tertians to bring supplies. When they arrived that morning, they set up chairs and gathered those of the ward's remaining patients who were able and willing. Finally, my Easter felt complete—Tom, my sisters, a handful of women in robes and slippers whose faces, like mine, were swathed in gauze and bandages, and the Risen Jesus, who promised life to the full and called me to freedom.

After Mass, I asked the sisters for a moment with Tom. I took his hand and asked him to return the next morning, Easter Monday, when we could be alone. The sisters would be busy with the big MC Easter gathering—all the sisters, priests, and brothers from MC houses throughout Rome together in Casilina for ten o'clock Mass and lunch. No one would come to the hospital until the afternoon.

Each time I heard footsteps in the hall that morning, I sat up straight in bed and adjusted my headpiece. I'd slept well. My head no longer ached and my sinuses didn't throb. I'd brushed my teeth three times and cleaned and adjusted the gauze around my nose more times than I could count. I'd chosen the most revealing of the three nightdresses the sisters had left me—short sleeves, and my collarbones showed.

Finally, excited by the waiting, I decided to close my eyes and rest once more in God, as I had so many times during the past weeks. In that godly quiet, I heard a voice.

"Sister Donata?"

Tom strode in, tall and handsome in his best clerics. I felt self-conscious with the gauze dangling from my nose, but he said, "You're looking very well for someone who just had her nose attacked for the second time in three weeks." In front of the patient in the bed next to mine, Tom pressed his lips against my cheek.

I introduced Tom to Signora Celina, and he extended his hand. Celina's throat surgery two days earlier limited conversation, which suited my intentions for that morning.

"*Facciamo una passagiata?*" I asked Tom.

"*Sì.* Let's go for a nice long walk."

I slid my feet into slippers and picked up my robe, blue rayon from the clothes go-down. Tom helped me into the sleeves. We walked together to an empty room at the end of the hall. I left the door slightly ajar.

Tom reached for a metal hospital chair and set it facing another chair in the tiny space between two beds. I reached for the window curtains and pulled them shut. We sat, knowing we would likely never again meet in circumstances so private, knowing also that each moment we lingered increased the likelihood of some unknown hand pushing open the door.

"Welcome," I said, spreading my knees ever so slightly.

He leaned back in his chair. "Are you sure?" he said.

"Very sure," I said.

We didn't say much, we didn't leave our chairs, we didn't remove our clothes. Still, our bodies found each other in our most private parts.

We knew pleasure.

We knew communion.

We knew love.

Then I stood and adjusted my robe. He put the chairs back in place. I reached for the curtains and opened them.

We walked into the corridor, and I led him to the little-used service elevator at the end of the ward, empty when it opened to us. I entered, and he followed close, his body warm and strong behind me. When the doors closed, we found each other again, eyes on the descending numbers, as attentive to the speed of the floor beneath us as we were to each other. We separated before reaching *piano terra*, sure that someone would enter, but the elevator kept going down. We made our way uninterrupted to the first and second basements. Tom's damp palms left wet spots on the sleeves of my robe. When we reached the bottom, we retreated to opposite corners. A woman entered, pushing a trolley stacked high with sheets. The smell of newly cleaned linen saturated the elevator. She got off at the first floor, and Tom and I rode up and down two more times. Finally he pushed the button for *piano terra*. I followed him out, walked him to the entrance, and watched through the glass doors until I couldn't see him anymore.

30

BULLIES

On a bright spring day, sisters from all over Rome had come to Casilina to celebrate a late morning feast day Mass. Sister Elena had invited Father Doug as the main celebrant, hoping to heal any bad feelings, and Sister Joseph Michael was back in town. I had settled on the floor next to a visiting sister who had studied at Regina Mundi several years earlier, and was just beginning to enjoy my chicken curry when Sister Joseph Michael approached. She asked us to accompany her to speak with Father Doug, who was eating in the parlor.

I said I'd rather not, and the other sister shook her head in a definite no, but Sister Joseph Michael begged. "I just want to feel him out and make sure things are all right. I'll do all the talking; you just stand there. I don't want to go alone."

When we got to the parlor, Sister Joseph Michael smiled and peeked inside. "Happy feast day, Father." Father Doug looked up, his mouth full. "Could we come in for a minute?"

"It's your house." Father Doug took another forkful of rice. He did not smile.

"Father, I am Sister Joseph Michael, and I'm in town for a few days. We met briefly in Calcutta when you came to give retreat last year."

"I know who you are." His eyes were as cold as his words.

"That was a very good homily you gave at Mass today." Sister leaned against the door jamb.

"Yes, Sister, it was. I pride myself on fidelity to the teachings of the Church."

Suddenly one of the tertians pulled my sari from behind. "Phone for Sister Joseph Michael, from Manila." It must have been the middle of the night there. I supposed it was urgent.

On the way out Sister whispered, "Stay here. I'll be right back." The other sister followed Sister Joseph Michael out, leaving me alone with Father Doug.

Father Doug pushed himself away from the table. He stood, his tall, thin figure blocking the door. "So you're on their side, aren't you?"

"Father, I know there are problems—"

"Yes, you're smart enough to admit that." He tilted his head and waited for more.

"But I can't understand why we didn't first try to settle the problems at the lowest level possible. If you had a concern, if Sister Frederick had a concern, why didn't you go to Father Attard or to the school to settle this?"

"You don't understand how these things work. He would have given some excuse, said he would change, and gone on as before."

"You don't know that. You didn't give him a chance. I don't think that's fair. I don't even think it's Christian."

"Defending the truth is the most important challenge in the world today, and you're not up to it. You hide behind being 'nice,' being 'Christian,' because you don't have the courage to take a stand." Father Doug spit the words out. I wanted to leave, but he was blocking the door, and I still had something to say.

"Father, isn't the whole point of this to find fault with the school so the sisters won't be allowed to attend anymore?" I should probably have kept my mouth shut, but I wanted him to know that at least someone saw through it all.

"You sisters don't need an education," he snarled. "You're here to do the humble works. Isn't that what Mother always says?"

"Mother has always insisted that some sisters be sent to study so they can teach the others."

"Well, she's certainly chosen the wrong sisters for that job, hasn't she? All of you—you're arrogant, you're cowards, you're unfaithful to the Church, and still you think you know everything." He exuded hatred so pure that my eyes automatically turned away, but I deliberately pulled them back.

"Father, I think that's enough. I'd like to—"

"You haven't heard the half of it." He continued in a steady crescendo, his eyes fierce. "Somebody should have put you in your place long ago. Sisters here think you're so wonderful, the tertians all love Sister Donata, but I know what's inside."

"Father, please, may I—"

"Truth is too much for you, isn't it? You want everyone to love you and you don't care about standing up for the truth." Even the men at San Gregorio, drunk and fighting, didn't shout as loudly as Father Doug was shouting. I began to tremble. "Does it make you nervous when someone sees through you?" I refused to answer. He wasn't going to listen, anyway. I only wanted out.

"Don't think it's finished here. You're going to feel the effects of this for the rest of your life." Of course, I knew Sister Frederick and Sister Priscilla controlled my future. I had known that for nearly twenty years.

"Get out of here. I can't bear the sight of you," he said.

I remained in place, silent, motionless.

"I said get out of here."

"Father, you're blocking the door." I was surprised by how calm my voice sounded.

He shifted to one side, giving me just enough space to turn sideways and squeeze past him.

I walked straight to the chapel, unable to think, unable to speak, unable to cry. I knew there were sisters eating, talking, but I existed on another plane where time and space, sight and sound, breath and consciousness had vanished.

In the chapel I prostrated before the tabernacle, remaining silent until sensation slowly returned.

God, God, where are You?

Oh, Sister Yvette, how many times did you endure this man's anger? I understand your paralysis now.

God, help him. Give me the courage of truth—Your truth, not his.

When I came out of the chapel, everything was quiet. Most of the sisters had gone to rest, but some were chatting in small groups at the end of the garden, and a few were preparing tea in the kitchen—at least an hour must have passed since I'd entered the parlor. I looked for Sister Joseph Michael.

"Where have you been?" she said. "I thought you were going to wait for me."

"Sister, you left me there with the devil. I've never seen such hatred, and all aimed at me."

"When I went back, Father Doug looked surprised, said he hadn't thought he'd see any of us again."

"He must have thought I told you what he said, but I couldn't do anything but go to the chapel."

"I suppose that is the only place we can do any good right now."

A few weeks later, over Thursday coffee, Tom told me, "Sister Juliana says the sisters in Calcutta have taken the Regina Mundi business to Ratzinger."

"No!"

"They saw that Laghi was trying to settle things quietly, so they took it to Ratzinger."

"I didn't think it could get any worse." Joseph Cardinal Ratzinger headed the Congregation for the Doctrine of the Faith, formerly known as the Office of the Inquisition. Cardinal Ratzinger was known for his uncompromising stands against theological dissidents.

"The Congregation for the Doctrine of the Faith won't let this go easily, you can be sure of that." Tom shook his head, and he had that sad look on his face that tore my heart apart.

"But isn't Catholic education under Cardinal Laghi? I thought Ratzinger only handled serious theological deviants. Father Attard may have been careless keeping his notes, but he's not a heretic."

"If Ratzinger's office pressures Laghi, he'll have to take firmer action. Ratzinger has power."

They were destroying the career of a good priest, prayerful and caring. As for the students, Mother would have the final decision, but Mother trusted Sister Frederick when it came to theological subtleties. Using the card of fidelity, Sisters Frederick and Priscilla could control Mother, for Mother would never give the appearance of being unfaithful.

Tom looked into his coffee. "There's something else I have to tell you."

"Oh?"

"The provincial has asked me to consider an appointment outside Rome."

"But you're not finished with your doctorate."

"I've finished the class work. I can finish the dissertation anywhere."

"Where?"

"Belfast."

"Belfast is dangerous."

"Nothing is decided yet. The provincial will visit in a few weeks. They will let me know."

In May, Mother came to receive the sisters' vows, accompanied by Sister Nirmala. Since my group of tertians was up for profession, I found myself at the head of the table, close to Mother and Sister Elena, and privy to many of their conversations.

At her first lunch with us, Mother looked very tired, more bent than usual. Right after the blessing, Mother asked Sister Elena, "Sister, do they know?"

"No, Mother," Sister Elena replied.

"Oh. They don't know?" Mother was surprised. "In Calcutta, all the sisters know." She bowed her head and took a few forkfuls of pasta, deep in thought. Then she rapped on the table for silence. "Sisters, while Mother is here, Mother has some very important decisions to make. You must all pray for Mother. You must write it on the board in the chapel, 'Mother's Special Intention,' and you must offer many sacrifices."

Mother paused, seeming to weigh her words before she continued. "It's about the school, Regina Mundi. A priest there has been teaching some very wrong things, and Mother must see about it. Please pray much."

That was all. We continued lunch.

Sister Juliana wore a simple navy dress, with no veil. She was in the office with Mother and Sister Nirmala for nearly an hour. When she came out, Sister Juliana told Sister Elena that Mother had agreed to give a talk later in the week to all the sisters at school, and they worked out the details.

Later, Father Doug spoke with Sister Nirmala on a bench in the compound for more than an hour. He did not shout, but he gesticulated fiercely.

The aging Father Hardon flew in from the States the next afternoon, the "solid" priest with his black cassock and shiny head. Father Hardon had seemed ancient the first time I'd seen him, eighteen years earlier in the contemplatives' chapel in the Bronx. Now he was so bent and his skin so transparent that he looked like a Dickens character from a wax museum. Because of his closeness to Sister Frederick, I assumed she had summoned him to urge Mother to fidelity and strength. He spoke at length with both Mother and Sister Nirmala.

With dozens of others waiting to see Mother, I found it impossible to grab a moment with her, so I turned to Sister Nirmala, hoping she would be able to talk sense with Mother. I told her I believed the charges against Father Attard had been trumped up. She said only, "Mother will decide. We must pray."

Father Matthew arrived at the gate that afternoon. Perhaps Sister Joseph Michael had told him Mother would be in town. I spoke to him for a moment, then positioned him next in line.

Mother came out of her room and took Father Matthew's hands, obviously delighted to see him. Then she excused herself, entered her room for a moment, and returned. She took Father Matthew by the elbow and led him close to where I stood. In her hand, Mother held a holy card that showed her standing under the cross, Our Lady at her side.

Mother showed Father Matthew the card. "It was like this," Mother said. "Father, it was just like this the day I heard Jesus say, 'I thirst.' "

I was shocked. As far as I knew, Mother had never affirmed so clearly to any of us sisters what we had all begun to suspect was true: that she had received a vision similar to the one someone had drawn on the card. Mother had never even told us whether she had seen anything at all.

Then I realized that Mother had brought Father Matthew within obvious hearing distance of me before she told him. Mother could have taken Father Matthew into her room. Mother had meant for me to hear about her vision.

I was still reeling from this revelation when the students arrived. Mother spoke with the six of them as a group, and then alone with Sister Yvette. When they came out, some were crying, and they all went straight to the chapel. When Sister Yvette came out, she looked for me.

"Sister, I know I shouldn't speak to you," she said, "but everything you said has come true, and much more. Mother says she may not allow the second-years to continue. She may even pull us third-years out before we take our last exams. She told us to be ready. No one quits school with only the exams left after three years of struggling." Sister Yvette's words poured out. "You know how we MCs are so much a part of the school. We're almost a legend. Sister Colombiere and you at the top of your classes, you leading the school liturgies, Sister Francis and I both elected as section representatives. It's like a scandal if we quit. And I don't care what they say—Father Attard is a good priest."

I had never felt so impotent. Sister Frederick and Sister Priscilla were hijacking the Society, and all I could do was stand below the plane and watch it fly, abused and broken, into their airspace.

When Mother returned from her talk at Regina Mundi, she appeared more peaceful than she had since she arrived from Calcutta. Sister Elena whispered to me, "Mother told the students not to worry—they can finish their studies."

"Thank God," I said, though I could hardly believe it.

"But," Sister Elena said, "there is still the meeting with the cardinal this afternoon, so you must pray."

At lunch Mother was in good spirits and told us that she'd had a wonderful time at Regina Mundi, that she'd given a talk and that all was well.

That evening, when Mother returned from meeting Cardinal Laghi, she went straight to the chapel, then to the office, where she closed the door. When the students arrived, Sister Yvette found me.

"Oh, Sister," she said, face finally relaxed, a smile on her lips, "Mother came to school today and she said we can finish our studies. Everything is going to be fine."

"That's good," I said. "Are you here to see her again?"

"Yes, we got a message to come here after school."

"I hope things are still fine," I said. "Mother looked worried."

"There you go again, Sister, always thinking there is trouble."

The students entered Mother's room. After what seemed a very short while they came out in tears. They left without saying anything to anyone.

Before too long, I found out what had made Mother change her mind. Everyone had said his or her piece and Mother had been pleased with whatever solution the cardinal had presented. Mother said that she had decided to let the sisters continue to attend Regina Mundi and she thanked everyone for their troubles. Then Father Hardon spoke. Father Hardon said that if Mother allowed the sisters' studies to continue, the Missionaries of Charity would split. Worried, Mother asked him to explain, but Father Hardon only kept repeating, "There will be a split. The Society will divide." Then he said the Missionaries of Charity's charism was to do humble works, that study of the catechism sufficed as an MC's education. He insisted that statistics showed the more education sisters received, the more likely they were to leave.

After sitting quietly for a moment, Mother said she would withdraw the sisters from the school. No MC ever studied at Regina Mundi again. Father Attard was prohibited from teaching moral theology.

Until that day, I had never been ashamed to be a Missionary of Charity.

A week later, Tom told me, "I saw Mark Attard today. He looks like he hasn't slept in weeks, and his arm is in a cast from falling off a bus."

"Did he say anything?" I asked.

"He said that now he would have time to see to his other duties, but he was sad. Sister Juliana is trying to schedule him to teach a course of some sort, but not moral theology."

I would later hear that none of the six Regina Mundi students studying at the time would be given a position of authority in the Society unless she signed a statement claiming that the school had been at fault in allowing Mark Attard to teach against the Faith. Some signed; others refused. I didn't think any of them really understood what was going on. Sister Yvette resisted for several years, even though the pressure on her was great. Then, after losing her mother in a family tragedy, when she was at her weakest, sisters increased the pressure even more, and Sister Yvette recanted. Since only current students were required to sign the statement, I was exempt.

The Missionaries of Charity didn't split, though the whole episode left me wondering if I could continue to belong to a group that had been taken over by corrupt politicians disguised as defenders of the Holy Faith. Father Hardon's claim that well-educated sisters were likely to leave also made me suspicious. Why did faith require such protection from scrutiny? If educated sisters left, wasn't it likely that their education had revealed some flaw in the system? What did it really mean when Jesus said, *You will know the truth, and the truth will set you free?*

31

Air

SUMMER 1995 TO WINTER 1996
SAN GREGORIO, ROME, AND FLORENCE

That particular June afternoon, after Tom had finished hearing the confessions of whoever hadn't yet been sent to their new assignments after profession, I was stirring sugar into his coffee. Before I could put the spoon down, Tom laid his hand over mine.

"The provincial came to lunch this week," he said.

"You're going?"

"Yes."

I stirred the coffee in his cup. "When?"

"Soon."

"For how long?"

"At least a year, but I have to come back several times—to defend my dissertation and to preach a retreat to the Holy Cross Sisters."

"It will be good for you to get out of Rome, and Belfast will be interesting."

"A little too interesting. A car bomb blew up two blocks from our house last week."

"But *you* are coming back. . . . Take a biscuit—these are good."

"At least twice this year."

"It's useless to ask you to write."

"Wouldn't Sister Constancia love that?"

"But you could send a postcard from time to time, to the whole community. You've come here at least once a week every week for five years, you know. You could say you miss us."

"Do you know why I've come here every week for five years?"

I smiled. "For the coffee?"

Tom shook his head. "I've never told you this," he said, "but after the first year, those twenty-eight sisters, all the confusion in that group, Niobe, all the pain . . . I didn't want to come anymore, but there was one sister who intrigued me, whom I admired very much. And after the second group—Niobe again, the hours and hours in the confessional, the time it took to prepare talks while I was supposed to be finishing my dissertation—I thought I shouldn't come anymore, but there was this sister who was just beginning to open, like the sun rising and shining on me every week, and the sun tantalized me. Then after the third group, with that depressed sister and her troubles, with your hand finally in mine, with the knowledge that you cared about me as much as I did about you, with my struggles in community and your battle with guilt and shame—"

"You knew you shouldn't come, but you did anyway. And then that fourth group, with Sister Agnel signing you up to give retreats all over Europe, with that 'seductive' accusation keeping me away from you far too long, with the phone calls at night, with an attraction—"

"Which I could no longer resist. With that fourth group, I continued to breathe only so that I could come here every week. And now, with the fifth group, which we have somehow survived and birthed together, my hands on your knees—"

"And mine on your neck."

"Our souls sharing each other's joys and pains—"

"And our bodies longing for a union we know we can never have."

"It is finally best that I don't come anymore."

"Because neither of us can bear it."

"I will never stop wanting it."

"Neither will I."

Kneeling on the floor at his feet, where no one could see me through the half-curtained windows, I wrapped my arms around his legs, laid my head in his lap, felt his hands on my shoulders, and let tears fall on his black trousers.

Two weeks later, Tom was gone, and I was in San Gregorio. Sisters mingled everywhere, hot and crowded in those remodeled chicken houses that retained heat like an oven. The weeks after professions saw hordes of sisters pass through this tiny house, newly professed from Calcutta and Africa and Rome, sometimes even from the Philippines and the States—it was a zoo. I was waiting for a new assignment of my own. When Sister Elena had phoned, she told me that I would stay in Italy, but she hadn't said where yet.

Some of the novices and one of the novice mistresses cried when they heard I was leaving Casilina. As new tertians arrived, several expressed disappointment—especially those who had been my novices. It was unusual for any MC to stay put more than a couple of years, and I had been in Casilina for five.

The outgoing tertians prepared a gorgeous scrapbook for me, each of them filling a page with words of gratitude and a photo. Their appreciation brought tears to my eyes, but scrapbooks were not on the list of acceptable possessions.

My family was in town. After I had again requested reassignment, I'd written them, offering to play tour guide to the Holy City if they could arrive before I left Rome. I wasn't sure I'd be reassigned, but I wanted to see them—I wasn't sure why, but I missed them more than I ever had. Kathy arrived with her husband and their two teenage children, and Margaret came with her new husband. When Mom and Dad arrived, Mom walked with a cane. I got permission to show them Rome and even Assisi. Everywhere we went, Dad took photos, including a few shots of the scrapbook before I reluctantly tossed it on the fire one evening. Sitting with me on a bench in the garden, Mom pulled out the piecework she'd brought along; she was quilting wedding vests for my sister Cindy's marriage that fall—another wedding I would miss.

Mom and Dad were still in town the day I followed Sister Elena into Mother's room, hoping for details of my new assignment. Sister pulled out a stool for me. She looked drained, her face pale. Even before she spoke, her small movements and less-than-enthusiastic smile warned me that she didn't expect I'd be happy when we were finished talking. After a little chitchat, she told me that she knew I had hoped for a small house, a little rest, and some work with the poor, but she needed me somewhere else. In San Gregorio.

I felt as though I'd been hit in the chest with several bricks.

Sister told me she needed a sister who could make herself understood in both English and Italian, could do passable paperwork, was willing to work while the others slept, and could keep confidences. I was the only available sister with the required qualities to take over the visa work.

Once I caught my breath, I looked at Sister. Sweat dripped from her sleeves, her shoulders slumped, and bags hung heavy under her eyes. Who was I to ask for rest?

"Yes, Sister," I said.

She went on for a bit. I would often miss community activities since embassies didn't keep an MC schedule. I would arrange not only visas but also travel tickets. I would buy and pack supplies for the missions. On Sundays I would visit Le Torri, a hotel that had been converted into public housing, where people were hungry for God.

My head was spinning. "If that's what you need, Sister, I'll do it."

"Thank you, thank you, thank you." Sister threw her arms into the air and shouted, *"Sant'Antonio Abate, ti rendo grazie."* Sister Elena invoked St. Anthony of the Desert the way Mother invoked the Blessed Virgin—in every circumstance, especially the most dire and exasperating—and after she'd finished thanking him, she gave me a big smile. She laid both her hands on my hand in a gesture I felt as both blessing and embrace. Her hands made it a little easier for me to begin to wrap my brain around life as a travel agent.

Within a week my parents had returned to Texas and I was in San Gregorio full-time. Each morning after breakfast I left the house with one postulant or another as partner. We traipsed all over town, filing visa applications, buying tickets, depositing donations in the Vatican Bank, leaving supplies and picking up letters at the office of the secretary of state.

In the bus or walking the streets, I prayed for guidance. A growing unease tugged at my soul. I often left the house with wads of cash in my bag and could have arranged a quiet getaway, but like it or not, God had called me to the MCs. *Mother's Instructions* and common sense told me I'd never find happiness apart from God's will. Each afternoon we returned to San Gregorio and quickly gobbled lunch in our respective refectories while the community rested.

Sister Patrick, who had been one of my first tertians, was superior of the house. When the first of August came, I asked Sister Patrick to renew my permission. She rolled her eyes a little before she nodded me into Mother's room.

She closed the door and sat down. I knelt, kissed the floor, and said, "I speak my fault for coming late so often for nearly everything, for not being present at community recreations enough, for often missing spiritual reading, for falling asleep during meditation, and for not being generous enough to help my sisters. For these and all my faults I ask pardon and penance, and I beg a renewal of my general permission."

"Sister, I can't do this." Sister Patrick had turned to stare at the ceiling, and she was wringing her hands.

I understood her apprehension, but I couldn't have cared less that she was several years my junior and that I'd once been her tertian mistress. "Just put your hands on my head," I said. "Then say, 'I renew your general permission,' and tell me to say one Hail Mary for all my faults."

"Sister, I can't—"

"Is that what your tertian mistress taught you?"

"Okay, okay." After performing the proper ritual, Sister Patrick invited me to sit.

"Congratulations," I said. "I hope having your tertian mistress in your community doesn't cramp your style."

"Having one of your tertians as your superior can't help but seem ridiculous to you."

"Sister Patrick, you may not believe this, but no one knows better than I do that it doesn't take a saint to counsel a sister."

"I can't—"

"Let's forget all this. I have a problem. You're my superior. I need help." I watched her swallow. "It's like this: I feel suffocated. You know, when someone needs air and they can't get it, and if they don't get it, they'll die. You know?" She nodded. "So now ask me, what is this air I need?"

"What air do you need, Sister?"

"I wish I knew." I watched her smile. "I think it has something to do with never being alone"—I felt my throat start to constrict—"and something to do with needing someone I can talk to, someone to relate to on a personal level."

"Sister, everybody loves you," Sister Patrick protested.

"Many sisters love me, and I love them, but a tertian mistress can't share her intimate thoughts with her tertians—it just doesn't work that way. And Sister Dorothy and Sister Constancia . . . well, you can imagine."

Sister Patrick nodded. "It must have been hard for you," she said. I worked to hold the tears back. "Not having anyone who understands is hard for most of us," she continued. "That's one reason I was glad to stay in Rome—because you were here, and even if I wasn't your tertian anymore, we saw each other sometimes and could talk, and you always understood me. And sometimes you even shared with me, didn't you?"

"Yes, Sister," I said through the tears that had escaped despite my efforts. "I trust you. You're a good person. I still think you're too demanding of yourself, and I'm afraid that if you keep it up you may fall apart one day."

"Sister, why are you crying?"

"Because I think I'm falling apart." Soon my handkerchief was so wet that it was useless, and Sister Patrick offered me hers.

"Sister, what do you need? Is there something I can do for you?"

"You can let me cry. Please don't run away."

"I'm not going anywhere," Sister Patrick said, though she was squirming in her seat. "You know, Sister tried very hard to find someone else to do this job because she knew you wanted something different, but the only sisters who were capable already had heavy responsibilities, and this is a full-time job. I know you can't be with the community so often, and you miss rest, and—"

"It's not the job," I said, shaking my head as I blew my nose. "It's true that it's not what I wanted, and that I miss the poor, but it gets me out of the house nearly every day, which is really important, and while I'm riding the bus I have plenty of time to think and to pray, and I like that I have to walk a lot, too. I finally get to see something of the city."

"What is it, then?"

"I'm not sure."

Each month when I renewed my permission, I cried. Sister Patrick usually cried, too. After the first two months, we each brought both our handkerchiefs as we tried to understand why I felt so oxygen-deprived.

The Regina Mundi affair weighed heavily upon me—but it wasn't just that incident. While Sister Frederick and Sister Priscilla glorified narrow-mindedness, I had become more open-minded. I didn't fit anymore.

Sometimes I dreamed of helping the Society return to Mother's emphasis on love, but I didn't want to settle for being a good influence on individual sisters in a bad system. Sister Priscilla controlled the appointments of superiors. I knew I would never be given a position where I could effect systemic change.

I missed Tom. I didn't begrudge him the change of scenery we both knew he needed—in Belfast Tom hoped to live among priests closer to his own age, men with whom he could speak in English, and eventually he would engage in more apostolic work—but I worried about his safety, and I missed him. I missed the occasional kisses and that one glorious morning in the hospital. But even more, I missed looking into his eyes and knowing he cared. I missed that he understood whatever I said almost before I said it. I missed his common sense and his wisdom. I missed his smile and even his sadness. And—I knew this was damning—I missed the thrill of breaking the Rules with him. On my bad days I wondered if that was all it had been, just an adolescent fling, but I knew our love was more than that. I kept telling myself that God loved me at least as much as Tom did, that I didn't need to feel God's love for it to be real, but as hard as I tried to believe, my faith left my soul cold. I was angry with the Church for demanding celibacy of her priests, and mad at God for giving me a vocation that demanded I sacrifice intimacy and intellect.

Though I ached for companionship, I also yearned to be alone, even would have welcomed a return to the hospital. Repetitive vocal prayers in the chapel irritated me. I wanted to be alone with God, at least every now and then, without any words—especially not someone else's words. On less than six hours' sleep, I struggled to stay awake through the 5:20 morning meditation. But when I did manage to empty my mind so that I could rest in God, I inevitably felt the press of sisters upon me. The times I came closest to experiencing God's presence in my heart were on the street or in the subway, far from the chapel and far from my sisters.

In September, when visa work had calmed down a bit, Sister Prema invited me to Madrid to teach "The Eucharist and the Poor." Now regional superior, Sister Prema had been a few groups behind me in the novitiate. Back in Germany, Sister Prema had a twin sister, and since I reminded her of her sister, she had always called me "my twin." Sister Prema had a quiet, steady presence, and I liked her.

In Madrid, no one seemed as overworked as everyone in San Gregorio did, and Sister Prema's respectful leadership seemed to call forth generosity and peace from the sisters. As I taught I realized how much I still believed in the MC vocation as I understood it. Nothing could be more precious than a call to live in union with God and to bring His love to those who needed it most.

Each Sunday back in Rome, as entire extended families emerged from their single rooms to join us for Mass in Le Torri, I could briefly touch what I so loved about being a Missionary of Charity. Mothers began to help each other, and the kids' faces lit up when I told them Gospel stories. The adults in Le Torri needed jobs, and I enjoyed imagining ways I could help them if I had been assigned there full-time.

Despite Sundays and the week in Madrid and moments on the streets, suffocation predominated. That summer and into the fall we didn't have a regular confessor, but made do with several different priests. I often found myself confessing temptations against my vocation. One priest told me not to listen to the devil, but to turn to the Blessed Mother and pray more rosaries. Another told me to give myself to hard work (if I worked any harder, I might have collapsed). Another told me a vocation always brought the cross. I told him I'd heard that before, but that this cross was more than I could bear.

To a priest who seemed more sensible than most, I described my problems as best I could. He told me, "Sister, bring your concerns before the Lord in peace. Don't go knocking on any doors, but ask Jesus to lead you, and listen very carefully." This advice gave me some peace. I no longer had to regard every thought of leaving as a temptation. Perhaps God wanted to bring me to fullness of life and was looking for a new way to do that.

Finally I got up the courage to tell a priest, "I think God may be calling me to something else." He wanted to know what. I said I didn't know. He said he would pray for me. Three days later he appeared at the gate, asking for me. Sister Patrick sent me to the parlor, where the priest told me, "I've been thinking a lot about what you said. It's not possible that God called you here and would now call you somewhere else without telling you specifically to what He is calling you. God doesn't work like that."

"What about Abraham?" I asked. "Didn't God tell Abraham, 'Leave this land and go to the place I will show you'?" The priest didn't have a reply, but left me a book about an early Jesuit missionary tempted to give up when Native Americans imprisoned and tortured him. The Jesuit had soldiered on.

Another priest laid his hands on my head and prayed for strength and wisdom. Hands still on my head, he said, "Sister, Jesus wants you to know that He appreciates the good you do for Him, and that He has a dream for you. This dream may not look good to you, but it is good for others. The cross did not look good to Jesus, but it was the way of salvation."

I tried to convince myself to walk in faith. I told myself that mine was a great pilgrimage with many tests along the way, but even that valiant story couldn't change the fact that I was tired and couldn't breathe.

Each day I gave myself to God again and again, and told Him that if He would make clear what He wanted of me, I would do it. But God didn't say anything.

When Tom came to town, I laid my head on his chest and gathered strength from the beating of his heart. When he left, I cried.

One fall night I fell quickly asleep. Before long, I saw a potter, her blond hair pulled back and fastened with a barrette, a few stray strands dangling on either side. As she pedaled her wheel, she hummed. The sleeves of her red plaid shirt were rolled to the elbows, her hands and forearms caked gray from the clay, her denim overalls spotted, too. The potter plied the clay into a curved roll, the length of her palm, then took the clay from the wheel and held it in her hands. She began pinching here, pulling there, her fingers moving nimbly, almost fluidly, over the clay.

She set the clay on a thick plank tabletop, where finished figures stood—humanlike figurines, a whole fleet of men and women, girls and boys, each one shapely and beautiful.

The potter smiled at the figures on the table, pleased with her work. She reached down and picked up a figure with long, flowing hair and supple curves. Turning the figure over in her hands, the potter examined it, as if for flaws, and then, holding the figure at the level of her heart, she bent her head and breathed into the figure's mouth. Slowly the figure acquired color: green eyes, blue-black hair, almond-hued skin. The figure shook her head and stretched her legs, as though waking from a long sleep.

The figure and the potter looked into each other's eyes for a moment, then the potter kissed the figure on the head. The studio floor dropped open in front of her, and she reached down to gently place the woman on a busy street—it looked like Paris. The woman waved, the potter waved back, and the floor closed. The potter returned to the table. In turn, she took each figure in her hands, breathed color and strength into each one, exchanged gazes with them, kissed them, and—as the floor opened out—set each one down, this one into a rain forest with banana trees, that one into a gray office with computers and filing cabinets, another into the warm kitchen of a small house at the end of a long dirt road, another on a busy Hong Kong street. She set a pigtailed girl onto the seat of a swing, giving a little push as the girl grabbed the ropes, threw back her head, and laughed.

Smiling, the potter returned to her wheel. Her feet trod the pedals, her hands worked the clay. She hummed more softly. Molding the clay with deliberation, she fashioned a figure with wide hips and a big belly. She lifted the figure from the wheel, then added little bits of clay all around. She studied the figure from various angles, then gathered up round breasts upon the figure's chest and added arms a little longer than average. The features of the figure's round face were pleasant but plain. The potter smiled and said, "Yes," pinching in dimples on both cheeks. Scrutinizing the figure from every angle, the potter lingered over the figure's delicate genitalia and began to hum more loudly. I enjoyed seeing the delight on the potter's face, though I couldn't understand what made this particular piece so pleasing. She cradled the figure near her heart for a long time. Then, taking a deep breath, she breathed into the figure's mouth. The clay skin pinkened, the eyes shone deep blue, and chestnut hair bounced on the figure's shoulders. The potter looked into the figure's eyes, wrinkled her forehead for a moment, then reached into the right side pocket of her overalls. From the pocket she drew out a tiny pair of glasses, which she balanced on the figure's nose. "Ah," the potter sighed with approval, and placed the figure gently on the table. A soft yellow glow emanated from this new feminine creature, as if she were clothed in light.

As the potter examined the figure again, I realized that she was looking at me, and I was both confused and pleased. The potter picked me up and kissed me on the head, on my cheeks, on my hands and feet. Her kisses sent warmth to every part of my body. She held me to her heart and I smelled the earthy clay, which was of her and of me at the same time. Then she set me down on the table again. *When the studio floor opens out, where will she place me?* I held my breath.

"I like this one so much," she said, voice resonant and deep, hands clasped at her chest, "that I am going to keep her all for myself." She reached down, placed her palm gently under my feet, and lifted me up, leaving me on a wooden shelf high on the studio wall.

Distressed, I stomped my feet and began to shout: "What are you doing? I'm not a collector's item." The potter continued pedaling the wheel, her back to the shelf on which I stood. I clapped my hands. I stomped my feet. I said, "I want to go through the floor with the others. I want to have adventures." Still she pedaled. I shouted louder and began to cry. Still she pedaled her wheel.

By Christmas I was so exhausted I could hardly pull myself into chapel, but the children I visited at Le Torri wanted gifts, and a few sisters still waited for visas, though we'd managed to send scores of others off fairly quickly after the early December professions.

After Christmas, I asked to go to Florence, thinking a week of rest with Sister Maria Lina would help me. I hoped that in talking with someone who had shared my initial enthusiasm as a postulant and novice—someone with whom I had taken my first vows some sixteen years earlier—I might be able to recapture some passion for my vocation. Instead, by the time Sister Maria Lina had told me of the jealousies that plagued her community, of the need to find a new location for the soup kitchen, of problems with volunteers who thought their job was to tell the sisters what to do, and of her stomach troubles, I didn't have the heart to tell her what was bothering me. After a week in which I did manage at least to sleep a bit, I was on the train headed back to Rome.

I shared the compartment with a single dozing teenager who looked like he'd enjoyed a long night on the town. Out the window, barren winter clouds hung low over grapevines.

The train pushed through a tunnel in the mountain. As darkness filled the compartment, I slid the crucifix out from its usual place at my side. I ran my fingers up and down its sides. *I am the spouse of Jesus Crucified.* Most scholars agreed that Jesus had died not of blood loss or pain but from lack of oxygen. If I felt I was suffocating, wasn't that what I was supposed to feel?

As the train emerged from the tunnel, I looked at Jesus' face. The bronze glob of His head was worn nearly flat after years of riding under the rope between my habit and sari, the bridge of His nose and a small hole for His mouth all that remained recognizable.

Silently, in the dark of another tunnel, I told Him what I hadn't been able to tell Sister Maria Lina: *I can't do this anymore.* I couldn't be just the spouse of Jesus Crucified. I wanted to be Mary Magdalene discovering the empty tomb in the garden, hearing the Lord call her name. I wanted to be the spouse of the One who said, *I came that you may have life, and have it to the full.*

I ran my thumbs over His torso. I gripped the cross so tightly that the loose nails at His hands left indentations in my palm.

I wanted intimacy, I wanted sex, I wanted to make a creative contribution, I wanted rest, I wanted to feel like myself. I was tired of looking at these desires as temptations. They seemed so full of God, not the devil. But it was temptation's nature to disguise itself as good. As long as I played hopscotch with my vocation—one foot in, one foot out—there was no way to know if the dissatisfaction I felt was due to my vows or to my failure to live them well. One thing was certain: I couldn't go on feeling out of sync with my own heart.

I looked down at the cross, His weight heavy in my hands again. There on the train I made a silent deal with Jesus. *Listen, Lord,* I said, *during the next year I promise to give myself completely to my vows, doing whatever is expected of me, trying to be a real Missionary of Charity. I won't even think of leaving. If during this year I can really be myself, I will remain and give up any thought of ever leaving. If not, at the end of the year I will go.*

32

FOLLOW THE STAR

WINTER 1996 TO SPRING 1997
PIOMBINO, SAN GREGORIO, TOR BELLA MONACA

At their core, my terms were contradictory. The paradox became clearer during a week in February with the contemplatives in Piombino. Sister Elena had sent me to clear my head, and the sisters gave me my own tiny room and my own tiny chapel. The only time I saw anyone was at Mass. During my retreat I often contemplated the phrase I'd framed as the condition of my remaining: *if I can be myself*. A nun was supposed to deny and transcend self, to lose herself in God and in service, but the more I prayed, the more I became convinced that God didn't want my immolation; God wanted me to flourish. Nonetheless, He had called me to be a Missionary of Charity. He and I had a year to reconcile the opposing terms.

For the time being, my new resolve to keep the Rules bestowed a sense of inner freedom. Tom was in Belfast and not scheduled for a return to Rome, which made keeping the Rules easier. I had asked him for a photo, and the last time he'd been in town he'd given me a glossy eight-by-ten head-to-toe portrait. When I'd packed for

Piombino, I'd stashed the photo between the folds of my spare sari. Settled in my chapel near the sea, I gazed on his smile, his broad shoulders, his long, lean legs. I gazed on a photo that violated three vows: Poverty forbade extra possessions, chastity forbade attachment, and obedience demanded my superior's knowledge of this possession.

There, before the Blessed Sacrament, I looked into Tom's eyes once more and for a moment let his smile caress me. Then I reached for the candle near the tabernacle and held a glossy corner above the flame. The paper curled as it burned. I gathered the ashes, cupped them in my hands, and blew them out the window.

After time away, it was hard to jump back into harried work at San Gregorio. I begged Sister Elena and Sister Patrick not to assign me any additional responsibility, and especially not to consider me as a candidate for superior when assignments were issued in May. "Sant'Antonio Abate," Sister Elena said, "don't even think it. I need you here."

Sister Elena was the truly harried one, responsible for twenty MC communities in Italy, often drafted as intermediary between Calcutta and the Vatican, de facto spiritual advisor to hundreds of sisters. I watched her grow thinner almost daily. A few days after Easter she met me as I returned from my morning rounds, her eyes bloodshot, her face as pale as her sari. "I, I—" she began.

Sister was trembling. I'd never seen her so distressed. I made her sit down and gave her some water. "Sister Letitia . . ." she said. "Sister Letitia has disappeared." As she daubed her face with her handkerchief, Sister told me that Sister Letitia had vanished in the midst of Easter celebrations. Her community in Tor Bella Monaca, on the northern edge of Rome, didn't have a clue about the whereabouts of their superior. Sister Elena had been looking for her for three days, without any leads. Sister couldn't understand. Sister Letitia hadn't appeared in distress.

Three weeks later, Sister had yet to locate Sister Letitia. Thinner still and just as pale, Sister Elena called me into Mother's room. "I know what you've asked for," Sister said with an all too familiar look of regret, "but I need you. I don't have anyone else I can trust with this. I'm asking you to go to Tor Bella Monaca as superior."

To me, the answer was simple. My vows required obedience; this was the year to keep my vows. "Of course," I said. Two days later I was installed as superior of the community in Tor Bella Monaca.

Tor Bella Monaca translates as "Tower of the Beautiful Nun." I was able to discover neither the story behind the beautiful nun nor any sign of her tower. What I did see were rows and rows of recently built apartment blocks, massive concrete conglomerations into which the poor of Rome had been packed tight. In a small prefabricated convent a ten-minute walk from the church, my new community cared for twenty refugee mothers and their children. We were a community of six sisters trying to find our way.

One of the youngest sisters, generous and cheerful by day, was haunted by childhood memories at night; no one could sleep through her shouts. My assistant superior ran the kitchen and obviously wanted to run more. Another sister cared for the refugees, the majority of whom had fled Africa and Eastern Europe, but tending these mothers didn't satisfy her; before entering the convent, this sister had been halfway through a Ph.D. in philosophy. I was grateful for the solid resilience of the most junior—and probably the most balanced—sister in the community, who poured her heart into caring for neighborhood families.

Eventually Sister Elena located the community's former superior. Sister Letitia didn't want to return and wouldn't allow Sister to tell us where she was, but at least we knew she was alive and safe, and that helped. If a sister had problems, she was supposed to pray and speak to her superior. If a sister still wanted to leave, protocol demanded she request permission for exclaustration, a year during which she would remain a vowed member of the community, but would live independently. At the end of that year, a sister could request an additional year or two of exclaustration, or she could ask the Pope for dispensation from her vows. To leave without the requisite permission was not only to abandon God and His call but also to disgrace oneself and the community.

Together, the six of us worked the Sinners Anonymous program. For the community's stability, I felt obliged to hide the details of my situation, which compromised the program. I felt other sisters holding back, too, but still the program helped. I let compassion guide my decisions. I gave everyone extra sleep on Thursdays. I consented to Sister Ewa's request for early coffee to fight drowsiness during meditation, and I allowed the kitchen sister to add more spice to our food than regulations permitted. I let particularly difficult Sister Kamini spend time working in the garden when she should have been visiting the poor; time among the cabbages and roses softened her a bit. As the weeks passed, infighting diminished, recreations actually became pleasant, and we all slept better at night. Watching each sister grow and the community gradually cohere brought a sense of satisfaction amid the inevitable squabbles.

The mothers and children in the house and the thousands of families in need kept us busy. The two-month limit on a family's stay was meant to motivate women to help themselves, and to make room for new families. It pained me that, despite our efforts and multiple extensions of stay, we often found ourselves releasing a woman and her children back to the streets with no job, no housing, no sure supply of food. We had to do better.

In May, when Mother arrived for professions, Mayor Francesco Rutelli proclaimed her a Roman citizen. Back in Calcutta three months later, Mother had an attack of malaria with high fever and such severe vomiting she required hospitalization. On the eve of the Society Feast, the night of August 21, Mother's heart stopped. She was resuscitated and then developed a lung infection. Two days later she was resuscitated again.

On September 8 Mother attended the brothers' profession in

Calcutta in a wheelchair. It was hard for us to picture Mother in a wheelchair. Ten days later we heard that she had injured her head; she was hospitalized for ten more days. Mother spent October out of the hospital but returned the third week of November with an irregular heartbeat, and underwent angioplasty to remove blockages in major coronary arteries.

We increased our prayers. We fasted, we prayed, we did double penance. Many sisters prayed for Mother's complete recovery. I prayed that this eighty-six-year-old woman who had done so much for the world would last at least through the beginning of the new year and the General Chapter. It seemed to me that Mother had more than earned her right to go home, but if Mother died before the elections scheduled for mid-March, Sister Frederick would succeed her.

While Mother was in the hospital in September, a Roman entrepreneur arrived at our door offering his services. Enzo drove the sisters for shopping expeditions, played catch with the young boys, repaired a broken window. When Enzo told me he wanted to do more, I told him the women needed help finding work and shelter. A week later, he came back with a plan for a cooperative in which he would supply knitting machines and a friend with expertise would teach the women to use them. We could set up the machines in a building already on the premises, with plans for moving to another as soon as feasible. The women would take turns with child care. Enzo would help market the products, with all proceeds going to the cooperative. No money would pass through Enzo's hands, and all his efforts and the work of a lawyer friend would be donated. Other friends in sales and real estate could be called upon. We would alter our two-month policy so that women who opted to form the cooperative could stay with us until they could stand on their own feet. In addition to the machines, Enzo wanted to donate all the start-up supplies and he wanted to begin as soon as possible.

I nearly leaped up and hugged him. His plan was exactly what we needed, and similar to what the sisters in India had done with the lepers who stayed with us, teaching them to weave cloth—including our saris and bedcovers—with proceeds going to the lepers.

I studied Enzo's plan, and we refined the details. I took our proposal to Sister Elena, and she told me she would think about it. A few days later, she had that familiar trapped look on her face. "This is not our work," she said. "We are to give immediate and effective service to the poor, not anything long-term."

"But, Sister," I said, "the *Constitutions* oblige us to give 'immediate and effective service to the poorest of the poor, as long as they have no one to help them.' When they leave us these women return to the streets with their kids. The lepers in India stay with the sisters all their lives. Once we get this started, the women should be able to keep it going on their own."

Her look told me everything I needed to know. She knew it didn't violate Mother's spirit of humble works and immediate service. She didn't say so, but her eyes told me she'd asked Calcutta, and they had said no. I knew Calcutta always hesitated to approve projects that required specialized knowledge, anything that couldn't be taken over by just any sister at a moment's notice, and that Calcutta didn't like partnering with outsiders—too much opportunity to lose control. I also knew that having my name on the proposal didn't help.

I couldn't understand how sisters could reject the opportunity to empower poor women, effectively returning them and their children to the street. I did understand their consciences wouldn't be bothered at all by having just knocked the heart out of my vocation one more time.

On December 8 the crowd, jubilant even without Mother's presence, applauded as the sisters filed down the aisle for the Mass of final profession. In years past, seeing the sisters in their new saris, hands folded at their chests, faces charged with terror and joy, had filled me with pride and a sense of belonging. This time I gripped the pew to keep from running down the aisle, from warning them to turn away.

The incense bearer swung gray sandalwood smoke throughout the church. The sisters formed a semicircle around the altar. The archbishop's golden chasuble shimmered in the candlelight.

My throat closed.

Always when sisters signed their vows on the altar I had silently renewed the gift of myself to God. I didn't know if I could do it this time. I wanted to do it. This was my year for a faithful and whole-hearted gift of myself—but what right did He have to take every-thing?

I screwed my eyes shut. God wasn't taking, I was giving. I was Donata, the freely given one. And I wasn't going to cry. The harder I tried to push the resentment from my mind and heart, the more the tears coursed down my cheeks. I tried repeating, *Jesus, I am Yours. I give You everything.*

But what had He given me? The good things in my life—Tom's love, the use of my mind, the awareness of my body, my desires to do more for the women under my care—these were all forbidden gifts.

The tertian mistress began the call and response: "Sister Jorrie."

"Lord, you have called me."

"Sister Ezra."

"Lord, you have called me."

The archbishop droned on: ". . . a call to perfection, to move be-yond the ordinary, to live the perfect love of God . . ."

God, I prayed, *I curse the day You placed that woman's wrinkled face on the cover of* Time, *proclaiming love for the poor and needy. This is not love.* I wanted to shout it, but instead I saw my hands clutching at my sari, balling it in my fist.

I forced myself to stay through vows, through the triumphal ringing of church bells, through the offertory procession, through the Eucharistic prayer and Communion. I couldn't stifle my feelings and thoughts, certainly couldn't repeat *I vow for life*, but I could force my body to remain in the pew. Back in Casilina, I formed part of the welcoming line that threw garlands of roses over the heads of the newly professed. When the others walked to the grotto to thank

the Immaculate Heart, I walked out the gate and took the train back
to Tor Bella Monaca.

I threw myself into work—there was plenty of it before Christmas,
including food parcels and presents and parties for the poor, con-
structing miniature crèche scenes for the shut-ins, urging everyone
to confession. I also asked permission to do double penance. My
year was about to expire. Soon I would have to make a decision, and
I wanted the clarity and strength penance offered. But when I
thrashed my thighs with the discipline and tightened the chains
around my arm and waist, I found myself no longer believing that
God took pleasure in my pain. I did it anyway.

When Christmas morning arrived, the carols dispelled the tension, at least for a moment. I loved the holiday melodies and the
story of God become man, born in a stable. A young MC father with
a round face smiled all through the Gloria. At the homily, Father
Marco introduced himself with a boyish grin and broad Italian hand
gestures. "This Christmas is a very special celebration for me," he
said, looking over our heads and then straight into my eyes. "Sometimes, like the magi, we don't know where we are going when we
start following the stars God sends us.

"A year ago, I left the Fathers." I watched as the sisters—even
those who had been dozing—sat straight and alert. "I had many
ideas and experiences, and I needed to sort them out. I didn't know
if I wanted to be a priest anymore. So I went away, praying and
thinking and struggling very much. I thought I might get married.
But a priest who knew me well told me that I would never be happier than if I was a priest, and the way he said it, in that instant I
knew it was true."

He paused for a long breath before continuing. "God has been
very, very merciful to me. I thank Him for the journey—it was part
of my path to God, because I could not live with the questions
anymore—and I thank God for bringing me back. This Christmas I
am born again, like the baby in the manger, with still so much to

learn and experience, but already with a mission in God's plan. What I wish for you sisters is that same knowledge of your mission, and that same experience of newness. God works in very surprising ways. We must not be afraid to follow the stars He sends us, even if the journey takes us unexpected places."

When Father Marco sat down, what I had to do was clear.

After a long day of celebrations for our people, when I finally crawled into bed, I pulled the pillow over my head so the sisters wouldn't hear me. Slowly the sobs and the tears released the pain. My year was over. I must keep my promise. Like the magi, I would leave this land called home and follow wherever He might lead.

The first of January was the day I'd chosen as my feast when I was still a novice—the Feast of Mary, the Mother of God, the Day of Prayer for World Peace, a day for new beginnings. The sisters took special trouble to make me happy. They invited all the Roman superiors for Mass and sang my favorite hymns. They made chapattis with potato bhaji. In the afternoon, when the community was preparing a little play for the evening, I took pen and paper to the chapel. Kneeling before the Blessed Sacrament, I wrote Mother a letter. I told her that I loved my sisters and was grateful for the time God had given me with the community. I told her I had prayed very much. I told her I believed God was now asking something different of me. I told her I would not change my mind. I asked for a year of exclaustration, for time away from the community, time in which I could pray and discern God's will. I also asked for time to prepare my community for my departure. I signed the letter to Mother as I always did: *Your loving child, Sister M. Donata, M.C.*

I folded the letter and stashed it in my Bible until I could hand it to Sister Elena in San Gregorio.

That night, though I usually cut my hair the first day of every month, I left the scissors in the cabinet. The next morning, when I should have fastened the chains, I left them in my bag, next to the discipline, which never stung my thighs again.

• • •

The last time Tom had been in Rome, he'd asked me to call him if I made any major decisions. The evening after I wrote the letter, I phoned him for the first time since he'd left for Belfast.

"Tom," I said, "I've decided to ask for a leave."

"Does that mean you'd consider marrying me?"

"What?"

"Would you consider marrying me?"

"I don't know. I mean, I hadn't thought of it that way. I don't know. Yes, I guess I would consider it."

He asked questions and I answered them, but I heard almost nothing else. Had he just proposed? I knew I loved him. I didn't know if I would marry him. Of course, we had sometimes spoken of marriage, and I'd imagined it, and even dreamed—often—of being together with him, but his question so floored me I couldn't even ask him to clarify.

Throughout the following days and weeks, Tom's question returned at odd moments. I thought maybe he was serious. But I wasn't sure he'd proposed—and didn't want to be sure. As long as I wasn't sure, I didn't need to answer.

The day I took my letter to San Gregorio, Sister Elena refused to look at it. When she handed the letter back to me, I refused to take it.

Then I reached for it. "I'll post it myself."

"You will not." She pulled the letter back and opened it. As she read, the paper shook in her hands. "How can you write such a thing?" she asked. "God does not change His mind, calling you here one day and somewhere else the next."

"Sister, God is free to do whatever God wants, and you know I have not made this decision lightly."

"Yes, I know. But perhaps your difficulties have blinded you. Do you know how this will hurt Mother's heart?"

"Sister, Mother will recover, and if I am making a mistake, it is my mistake, and I am entitled to make it. Please, mail my letter."

"Sant'Antonio Abate," she murmured. "Sant'Antonio Abate."

I bowed my head for her blessing, and she took my head in both hands and shook it.

Though we had a regular confessor at Tor Bella Monaca, I knew that when I left the convent my sisters would need more help than this priest could give. I arranged for Father Marco to replace him. Father Marco was easy to talk to and insightful beyond his years. The fact that he had returned might give the sisters hope.

A week later, when sisters arrived from Calcutta, I asked Sister Elena if they had brought an answer to my letter. "No, nothing yet," she said. It was still early, but I hoped for an answer before the General Chapter, scheduled to begin in Calcutta later that month.

Days later, Sister Elena, Sister Dorothy, and Sister Agnel left for the Chapter. At the airport, I begged Sister Elena to get a reply for me soon. I didn't think it likely that Mother and the councilors would refuse my petition. Sister Frederick and Sister Priscilla would interpret my request for time away as proof that education destroyed vocations, but I wasn't willing to retract my request simply because they could use it for their own ends. Sister Joseph Michael would be sad, and I didn't know if she would understand, but I suspected she would still respect me. I knew Mother was always upset when a sister left, but I couldn't help that.

In February I asked Sister Patrick, whom Sister Elena had left in charge, if she had news for me from Calcutta. "Nothing," she said.

My hair was growing longer. Each morning I ran my fingers along the edge of my headpiece and stuffed the wayward curls inside, hoping they didn't show.

Waiting for an answer grew more and more difficult. I was no longer too concerned about whom the Chapter might elect as superior general, or what decisions they might make. I only hoped that when the sisters returned, they would bring a letter for me.

The days dragged into weeks. I told Sister Patrick I was afraid that between the pressure of waiting and the tension in my community, I might explode. She decided to send me to L'Aquila for a week.

The sisters gave me a little room with a bed and a table. They distracted me during the day with walks around the quaint town, and I read when they worked. Toward the end of the week I began to relax a little. On Valentine's Day, the day I was to return to Rome, I struggled to get out of bed, paralyzed by an intense pain in my right side. Eventually the sisters called a doctor. "You've got to take her to the hospital, *presto*," the doctor said. "I think it's appendicitis."

Two hours later I was naked on a gurney, covered with a green sheet, an oxygen mask over my face. When the sisters from Tor Bella Monaca came to visit, Sister Kamini stuffed my nightstand with sweets. "Sister," she said, screwing her nose up tight and shaking her head, "when we told Father Marco that you were having an appendix operation and wouldn't be back for another week, he laughed and laughed. I told him it wasn't funny, but he just kept laughing. He said it was the best thing he had heard in a very long time, and that the ways of God are very strange." She looked away for a second, then said, "I think Father Marco may be a little loose in his head."

The ways of God were strange indeed. I was at peace with my decision, but time in bed forced me to ponder the question I'd been avoiding: *Does this mean you'll consider marrying me?* Tom had phoned once after that conversation, and he'd sounded excited about the possibility of seeing me, but I still hadn't asked him to clarify his intentions. The thought was too much for me, and not only because I couldn't yet envision my life without a sari. I wasn't sure Tom would be happy without the teaching and preaching he'd always been so passionate about, without the opportunities for counseling and forgiveness, without service behind the altar. I didn't want to be the one who took that away from him, and from the people he served.

I knew that Tom had made the thought of leaving possible for me. Jesus' call to fullness of life could echo as it did only because Tom had given me a taste for fullness. But I wasn't leaving *for* Tom. I was leaving to survive. I didn't have much sense of what I would do outside the convent, but I could follow God out because I trusted He would lead me.

Sometimes I imagined life in a new community made of all sorts of people—married and single, young and old, Christian and non-Christian. Each member would be free to love God as he or she understood Him, and together we would serve those in need. I didn't know if this imaginary community was God's call or my own longing to remain attached to the good parts of MC life. I certainly didn't know if the new life God was calling me to involved marriage to Tom or not. I feared that proximity to Tom might make hearing God's voice and becoming myself even harder than it already was. For days after talking to him I could think only of his smile, his lips, his hands in the elevator.

Anything that got in the way of God's voice and my self-possession had to be avoided, even if what got in the way was the person I loved more than any other in the world. I took out paper and pen. I thought for a long time. I wrote pages and pages. I told Tom I loved him, that I would always love him, but that I needed to love myself better before I could truly love him well. I told him I didn't want to stand in the way of his priesthood. I suggested it would be best if we had no contact, not even a phone call or letter, except to keep each other informed of our physical locations, for a year. By that time we should be able to see the way forward.

When I put the pen down, a sad and grateful peace filled me.

The General Chapter elected Sister Nirmala to succeed Mother as superior general and Sisters Fredrick and Priscilla as first and second councilors. Sisters Lysa and Martin de Porres were elected third and fourth councilors—both of them compassionate, honest sisters, but sisters we all knew posed no serious threat to the first two. The Italian contingent returned to Rome on March 19, the Feast of St. Joseph, with eight other sisters, six babies and two toddlers for adoption, and nearly thirty boxes crammed with printed copies of Mother's *Letters* and other books for distribution throughout Europe and Africa. I was fairly certain that Sister Elena would also be carrying a letter for me.

The plane had been delayed by bad weather in Bombay, the babies had cried most of the way, and the sisters were obviously exhausted. During tea in San Gregorio the sisters gave us as much news as they could squeeze into half an hour, then we left to let them rest. I would return another day to ask for my letter.

As I neared the lower gate, I heard my name. One of the postulants beckoned me back. "Sister wants you," she whispered.

Sister Elena stood at the threshold of Mother's room, waiting for me. "Here," she said, taking an envelope from her bag. "Of all the things I brought back today, this was the heaviest."

Sister Elena stepped back into the office, and I sat on the steps.

The letter was typed, a form letter with my name inserted on the appropriate lines. Mother and Sister Nirmala had both signed it. The letter granted me exclaustration for a year—but said I would have to postpone my departure until after May professions. Only then, according to the letter, could someone be appointed to take my place in Tor Bella Monaca.

My heat sank. After the May professions? I had asked for time to prepare my community, but I had meant a week or ten days. Making me wait more than two months after I'd already waited so long seemed cruel. I wanted out. I wanted it now.

33

CHURCH BELLS

SPRING 1997
ROME

Professions were finally drawing close. Whenever I asked Sister Elena for a departure date, she invoked Sant'Antonio Abate and changed the subject. Mother and Sister Nirmala were supposed to come for professions, and Sister Elena hoped they would convince me to stay. Each day until their arrival was an exercise in patient endurance. Some days I did better—soothing the tensions in community, helping connect a mother with a job and a room, reciting my prayers with patience if not fervor. Other days I could barely drag myself out of bed. I was ashamed to find myself sneaking chocolate from the cupboard on a regular basis. Thankfully, morning meditation and the few moments of quiet during adoration often brought solace. When I was able to still myself, I knew God was taking care of me, that He had something marvelous waiting for me outside the convent.

Every superior was expected to speak with Mother when she was in town. I told Sister Elena that I was more than willing to speak with Sister Nirmala but that I'd rather not speak to Mother. Mother was eighty-six years old, her health more frail than ever. She would be upset if she realized I was going, and I didn't want to give Mother the heart attack that would finally send her home to Jesus. Sister Elena said we would handle my departure quietly; I didn't need to talk with Mother.

At that point she also admitted that she hadn't sent my letter when I'd given it to her, hoping I would change my mind. During the Chapter, several sisters had approached her, asking if I would make a good general councilor. "I had to tell them not this time," Sister Elena told me, her voice shaking. "After the election, when I knew I couldn't delay any longer, I told Sister Nirmala and the new councilors that I thought you should be appointed to write and teach full-time. No one helps the sisters like you do. I thought an assignment like that could convince you to stay—and I knew it would be good for us, too. Only when they told me no did I give them your letter." Sister looked me in the face. "It's not too late to change your mind," she said.

"Thank you," I said, "but no."

When a crowd of us went to fetch Mother and Sister Nirmala from the airport, we were surprised to see that an entourage of twelve, including Sister Joseph Michael, Sister Gertrude, and several other very senior sisters, had arrived with Mother.

We called more Co-Workers with cars and eventually got everyone back to Casilina. Sister Joseph Michael and the others were talking in the compound while Sister Gertrude ran around making sure everything was all right for Mother: "This room is too damp. . . . You mustn't serve beans for lunch. . . . Do you have any grapes? . . . Mother must have a tiny stool in the chapel." I waded through the sisters, making my way to Sister Joseph Michael.

"What a surprise to see you here," I said.

"You didn't know I was coming?" She looked surprised now. "Well, isn't that the strangest thing? I've come to take your place."

I panicked. "Does everyone know that?"

"Why, yes, everyone who's come from Calcutta knows."

"So they all know I'm leaving?"

"Yes."

Though I knew I shouldn't travel alone, I grabbed a ticket from the box in the refectory and rode the train home. I had to tell my sisters before they heard it from someone else.

Back in Tor Bella Monaca, I rang the bell for lunch, though it wasn't yet time. Around the refectory table, I told the sisters I appreciated their efforts to make a beautiful community and to help our poor. I told them I was proud of the ways they'd grown in the year we'd been together. Then I told them that for a long time I had felt God calling me to something different. I was taking some time away to ponder the next steps. Stunned silence followed. Finally Sister Kamini, who normally spoke in a gruff, defensive voice, wailed like a three-year-old about to lose her mommy: "You can't go."

While one sister played with her pasta and the others looked blankly ahead, Sister Ewa locked eyes with me and said, "You can't do this."

"I'm doing it," I said. "I can't say I understand it myself, but I know I have to go."

No one looked at me.

"Where are you going?" Sister Trina, the most junior sister, demanded.

"For now, to my sister's house in Texas."

"And when are you going?" another sister asked, fork sliding from her fingers.

"I'm not sure. Soon."

That afternoon Sister Trina found some cloth in the storeroom and began stitching the blouse and skirt that were to be my getaway clothes. Over the next few days she had me try them on several times, adjusting hems and necklines. The sight of me in those clothes seemed to be her way of getting used to the idea that I was going. It helped me, too, though it still wasn't easy.

When I told my assistant I would miss her, she slammed the pots onto the big commercial stove with extraordinary vigor. "Sister, you can't go," she said.

Sister Ewa wouldn't look into my eyes, wouldn't speak to me. Finally, as she passed me on the steps, she said, "Why didn't you tell me before? You always said, 'Pray for me and my intention,' but you never said what was really going on."

"I asked permission to leave five months ago. They gave me permission only now. Could you have lived with that insecurity for five months?"

She stared over my shoulder and asserted, "I would have wanted to know." Sister Ewa shifted her stare to my throat, looked down, then continued up the stairs.

Sister Kamini found a dark corner in the storeroom and cried.

Back in Casilina, the excitement was palpable. Sisters were grateful for Mother's recovery, and everyone wanted to congratulate Sister Nirmala on her first visit to Rome as superior general. In the morning and at night there were two lines for blessing—one in front of Mother and, at Mother's insistence despite Sister Nirmala's objections, one in front of Sister Nirmala. I spoke with Sister Nirmala, who said she would pray for me and then reassured me that I needn't mention anything to Mother.

Sisters murmured in corners as I passed, and every now and then someone elbowed me and asked, "Is it true?" I just nodded. Sometimes a sister would plead with me, urge me to change my mind, insist I was about to make a mistake I would regret for the rest of my life. Then I pulled out the envelope I'd kept in my bag since Mother's arrival. Sister Sajani, who had taught me to work in the kitchen when I'd been a postulant, couldn't look at the letter through her tears, but the letter was enough to stop most sisters from arguing.

It pained me to see sisters from other communities murmuring to my sisters. Sometimes I overheard others blaming my community, an accusation I quickly refuted when I heard it. The longer I hung around, the longer the whispers would continue. I needed a date and a plane ticket. I returned to Casilina for Mass and breakfast twice, hoping to convince Sister Elena to put me on a plane as soon

as possible—preferably before professions, just a few days away—
but Sister just kept saying, "We'll see." On my third try, Sister left
the house with Mother right after breakfast, and Sister Joseph
Michael grabbed my arm. "Come with me, Donata," she said. "I
want to take Dr. Patricia on a tour of Rome."

Before she finished speaking, Sister Joseph Michael pulled me
into the front compound and I found myself before the cardiologist
from Scripps Clinic who had several times saved Mother's life. This
time, Dr. Patricia Aubanel had traveled with Mother from Calcutta.

"Sister Donata will show us Rome, Doctor," Sister Joseph
Michael said. "She's been here so long she knows all the history."

"Sister, no one knows *all* the history of Rome." I laughed, relieved to escape the sideways glances of Casilina. Sister hadn't asked
any prying questions since she'd arrived, hadn't thrown me any guilt
trips. She'd asked a little advice about the community, and that had
been it.

I took Sister Joseph Michael and Dr. Patricia to the Colosseum,
San Clemente, San Giovanni, and Santo Stefano Rotundo, the
round church with the frescoes of early martyrs—St. Agatha having
her breasts sliced off, St. Catherine of Alexandria tied to the wheel
of a horse cart, anonymous Christians bound spread-eagle to two
tall saplings that had been pulled together and then released, literally tearing them apart. "I thought I'd seen everything in my emergency room days," Dr. Patricia said, "but these early Christians
certainly did come to some imaginative ends."

Sister Joseph Michael looked at me. "Imaginative ends. What an
interesting phrase."

Back in Casilina we'd missed lunch and everyone was at afternoon
siesta. Sister Joseph Michael wandered off somewhere and I foraged
some pasta. I was swallowing quickly, hoping to make it to bed for at
least a few minutes before the bell rang, when the refectory door
squeaked open. Mother stood firm, all five feet of her looking
straight at me—then she grabbed the door jamb for support. Indignation massed in her eyes.

I nearly choked.

Mother raised her hands, palms imploring. "What is this Mother hears about you?"

I put down my fork and tried to swallow. I spotted Sister Joseph Michael slinking down the hall. What was I going to say? *God, where are You?*

"Come to Mother now," she said, and led me toward her room.

I grabbed my bag from the bench beside me and followed Mother, making sure to close the door behind us. Mother walked to her desk but did not sit. She put her hands on the desk and leaned into them to steady herself. Despite what I'd heard about Mother not always getting enough oxygen to her brain, she seemed fully alert, completely aware.

She looked right through me. "Sister, tell Mother what's going on."

I swallowed.

"Mother, I'm going home."

"Why, Sister?" Mother lifted one wrinkled hand in an expression of incomprehension. "What's wrong?"

"Mother, I just need to go." I began praying for an interruption—a knock on the door, a phone call from the Pope, an earthquake, anything.

Mother fixed her eyes on mine, and I sensed her trying to understand. Part of me wanted so much to explain.

"Tell Mother why." Her voice was softer now, pleading more than insisting. "Has someone been unkind to you?"

There had been other sisters who, when they left, had told Mother they couldn't bear the unkindness they felt in community. I knew that's what they'd said because Mother had written several general letters over the years in which she'd told us we'd driven the sisters out. She had begged us to love one another.

The sisters in Tor Bella Monaca loved me and I loved them. We had our spats, but nothing to complain to Mother about.

"No, Mother. No one's been unkind."

I searched for something to help her understand, but I knew that nothing I might say would satisfy Mother. For Mother there never was nor could there ever be a sufficient reason to leave a God-given vocation. And none of the particulars I might point to were really why I was leaving, anyway. It was far bigger than any one thing.

"Mother, God is asking something else of me now." That sounded safe. How could Mother argue with God's will?

"You mean you want to join another community—the Carmelites or Poor Clares?"

Joining a cloistered community would have made some sense to Mother. I would still be married to Jesus, just realizing a different calling. "No, Mother. I don't want to join another community."

She shook her finger at me, pain and confusion in her face. I was hurting her. She had trusted me; she had plans for me; she thought she knew me. She had promised to give Saints to Mother Church, and I was disappointing her in the worst way possible.

"Don't you know that you belong to Jesus?" Mother said, playing what she must have considered a trump card. I had no right to make such a decision. I was Sister Donata, the freely given one. Jesus owned me.

I wiped my sweaty palms on my sari. "Yes, Mother. I belong to Jesus, as any Christian does."

I might have asked Mother to sit down, to calm down, so that we could have a heart-to-heart. I didn't. Mother's black-and-white convictions, the power her words held over my psyche, and the simple fact that I loved her so much would best me in any discussion. My only way out was to refuse to engage.

Mother began to look around the room, her eyes searching the plaster walls for an answer. Finally she looked at the desk, then up at me, and said, "Mother could believe this about anyone, but she cannot believe it about you."

These were hard words, and I couldn't be sure what they meant. I had wanted to believe that Mother knew who I was, knew that I had wanted to be a good MC more than I had ever wanted anything. Others had told me Mother knew me. Certainly the jobs she'd assigned me spoke of her trust in me. On the other hand, I'd never heard Mother even call my name. I was thirty-nine years old. I'd known and followed Mother for twenty years, and for each of those years I'd longed to hear Mother call me "Sister Donata." I'd often seen her look my way when some sister pointed me out as the one who composed the hymn sung at profession, or the one who was in charge of a sister's formation, the one who worked so hard to get approval from the city council for the women's shelter, the one who taught such good classes to the sisters. But Mother had uttered my name when she gave it to me as a novice—and never again. In twenty years, even when we traveled together, even during the three-day trip to Sweden where I was the only sister with Mother, she never once called me Sister Donata. I was just "Sister."

I could imagine Mother saying "Mother can't believe this about you" to any sister in an attempt to keep her in the community. Did she remember how she'd scolded me the day I'd walked barefoot across the grass in Washington, how she'd told me to let Jesus use me without consulting me? Did she remember my letter confessing my relationship with Niobe? Did she remember how I'd pleaded with her not to admit Niobe to final vows, and how she had admitted her anyway? Did Mother know how much I loved the sisters, how much I loved the poor, how much I loved her? Did she know that throughout it all, my love for God had never waned?

Did she know how much I hated to disappoint her?

"Sister, listen to Mother. Talk to Mother." She was beating the desk with the flat of her hand, every beat emphasizing every word. "Why do you want to go?"

It all flashed through my head. The suffocation, the disillusionment, the frustration, the thirst for more.

Mother, I wanted to say, *Mother, my God isn't like yours. Your God asks you to deny yourself. He counts each sacrifice and will reward each act of self-denial. Your God is Jesus Crucified. My God is the God of the resurrection— the God who says, "Enough of this suffering. Let's heal the world."*

Your God is a jealous God, one who says, "So long as you never get too close to any human being, I will be close to you. You may not feel my close-ness on earth, but I will be close in heaven." My God says, "I offer you friends, I offer you lovers. I am present in the people I give you now, people in whom I hope you will delight, as I do."

Your God says, "I bind you to this life forever. You are my spouse. Marriage is an unbreakable covenant." My God says, "I invite you to walk with me. I'm not sure where we'll end up, but we'll walk together, and others will join us on the way."

Mother, I'd like you to understand. But I can't take the chance that you won't. I don't want your God anymore. My God says, "I came that you may have life, and have it to the full." I'm following my God out the door, Mother, and you can't stop me.

I said none of this, of course. What I said was, "Mother, I am going home." I reached inside my bag. "Mother has already given me permission." I pulled out the letter. Mother took it from my hand.

Mother's expression of surprise as she read the letter confirmed my suspicion that this had been just one in a pile of hundreds of papers Mother signed every day. Mother had never read it, or if she had read it, she hadn't recognized my name, or perhaps she had read it and then, given her frail physical state, forgotten that one of the sisters she trusted most had decided to turn her back on Jesus.

"Mother," I said, taking a deep breath, "if Jesus wants me to, I will come back." Even as I said this, I knew I would never return.

"Of course Jesus wants you. Don't go." I saw the determination and frustration in her eyes as she looked at me.

Then Mother closed her eyes for a moment. Perhaps she was praying. Perhaps she realized I was not going to give her anything with which she could engage, or perhaps she was just not able to take any more of the conversation. "Mother will speak with you later," she said.

As I knelt for Mother's blessing, I felt her hands press my veiled head, both blessing me and pushing me out.

The church bells rang, steady and clear, calling the faithful to the Church of San Luca. In just a few minutes, on the eve of Trinity Sunday, in the presence of the living Saint Mother Teresa of Calcutta, eighteen young women would irrevocably vow their lives to God and to the service of the poor.

We rarely had professions in San Luca, and rarely on Trinity Sunday. Yet exactly eleven years earlier, on Trinity Sunday, May 25, 1986, I had climbed those very same steps. Already having lived as a Missionary of Charity for nine years, dressed that day in my best sari, hair newly shorn, eyes bright with joyful love, heart trembling in fear, I had vowed to live my remaining days as a Missionary of Charity.

The crowd gathering on the eve of Trinity Sunday in 1997 did not know that the bells rang again for me, too. I could no longer hide the curls that poked from beneath my headpiece, and I had not bothered to darn that week's holes in my ever-thinner sari, but I climbed the steps with more determination than I had ever known, about to set out on a great adventure with God, because He wanted me to have life to the full.

I surprised myself by how calmly I sat through the first half of that profession. These sisters were following their path; I was following mine. As they began reading their vows, Sister Patrick came to my pew and knelt beside me. "Sister," she whispered, "not all the sisters from San Gregorio could come. They want to say good-bye. If we go right now, we can catch them before they leave for work."

Driving a borrowed van, Sister Patrick dodged cars on the narrow Roman streets with the same skill with which she must have carried the rugby ball down the field through less exceptional players. "I'm sorry to have pulled you away from professions," she said.

"It's fine."

"Your plane leaves early tomorrow."

"Sister Elena asked who I wanted to accompany me to the airport. I said you and Sister Joseph Michael."

"It will be a privilege, but I still don't understand." She was trying very hard to be brave, but I could see and hear her choking up.

"Sister Patrick, the ways of God are strange. There are no guarantees. I can't say I understand it, either. I only know I have to go."

"We'll miss you so much. You know that, don't you?"

"I'll miss you, too. Better not cry right now—that was a red light we just went through."

"Sister, this is Rome. Red lights are made to be run."

"Exactly right."

We parked in the piazza and climbed up those wide stairs for what I supposed would be my last time. When we reached the first gate, I told Sister Patrick, "Do you see these trees, the grass, the roses, the little path with gravel?" She nodded. "When I came here as a postulant there was only dirt and a few slabs of broken marble. See how things change, see how they grow?"

"Sister, you're not crying anymore."

"No, I'm not, though part of me is sad."

"Every time you used to renew your general permission, you cried. Do you remember that?"

"Oh, yes."

After a quick visit to the chapel, Sister Patrick led me to the refectory, where the sisters looked up from their spiritual reading. "Sister Donata," one of them said, holding out the last *a*, stretching it as though she didn't want to let it go. They all began to stand, but I quickly sat on the bench.

They started up at once: "Are you really going, Sister?" "You cannot go." "It was such a surprise."

"Yes, it is something of a surprise for me, too."

They wanted to know why, and if I was bitter. I told them I was excited because God was doing something new in my life.

"I love you all," I said, "and I'm going to miss you. I hope you will pray for me."

One of the sisters looked at Sister Patrick, then cupped her hand over her own head. Sister Patrick nodded, then put herself first in line. "Sister," she said, "please give us your blessing."

As my hands rested on each of my sisters, I prayed that she might find happiness and true freedom. Energy flowed through my palms, in a way I hadn't felt for a while.

Back at the profession, on the steps of the church, Sister Patrick handed me an envelope. "I'm afraid this is all we have in the house at the moment," she said. "The banks are closed till Monday."

I looked inside: five crisp one-hundred-dollar bills. "Thank you," I said. I knew this wasn't going to go very far, but I didn't ask why she hadn't gotten more. She'd known for a few days that I was leaving Sunday, but no one wanted to believe it. I'd had to ask Sister Elena four times before she finally scheduled a flight.

Back in Casilina at the reception after professions, I told the priests and Co-Workers what I had been told to tell them: "I'm going to America tomorrow to be closer to my family, as there is some trouble." The sisters wanted damage control, and I didn't blame them for that, though it was hard for me. To keep up the charade required I behave like any sister who was transferred: no contact with people she left behind. In one moment I lost relationships I'd formed over twenty years.

The next morning when the community scrambled out of bed, I didn't reach for a white habit. I didn't cinch a rope around my waist. I didn't tie a headpiece around my head or drape a sari from my shoulders. I didn't place a crucifix at my side.

I got up. I stretched my arms into the sleeves of a dark gold blouse and shimmied into a brown paisley skirt. I combed my hair. I reached under my pillow, cradled the cross in my hands, kissed it, and put Jesus in my bag.

EPILOGUE

It's September 2007. Ten years ago I donned a brown paisley skirt and left the Missionaries of Charity. Today I approach an imposing church on a hill in Latrobe, Pennsylvania, on the campus of St. Vincent College. I've been avoiding church for several years—I went for my parents' fiftieth anniversary a few weeks ago, and four years before that for Mother's beatification in Rome—and now I've driven several hundred miles to be in this particular church. I have a mission.

I dip my hand in the huge holy water font and genuflect, out of habit and a lingering respect. Part of me still feels very much at home as I slide into a pew toward the back, just in front of a confessional. I spend a moment resting in gratitude—and trying to calm my nerves. The church's simple Romanesque lines and soaring ceilings invite honesty and humility, virtues I know I'll need this weekend.

Past the heads of worshippers who crowd the pews, I spot two rows of white-draped figures up front. From the back, an untrained eye might notice only slight differences in size and shape among two rows of Missionaries of Charity; I note one sister's characteristic list to the left, the telltale slump of the next sister over, how another leans desperately forward as she prays. I recognize Sister Nirmala, even smaller than I remember her, now in her second term as superior general. Sister Prema kneels tall and confident behind her; this German sister who used to call me her twin is now one of Sister Nirmala's councilors. I recognize Sister Dorothy and several others. If things had gone differently, I might have knelt in one of the front pews, too. A realization like that might have filled me with regret or guilt a few years earlier, but no more. I'm pleased with my spot at the back, pleased with my decision not to go to Communion, pleased with the wedding ring on my finger and with the blouse that drapes my shoulders in green, not white. When Father Brian agreed to my request for an invitation to this weekend conference marking the tenth anniversary of Mother's death—or, as they say, Mother's entrance into heaven—I was glad. I want to celebrate the life I led before so that I can more fully leave it behind.

I join in the singing and some of the responses. When Father Bob approaches the ambo to preach the homily, my heart beats a little faster, remembering the hours we'd spent in frank discussion over the years. Now superior general of the MC Fathers, Father Bob speaks with fluid assurance, a smile illuminating his still-boyish good looks. In what will become a recurring theme this weekend, Father Bob mentions the recent revelations about Mother's dark nights, the article in *Time* magazine and the book so boldly titled *Come, Be My Light*. In a series of e-mails and phone calls nearly five years earlier, Father Bob and I had discussed Mother's darkness. From the pulpit Father Bob says that if St. Teresa of Avila were living today, she would expand her sixteenth-century scheme of the soul as a castle with seven mansions—seven progressive stages of mystical union with God—to include an eighth mansion for Blessed Teresa of Calcutta, who, in her extraordinary sanctity, endured nearly fifty years without consolation in prayer. I smile at what I've come to recognize as MC grandiosity.

Father Bob says one thousand sisters have been added to the Missionaries of Charity in the ten years since Mother's death, that the MCs have opened more than a hundred new homes in fourteen more countries. The growth is impressive at a time when most congregations of sisters are in decline, but I know the figures represent a diminishing growth rate and say nothing about the number of sisters who have left, a number I've heard is increasing but which I cannot quantify.

After Mass I approach the front pews—I need to talk to the sisters—but I can't get close before they're all whisked into a van and driven off campus. I'm disappointed, but I assume they'll return in the morning, when Sister Nirmala is scheduled to speak. And frankly, though I want to meet them, I'm still a little hesitant about declaring myself. The sisters in Rome (after the initial shock of seeing me with hair, in pants) had met me with pleasure and kindness when I'd sought them out. I'd had long conversations with Sister Joseph Michael and Sister Elena, and a too-brief talk with Sister Patrick. But on another occasion, after Mass with the MCs in Washington, when any visitor would have been offered coffee and a little breakfast, the sisters told me that if I was hungry I could wait a couple of hours and eat with the soup kitchen people. Since then, I've avoided MCs in the States.

I follow the crowd out of church. At the entrance to the gym that serves as cafeteria for the conference, smiling people in frumpy clothes sit behind tables hawking Mother Teresa books, photos, CDs, medals, calendars, dolls. It's a more modest, less imaginative array than that offered in St. Peter's Square at Mother's beatification four years earlier: Mother Teresa scarves, Mother Teresa puppets, Mother Teresa candles, Mother Teresa postcards, Mother Teresa key chains, coffee mugs, posters, T-shirts, caps, stamps, flags, commemorative plates, umbrellas, buttons, magnets, bumper stickers, coins, patches, bracelet charms, and hooked-rug kits. What would Mother think?

I pass the merchandise and fill a plate at the steam tables. The basketball court is packed with dozens of round tables—color-themed with white cloths and blue napkins—but I recognize no one. I know that Sandy McMurtrie, who was so kind to me in Washington, is scheduled to speak tomorrow, as are Jan Petrie the filmmaker, Mother's physician Patricia Aubanel, and Mother's niece Aggie— but I don't see any of them, or Jim Towey, either. Years earlier, Jim lived with the MC Fathers in Tijuana, then worked with the sisters, and eventually became Mother's lawyer. He recently finished four years as George W. Bush's "faith czar"—director of the White House Office of Faith-Based and Community Initiatives. Now Jim is president of St. Vincent College, and this conference is his idea— a "family reunion," he'd called it.

I've almost resigned myself to dinner with strangers when I catch a glimpse of a tall priest with white hair and one of the world's kindest smiles—Bishop William Curlin. When I knew him, Bill Curlin was parish priest of St. Mary's, just blocks from the Capitol in D.C. I made my confession to him a few times, and he impressed me as warm and kind, the sort of fellow who made God's love seem tangible.

I have this strange idea that if I can reveal to at least one member of the MC family more about my current life (what they would call the state of my soul), then that act of honesty will somehow free me to be more completely myself. I want to silence the guilt and the re-curring dreams in which I'm wrapped tight in a sari, my curls shorn again to nubs, the sisters expecting things of me. Though he's not an MC, Bishop Curlin may be the ideal person to begin to hear my story.

Between bites of chicken and broccoli, people around the table introduce themselves. When my turn comes, I say I'm Mary Johnson, from New Hampshire. I want to say more, but nothing comes out.

"What brought you all the way from New Hampshire?" a local woman asks, drawing forth what I'd been unable to volunteer.

"I wanted to be around people who love Mother," I say, then clear my throat with a little iced tea, in preparation to tell more of the truth. "I used to be a sister."

"Really?" a Co-Worker from Little Rock asks, in a southern accent that would charm me if I weren't so nervous. "If you don't mind my asking," she continues, "why did you leave?"

I'm used to this question, and it's what makes talking about my past difficult when I'm with Catholics. When I tell non-Catholics that I spent twenty years as a nun in Mother Teresa's congregation, they ask for my impressions of Mother and tell me I've done something wonderful with my life. Catholics always want to know why I left.

"It's a long story," I say.

"You're married now," she says, glancing at my ring finger.

"I am."

"Good for you," Bishop Curlin interrupts with an authoritative, grandfatherly smile.

"Bishop," I say, emboldened by his protective intervention, "I was Sister Donata when you knew me in Washington."

He tilts his head to one side. "Bless my soul," he says, poking the air with his empty fork. "So you were."

I'm grateful he remembers me, or seems to, anyway.

"My heavens, what are you doing now?" he asks.

"Teaching," I say. "Teaching Italian and creative writing."

"Are you? Have you written a book about this crazy group yet?" He smiles.

Flabbergasted, I stare at him, my fork hovering in front of my mouth. Surely he doesn't know that two months earlier I approached a literary agent about a book on that very subject.

"I think you should write a book," he continues, nodding and smiling, his eyes bright behind his glasses. "I think you should call it *Cracks in the Convent.*"

He laughs, and so do I. When Bishop Curlin calls the Missionaries of Charity "crazy," he does so in an affectionate way, but I also hear frustration—he knows the sisters well. Surely Bishop Curlin knows they would frown on a book revealing an MC's day-to-day struggles, the community's politics, the human foibles, but he sees the value of a book like that. I finish my pudding in an astonished haze.

I join the crowd in the auditorium for Jan and Ann's film about Mother. I've seen this film half a dozen times since I first watched it in Rome, immediately after its premiere at the United Nations. I don't know why I stay to see it again. I've driven nearly six hundred miles, and now that the adrenaline is beginning to wear low, I'm not sure I wouldn't be better off resting in my hotel room. So far—I hate to admit it—the conference has been rather boring. I've heard a couple of new stories, but not a single new thought about Mother. Even explanations of her dark night just repeat the analysis in Father Brian's book. Maybe it was unreasonable to expect that this conference would be more intellectually stimulating than most of my years in the convent had been. After all, Mother and those who surrounded her were always more concerned about getting things done than about thinking things through.

As the lights dim and Mother's image flickers on the auditorium's large screen, I hear her say, once more, *God has made us to love and to be loved.* Her throaty voice tugs at my heart.

I can't take my eyes off the screen. There is Mother, kneeling in the chapel, walking the street, bossing everyone around again. As I watch, I realize how much I miss her—not the bossing around, but her voice, her eyes, the feel of her hands on my head. I miss our exchange of greetings: *Welcome, Mother,* followed by, *Very good, Sister.* I miss the way she always implored us to do better. I miss how everything seemed urgent and necessary and important when I stood beside her. I miss her passionate idealism, and mine.

Three months after I left Rome, a new friend came to tell me—since I hadn't yet developed the habit of listening to the radio or of watching television—that Mother had died. It took a while for the news to sink in. I called the sisters in Rome but couldn't get through, despite many attempts. At a memorial service in Houston's Sacred Heart Cathedral, the bishop spoke at length of the privilege of having met Mother Teresa at the airport during a layover. I knew no one in that church, and no one knew me. I knelt at a pew in the back and cried.

On the screen in front of me, sisters clip the novices' hair, pronounce vows, wash their clothes. A sister I know visits an old woman in the Bronx. I miss waking up surrounded by my sisters, hurrying to the chapel together, eating elbow to elbow in the refectory. I miss the singing, the smiles, the easy laughter. I even miss squatting outside around buckets of soapy water, scrubbing shoulder to shoulder with my sisters—though lavishing twenty minutes on laundry each morning and half an hour on darning each night now seem a ludicrous extravagance.

I watch as Mother rescues handicapped children in the midst of a Beirut war zone—Mother so full of faith, determination, and purpose. I recall the brave stories sisters told of work in Rwanda, Sudan, Iraq, Pakistan, and even the gang-infested projects of Chicago. It felt good to be part of the family who walked into danger and poverty armed with rice, a smile, and faith that everything would be all right in the end.

I understand a little more viscerally something of the hold Mother and her message continue to exert on me and on so many. What human heart doesn't long for love, purpose, and the opportunity to make the world a better place?

After the screening, I wander outside, where eventually I find Father Bob under a street lamp, talking with a young couple. I linger, pulling my wits together, and when the others leave, I walk up and say, "Well, your homilies have certainly improved."

He looks at me, a blank expression on his face.

"I mean, your homilies were always good, but building an eighth mansion for Mother takes real imagination."

Father Bob stares.

I smile and look him straight in the eyes. "I think you should know that it's not true what they say—that bit about never being happy if you leave the Society. Not true at all." I laugh.

"Sister Donata," he says, shaking his head and grabbing my arm. "I mean *Mary*." He grins. His brotherly grip surprises me. "I recognized you by your laugh," he says. "You have the most distinctive laugh."

We talk for a while, catching up on each other's lives. I feel no trace of judgment in his words or expression. He smiles a lot, and it feels good that he's so obviously happy to see me. I ask about the sisters and the fathers, and he doesn't ask anything—just waits for whatever I'm ready to say. I tell him that I'm married, to a great guy I met while we were both doing graduate studies in writing. I'm not ready—and don't know if I will be—to tell him about my visit to Tom, a little over a year after I left the sisters. At that time I was ready to say yes if Tom mentioned marriage again; instead, Tom told me he wanted to remain a priest.

"You look really good," Father Bob says, and once more I feel how happy he is for me.

At this point, another priest approaches. This round priest with a little white goatee is scheduled to lead meditations during the rosary the next day. He hardly acknowledges my presence and starts talking to Father Bob about how wonderful it is to be at a Catholic gathering where he needn't worry about dissenting theology. After taking a few swipes at several priests, whom he names, he starts talking about a woman, whom he also names, who had submitted to him a doctoral dissertation purporting to find Scriptural support for female priests. "These lesbians aren't content to pervert themselves—they want to pervert our Holy Church as well."

His monologue continues for five, ten, fifteen minutes, with increasing references to immoral women, scandalous lack of virtue, and a dearth of intellectual rigor among many who pretend to be Catholic. I don't know what Father Bob thinks, but I want to hit this priest.

He reminds me of Sister Priscilla and Sister Frederick, neither of whom I've seen since I left, not even at Mother's beatification. I did receive a note from Sister Frederick early on. She had enclosed a form letter, requesting that I fill in the blanks so that they could process the dispensation of my vows posthaste. I know she still terrorizes the sisters—several of them had told me in whispers of the course she conducts for ex-superiors, designed to retrain them in humility and obedience. I wonder if she knows that Mark Attard was eventually cleared, despite her attacks, and that he is currently head of the Pontifical Gregorian University's Moral Theology Department. I hope her defamation of Regina Mundi's reputation had nothing to do with the school's closing in 2005.

I turn to Father Bob, who looks sheepishly at me. I can tell the priest's comments have made him uncomfortable—or maybe I'm only projecting. I'm ashamed of my silence, but I wasn't ready for the sort of attack my credentials as a married ex-nun might have provoked.

"It's really good to see you," Father Bob says again.

"Likewise," I say. I leave for my hotel, grateful for his smile.

The next day, while the congregation sings the final hymn of morning Mass, I hurry to the front. The sisters have gathered in the center aisle, discussing something. Looking over her shoulder for a moment, Sister Nirmala—despite being surrounded by a dozen sisters and several other people—spots me. "Donata," she says immediately, no hesitation in her voice.

I come forward and bow my head for her blessing, but she puts a finger under my chin and shakes her head. I know I'm no longer a member of the family, but I hadn't realized I didn't deserve a blessing. She's next on the conference schedule, and someone leads her away. "We'll talk later," she says.

Sister Prema is the person I really want to talk to. Of the gaggle of MCs present, she's the sister who knows me best. When Mother died, Sister Prema sent me a small cloth with a drop of Mother's blood, a relic she'd been privileged to receive as regional superior but sacrificed for me, though it spooked me when I opened the envelope. Over the shoulders of sisters in the aisle, I call Sister Prema's name, and eventually she recognizes me.

"Donata, Donata, Sister Donata," she says, smiling and taking both my hands in hers. One of the sisters motions her away, and Sister Prema tells me, "Please do find me later." I nod, again disappointed. As always with the MCs, duty calls. The sisters exit through a side door, and I head out the back, knowing that news of my presence will spread quickly enough. The sting of that withheld blessing still fresh, I feel less eager to meet them.

In the auditorium, the sisters take seats together in one long row, at the front. I choose a place close by, but out of range of the older ones. I overhear bits of conversation from a few youngsters. They exude a sense of resentment and superiority, though I don't know why. These sisters are too young to have known Mother personally. I wonder what novice mistresses tell young sisters these days—that they must now be Mother Teresa for the world?

Sister Nirmala, flip-flops dangling from her toes as she sits in an armchair on the stage, talks of the day she met Mother, of the way the light in Mother's eyes belonged "not on earth, but in heaven." Unlike Mother, Sister Nirmala speaks not extemporaneously but from a prepared text in a blue folder. She says that though the Lord chose darkness for Mother, Mother had no worries and always shone with joy.

It's that *always* that bothers me. Mother did not always shine with joy. I saw Mother angry, confused, worried, disappointed, and lonely. I never saw Mother show those emotions to anyone outside the convent, but with us—strange how I still think in terms of *us*—Mother was human. If we're here to remember her, why can't we remember all of her?

When Sister Nirmala finishes her talk, a massive priest with silver hair takes the stage, the postulator of the cause of Mother's beatification and canonization. Thin when I first met him, Father Brian often sparkled with quiet mischief when we were postulants in Rome. Today only his smile is thin, and the sparkle is gone. It saddens me to see him so worn.

Father Brian wrote the book everyone is talking about, having pieced it together from Mother's letters and conversations. As Father Brian begins his lecture, I realize there will be no new revelations today. He's just summarizing *Come Be My Light*, with its startling admission that Mother lived for fifty years without consolation in prayer, in a state of spiritual emptiness that led her even to question God's existence. Mystics have long considered temporary spiritual aridity a necessary purification leading to deeper union with God, but theologians struggled to understand the saintly Mother Teresa's claim that her darkness lasted decades.

Of her relationship with God, Mother wrote to one of her early spiritual directors: "I call, I cling, I want—and there is no One to answer—no One on Whom I can cling—no, No One. Alone . . . The loneliness of the heart that wants love is unbearable."

When I first read that phrase from Mother, it broke my heart.

As Father Brian talks, I'm particularly annoyed by the way he downplays Mother's doubts. Father Brian claims Mother suffered "not a crisis of faith, but a trial of faith," emphasizing that Mother's doubts were merely in her emotions, never in her mind or will. It seems to me that Mother's doubts were real, wherever they resided. In 1959 she wrote, with her characteristic proliferation of dashes, "Where is my faith?—even deep down, right in, there is nothing but emptiness & darkness . . . —I have no faith.—I dare not utter the words & thoughts that crowd in my heart—& make me suffer untold agony. So many unanswered questions live within me—I am afraid to uncover them—because of the blasphemy."

I suspected when I first read those words, and I suspect now, that Mother's refusal to uncover those questions may have caused her darkness to linger. Contemplating for even a moment that God might not exist required enormous courage for Mother. Something in Mother's life—perhaps daily exposure to the sufferings of Calcutta's poor, or the emptiness that had replaced "sweetness and consolation and union" during prayer—provoked questions about God. If God wasn't real, what had she done? I understand some of the terror in that question. Unwilling to explore her doubts, Mother wrote that she feared the contradictions within would "unbalance" her—and perhaps they would have, if a Jesuit priest hadn't told her a story.

As Father Brian talks, I can almost hear the priest's spin: *This darkness, dear Mother, is a sign of your union with God. Others need the darkness to purify them. Your darkness is not meant as purification—you are already pure. Your darkness is the divine gift of union with Jesus in His suffering. Your pain brings you close to your Crucified Spouse, and is the way you share His mission of redemption. There is no higher union with God.*

Though Mother had felt relief at this priest's words, my belly tightens with anger. Darkness now interpreted as holiness, Mother came to believe that her feelings of "torture and pain" pleased God. Over the years, she encouraged her spiritual daughters to become "victims of divine love." Mother often told the sick, "Suffering is the kiss of Jesus."

Mother's questions gave way to a dogmatic decision to believe. She would avoid future doubts by uncompromising insistence on Church teaching, including doctrines on birth control, marriage, and the place of women, regardless of the suffering or injustice these and similar teachings perpetuated.

According to Father Brian, Mother's darkness continued until the day she died.

I have questions for Father Brian, but the audience is not offered an opportunity to respond. I will find a way—if not today, one day soon—to enter into dialogue about the big questions.

So much depends on the stories we tell ourselves, and on the questions we ask, or fail to ask.

I'm leaving the auditorium, lost in my thoughts and feelings for Mother, avoiding the sisters because I'm not sure I'm ready for them, when a quiet woman who'd been just six months ahead of me in the novitiate taps me on the shoulder. "Walk with us," she says. "Sister Prema wants to see you."

I take a deep breath, and while the conference attendees head to the gym for lunch, I follow the sisters in the opposite direction. The Rule prohibiting MC sisters from eating with outsiders seems a particular pity today, when so many people would love to chat with a real Missionary of Charity. I tell myself to stop fussing about Father Brian and dark nights and Rules, and I let myself hope for a tiny instant that the sisters might invite me to lunch.

As I walk, a sister I hardly know grabs my elbow and says, "Sister Donata, you must come back to us." She pulls me away from the others and looks into my eyes. "You never should have gone. You must talk to Sister today and you must come back."

I received dozens of letters from sisters across the world when I first left. The most adamant missives were from sisters I knew only by name, sisters who felt a need to impress my sinfulness upon me. They insisted on my duty to Jesus and to the Society. They accused me of betraying the love of God. They told me Jesus thirsted for me and wanted to share his passion with me, and that I ought not run from the cross. Letters from sisters I had known better read, *Sister, I don't understand what you're doing, but I trust you. If you come back, we will welcome you. We miss you.*

I smile at the insistent sister clinging to my elbow and I shake my head. She moves on.

Sister Prema and Sister Nirmala don't seem to be walking with the group. I've been watching Sister Dorothy out of the corner of my eye—she was at the front but has fallen behind. She walks slowly, but with the same dogged purposefulness she exuded back in Casilina, when her daily scolding had so irritated me. She takes my hand. "Donata," she says. "Sister Donata." She looks me up and down, shakes her head, then slips her hand onto my arm. "Donata," she repeats. She walks slowly, in some pain, I think.

"Sister," I say. I know that Sister Dorothy has been trying to reach me; a friend told me she'd phoned, asking for my number, but I didn't want to talk. Now whatever she wanted to say seems to have melted away. Sister Dorothy clutches my arm and pats it from time to time as if checking to see that I'm real. The remnants of my old animosity melt with each pat. In the silence, we are just two women whom years have made gentler.

As we reach the room where the sisters are to eat, Sister Dorothy looks around for a moment. I sense she wants to invite me in, but Sister Nirmala and Sister Prema approach from another corridor, and Sister Nirmala shoos Sister Prema in my direction.

"Mary," Sister Prema says. "That's your name now, isn't it?"

"Yes," I say, a little disappointed. Even though I've come here hoping for a cleaner break with the MCs, something in me enjoyed hearing the others call me Sister.

"I wish I could invite you to lunch," she says, "but, well, you know the Rules."

I nod. The Rules. At the beatification I'd asked Sister Martin, who was again stationed at Casilina, if I could enter Mother's old room for a moment. It was the first room in the house, and Mother received visitors there sometimes, and I'd lived in the place for six years, after all. I had hoped a few minutes in that room might help me come to peace with some of the things that had happened there. I could tell Sister Martin wanted to let me in, but—the Rules.

Sister Prema leads me to a little courtyard. She asks about my life now, and about the community back in Texas that I had tried to form with two other ex-MCs. She seems to understand when I tell her that the three of us had different visions, and that during the two years we were together my desires changed. She asks about my family, and I ask about hers. Then she turns to me and says, "You were tired, isn't that it? You were capable and we gave you too much work, and you were tired."

"Well, yes, I was tired"—I don't tell Sister Prema that it took nearly four years for me to begin to feel energetic again—"but it wasn't mostly that. I felt I was dying a little every day, and I couldn't believe God wanted that."

"But suffering is an important part of our life." She says these words with certitude and generosity. I once said these words.

"Yes, but I wanted to live fully, and I thought God wanted that, too. I still want life."

She looks without saying anything.

"And I didn't fit anymore," I say. "I watched the Society grow more and more narrow-minded. It wasn't what I signed up for. I wanted to make a personal contribution, but the Society didn't seem to want what I had to offer."

She says nothing. I know my reasons make little sense to someone convinced that obedience and renunciation are the true path to God.

"I'm worried," I say. "All this talk about Mother's dark night."

She nods. "Quite extraordinary," she says. "Mother always looked so happy. Who knew?"

"Yes, but I worry for the sisters, and for the poor, but especially for the sisters. I worry that when someone is depressed or really lonely or suffering in some other way, Mother's dark night will be one more excuse not to get help. Sisters may think they just have to suffer, or others may tell them that."

"We're trying our best for sisters in trouble," she says, and explains about days of prayer and doctors and time away with other nuns.

It seems a step in the right direction, but I still worry. When I'd requested dispensation from my vows, I'd sent a long letter voicing my concerns to Sister Nirmala and the councilors. I never received a reply.

Sister Prema looks at me intently. "You still love the sisters, don't you?"

The question touches me, as it always does. Inevitably, whenever I see sisters who have known me before, someone asks, "Sister Donata, do you still love us?" I take issue with so much of MC life, but I can't deny what I feel for the brave and generous women who lived it with me for so long.

"Of course I love the sisters," I say.

She sighs, and we both stand silent for a few moments, the sisters' presence and our love filling the space between us.

In the auditorium that afternoon I sit through two and a half hours of Co-Workers sharing memories of Mother. Each tells the story of how his or her life was completely changed by one meeting, how each felt completely loved when in Mother's presence. A few of them mention Mother's stubbornness, which they see as a virtue, even when it was inconvenient. The hours of stories are broken only by a young man who plays the piano and sings songs of Mother's words he's set to music, just as I used to do for professions.

After the panel, we head to the chapel for the rosary, where the obnoxious priest who pontificated about dissident lesbians leads the meditation. I don't like the thought of being in the same room with him, much less listening to him consider Our Lady's virtues, but Father Bob has consented to my request for a private talk, and we agreed to meet here.

I kneel at the back. I know how to find my way to a quiet interior space similar to what I used to feel in prayer, though I no longer identify that peace with a supreme being. Before long, Father Bob taps my shoulder and I follow him out into the sun. I hadn't managed to tell Sister Prema everything—I cared too much what she thought of me. I have another chance with Father Bob, and I want to take it, but something he said years earlier still bothers me enough that I'm not sure I can talk freely to him, either.

"You know," I say as we walk a path through campus, "you once said you thought I left because MC life was too hard for me."

"It *was* hard for you."

"It was hard for all of us, but I lived it for twenty years—longer than you had at the time."

"I had to say something. We all struggled to understand." He looks down. I sense that my departure was a challenge in more ways than I know. "But I think what you're doing now is even harder," he says. "Trying to build a new life after you'd given yourself so completely to the community—I can't imagine it."

I tell him a little about the confusion of those early years, the depression, the despair, the guilt, the regrets—what I might call a dark night, if I were so inclined. As we sit on bleachers surrounding an athletic field, I talk about months at a residential center for priests and sisters in crisis, where they told me I looked like someone recently escaped from a war zone. I tell him that I cried my way through my first family gatherings, my siblings' families, careers, and homes a stinging reminder of my isolation and minimum-wage job. I tell him about working on an undergraduate degree, surrounded by teenagers. I tell him about falling in love and about refusing the first proposal because I didn't trust myself to keep vows again. I tell him that sometimes the old stories about being Jesus' spouse would torture me with so much guilt that I begged my lover to hit me, though he—wise and gentle soul—never obliged. I tell him about finally feeling secure enough in my lover's arms that I began to fall apart.

I don't look at Father Bob; I look at the sky as I talk about the tunnel I entered, where nothing looked sure and God disappeared, where no one heard my prayers or guaranteed a happy ending. During that time I fell frequently, once so badly that I couldn't sit for weeks; the bruise took months to heal. I fainted, for no medical reason anyone could divine. Sometimes I woke up at night, unable to breathe. For years I dreamed my house was on fire as I rushed to rescue sleeping babies from the flames. Other nights I struggled to emerge from a locked train hurtling over a cliff or into the ocean.

Eventually I find the courage to look Father Bob in the face. A kind, open face. I tell him I don't go to church anymore.

I expect this news to sadden him—I know the sisters would be disturbed—but Father Bob doesn't flinch. He says he will pray for me. Despite his goodwill and my sense that no matter what I say he will not condemn me, I don't have the courage to tell him about the afternoon near dusk when I sat on a hill overlooking a pond in Vermont. That day I called out to God, loudly. I yelled, "So are you out there? And if you are, what are you like? Tell me. I've got to know." I don't tell Father Bob about the still, small voice I heard within. *Look inside yourself*, the voice said. *God is like the best parts of you.*

From there it was a short step to *God is the best parts of you.*

I don't tell Father Bob how the stories about God no longer ring true, how physics and literature and music feel so much more honest than theology. I don't tell him that I've learned to be content with mystery, that the universe and its secrets excite me. I don't mention that living mindfully, trying to do good while avoiding harm, works better than keeping the Rules ever did.

I do tell him that life has been remarkably kind to me, that my husband is the best person I know, that I'm still determined to live a life of love. He smiles. I speak about the kindness of a woman I hardly knew, who believed in me and my story so much that she paid my graduate school tuition. I tell him how we started a foundation to help women writers tell their stories, and that I've found community among these funny, resourceful women. "It's wonderful not to worry about becoming a saint," I say.

I tell him that the freer I become, the more beautiful I grow. I tell him that eventually I will find the courage to tell all my secrets, that the things we don't tell eat us up inside.

I tell him the story of my journey is a gift I want to offer others.

I sit through the last panel of the day, as Sandy and Jan and Dr. Patricia and Aggie tell their stories of Mother. They're all so happy to remember this woman they loved so much. So many people throughout the world have been moved by the stories of a perfect Mother, a holy Mother who loves each person, and who always smiled, even when she didn't feel like it. I feel odd to prefer the human to the perfect; maybe that's part of why I don't fit anymore. I want earth, not heaven.

I get in my car and take a last look at the crowd. I watch the basilica on the hill slowly disappear through my rearview mirror. I move on. I head home.

ACKNOWLEDGMENTS

This book exists because of the generosity, support, and skill of more people than I can name—or perhaps even remember. Thanks to you all.

For early and continued support, both financial and moral, and for their friendship, I thank Kathy Johnson, Vickie Giblin, and Darlene Chandler Bassett, a modern visionary.

For insisting I tell my story (succinctly—250 pages!) and for nudging me forward at every step of the process, I thank Kenny Fries.

For commenting on early drafts, for encouragement in times of doubt, and for sharing their expertise and talent with generosity and wisdom, I thank Mira Bartók, Liz Bedell, Jayne Benjulian, Mary Rose Betten, Rebecca Brown, Doris Cheney, Karen Desrosiers, Kayleen Dunson, Laurel Earnshaw, Carol Franzblau, Kate Gale, Melissa Gould, R. S. Gwynn, Meredith Hall, Robbie Harold, Rachel Holmes, Heliene and Gary Houdek, Cathy Kirkwood, Jenn Mattson, Gail McMeekin, Charlene Pollano, Kim Ponders, Deborah Regan, Jody

Rein, Marilynne Robinson, Jim Sanderson, Bill Schmidt, Sarah Schulman, Mimi Schwartz, Sallye Sheppard, Michael Steinberg, Dan Stollenwerk, Cheri Valentine, Martha Walsh, Summer Wood, Sue Wreska, and Stuart Wright.

For supporting writers and artists and especially for supporting me, I thank Goddard College, Grub Street, Lamar University, the MacDowell Colony, the New Hampshire Writers Project, Literature and Latte, and the valiant women at the A Room of Her Own Foundation.

For soulful sustenance, I thank writers whose courage and craftsmanship have inspired, enlightened, and entertained me over many years of reading.

For ready assistance, I thank librarians and supporters of libraries.

For enriching and complicating my life in invaluable ways, and for becoming my sisters and brothers, I thank the Missionaries of Charity.

For standing behind me and this book, and for their skill, generosity, and professionalism, I thank everyone on the extraordinary team at Spiegel & Grau, especially Laura Van der Veer (whose ready help and smile saved me more than once), Margaret Benton, London M. King, Kirk Reed, Susan Warga, Amelia Zalcman, and, from the depths of my heart, Julie Grau, whose faith in me and insight into this project have made all the difference.

For his wit, expertise, and true friendship, for guiding and protecting me through many perils on this odyssey to publication, I thank my agent Dan "the Wizard" Conaway, with special thanks also to Dan's inestimable assistant Stephen Barr, and to all the team at Writers House.

For being my first and most crucial reader, for insisting on grammar and punctuation and just the right word, for urging me deeper and never letting me take the easy way out, for believing in me from the beginning and all the way through, I thank my husband, my partner, my love. *Luca, ti ringrazio.*

An
Unquenchable
Thirst

A Memoir

Mary Johnson

A Reader's Guide

A Conversation with
Mary Johnson

Mary Johnson sat down to discuss *An Unquenchable Thirst* with her longtime friend Mira Bartók, author of *The Memory Palace*, winner of the 2012 National Book Critics Circle Award for Autobiography.

Mira Bartók: I've often thought of the writing process as a kind of monastic experience. You spend long stretches of time alone, wrestling with the angel of creation and sometimes with your demons. Writing also requires an immense amount of discipline and sacrifice, not unlike being a sister with the Missionaries of Charity. I couldn't help wonder, while I was reading your book, whether or not you found some similarities between these two dissimilar vocations.

Mary Johnson: I do find some similarities. As a nun I had to censor myself all the time, and as a writer I get to speak my mind, but the ritual of writing and the introspection that it requires are familiar to me from my time as a sister. I usually write first thing in the morning, just as I used to pray first thing. To get to the best writing,

I need to enter a space deep within myself, and I'm sure that years of meditation and confession prepared me to access that sort of naked honesty. I like that now I can eat more dark chocolate, the elixir of many a good writer.

MB: Is there anything that you miss about life as a nun?

MJ: I miss my sisters. I miss the shared purpose that comes from living so intensely in community. Sometimes I miss the simplicity of having only two sets of clothes, but most days I love having choices.

MB: Speaking of choices, before I began my memoir, *The Memory Palace*, I kept trying to write other things, but I eventually realized that my mother's story needed to be told. I'm curious to know if you started with the intent of writing *An Unquenchable Thirst* or if you tried to write something else but your memories of life with Mother Teresa got in the way.

MJ: I knew I wanted to write about the Missionaries of Charity, but I didn't start out telling *my* story. Marilynne Robinson read one of my early pieces, an essay about my experience as a sister, which was an immense privilege. More than a decade later Marilynne told me that she'd never forgotten that essay because it was the only piece of autobiographical writing that she'd ever read that abstained from the use of the first person singular pronoun. As a good sister, I had obliterated the word "I" from my piece. I wrote about Mother, about the life of a sister, about the poor. It took a long time before I realized that I needed to write about me.

MB: Since your book came out, have you heard from anyone you knew before you left the order? If so, what has their response been?

MJ: I don't imagine that sisters are encouraged to contact me, but those who have written are mostly concerned that I've lost my faith. Father Joseph phoned me when I was still working on *An*

Unquenchable Thirst. We had several long, beautiful conversations. He died shortly before my book was published, and I feel that loss very keenly. Sister Prema, the current Superior General of the Missionaries of Charity, told a journalist that my book was an opportunity for the sisters to examine themselves—probably the best reaction I could have hoped for. Sister Priscilla died two weeks after the book came out—when I heard, I worried that my not-always-flattering portrait of her might have killed her. Several former sisters and brothers told me my book has helped them come to terms with their own experiences, and that their friends and families understand them better after having read my story.

MB: If you could go back and give your nineteen-year-old self advice, what would you say?

MJ: If I could, I'd tell my nineteen-year-old self, "Mary, I know you think God wants you to do this, but isn't it a rather strange God who would give you a mind and a will and the ability to connect deeply with others, then ask you to renounce these gifts? Is that the sort of God you want to dedicate your life to?" I would hope that teenage Mary might reconsider, but I have my doubts.

MB: If I had known you back then, I would have suggested you start keeping a journal to help prepare you for becoming the writer you are now. I'm so thankful that I kept all my old journals because I constantly referred to them while working on my memoir, particularly because, as you know, I suffer some memory loss from a past brain injury. Was it difficult for you to remember your past, given your limited access to writing materials with the Missionaries of Charity?

MJ: In the convent we didn't have journals, but neither did we have distractions—no TV, radio, newspapers, novels—just our own little lives. As sisters we reviewed those lives all the time: examination of conscience twice a day, confession every week, general confession at the annual retreat. I had plenty of opportunities to commit my experiences and thoughts to memory. Also, my parents had kept my letters to them—imagine how excited I was to discover twenty years of letters in old shoeboxes and files! As I wrote my book, I was also able to tag events in my life to the public records on Mother Teresa, which helped me work out the chronology. My memory had a lot of help.

MB: Mary, rumor has it that one early version of *An Unquenchable Thirst* was around a thousand pages! I read part of an earlier draft of your book and when I read the final version, I was struck by how many amazing scenes you had cut. How did you decide what to cut? Did you have help along the way?

MJ: My MFA advisor Sarah Schulman told me to write everything down before I forgot it, so I did, during my MFA work and for several years after that. My other MFA advisor, Kenny Fries, kept insisting that my manuscript be no longer than 250 pages, but, despite his advice, I ended up with this behemoth of a first draft, mostly dialogue, because that's what comes to me first. My husband and I read through everything—yes, all thousand pages—then marked what each of us thought could stay and what could go. I called this Mary's *Unquenchable Thirst* Fat-Reduction Plan. My editor, Julie Grau, and her assistant, Laura Van der Veer, helped make it even leaner, and my agent, Dan Conaway, was a huge support always. I've got enough outtakes on file to fill another book, if I wanted to.

MB: I always tell aspiring writers to cultivate a supportive artistic community, otherwise you run the risk of writing in a vacuum. I think it's also crucial to champion others, especially emerging writers. Would you mind talking about the community of writers at AROHO (A Room of Her Own Foundation), the nonprofit organization that you helped found to support women writers? How significant a role do AROHO women play in your writing process?

MJ: I think you and I are especially supportive of other writers—you through the tremendous resources of your Mira's List blog and I through AROHO—because we've each experienced our own need for support. Darlene Chandler Bassett originally founded AROHO to help me write *An Unquenchable Thirst*. That she believed in my story meant everything to me. That women at AROHO retreats leaned forward in their seats whenever I read, that they gave me feedback on early drafts, that I found a group of local women writers unconnected with AROHO who read draft after draft of my book proposal—all of this was essential, not only to the quality of my work, but to keep me motivated during those ten long years of writing.

MB: Obviously, the name of your organization, A Room of Her Own Foundation, comes from the much-loved seminal essay by Virginia Woolf. At AROHO retreats one can feel Virginia's vibrant spirit just about everywhere. I'd love to know which other writers, living or dead, inspire you the most.

MJ: When I need to be urged toward raw honesty, I read Meredith Hall and Toni Morrison. When my imagination needs to be shaken loose I read Jeanette Winterson and Marguerite Duras and Gabriel García Márquez. To make my language more robust I read Rebecca Brown. For elegance and honesty, I read Joan Didion, Mary Gordon, Natalia Ginzburg, Kate Gale, Kathryn Harrison, Ruth Kluger, and Marilynne Robinson. For life guidance I read Alice Walker, Kathleen Norris, Viktor Frankl, Pema Chödrön, Karen Armstrong, and Joan Chittister. When I need to remember why I write, I go to an open mic of beginning writers with the courage to put their hearts out there. When I need a laugh I read Christopher Moore and Christopher Buckley and Caitlin Moran. For poetry in my prose I read Alessandro Baricco (in Italian). There was a time when I read St. Augustine's *Confessions* every year, but now I'm more likely to turn to Sam Harris to provoke thoughts about life's important questions.

MB: That transition from Augustine to Harris describes your spiritual journey fairly well, but I don't sense any bitterness in you.

MJ: Life is too short to waste in bitterness. I just want to live and to love well. I keep growing toward honesty, toward living without illusion—it's a great life!

MB: So, Mary, here's my million-dollar question: What's your next project? I'm dying to read more of your work.

MJ: I'm working on a follow-up memoir about life outside the convent walls—navigating the guilt and doubt, learning to pump gas and use a microwave, falling in love, gaining a sense of inner freedom, and building new communities. Like so many other people, I've abandoned organized religion, but the yearnings for meaning and purpose, strength and connection remain. I hope that my continuing journey can be a gift to folks hungry for an honest, fulfilling life beyond religion. And it won't take me ten years to write this time, I promise!

QUESTIONS FOR DISCUSSION

A Note from Mary Johnson

As I traveled around the country after the publication of the hardcover edition of *An Unquenchable Thirst* and spoke with readers everywhere from Harvard University to small book groups in friends' living rooms, I was thrilled to hear people talking from their hearts about the ways my story resonated with them. The more I listened, the more I realized that readers tended to approach my story in one of two ways: either as a coming-of-age story or as a spiritual memoir. So, for this paperback edition, I've decided to create two sets of discussion questions, one for each approach.

If you find yourself relating to my struggles within a faith community—whether you've abandoned organized religion or have found reasons to remain—you may find the first set of questions helpful. If you identify with my journey to discover myself as an independent woman within a rather repressive system, the second set of questions may be for you. Or you might prefer to dip into both sets and discover new ways of looking at my story.

For Groups Reading An Unquenchable Thirst
as a Spiritual Memoir

1. *An Unquenchable Thirst* in many ways follows the classic shape of a spiritual memoir, though Mary Johnson's story ends with her leaving the church. Does the endpoint of Mary's story undermine it as a work of spiritual memoir? Do you relate to Mary's struggles? How does her story make you feel about your own sense of faith and your feelings about organized religion?

2. Mary Johnson joined the Missionaries when she was a teenager, still trying to figure out who she was and not yet comfortable with the woman she was becoming. What were some of her motivations to leave home—where she was considered the "most likely to succeed"—and enter a world of deprivation as the "spouse of Christ crucified"? How did her expectations differ from her actual life with the Missionaries of Charity?

3. The Missionaries of Charity (MC) sisters took vows of poverty, chastity, obedience, and service to the poor—vows that proved very difficult to follow absolutely. Discuss the theoretical basis of the vows and how they were practiced in Mother Teresa's order. Which of those practices was the most difficult for you to understand? Why?

4. After struggling to find meaning in the Jesus Prayer, Sister Donata discovers a book called *The Cloud of Unknowing* that encourages a form of prayer that Mary has already been adopting—"prayer without images, prayer with very few, if any, words" (p. 118). Discuss the differences between reciting prescribed prayers and those with few or no words. Do you think one form is more authentic than the other?

5. At one point Mother Teresa repeats to the MC sisters what she often told audiences of all sorts: "Holiness is a simple duty for you

and me." What do you think she meant, and what implications did that have on her order? Do you think that particular philosophy is essential to or counterproductive for the MCs?

6. Mother Teresa believed that "for love to be real it has to hurt." Discuss the psychological implications of this perspective in the lives of the MC sisters. What was your reaction to "The Discipline"?

7. While on retreat in Casilina soon after her initial encounters with Timothy and Niobe, Sister Donata feels herself "drawing closer to Jesus" as a result of those relationships. Do you believe her? Do you think that physical intimacy can be analogous to being close to God? Is there a place in religion for the feelings that intimate relationships inspire?

8. When Sister Donata confesses to Father Tom that she has sometimes thought more about her own needs than those of others, his response is that she should focus on loving herself. "You're just as worthy of having your needs met as anyone else is," Father Tom says (pp. 276–77). Do you think Father Tom's advice is sound? Does it necessarily contradict the principles of the Missionaries of Charity? To what extent is serving others dependent on loving oneself?

9. The leaders of the MCs suspected that education destroyed many women's dedication to their vocations. Why? Discuss the consequences of this for the MCs.

10. In the Epilogue, Mary Johnson says, "I've learned to be content with mystery. . . . The universe and its secrets excite me." Do you feel that in leaving the church, Mary turned her back on faith and God, or do you think she incorporates her faith in her secular life?

For Groups Reading An Unquenchable Thirst
as a Feminist Coming-of-Age Story

1. *An Unquenchable Thirst* is a spiritual memoir, but it is also a coming-of-age story. How does the book mirror the traditional story of a feminist awakening? Do you consider Mary Johnson a feminist?

2. The narrative of *An Unquenchable Thirst* pulls the reader through extreme situations, intense emotions, and quietly fought battles. When did you empathize most with Sister Donata? What experiences in your life allowed you to understand some of what Sister Donata went through? Were there also times when you found her hard to relate to?

3. Discuss the book's title. What do you think Mary Johnson was really thirsting for all along? Does she succeed in finding what she was looking for, or is her thirst inherently "unquenchable"?

4. Mary Johnson believed, as a teenager, that she was "too ugly to have a boyfriend," then goes through a sexual awakening during her years with the MCs. Discuss the trajectory of each of her affairs, the motivating force behind them, and how they represented different aspects of romance, lust, and mature love. Can you relate to her experiences?

5. Mary Johnson chooses to join the Missionaries of Charity—and stays even when she experiences doubts—because she believes it is her calling. Discuss the concept of a having a "calling" in life. Do you believe there is such a thing? Is there a secular equivalent? Is experiencing a "calling" freeing, or can it inhibit growth? Discuss the implications of the concept as it relates to Mary's story and to your own experiences.

6. For Mary, the lack of stimulating reading material and the lack of value placed on scholarship was one of the most challenging constraints of being an MC, and she seizes any opportunity for intellectual development and creativity. Discuss the different outlets for intellectual stimulation that Mary encounters. What does she learn from each of them, and which had the greatest effect on her personal development?

7. Mary Johnson's trip to Sweden with Mother Teresa is a turning point in Mary's development. How does that trip change Mary's perspective? What does she learn about Mother Teresa, and what does she learn about herself?

8. Among the reasons for Mary's decision to leave the MCs is her desire for intimacy and connection. Are those feelings universal? Do you think the other sisters were suppressing similar desires?

9. Mary has doubts about the way the MCs minister to the poor, questioning whether the order makes the best use of their resources and funds. What do you think the best way of giving is?

MARY JOHNSON'S
READING LIST

Books have always been important to me. Here are a few titles that have marked my journey.

As a child, I read Jean Craighead George's *My Side of the Mountain* when I was supposed to be asleep, under the covers, by flashlight. Both young Sam Gribley and I came from big families. While I sometimes dreamed of running away, Sam set up house in a huge hollowed-out tree in the Catskill Mountains. Later, when I was in the convent, Sam's self-reliance often returned to me, telling me that I could survive on my own if I would just give it a try.

Something Beautiful for God by Malcolm Muggeridge was the first Mother Teresa book I read. Muggeridge's infatuation with Mother Teresa—she shone with "all the beauty and joy in the universe"—led my seventeen-year-old self to be smitten, too. Today when I read Muggeridge I understand yet again how the yearning to love and to be loved can overcome us all.

The first book I read after leaving the convent was Kathleen Norris's *The Cloister Walk*. In my journal I wrote, "Beautiful book, so funny at times, full of insight and simple wisdom from a woman who lives with her humanity. It leaves me wanting to write." In Kathleen Norris I found a Protestant who understood the monastic life better than did most of the sisters I'd lived with. Norris was an antidote to MC rigidity and an inspiration for me to tell my own story.

I hadn't yet read more than the back cover of Virginia Woolf's *A Room of One's Own*, but Woolf's argument was in my mind the day someone at a retreat asked me, "What do you need?" When I responded that I needed privacy and financial support so that I could write my story, that I needed "a room of my own," Darlene Chandler Bassett volunteered to pay my graduate school tuition if I'd help her start a foundation to help women writers. Thus was born A Room of Her Own Foundation, which has since channeled more than $750,000 to support and challenge women writers. Sometimes just reading a book's jacket is enough to change your life.

When a friend gave me Sam Harris's *The End of Faith*, she gave me permission to explore my own doubts. Though I don't always agree with Harris's conclusions or his methods, I always feel intellectually invigorated by his words, ready to question and argue and find my own conclusions. This, too, is a great gift.

When I read Ayaan Hirsi Ali's *Infidel*, I felt as though I'd found a kindred spirit from the Islamic world. In moments when I wanted to hide, Hirsi Ali's courage and her need to have her outer reality express her inner convictions helped me overcome my fears as I wrote my story.

The day my husband brought my first Christopher Moore book into the house was a very happy day indeed. Moore is zany and sweet and *Fluke* talked about humpback whales and human hearts

.nd the nature of the world—all while making me laugh out loud. Moore offers me the gift of laughter whenever I need it, and for that I'll be always grateful.

Sister Joan Chittister's spiritual memoir, *Called to Question*, showed me that it was possible to be both a good nun and a real person whose heart and mind flourishes in honesty and conviction. Chittister asks tough questions and lets the answers take her where they may.

For twenty years, MARY JOHNSON was a Missionary of Charity, a nun in Mother Teresa's order, until she left in 1997. A teacher and public speaker, she has been named a Fellow of the MacDowell Colony and is on the board of the A Room of Her Own Foundation. Johnson's work has been featured in *O: The Oprah Magazine*, *The Washington Post*, The Daily Beast, and The Huffington Post, among other publications, and on National Public Radio and *The Rosie Show*. She lives in New Hampshire. Visit her online at www.MaryJohnson.co.

To help the A Room of Her Own Foundation in the work of supporting women who tell their stories, visit aroho.org.